CONNECTIONS BETWEEN SEX AND AGGRESSION

CONNECTIONS BETWEEN SEX AND AGGRESSION

WITHDRAW

DOLF ZILLMANN
Indiana University

LEA LAWRENCE ERLBAUM ASSOCIATES, PUBLISHERS
1984 Hillsdale, New Jersey London

Lawrence Erlbaum Associates, Inc., Publishers
365 Broadway
Hillsdale, New Jersey 07642

Library of Congress Cataloging in Publication Data

Zillmann, Dolf.
    Connections between sex and aggression.

    Bibliography: p.
    Includes indexes.
    1. Sex (Psychology)   2. Sex (Biology)   3. Aggressive-
ness (Psychology)   I. Title.
BF692.Z54   155.3   83-20633
ISBN 0-89859-333-6

Printed in the United States of America
10   9   8   7   6   5   4   3   2   1

Contents

Preface

Sexual and aggressive behaviors have received much scholarly attention. Numerous recent and not-so-recent monographs and anthologies on the one or the other subject are available. The possibility of interdependencies between these behaviors has received considerable attention also. Oddly enough, however, theory and research on the interdependencies in question have not been brought together in an organized fashion. The literature concerning connections between sex and aggression is eclectic and scattered through various disciplines. Characteristically, there has been little exchange of information between investigators in different disciplines, and nonintegrated, esoteric research has often been the result. At the very least, investigators in any particular discipline had little knowledge of what their colleagues in other disciplines were doing and had accomplished in their efforts at understanding sex-aggression linkages.

The present monograph seeks to overcome this state of affairs by covering the pertinent theoretical and research developments in all disciplines that have significantly contributed to our understanding of interdependencies between sexual and aggressive behaviors. Moreover, it attempts to integrate advancements in our understanding as much as this is possible. Incompatibilities in theory and empirical findings are pointed out, of course, where efforts at integration cannot succeed.

A glance at the table of contents shows what is covered where in the book.

Chapter 1 introduces basic proposals about sex-aggression linkages. It also outlines the grand and mostly dubious speculations about these linkages. Thereafter, it develops a conceptual framework for things to come.

Chapter 2 puts sex-aggression linkages in perspective. It first covers the wealth of relationships between sexual and aggressive behaviors in nonhuman species. Special attention is given to nonhuman primates. It then addresses sex-aggression interdependencies in humans. Much information from comparative behavior analysis and anthropology is used to probe the likely evolutionary path of aggressive-sexual behaviors in humans.

Chapter 3 presents significant developments in sex-aggression theory and research in neurophysiology. Autonomic commonalities in sexual and aggressive behaviors are scrutinized in preparation for later theoretical proposals.

The basic endocrinological work on sexual dimorphism, both normal and aberrant, and its implications for aggression are discussed in Chapter 4. Again in preparation for proposals advanced later, endocrine commonalities in sexual and aggressive behaviors are detailed.

Chapter 5 covers theory and research on sex-aggression linkages of mainstream psychology. As social-psychological notions of love-enhancement through hostile and aggressive actions have drawn much attention recently, the pertinent reasoning and empirical findings are subjected to close examination.

Chapters 1 through 5 might be construed as a response to a gaping void in the book market. These chapters finally bring together, relate, and integrate the hitherto sporadic efforts at delineating and comprehending connections between sexual and aggressive behaviors. Chapter 6 is different in that it proposes a new solution to the interdependency problem concerning sex and aggression. This solution derives from the realization that a paradigm that had proved useful in the study of various emotional behavior sequences also might prove useful in studying sexual/aggressive and aggressive/sexual behavior sequences, but especially in exploring behaviors in which sexual and aggressive actions are intertwined and fused. It was the expanded use of the paradigm that motivated the writing of this book and that ultimately gave impetus to covering and integrating theory and research on sex-aggression connections, once it was realized that such coverage and integration was sorely needed.

Chapter 6 develops the excitation-transfer paradigm for sex-aggression connections specifically. Much of the information on autonomic and adrenal commonalities in sexual and aggressive behaviors that was presented earlier is fully utilized at this point. The paradigm's unique projections are compared and contrasted with predictions derived from other theories and models. Research findings that directly support the transfer paradigm, or that are at least consistent with its projections, are reported in some detail. The manipulability of sex-aggression connections (that is, the possibility of undoing undesirable connections and of creating desirable ones) is also given much attention.

In contrast to alternative models, the transfer paradigm projects great plasticity of most connections between sexual and aggressive behaviors. Interdependencies are not construed as fixed and undeniable response sequences. Rather, these interdependencies are seen as resulting, for the most part, from insufficient differentiation in the autonomic response components together with the somewhat archaic stimulus control of excitatory reactions. Although the processes under consideration elude voluntary control to a high degree, intervention and manipulation are readily accomplished by particular stimulus arrangements. In fact, owing to the superior anticipatory skills of humans, specific stimulus arrangements tend to be exploited for pleasure, and this exploitation often results in the development of aggressive-sexual behaviors. Such exploitation, especially that of aggressive acts in the enhancement of sexual gratification, has been deemed desirable by some and undesirable, if not abhorrent, by others. As values concerning what, in the sexual realm, is proper and desirable, and what is not, differ enormously between and within cultures, and as these values are bound to be applied to aggressive-sexual actions, the value issue seemed unavoidable. At any rate, I elected to address it on different occasions. I found myself unable to follow other authors of publications on human sexuality in declaring—categorically and despite their promotion of extremely liberal sexual views—that the discussion of aggressive-sexual behaviors, including the so-called aberrations, is devoid of a value component. I thought it better to reflect on values and to exhibit diverse and potentially opposing views, concentrating on the criteria used in making such value judgments. I hope that the reader appreciates my efforts in presenting many conceivable value positions—rather than my own point of view. I also hope that my own values are not spotted too easily, as I attempted to be sensitive to the full range of basic value positions that might be taken.

In writing this book, I enjoyed the support and assistance of many of my colleagues and friends. I feel greatly indebted to them. My longtime collaborator in sex-aggression research, Professor Jennings Bryant, spent much of his time responding to the first draft. He is responsible for uncounted improvements in the text. The actual manuscript was then read in full by Professors Robert Baron and John Cacioppo. Both provided insightful commentary that greatly enhanced the clarity of presenting and discussing theories and research findings. Professor William Timberlake read the portions of the manuscript that concern animal behavior and made valuable suggestions. Professor James Holland scrutinized the portions on endocrinological work. I am indebted to him for valuable advice and corrections. I am also indebted to Professor Paul MacLean for catching an error in the presentation of his own, fascinating work. Professor Donn Byrne served as my editor. I am deeply grateful to him for his thorough and prompt analysis of the manuscript. His informed commentary has led to numerous clarifications and extensions that, I feel, have greatly improved the book. Last but not least, I am indebted to my copyeditor, Ms. Sondra Guideman, for her fine work in finalizing the manuscript. Her extremely careful reading of the text prompted numerous refinements, and her substantive queries led to some late, clarifying modifications. My deeply felt gratitude goes to all. Needless to say, however, I solely am to be held responsible for any errors that may have escaped our concerted efforts at eliminating them. More importantly, I alone am responsible for any shortcomings the reader may detect in the interpretations of particular theories and findings or in my own proposals. I solely am to be held accountable, too, for the exposition of extreme value positions. As some of these positions must clash with those espoused by the reader, I can only hope that the annoyance that is likely to be felt will be curbed by the recognition of the purpose for juxtaposing divergent value positions.

Finally, I must express my gratitude toward my wife, Valtra. She motivated me to persevere, giving me comfort and encouragement when I got annoyed with all those not-to-be-named little things that kept me from writing. More importantly, however, I greatly benefitted from her knowledge of biology, especially primatology, and anthropology. We collaborated on the sex-aggression connections in nonhuman and human species. It was she who gathered and organized all pertinent data. Had she not done so, I probably still would be doing my library work for Chapter 2.

Dolf Zillmann

CONNECTIONS BETWEEN SEX AND AGGRESSION

.

1 Connections Everywhere

Relationships between sex and aggression seem both obtrusive and abundant. Not surprisingly, then, they have been the subject of much contemplation and debate. In this opening chapter, I attempt to provide an overview of various principal connections and discuss the ways in which they have been construed in grandiose speculations and in popular theories.

I. SEXUAL ACCESS AND AGGRESSION

> In the midst of the applause . . . the king gave to the people the expected sign of rape. Straightway they leap forth . . . and lay lustful hand upon the maidens. As doves . . . flee from the eagles, and the weanling lamb when it spies the wolf, so feared they the men rushing wildly on them; in none remained her former colour. For their fear was one, but not one was the appearance of their fear: some tear their hair, some sit crazed; one is silent in dismay, one calls in vain upon her mother; this one bewails, that one is struck dumb; . . . and to many their very fear had power to lend grace. . . . Ah, Romulus, thou only didst know how to bestow bounty on thy warriors; so thou but bestow such bounty upon me, I will be a warrior [Ovid, *Artis amatoriae,* i, 110–135].

With this comment on early Roman history, the author of the first Western manual on the joy of sex made reference to the well-known fact that in the ascent of civilizations, aggression and sex tended to join forces on a grand scale. Today's teachers of history are likely to characterize events such as those eluded to as barbaric and inhumane. Ovid, however, reveled in the imagination of coercive sexual action and could see no wrong in the use of coercion in a sexual context. In fact, if there is a recurrent, dominant theme in Ovid's tutoring, it is that women just wait to be violated. The use of force in achieving their compliance with the eager males' demands is not merely viewed as being above reproach, but is considered part and parcel of lovemaking: a welcome enhancement of the passions, ultimately for women as well as for men. Ovid insisted that the ravisher will find favor with the ravished, and that forceful seduction accomplishes admiration in the end:

> Perhaps she will struggle at first . . . yet she will wish to be beaten in the struggle. . . . You may use force; women like you to use it; they often wish to give unwillingly what they like to give. She whom a sudden assault has taken by storm is pleased, and counts the audacity as a compliment [Ovid, *Artis amatoriae*, i, 665–675].

No doubt, most women might be inclined to accuse Ovid of callousness toward females. But such accusations, it seems, could be levied as readily against the majority of men in contemporary society, not to mention men of civilizations gone by. Beliefs about what women tolerate and enjoy within the sexual sphere and about what men need and must do within this sphere appear to have changed little over the ages. In more or less all known cultures there were and are institutions such as today's young men's bull sessions (i.e., big-talk of sexual adventure in gatherings on street corners, in locker rooms, around pool tables, in camps, clubs, and bars) that have promoted and promote beliefs about male and, in particular, female sexuality that are essentially those implicit in Ovid's recommendations. All such institutions, it seems, have encouraged, if not created, callous, exploitative, aggressive attitudes and dispositions toward women—dispositions that serve one goal only: *sexual access*.

To men, Ovid's caution that he who is noble and gentle shall be a lover last apparently has not lost its threatening quality. Forceful attempts at intercourse, short of full-fledged rape, still are very common. In contemporary society many young men—indeed a surprising proportion—trust their physical powers in subduing reluctant partners more than their communicative talents in gaining cooperation (e.g., Kanin, 1957, 1967; Mosher, 1971). This preference for aggression in achieving compliance is by no means limited to young men, however. It cuts across age levels. It is in evidence even among intimates who have known each other for some time and who should have had ample opportunity to develop and refine nonviolent bargaining techniques to achieve their partners' collaboration in sexual endeavors. Recent research on forced sexual intercourse in married couples, for example, suggests that women are far more frequently forced into compliance, through violent action, than previously had been thought (Finkelhor & Yllo, 1982). Characteristically, they take a beating whenever persuasion fails, and persuasion tends to fail most often when males demand and insist on their participation in some of the more uncommon sexual practices.

There can be no question that through the ages a great many men have sought and achieved sexual access through violent action or the threat thereof. No civilization, regardless of the degree of punitive sanctions against forceful access and the extent of access-accommodating promiscuity among women, has been without rape. Rape—that is, the sexual assault of strangers, acquaintances, friends, and relatives alike—has been a most ubiquitous phenomenon through the history of human kind, and it has remained a ubiquitous phenomenon in contemporary societies (e.g., Brownmiller, 1975; Gager & Schurr, 1976; Groth, 1979). And though there is little, if any, argument about the ubiquity of rape, the appraisal and evaluation of rape has varied greatly among and within societies. Legal records of sanctions against rape in ancient societies (e.g., Bullough, 1976) would seem to suggest that rape has been consensually condemned in most civilizations. Rape is likewise consensually censured in contemporary societies, although many inadequacies in the application of punitive sanctions may exist (e.g., Russell, 1975). There always seem to have been some individuals, however, who have celebrated rape as the ultimate expression of sexual freedom. Sexual violence was hailed by de Sade (1799/1955), who viewed it as a basic and common human desire. Modern political radicals such as Marcuse (1957) have similarly endorsed it and urged that the pleasurable yielding to violent, sexual impulses be recognized as a civil liberty, if not as an inalienable human right. In stark contrast, others have deemed rape an undesirable, intolerable expression of human sexuality and have tended to view it as a grave illness: a form of sexual psychopathy (e.g., Groth & Burgess, 1977). Still others have seen it as a comparatively minor aberration: a deplorable inability on the part of some men to check urges that presumably all men experience at one time or another (e.g., Clark & Lewis, 1977). But regardless of the particular evaluation of rape and quasi-rape in terms of social unacceptability and pathology, sexual access through the use of physical force undoubtedly constitutes a domain of behavior in which aggression and sex appear to be intimately linked.

In his influential essays on sexuality, Freud (1905/1942) sought to put this intimate linkage into perspective theoretically. He suggested that the intertwining of sexual and aggressive impulses constitutes a remnant of times when communication skills were not sufficiently developed to assure sexual access and, hence, reproduction. The linkage, then, is seen as a reflection of an archaic but nevertheless functional and natural inclination to take women by force. Freud (1905/1942) thus viewed the tendency to behave forcefully toward the sexual object as characteristic, not as abnormal: ''An admixture of *aggression* characterizes the sexuality of most men. There is an urge to overpower the sexual object. The biological significance of this urge lies in the necessity to overcome the resistance of the object by means other than *persuasion* [p. 57; author's translation].''

Freud's contentions regarding access in humanity's darker hours might be cast aside as idle speculations. Records of such presumed, ancient behaviors do not exist, and any demonstration of the contention's validity is thus impossible. The situation seems to be different, however, for related contentions that have emerged from ethology. A wealth of behavioral observations on a vast number of species (e.g., Hinde, 1970; Marler & Hamilton, 1968) has led investigators such as Lorenz (1963, 1964) and Eibl-Eibesfeldt (1970, 1973) to propose views that in many ways resemble the one espoused by Freud.

Lorenz (e.g., 1963) promoted the idea that specific forms of aggression have evolved in the service of sexual access. Obviously, in order to gain access males not only must achieve compliance in females, but also must ward off competing males. Lorenz apparently assumed that aggression initially served both of these ends; he further assumed that the amount of aggression thus necessitated must have been excessive and maladaptive for any species. Lorenz then proposed that reproductive success favored those animals whose fighting was less destructive. As ferocious fighters mutilated and devastated each other, those who fought less ferociously reproduced and shaped their species. Similarly, female victims of destructive assaults participated less efficiently in the reproductive process than those treated somewhat more gently. Following Darwin's (1859/1887) proposals concerning natural selection, this selective bias certainly should produce a less aggressive species. Lorenz's suggestion is more specific, however. Applying evolutionary considerations a bit selectively, he proposed that in the evolutionary adjustment only the destructive goal reaction dropped out, not the action patterns of aggression. As a result, animals still fight, but they do so in a *ritualized* fashion. Analogous to the tournaments of medieval knights, in which destructiveness was curtailed by honor codes, animals are thought to fight in a controlled manner, with built-in constraints against maiming and killing their own kind. The strongest, swiftest, most enduring fighter thus emerges an unharmed victor from ritual combat, his victory giving him sexual access.

Lorenz's proposal accommodates the fact that intraspecific intermale fighting rarely produces severe injury. The competition for sexual access is indeed often settled in skirmishes that leave the participants exhausted, but unharmed. Also, females are often without a choice in the matter, taking their lot with the outcome of the combat over access. Ruminants such as deer are usually called upon to illustrate the outlined solution to the sexual-access problem. Males engage in combat spectaculars, locking horns to the point of total collapse, but maimings are rare despite the apparent capacity for it. The victor is granted sexual access, presiding over a harem of accommodating females. Many species of birds, although the male–female pair constitutes the reproductive unit, exhibit essentially the same approach to sexual access. The males fight over territories in skirmishes that hardly ever produce bodily harm. The females are then attracted to these territories. Once co-occupants, they seem to offer little resistance to the landlord's sexual advances.

More than Lorenz himself, Eibl-Eibesfeldt and others (e.g., Morris, 1968; Storr, 1968) have popularized the view that ritualized aggression is not limited to subhuman species, but permeates more or less all facets of human life and culture. Regarding sexual access, anything that men can do to impress favorably upon the opposite sex has, it seems, been interpreted as an element of ritualized aggression that somehow evolved from initially destructive fighting for reproductive privileges. Anything that smacks of competition is construed as a derivative of such fighting. Playing a game of tennis becomes a ritualized exercise in violence. So does any other game that entails elements of ancient combat: strength, quickness, agility, accuracy, or endurance. Although devoid of similarities with physical fighting, assertive behavior in any kind of business endeavor also has been interpreted as ritualized aggression, as have behaviors such as "pumping iron" to build a supernormal chest or wearing a jacket with padded shoulders to achieve similar impressions. The skillful can, no doubt, spot an element of aggression that serves sexual access even in a tender love song.

It may appear that Lorenz's ritualization concept has taken the element of destructive violence out of the fight for sexual access. Aggression is trivialized, so to speak, and rendered innocuous through miraculous selective adjustments. More recent research has made it abundantly clear, however, that fighting for access is by no means innocuous. Intraspecific maiming and killing may not be common, but they seem to be less rare than presumed by Lorenz (e.g., Estes, 1969; Schaller, 1969). If, among species as diverse as cichlid fish, hamsters, langurs, baboons, and gorillas, the inferior fighter fails to submit and escape in time, the victorious animal is likely to fight to the point of the opponent's incapacitation or death (e.g., Dart, 1961; Eibl-Eibesfeldt, 1970; Hall, 1968a; Lawick-Goodall, 1968; Sugiyama, 1967; Yoshiba, 1968). The fact that fighting for access often proves harmless is apparently more the result of nimble feet (i.e., a capacity for quick withdrawal), sturdy skulls, and thick skin (cf. Johnson, 1972) than of "knowing" when to stop. The so-called tournamental fighting, then, can readily turn into gladiatorial combat. Even the subduing of the female, notwithstanding spectacular courtship rituals precipitating it, can become a bloody affair (cf. Ford & Beach, 1951).

Lorenz's concept of ritualized aggression for sexual access might be considered a magnificent abstraction. But it should be recognized as one that does not correspond too well with the facts at hand. It understates the infliction of pain and injury associated with access fighting. Freud, on the other hand, may well have overstated the role of physical force and coercion in the presumed conquest of the female. After all, in many of man's closest relatives, both monkeys and apes, combat over access is conspicuously absent; and the females, at least early during estrus, actively *solicit* sexual engagements from the males in their troop (e.g., Carpenter, 1965; Hall & DeVore, 1965; Jay, 1965).

Regardless of the extent to which the one position underestimates and the other overestimates the actual involvement of aggression in the striving for sexual access, especially for humans, both positions entail a projection of archaic sexuality that may be as erroneous and misleading as it has been influential. Clearly, both positions are based on the assumption that, once upon a time, sexuality was a behavioral problem to be resolved among initiative, hyperaggressive males and passive, submissive females.

Without such an assumption, the concept of ritualization—as it has been applied to this sex-aggression connection—becomes meaningless. For ritualization to occur, the aggressive behavior that becomes pseudo-aggressive via ritualization obviously must have existed initially (e.g., Lorenz, 1950, 1961, 1965). Additionally, the fact that ritualized aggression has been detected mostly, if not exclusively, in the behavior of males suggests that females have never been considered to have much to ritualize (i.e., they must have been thought to have been rather nonaggressive in the first place).

Freud similarly singled out the male as the active, aggressive agent. Libidinal urges (i.e., the forces of the life instinct, *Eros*, focusing on reproduction) were viewed as impelling the male to action—more so than the female (e.g., 1905/ 1942, 1915/1946, 1917/1940). Aggression was clearly secondary, a force in the service of *Eros*. This situation did not critically change with the later (e.g., 1920/1940, 1933/1950) addition of a death instinct, *Thanatos*. The forces of this death instinct, unlike those of other aggression instincts, were said to operate toward the destruction of the self. For life to be maintained, these instinctual forces had to be continually converted into outwardly-directed destructive actions. Males apparently manage this conversion better than females do. More specifically, they manage to exploit it by placing the resulting energies into the service of *Eros*. According to this Freudian thinking, then, females not only become the victims of the greater conversion efficiency on the part of the males, but are additionally victimized by letting themselves too often be the target of self-destructive impulses. The latter aspect, in particular, has opened the door to much speculation concerning a greater propensity for mental illness in women (e.g., Bardwick, 1971; Deutsch, 1944).

The *Urzustand* (i.e., the "primal state") regarding sexual access may, of course, have been quite different from that projected by Freud and Lorenz, and all the derivations can legitimately be questioned. Freud's projection can indeed be branded idle speculation, and Lorenz's can be considered based on faulty reasoning. The fact that gazelles, for example, fight for access in seemingly vicious snout-pushing rituals (Walther, 1958) does not mean that in earlier days they engaged in injurious biting. Similarly, from the fact that oryx antelopes, who use their spearlike horns to stab predators, do not use these weapons in their conspecific head-to-head pushing contest, it does not follow that they ever used them in sexual-access fighting. The unwarranted, interdependent inferences of both ritualization and primal state, it appears, were invited mainly by redundancies in the expression of social conflict that are due to a limited capacity for locomotion and signal production. Destructive interspecific fighting and comparatively nondestructive conspecific fighting are bound to share many manifestations in any particular species. Rather than "inferring" ritualization from the necessary behavioral similarities, the affinity might actually be interpreted as reflecting an evolutionary adjustment in the opposite direction: The nondestructive forms of aggression that are characteristic of conspecific fighting may have been abandoned in defensive, interspecific fighting, making this type of fighting increasingly destructive. Such an interpretation circumvents the assumption of mayhem in the *Urzustand*, an assumption that meets with great conceptual problems. Indeed, it is difficult to imagine how any species could have survived the presumed initial chaos and its devastation. But it is even more difficult to imagine why, in the mutational advancement of species, a reversion to seemingly indiscriminate destructive aggression would occur and recur. Why, after the nonhuman primates found ways of dealing with sexual access in essentially nonviolent ways, should the humanoids have fallen back on the instinctual use of violence to solve their sexual problems?

Projections of a violent beginning undoubtedly have great dramatic appeal. Presumably because of this, and despite their indefensibility from a scientific point of view, such projections tend to leave deep impressions. Uncritically accepted, they provide an orientation as to what is "natural" and what is not. With human sexual violence looming so large in these projections, the somewhat forceful pursuit of sexual access may appear innocuous, if not civilized. Truly forceful, violent attainment of access, moreover, might be construed as the expression of culturally unmitigated "human nature." Sexual violence thus might be deemed more tolerable and acceptable than it would if beliefs about a primal state of such violence had not been adopted.

The provision of an orientation is likely to have significant social implications. For that reason, I return to this issue in the next chapter and try to put human aggressive sexuality in perspective. In a comparative analysis, I attempt to delineate our position in the animal kingdom and suggest an orientation in line with the evidence at hand rather than with speculations about what might have been.

II. FRUSTRATION IN SEX AND AGGRESSION

In the human species, the use of force to achieve sexual compliance is certainly not limited to overpowering resistant strangers and acquaintances. Such use of force, as indicated earlier, is rather common among so-called intimates. Research into violence within the family context, especially into marital violence (e.g., Gelles, 1979; Straus, Gelles, & Steinmetz, 1980), leaves no doubt about the ubiquity of sex-related conflict which is capable of escalating into injurious fighting. Quite frequently, men accuse their wives of frigidity; similarly, though less often, women accuse their husbands of sexual disinterest. On occasion, continued teasing leads to shouting matches, and in the heat of the argument, punches and bottles may be thrown.

Surely, such fights can be viewed as efforts at gaining sexual access. Presumably because of greater strength and more experience in fighting, males succeed in these efforts often enough (e.g., Russell, 1980b). More frequently, however, access is not gained, and one party's sexual intentions remain thwarted. Such *sexual frustration* seems widespread among intimates, both in martial situations and in any other kind of nontransitory cohabitational arrangement. But it appears that sexual frustration often derives not so much from the outright denial of sexual access as from the denial, almost always on the part of females, of collaboration in sexual endeavors that are deemed objectionable and repulsive, unenjoyable or plainly painful (cf. Faulk, 1977; Finkelhor & Yllo, 1982).

Sexual frustration, it seems, strains many relationships. Characteristically, it motivates the party whose intentions have been thwarted to use all available powers to overcome the resistance. Withholding incentives and affection, being nonsupportive, responding with strong irritation to minimal provocation, and exploiting every opportunity for hostile action are all part of bargaining among intimates. Such bargaining can go on for days, weeks, and even months. Regardless of whether or not the denying party finally yields to the coercive pressures and accommodates the thwarted party's specific sexual demands, these periods of conflict can be viewed as times of sex-precipitated fighting in which much hostility and aggression that does not serve sexual access directly can be liberated. The research on family violence suggests that fighting tends to become somewhat indiscriminate. Not only does it seem to generalize to conflicts that are unrelated to sexual behavior, but also to any suitable target that is available. Most often, these targets are the intimates' children (e.g., Gil, 1973). Aggression against children and other bystanders, then, has been linked to sexual frustration. It thus appears that sex-precipitated conflict can foster, or at least facilitate, aggressive behavior that is entirely devoid of sexual elements. It should be recognized, however, that aggression precipitated by sexual frustration often maintains its sexual character. Sexual molestation and rape (e.g., Groth, 1979) and the sexual abuse of children (e.g., Finkelhor, 1979) are often viewed as based on sexual frustration. In this interpretation the potentially nonaggressive male who is denied sexual access (more likely, who is denied the performance of highly specific sexual acts that he, for whatever reason, deems particularly enjoyable) turns, in his frustration, to alternative targets and uses force, if necessary, to achieve compliance.

The mechanics of this sex-aggression connection have received much attention from Freud (e.g., 1905/1942, 1915/1946, 1917/1940). He suggested, essentially, that the blockage of libidinal urges leaves the associated subservient, outwardly-directed aggressive impulses active and that these impulses seek outlet in the assault upon more or less any substitute "object." Presumably, if the alternative object is capable of satisfying libidinal urges, the assault will be sexual and destructive impulses will be partly or fully repressed. If, however, this object is not capable of satisfying the libidinal urges, the assault will be destructive and the sexual impulses will be repressed. In view of Freud's (1938/1958) famous contention that "the repression of aggressive impulses is altogether unhealthy and causes illness [p. 12; author's translation]," one would think that aggression, in the interest of the individual's well-being, is always expected to follow sexual frustrations.

Although Freud proposed a set of processes that, if inventively combined, can post facto account for any other conceivable outcome, it is the foregoing interpretation that proved most influential. Freudian thinking on repression entered into the reasoning on aggression generally, and it found expression in the so-called frustration-aggression hypothesis (Dollard, Doob, Miller, Mowrer, & Sears, 1939), which has dominated conceptions of human aggression for decades (cf. Geen, 1972). According to this hypothesis, frustration *always* leads to aggression; moreover, aggression *always* derives from frustration. These sweeping claims made frustration both a necessary and a sufficient condition for aggression. It was soon recognized, however, that frustrations do not by necessity produce aggression. As a result, Miller (1941) retracted the contention that frustration always causes aggression and modified the hypothesis to state that frustration instigates a variety of aggressive *or* nonaggressive responses. But the revised frustration-aggression hypothesis continued to maintain that any aggressive behavior that occurs *is caused by* frustration. Thus, frustration was no longer considered a sufficient condition for aggression; however, it was still considered a necessary one.

Although the frustration-aggression hypothesis proved highly controversial (cf. Buss, 1961) and failed to be unequivocally supported by the research evidence it generated (cf. Bandura, 1973), it has remained enormously influential—especially in clinical circles. The claim that any and every aggressive response ultimately derives from a frustrating experience has invited much uncontrolled speculation. Tracing someone's aggressive outbursts to frustrating incidents in his or her life is common practice. At times, such tracing may be revealing. More often, however, behaviors are ascribed to doubtful "causes." The validity of attributions of this kind is usually entirely spurious. In many instances such attributions prove to be erroneous, and the projected misconception of someone's aggressiveness may have harmful consequences for the person who is led into misconstruing the causation of his or her aggressive actions.

In the context of frustration-aggression theory, sexual frustration is just another form of frustration. But in view of the strength of sexual motivation, it may be assumed that sexual frustrations are experienced particularly intensely. It may be expected, consequently, that they powerfully instigate substitute actions, aggressive actions being likely choices. Additionally, because all aggressive actions—whether they are associated with sexual behaviors or not—are viewed as deriving from frustrations, the intensity or magnitude of sexual frustrations should make this type of frustration a prime target for causal attributions. It should thus be no surprise to find that wife and child beating have been ascribed to sexual frustration—rightly or wrongly. But the contentions have gone even further. Curtailing sexual behavior has been held accountable not just for the behavior of some individuals who are excessively violent, but for high levels of aggressiveness in entire cultures. For instance, a comparison of sexual freedom in a number of cultures led Prescott (1977) to the conclusion that sexual deprivation, especially the repression of female sexuality, "constitutes the single greatest source of physical violence in human society [p. 449].'' Sex and aggression, then, are viewed as being inversely related. The repression of sex creates mayhem, and the free expression of sex secures tranquility. Oddly enough, it has not yet been contended that the documented increase in sexual activity in contemporary society (cf. Hunt, 1974; Kinsey, Pomeroy, & Martin, 1948; Kinsey, Pomeroy, Martin, & Gebhard, 1953) should yield a reduction in violent crime and in abusive behaviors among intimates. Nor has it been claimed (as it could on the basis of frustration-aggression theory) that the increase in sexual activity is due to increased frustrations in everyday life in modern society.

Notwithstanding the fact that some societal implications of the presumed inverse relation between sex and aggression have not been articulated, the various dependencies of this relationship have been expressed for the individual. Nonsexual violence among intimates is apparently considered the principal domain for aggression that is motivated by sexual frustration. A case in point is child beating by mothers, a phenomenon alleged to be the province of nonorgasmic women (Prescott, 1977; Steel & Pollack, 1968). In contrast, sexual violence is treated as a more or less exclusively male preoccupation, and it has been derived from nonsexual frustrations (e.g., failure in professional endeavors) as much as from sexual ones (cf. Groth, 1979). In the light of all these proposed influences, it appears that the frustration concept has been called upon to make any conceivable connection between sexual discontent and aggression.

III. FUSION OF SEX AND AGGRESSION

Up to this point, I have dealt with sexual and aggressive behaviors as distinct, discrete events. A first behavioral event was thought to terminate prior to the onset of a subsequent one that it was expected to influence. In fact, the reasoning on frustration often implied that behaviors could be influenced by events from the past as well as by recent events. Even in the case of sexual violence, it was implied that after access has been gained through force or by the threat of force, the subsequent behavior would be essentially sexual.

Such discrete separation of sex and aggression may occur, but it certainly cannot be assumed to be the rule. It seems that more often than not, elements of one type of behavior enter into the other type. Sex and aggression may overlap and intertwine to a high degree, producing a *fusion* of the two behaviors.

The literature on rape (e.g., Cohen, Garofalo, Boucher, & Seghorn, 1971; Groth, 1979) leaves no doubt about the fact that violent action often continues and even escalates after sexual access has been accomplished. In rape, aggressive impulses may dominate sexual ones to the point where the sexual activity becomes entirely secondary. Sexual activity, it seems, can become a means of expressing violence—a means of debasing (cf. Wickler, 1972) and of humiliating a person (cf. Brownmiller, 1975).

Probably the most perplexing and confusing sex-aggression fusion, however, has been that in sadomasochistic behaviors (e.g., Lester, 1975; Stekel, 1929). In such behaviors, aggression is placed in the service of euphoria. Pain is converted to joy. Thinking in motivational terms, von Schrenck-Notzing (1892) spoke of a lust for pain (algolagnia), and he distinguished between an active lust (i.e., euphoria deriving from inflicting pain) and a passive lust (i.e., euphoria deriving from receiving pain) of this kind. Although the concept of algolagnia was initially independent of sexual considerations, the sexual undercurrents of such behavior were so strong that the concept was soon transformed to a sexual one. It appears that von Krafft-Ebing (1886), in coining the terms sadism for active sexual algolagnia and masochism for passive sexual algolagnia, has virtually immortalized the two European noblemen (i.e., de Sade and von Sacher-Masoch) who had confessed to their somewhat unusual sexual preferences and promoted them in their philosophical and literary work.

Sadomasochistic behaviors used to be regarded as sexual aberrations (e.g., Freud, 1938/1958). Psychoanalytically inclined writers such as Fromm (1973) emphasized the element of destruction in sadomasochism, insisting that the sexually aberrant person is a sadist first, that is, a person "with an intense desire to control, hurt, humiliate another person [p. 282]." In contrast, more recent texts on human sexuality (e.g., Luria & Rose, 1979; Walster & Walster, 1978) have granted such behaviors normalcy. The destructive component in sadomasochistic behavior is played down, if it is acknowledged at all. It appears that sadomasochism is made palatable as a game in which no one gets hurt: a scenario in which all actors know where to draw the line. Much of the typical bondage rituals seems "pure theatre" indeed. However, things can and occasionally do get out of hand. Clinical records are laden with reports of accidental mutilations (e.g., Friedman, 1959; Stekel, 1929), but reliable quantitative documentations are not available. Probably the most reliable and compelling evidence, suggesting that sadomasochistic activities tend to go beyond the innocent ritual that they have been portrayed as being, comes from accidental deaths. Young masochistic men are known to hang themselves to enhance masturbatory excitement and pleasure. Some strangulate themselves to death in the process (Resnick, 1972). Women seek to accomplish a similar enhancement of such pleasure by partially suffocating themselves, and they too kill themselves on occasion (Weisman, 1967). The number of such accidental deaths (cf. Litman & Swearingen, 1972) may not be alarming. But if one considers how infrequently death is likely to result from the performance of sadomasochistic behaviors and, should it result, how infrequently it is likely to be recorded as more than a common suicide, the figures (about 50 deaths annually in the United States) can be taken to suggest that the exploitation of pain for sexual enjoyment is not a trivial social phenomenon. The problems with violence in marriages in which one or both parties develop a sadomasochistic preference (e.g., Kaunitz, 1977) give further testimony that such behavior is not always a form of controlled play in the service of the maximization of pleasure.

Flagellation might be regarded as one of the less destructive, comparatively safe techniques in sadomasochism. It also seems to be the most preferred. Henriques (1968) describes mid-19th-century London as "the flagellation capital of the world [p. 243]." This behavior was enormously popular in the brothels, inspiring many respected writers to comment on what appeared to be a complete and perfect transformation of painful sensations into pleasurable ones. Recent surveys of preferred sadomasochistic activities (e.g., Spengler, 1977) continue to show a fascination with the basics: whipping and caning, with bonding next in line. More elaborate alternative practices follow far behind. Such choices seem to suggest a preference for direct, uncomplicated access to pain or the satisfaction of inflicting it.

The populus at large seems to disdain sex-related beatings. But scratching and biting prior to and during intercourse are not uncommon (e.g., Eysenck, 1976; Gebhard & Johnson, 1979). As was indicated earlier, biting during copulation is common in many species (usually, the male bites the female to restrain her—a circumstance that led those who like to anthropomorphize to speak of rape as the rule in the animal kingdom), and this biting can be injurious. Likewise, such aggressive behavior has been found to be closely associated with sexual activities in several preliterate cultures (cf. Ford & Beach, 1952). It is unclear, however, to what extent the reports of sex-related pinching, scratching, squeezing, and biting in contemporary society reflect inclinations to inflict or receive pain. Conceivably, most of these "aggressive" behaviors constitute variations, though forceful ones, of touching and kissing. Most bites, then, might be nibbles. And the scratching and striking might be more in line with the recommendations of the *Kāma Sūtra* than with the suggestions of de Sade. Be this as it may, the inventory of sexual practices in the United States taken by Hunt (1974), which entailed specific questions about the infliction and the reception of pain during sexual activities, revealed that pain is with some regularity placed in the service of sexual joy.

But bodily pain is not the only aversive experience considered capable of enhancing sexual pleasures. Seemingly all other aversive experiences have been implicated as well. Long ago, Ovid (*Artis amatoriae*) gave detailed descriptions of the extraordinary male delight of coitus with a frightened maiden in tears. More recent discussions of sexuality (e.g., Janda & Klenke-Hamel, 1980; Luria & Rose, 1979; McCary, 1978) echo such observations in treating it as a truism that sex "is never sweeter" than right after an argument or a fight. The British philosopher Bertrand Russell (1969) chipped in his wisdom concerning fear and sex. He held the anxieties he experienced during a war night—bombardment, flaming skies, and all—accountable for the special passion of an extramarital love affair.

Ovid is usually called upon to validate the point that mere exposure to blood and gore enhances the passions. His comments on the high likelihood of inciting passionate love in the presence of gladiatorial combat are often interpreted as showing that the excitement from witnessing mayhem facilitates sexual behavior. But actually, he talked only about dating, and his comments suggest that the excitement produced by exposure to the bloody events in the arena furthered passionate love in the sense of creating intense mutual *attraction* between lad and maiden.

Fromm (1956) contended that any strong emotion (in his view, the anxieties of loneliness, the wish to vanquish or be vanquished, to be hurt or destroyed, vanity, love, etc.) readily blends with sexual desire. Walster (1971) and Berscheid and Walster (1974), in developing a theory of romantic love, analogously proposed that potentially all emotions, negative as well as positive ones, can fuse with sexual desire. Specifically, they applied Schachter's (1964) two-factor theory of emotion to emotional attraction or romantic love. This theory is based on the assumption that peripheral arousal is not specific to emotion. To the extent that romantic love, as Walster and Berscheid proposed, is influenced by feedback from peripheral arousal, it stands to reason to expect that other emotions, by contributing to peripheral arousal, enhance love. And to the extent that adrenalin (a catecholamine impacting sympathetic activity in the autonomic nervous system) controls peripheral arousal, it appears indeed—as has been proclaimed (Walster & Walster, 1978)—that: "adrenalin makes the heart grow fonder [p. 83]." Similarly, it stands to reason to expect that unpleasant emotions, as long as they produce comparable amounts of peripheral arousal, can contribute as much as positive emotions to romantic love. And if romantic and passionate love are thus affected, should one not expect the same facilitating consequences for romantic and passionate lovemaking?

The possible fusion of sex and aggression applies to both men and women. It has been suggested, however, that it applies to men and women in different, unique ways.

Freud (1938/1958), as might be remembered, considered sex-related aggressive inclinations a universal male trait. He thought it obvious that sadism is nothing more than the occurrence of this trait in exaggerated form, and he regarded sadism as a male trait. Freud's reasoning on masochism is less straightforward. In his earlier writing (cf. 1938/1958) he suggested that masochism is a secondary dynamic that results from the inversion of sadism. Later he felt compelled to revise his position (1940). Although he continued to maintain that masochism could, at times, derive from sadism and have secondary status, he then suggested that masochism is as primary a force as sadism. However, Freud left no doubt that in his view masochism is a universal female characteristic that grows from primary sexual inclinations to engulf all of womanhood (the so-called "feminine" and "moral" masochism) and that it is antithetical to male features. Masochistic males, he felt, place themselves into a situation of womanhood, subconsciously seeking castration, playing the passive part in coitus, and giving birth. But Freud (1940) also likened masochistic inclinations to the behavior of children in awe of a dominant, potentially sadistic father: "The masochist wants to be treated like a little, helpless, and dependent child, especially like a naughty child [p. 374; author's translation]." Such Freudian thinking is still very much alive in contemporary psychotherapy (e.g., Klein, 1972).

Not surprisingly, these Freudian contentions have been on a collision course with the intuition of feminists (cf. Lederer, 1980). If Ovid can be accused of having promoted callous attitudes toward women by portraying them as beings without sexual initiative who yearn to be ravished, Freud—because of his theorizing on masochism—can be accused of having contributed to making such attitudes respectable. Clearly, many behavioral gender differences along the lines implicated by Freud (e.g., activity–passivity, dominance–submission) exist in many cultures (cf. Maccoby & Jacklin, 1974) and cannot be denied. The extent to which these differences are biologically founded or simply the result of acculturation is quite unclear, however. Freud may indeed have been hasty in extrapolating the "nature of femininity" from his observations on the largely culture-bound sexual practices of his Vienna clientele. He may have grossly overestimated the degree to which gender differences regarding sexuality are biologically determined, and by ascribing to women an inescapable masochistic nature, he may indeed have committed a grave injustice to women (cf. Shainess, 1979).

It has been suggested that the Freudian portrayal of women as ready-made targets for sexual assaults has aided in creating a climate hostile to women who have been victimized by callous and forcefully aggressive males. In particular, it seems to have helped to perpetuate the so-called "rape myth" (i.e., the belief that women ultimately enjoy being violated) and thereby kept women vulnerable. It has been observed that men who endorse aggression as a means of settling issues also tend to believe the tale of the masochistic female (e.g., Burt, 1980). The myth is thus highly self-serving to some men. But more generally, and despite the telling evidence at hand concerning the devastating consequences to women who have suffered through traumatic rape (cf. Brodyaga, Gates, Singer, Tucker, & White, 1975; Burgess & Holmstrom, 1974, 1976), most men seem to believe that the rape myth is more than a fling of male imagination and that there is some truth to it (e.g., Brownmiller, 1975). Surely, the popularity of these beliefs cannot be attributed to Freudian influence alone. It appears, however, that the psychoanalytic insistence on masochistic sexual inclinations of women has, as alleged, not exactly promoted sympathy and understanding for sexually victimized women where it counts: in police stations, in emergency rooms, and perhaps most importantly, in courtrooms (cf. Russell, 1975).

Rape can be an act of the utmost cruelty, aimed at demeaning the victim rather than at satisfying any immediate sexual urges of the assailant. Violent men have thrusted bottles and gun barrels into the vagina and the anus of their victims (cf. Schram, 1978). They have performed oral coitus with such force that their victims have vomited, urinated, and defecated in terror. They have bitten and burned their victims' breasts and labia. And on occasion, both prior to and after a sexual assault, they have killed their victims (cf. Groth, 1979). In view of such destructiveness, one would indeed expect a consensus, at least on the part of women, in efforts at dispelling the rape myth.

Interestingly, however, the controversy concerning women's masochistic inclinations promises to continue in domains of behavior, especially sexual behavior, other than violent rape. In fact, new contentions regarding such inclinations come from within the psychology of women. Relatively independent of Freudian suggestions, Bardwick (1971), for instance, has argued that women have a biologically rooted propensity for bearing pain. Women, according to this view, are equipped to cope with the pains of menstruation, pregnancy, and childbirth, and the experience of these pains is believed to make women more tolerant of pain. Bardwick acknowledges that acceptance of extreme levels of pain may be pathological but suggests that moderate levels may be stimulating. Pain, in her reasoning (Bardwick, 1971), can fuse with sexual excitement and enhance the sexual experience of women: "During coitus, women find moderate amounts of pain erotic, perhaps because the vagina is not very sensitive. In that case pain would heighten the physical sensation of genital fusion [p. 14]." Pain, then, is not viewed as enjoyable in and of itself, but as capable of facilitating pleasurable sensations—at least in women. Deutsch (1944) had presented a similar view.

It seems that Bardwick's proposal swings full circle back to Ovid's beliefs about female sexuality. Ovid may have been preoccupied with the male perspective on sex, but his tutoring did not fully anticipate de Sade. He may have had the males' pleasures at heart, but he was apparently convinced that women's distress and emotional upheaval would enhance their pleasures as well as those of men.

IV. PROVING THE LINK

Freud (1938/1958) felt that even a cursory look at human recorded history should leave no one in doubt that cruelty and sexuality are intimately linked. At the same time, however, he felt that "in explaining the connection, no one has gone beyond emphasizing the element of aggression in sexual motivation [p. 58; author's translation]." Since then, many have responded to the challenge and offered both theoretical proposals and research data. "Proving the link," if it is not a proclamation of achievement (e.g., Feshbach & Malamuth, 1978), has become an often stated objective. Laudatory as such an objective may be, it is not necessarily a particularly meaningful one. First of all, proof of *a* linkage appears to be superfluous. Fighting for sexual access, for example, has been so obtrusive a phenomenon that it could not escape the attention of early philosophers, and more recent records of biologists should have amply proven a linkage between sex and aggression. Second, proof of *a* linkage is of questionable value conceptually. Some form of relation is likely to exist between almost any two forms of behavior. A degree of relatedness is certainly more likely than complete independence. Sexual behavior, for example, can be expected to be specifically related to such activities as sleeping and feeding, grooming or preening, as well as to aggression. In many species, for instance, the well-nourished animal might be sexually more active than its starving counterpart, and continued sexual engagements might stimulate food seeking and food intake. Similarly, many bird species are likely to preen themselves after copulation. Both a connection between feeding and sex and between preening and sex could therefore be proclaimed.

It seems a moot undertaking, therefore, to prove *a* connection between sex and aggression. Not only one but several connections can readily be granted. In fact, many can be considered empirically well established (e.g., fighting for sexual access, sex-related fighting among intimates, sadomasochistic activities). The issue, consequently, is not so much the proof of a general connection as the determination of *many specific connections between sex and aggression*. And the challenge is to understand the *mechanics* of any particular connection between these behaviors. How does a sexual trait influence aggressive behavior? How does an aggressive trait influence sexual activity? How does a state of sexual motivation affect aggressive action? And how does a state of aggressive motivation influence sexual behavior? To what extent are the traits in question genetically fixed or subject to individual development? To what extent are the states under consideration biologically determined or due to learning? In short, what of the likely connections between sex and aggression is nature, and what is nurture?

A statement on what is to be considered evidence and a commitment to particular methodologies seems unavoidable at this point.

Theorizing and research in the psychoanalytic tradition and in similar approaches may have been provocative and inspiring in many ways, but they have—with few notable exceptions—failed to produce predictive models that have any acceptable degree of precision and have survived rigorous attempts at falsification (cf. Eysenck & Wilson, 1974). Regarding the sex-aggression connection, the thinking of Freud and others (e.g., Fromm, 1973; Stoller, 1975; Szasz, 1957) is laden with imaginative suggestions—but no more. Careful, controlled observation is almost nonexistent, and the critical experimental testing of theoretical proposals is definitely nonexistent. Fromm's (1973) efforts to validate the linkage between sexuality and aggression can be considered characteristic. To back his ideas, he employed—among other things—fantastically creative interpretations of the motives of such violent eccentrics as Hitler, Himmler, and Stalin; he also drew heavily from fiction such as Pauline Reage's *The Story of O*.

The study of the relationship between sex and aggression has, without a doubt, been greatly curtailed and hampered—at least in Western societies. Until recently, sexual behavior was cloaked by privacy. Aggression, on the other hand, largely eludes experimentation because of the destruction such research would entail. As a consequence, compelling tests of theoretical proposals are scarce. But such tests do exist, and they are complemented by a wealth of systematic observation. It seems possible, then, to make a commitment to rigorous empiricism and to honor it in the process of extracting and aggregating the contributions that various disciplines have made to the exploration of sex-aggression connections.

In the chapters to follow, I pursue this very possibility and try to establish sex-aggression interdependencies in humans by comparing them with those in other species. I outline the similarities and the differences of these interdependencies in various species. Then, I review principal theories of the sex-aggression linkage and critically analyze the pertinent research evidence. This undertaking leads us from contributions made in neurophysiology and endocrinology to advances in the theory of emotion and motivation. Finally, I develop a theory of sex-aggression interactions, apply it to project the conditions under which specific mutual influences occur, present research findings in support of the theory, and discuss the implications of theory and evidence.

V. DEFINITIONAL CONSIDERATIONS

Before turning to the discussion of the contributions of various disciplines to the sex-aggression issue, a brief clarification of exactly what is meant by aggression and sex seems in order.

The common usage of the word *aggression* is so broad as to render the concept vague and useless for scientific inquiry. Aggression has been conceived of as anything from killing and maiming through the destruction of valued inanimate commodities and the refusal of compliance to being assertive and initiative without directly harming anybody. Aggression and aggressiveness, it appears, have been equated with mere vigor and persistence as well as with violence and destructiveness. Attempts at delineating the concept more rigorously (e.g., Carthy & Ebling, 1964; Kaufmann, 1970; Scott, 1958a) have emphasized the goal-directedness of the behavior and the destructive nature of the goal response. Aggression became ''behavior with injurious intent.'' But whereas biologists concentrated on the behavior's propensity for inflicting *physical* injury (Hinde, 1970), psychologists employed broad and vague definitions of harm and injury. Dollard et al. (1939), for example, included under the infliction of harm such expressive behaviors as ripping a doll to pieces, and Buss (1971) included saying ''no'' to a request under injurious behavior. To make the conceptualization of aggression more useful, it became necessary to distinguish forms of harm. In particular, a distinction between bodily harm (i.e., pain and physical injury) and other forms of harm (e.g., destruction of possessions, demeaning treatments) seemed indicated. Also, it appeared desirable to involve *coercion* (e.g., Tedeschi, Smith, & Brown, 1974) as a definitional criterion to distinguish pain- and injury-inflicting behaviors that are requested and consented to from those that are forced upon a victim. The latter distinction seems especially important for the theoretical treatment of interrelationships between sex and aggression.

For the purpose of the discussion of these interrelationships in humans, I thus adopt the following definition, which entails all these criteria and distinctions (cf. Zillmann, 1979): *Aggressive behavior* is defined as any and every activity by which a person seeks to inflict bodily damage or physical pain upon a person who is motivated to avoid such infliction.

Clearly, this definition does not include the infliction of pain and injury in the context of sadomasochism. Sadomasochistic behavior may prove destructive, but it is not to be considered aggression as long as it does not meet the coercion criterion. The infliction of pain and injury, if it occurs *among consenting persons,* constitutes just that—but not aggressive behavior. Analogously, the self-infliction of pain and injury is to be regarded as self-torment and self-injurious behavior rather than as aggression.

A parallel definition classifies the infliction of nonphysical forms of harm as hostility: *Hostile behavior* is defined as any and every activity by which a person seeks to inflict harm other than bodily damage and physical pain upon a person who is motivated to avoid such infliction.

Regarding sex-aggression linkages, hostile behaviors appear to play an important part in the frustration-motivated bargaining among intimates for sexual privileges. More generally, interpersonal conflict tends to be permeated with hostility, and to the extent that many psychological and physiological manifestations of hostility—along with their motivational consequences—are similar to those of aggression, hostile and aggressive inclinations and reactions should similarly affect sexual behavior.

It should be recognized that these definitions apply to human behavior. Related definitions have been proposed for the behavior of nonhuman species. The concept of *intent,* however, has been deemed unworkable for these species (cf. Hinde, 1970; Zillmann, 1979); consequently, it has been removed from the definitions. Aggression is thus construed as any and every activity of an animal directed toward another animal that inflicts partial or complete destruction upon that animal or is associated with a high probability of so doing. Similarly, hostility is construed as any and every activity of an animal that involves behavioral elements characteristic of aggression without, however, involving the infliction of destruction upon another animal (enacted in situations of social conflict).

If definitions of aggression were initially too inclusive, early definitional approaches to *sexual behavior* tended to be too exclusive. The concept, it seems, has been successively expanded from strictly reproductive activities (the biological perspective) to anything that produces pleasure (the psychoanalytic perspective). I bypass a lengthy discussion of the divergent views and simply define sexual behavior in terms of its unique physiological manifestations. In so doing, I understand *copulation* to mean the penetration of the male into the female genitalia for the general purpose of insemination. Hence: *Sexual behavior* is defined as copulatory behavior and as any and every activity that simulates such behavior and that produces the physiological concomitants of copulation in full or in part.

This definition is broad enough to encompass any conceivable kind of heterosexual intercourse (including oral and anal intercourse), any homosexual emulation of such intercourse, any manual or oral contact with genitals or secondary erogenous parts of the body that fosters sexual excitement, any form of masturbatory activity, even sexual excitement generated by exposure to symbolic mediators of immediate sexual stimuli (e.g., erotica, fetishes). In the nonhuman primates, for instance, masturbation by manual or oral means (e.g., Harlow, 1975; Wickler, 1972) would, along with copulatory activity, be included under sexual behavior. But the routine mounting (without thrusting and without indication of sexual excitedness) that serves to establish and maintain social rank would not be included. At the human level, mutual oral contact among intimates that serves to generate sexual excitedness in the parties involved would be classified as sexual activity. But a kiss that expresses general affection or gratitude among intimates (e.g., between children and parents) and acquaintances would not.

Disagreement about definitions of sexual behavior concern not so much the delineation of what is to be considered sexual activity as it concerns the classification of what is to be considered "normal" and what "abnormal" or "deviant." This issue is, of course, extremely value-laden, especially with regard to human sexual behavior. Not surprisingly, then, authors have tended to view as abnormal those behaviors that were deemed inappropriate, if not objectionable and repulsive, during their upbringing; and on occasion, such behaviors were plentiful. In recent years, however, an extreme liberalization of sexual standards has taken place in Western societies, and authors tend to apologize for using the qualification "deviant," if they dare to use it at all. But despite the apparent reluctance to label behaviors as deviant, it seems that a consensus on this issue is emerging, and I attempt to articulate this consensus.

First of all, normalcy is to be interpreted in statistical terms. For a behavior to be normal it simply has to be practiced by a substantial majority of the people in a particular social aggregate. Normal, therefore, means frequent and typical. By implication, abnormal and deviant mean infrequent and rare. Clinical definitions of deviancy generally follow statistical lines, because persons usually do not seek treatment for sexual habits that are shared with a majority of people and are likely to be endorsed by this majority. Needless to say, the popularity of sexual practices may change in society, and the assessment of normalcy would vary along with such changes.

The real issue, which is usually confounded with considerations of normalcy, is that of deviant behavior that is subject to social reproach. Which human sexual practices are to be considered unacceptable and objectionable? Which are deviant in this sense?

In a much cited definition (Suinn, 1970), all sexual activities in which gratification of sexual impulses is achieved by practices other than heterosexual intercourse with a person who has reached the age of legal consent are ruled deviant. In view of the documented sexual practices in contemporary society (e.g., Eysenck, 1976; Hunt, 1974), this would leave a small minority of persons who could be found not deviant. Texts on human sexuality (e.g., Luria & Rose, 1979) have thus countered with "everything goes." Usually, however, the qualification has been added that sexual activities, whatever their nature, be based on the *consent* of the persons involved.

The value position for which a consensus seems to exist is this: Any conceivable form of sexual behavior is acceptable (i.e., nondeviant) as long as all participants are free to do whatever they do. It is the involvement of *coercion*, then—the *use of aggressive and hostile means or the threat thereof* to force compliance—that makes sexual behavior deviant and societally unacceptable.

The concern for the welfare of the participants in sexual engagements has led Byrne and Byrne (1977) to include the stipulation that, notwithstanding initial consent, any sexual activity that proves truly distressing to a party involved be considered deviant and unacceptable: "Abnormal sexuality consists of any sex-related behavior that causes psychological distress or unwanted physical pain for the individual engaging in the act and/or for an unwitting or unwilling participant [p. 345]."

This *hedonistic* definition renders acceptable all sexual activities that produce pleasure, and it renders abnormal all such activities that result in displeasure. However, of potentially pleasurable sexual engagements only those in which all participants act "voluntarily and knowingly [p. 345]" are deemed acceptable. Byrne and Byrne (1977) elaborate the implications as follows:

> Any violence or threat of violence or any force applied to coerce an unwilling victim are unacceptable. Any sexual act that takes advantage of another's weakness, fear, poverty, inexperience, ignorance, or state of consciousness is unacceptable—therefore, sex with animals, or children, or someone who is mentally incompetent is not acceptable. Equally abnormal is sex with someone who is drugged, not in contact with reality, unconscious, or dead. Any sexual act that is unpleasant, anxiety evoking, or guilt inducing is unacceptable. Any sexual act that results in delayed negative consequences such as venereal disease or an unwanted pregnancy is unacceptable [pp. 345–346].

Any sexual activity, regardless of its particular physical manifestations, is thus considered acceptable as long as it is based on *informed consent* and does not produce *distress* in any of the participants. If it is assumed that genuine distress is—as a rule—not consented to, both stipulations merge into one criterion: the absence of coercion. And inasmuch as coercion is by definition the use of hostile or aggressive means or the threat thereof to achieve desired ends, the definition can be rephrased to read: *Acceptable sexual behavior* is devoid of hostility and aggression or the threat of hostility and aggression.

It should be remembered that the infliction of pain and injury in sadomasochistic activities (i.e., such infliction being approved of and sought out) is considered torment and destructive behavior, but not aggression. Sadomasochism is thus not ruled abnormal, regardless of how strongly one might object to such activities on aesthetic and moral grounds.

The criterion of informed consent, useful as it may be in making a consensual evaluation of human sexual behavior appear feasible, is not without problems. First, the notion does not apply to nonhuman species. Second, it is often unclear what "informed" is to mean. Is it the comprehension of *all* possible or likely consequences of specific acts? Third, the question may be raised whether the expression of consent is really more than a failure to express reluctance and unwillingness. If the latter is considered essentially identical with the former, the consent concept can be operationalized in more behavioral terms and applied more universally. Analogous to our definition of hostility and aggression, it could be stipulated that acceptable sexual activities be free of victimization in the sense that no one is coerced into doing something that he or she is *motivated to avoid*. Sex, in other words, must be a *victimless* activity in order to be societally acceptable.

The criterion that sexual activity be victimless is offered here as a "conservatively biased" criterion for which a general consensus can be assumed. In all probability, large segments of the population will find this criterion to be far too inclusive. More stringent, ethical criteria may seem desirable. I do not discuss such criteria, however, because they tend to vary enormously among individuals and thus defy consensus.

2
Connections in Comparative Behavior Analysis

The purpose of this chapter is to review the pertinent and representative occurrences of sex-aggression linkages in different species, including preliterate and literate humans, and to provide an overview of the degree of generality of essential linkages. I concentrate on extracting the principal forms of connections between sex and aggression and on documenting their variability and their range in nonhuman and human behavior. Finally, I place sexual-aggressive behaviors in contemporary society into the context of such behavior in other species and in earlier human societies, and I try to determine the relevance or irrelevance of these comparisons for present and future human behavior.

I. BEHAVIOR OF NONHUMAN SPECIES

The principal biological advantage of sexual reproduction is the wealth of genetic permutations associated with it. The progeny from sexual unions, due to genetic segregation and recombination, exhibit far greater genetic variability than the progeny from asexually reproducing organisms (Crow & Kimura, 1970). As a result, the progeny from sexual unions are capable of surviving under a greater variety of environmental conditions (Brown, 1975), and the genes of the offspring are favored by a higher probability of being represented in the next generation. For this reason, sexual reproduction has been viewed as a master adaptation for survival (Adler, 1978). The adaptive advantage comes at a considerable behavioral cost, however. Comparatively elaborate mechanisms are necessary for attracting the parties of sexual unions to one another and for coordinating the enormously complex social interactions involved in both the sexual union as such and the caretaking of the offspring (cf. Dobzhansky, 1970; Hinde, 1970).

Additionally, the adaptive advantage seems to come at a high cost in aggression and destructiveness. It is this latter idea of apparent "cost" that I consider in more detail.

The social conditions under which sexual unions occur vary vastly across species. In many insects, for instance, reproducing females mate with what seems to be the male that, by chance, is immediately available. Without an apparent selection procedure used by the female and without any apparent competition for sexual privileges among males (other than the active pursuit of the female), mate selection seems random and is without conflict and aggression. Characteristically, the social relation is dissolved immediately after mating. The male has become superfluous and, especially in systems in which one or a selected few females carry the burden of reproduction, is often abandoned. As is well known, for example, bees eject drones from their colony after one of them has fulfilled its reproductive mission. Such postmating behavior can be construed as sex-related aggression. It is, however, without cost as far as the survival of the species is concerned.

Similarly short-lived social arrangements for the purpose of sexual union can be found in most arachnida. The cannibalistic habits of the famous black widow, for instance, demonstrate the disposability of the male after mating. Again, such aggression is without cost to the species. If anything, it is beneficial in that it provides food for the parenting female, a resource that would otherwise be lost to another species.

Much has been said about the extraordinary sexual-aggressive behavior of the praying mantis (cf. Marler & Hamilton, 1968; Wendt, 1965). The female may start to ingest the front part of the sexually attracted male. Yet, the beheaded male manages to avoid further mutilation by turning away from the female's mandibles, to eventually mount the female, to perform vigorous sexual movements for minutes, and maintain copulation for hours (Roeder, 1963). The fact that the beheaded male performs vigorous abdominal movements that have not been observed in the intact male might be construed as an indication that bodily injury somehow facilitates sexual behavior in this and possibly other species. Generalizations of this sort are utterly unwarranted, however. It appears that a highly specific injury, namely, the destruction of the protocerebral ganglia that mediate the inhibition of locomotor activity in the mantis' central nervous system (Roeder, 1937; Roeder, Tozian, & Weiant, 1960), accounts for the observed "hypersexuality." The peculiar sexual behavior of the praying mantis attests to the robustness of the neural endowment for motor activity in arthropods. But it is without apparent implications for the sexual-aggressive behavior of different orders of species. In terms of aggression, the mantis' behavior is another illustration of the dispensability of the male after mating—although, admittedly, the demonstration of this dispensability comes unusually early.

It is generally agreed that the female's parental investment is much greater than that of the male (cf. Trivers, 1972). Notable exceptions can be found in fish. For example, the male pipefish virtually carries and breeds the young. In mammals, however, the male's reproductive contribution tends to be limited to comparatively brief copulatory engagements. It is the exception that the male, as for example in the red fox (Brown, 1975), is significantly involved in caring for the young. In stark contrast, the pregnant female's reproductive physiology undergoes drastic, often incapacitating changes, and after giving birth, the female's behavior is dominated by nurturing the developing young for considerable periods of time. Even if breeding and caring for the young is shared by a male and a female as a parenting pair, as is the case in many bird species, the reproductive effort of the female by far exceeds that of the male. Repeatedly, the female invests her resources into producing an ovum containing a large energy store for the embryo. A single egg has been shown to weigh up to 20% of her body weight (Alcock, 1975), restricting her mobility in the same way that pregnancy restricts the mobility of the mammalian female.

In many species, then, the female seems vulnerable to accident and predation for some time during the reproductive phase. Even her food-gathering capacity may be impaired, rendering her somewhat dependent on care and protection. The quasi-random short-lived encounter for the purpose of sexual union may thus not be particularly adaptive. It may suffice for wasteful systems, such as in fish, where offspring come in enormous numbers (and do not require parental care). But it seems inadequate for species that produce offspring in limited numbers, especially when reproduction cannot be repeated without much delay (e.g., once per season) and the young are vulnerable and dependent during a comparatively long period of development. It would seem advantageous for such species to establish social relations that outlast the mating encounter and that afford a degree of protection to both the reproducing females and the offspring.

It appears that every conceivable social system of reproductive affiliation has evolved and that the various principal forms have unique implications for aggression.

Monogamy, a lasting bond between a male and a female, can be found in many birds. South African black eagles, for example, form lifelong pairs (Cowden, 1969). Similarly, zebra finches pair for life in a remarkably harmonious fashion; fighting among the two parties is virtually nonexistent (Butterfield, 1970). More characteristically, however, pairs are formed for particular reproductive cycles.

The formation of reproductive pairs resolves the problem of sexual access in a population. Once the pair is formed, fighting for access is no longer an issue, although it may be one prior to pair formation. In many marine birds, pairs are formed after elaborate but usually nonviolent courtship rituals. More generally, as indicated earlier, a great many bird species attract a female to a territory over which the males fought—usually employing more threat than actual aggression. The social solution to the reproduction problem is thus at a very low cost in intraspecific aggression. A disadvantage might be incurred in the somewhat limited genetic recombination provided by the system. This possible disadvantage is likely to be a problem only in rather small populations, however.

Independent of the particular duration of the monogamous relationship, it is a system that minimizes conflict and sex-related aggression, especially when the pairs are territorially segregated, as long as the male–female distribution within a population approximates equality (Selander, 1965).

Polygamy, the mating arrangement between a member of one sex and several members of the other, is far more conducive to sex-related aggression. In principle, the claiming of exclusive access to multiple partners by some comes necessarily at the expense of others, and the parties denied sexual access are likely to continue to challenge, by violent means, those who control access.

Polygamy subdivides into polyandry (i.e., a female's affiliation with several male mates) and polygyny (i.e., a male's affiliation with several female mates). Generally speaking, polyandry is rather rare. It occurs, for example, in some quails and pheasants. Polygyny, on the other hand, is very common. It is practiced, among other species, by antelopes, buffalos, camels, deer, goats, hippos, horses, pigs, sea lions, sheep, sperm whales, and zebras (Wynne-Edwards, 1962).

The dominance of polygyny over polyandry across species corresponds with the greater physical strength of males over females within many species. Particularly in mammals, but in other orders as well, the males tend to outsize the females and to be stronger and more aggressive (Scott, 1958a, 1958b). In the elephant seal, for example, the male may be up to 10 times the size of the female (Bartholomew, 1952). Ratios slightly above unity are far more common, however.

In polygynous species, control over sexual access is exerted, as a rule, through intermale fighting. So-called harems or sexual monopolies are established and maintained through combat with rivaling males. Such combat, counter to popular beliefs, frequently injures the combatants, sometimes severely. On occasion it leads to death. The monopolization of females, therefore, comes at considerable cost in aggression and its consequences to the species.

The prime example of a polygynous system, it seems, is the red deer (Tinbergen, 1953). As the breeding season approaches, the males round up harems of females. Competition over these females is fierce, and the males engage in exhaustive battles to maintain control over their harems. Using their huge antlers they inflict injury upon one another with some regularity. In addition, it has been observed that these antlers get entangled and that the combatants are unable to disengage themselves, resulting in the death of both animals. Nonetheless, sexual access is accomplished through fighting only, as animals whose antlers were removed experimentally generally failed to gain access (Lincoln, 1972).

Whereas the red deer is thus polygynous and aggressive, the roe deer, interestingly, is monogamous and does not form harems (Darling, 1964). In this related species, the males' antlers are considerably smaller, the males' body size is reduced, and the species exhibits far less aggression altogether.

The monopolization of females by polygamous males can entail aggression against females as well. It has been observed, for example, that in wolves the dominant animal may deny competitors sexual access by incapacitating particular females (Ginsburg, 1970). As an alternative to fighting off male rivals, wolves have attacked and injured members of their harem that come into heat. The injured females fight off sexual advances, and once recovered, they are no longer receptive. Such seemingly "calculated" aggressive behavior against females appears to be extremely rare, however.

The monopolization of females not only comes at the expense of excessive intraspecific fighting, but at the cost in genetic recombination as well. Obviously, only the best male intraspecific fighters attain sexual access and reproduce. The evolutionary consequences of this process are known as "sexual selection" (Campbell, 1972; Darwin, 1859/1887; Fisher, 1958). The process tends to perpetuate and promote the selection-governing behaviors (i.e., intermale fighting), and it proves adaptive only to the extent that essential survival faculties covary with the fighting skills in question. Specific faculties manifest in inferior fighters may be vital, but are lost to the species.

Extreme reproductive selectivity has been observed, for example, in elephant seals of the Pacific coast (Le Boeuf & Peterson, 1969). In their natural habitat, 85% of the females were found to be inseminated by only 4% of the males. More characteristic ratios of "genetic participation" may be found, for instance, in the American chameleon. In this species, males commonly attract 8–10 females to their territory and, warding off any competition, mate with them exclusively (Cloudsley-Thompson, 1965).

Sexual affiliations of limited duration and with multiple male and female partners (bilateral polygamy, so to speak) is usually referred to as promiscuity. Promiscuity within social aggregates of a species, because it provides seemingly unrestricted sexual access, can be viewed as a reproductive arrangement that most effectively curtails sex-related aggression. Indeed, promiscuous species appear to exhibit little intraspecific fighting. In addition, promiscuity promotes the highest degree of genetic recombination and is thus advantageous to species whose effective adaptation and survival depend on maximal genetic variability.

Promiscuity is evident in a great many mammalian species. Most rodents and ruminants are promiscuously inclined (Johnson, 1972). In fact, for many such species it has been observed that the provision of novel sexual partners leads to a significant enhancement of sexual activity (e.g., Beamer, Bermant, & Clegg, 1969; Fowler & Whalen, 1961; Schein & Hale, 1965; Wilson, Kuehn, & Beach, 1963). These observations, however, attest more to promiscuous inclinations in males than in females. It should also be noted that contradictory data do exist (Dewsbury, 1975) and that the projection of universal promiscuity in these species may understate their capacity for diverse, adaptive social organization in the service of reproduction.

Promiscuity is characteristic of most species of nonhuman primates (Jensen, 1973). In bonnet macaques, for example, all males are free to mate with all females of the troop that are in estrus (Simonds, 1965). Social rank is of little moment, and fighting is conspicuously absent. The situation is similar in most chimpanzees (Goodall, 1965; Reynolds & Reynolds, 1965). In some chimpanzees, however, social rank is of importance. It has been observed that when several males copulate with the same female the higher ranking males take precedence over the lower ranking ones (Sugiyama, 1969). Regarding sexual initiative, there are striking differences in chimpanzees. In the Gombe Stream Reserve in Tanganyika (Goodall, 1965), sexual activities were found to be mostly initiated by males. Only in 15% of the copulatory incidents recorded did a female approach and solicit the males. In the Budongo Forest in Uganda (Sugiyama, 1969), on the other hand, the females were found to be mostly responsible for initiating copulations.

Solicitation by females in estrus is common in other species as well. In howlers (Carpenter, 1965), for example, females solicit without apparent preference for particular males. If unsuccessful with one male, they approach the next, and so forth, until cooperation is gained. Langur females practice similar solicitations (Jay, 1965). At midestrus, however, they display a preference for dominant males.

The degree of promiscuity can vary substantially during estrus. In baboons (Hall & DeVore, 1965), for example, females are fully promiscuous at the onset of turgescence. All males of low rank are sexually accommodated at this time. When in full estrus, however, they affiliate and mate exclusively with the most dominant male of the troop or with a particular male consort. Consort relationships that emerge from a milieu of sexual promiscuity are not limited to baboons. They have been observed in chimpanzees (Bower, 1971) and macaques (Carpenter, 1942; Hall & DeVore, 1965), among other nonhuman primates.

Consort relationships can be construed as reproductive pairs. Considering sex-related aggression, it is most significant that such relationships can be formed without any apparent fighting. It has been noted that consort pairs tend to be secretive about sexual activities (Jensen, 1973). This inclination to conduct sexual affairs in privacy (i.e., without being witnessed by the troop) may be essential in that it helps circumvent the aggression-promoting conflicts that are created by the monopolization of the female and possibly the male consort.

Promiscuity in the nonhuman primates, then, is somewhat less than "total sexual freedom." Monopolization of sexual partners does occur. In fact, monopolizing consort relationships can result in lasting pairs. The tree shrew, a primitive primate, is known to form such pairs (Martin, 1968). Gibbons, moreover, can be characterized as monogamous because the consort relationships established tend to be permanent (Berkson, Ross, & Jatinandana, 1971; Mason, 1971).

It should further be noted that many nonhuman primates observe, without any involvement of fighting, promiscuity-limiting "incest taboos." Male chimpanzees (Goodall, 1965) and male rhesus monkeys (Sade, 1968) do not copulate with their mothers, although they are promiscuous with all other females of their troops. On the other hand, fathers tend to mate with their genetic daughters—presumably because they cannot be identified as such. There are, nonetheless, reports that father-daughter incest taboos have been observed (e.g., Alexander, 1970).

It appears that social organization exerts a most powerful influence on the resolution of the sexual-access problem. The establishment of enduring social ranks through comparatively innocuous intragroup fighting, in particular, not only minimizes destructive fighting over the vital resources of food and shelter, but over sexual access—another vital resource—as well (cf. Zillmann, 1979). In the nonhuman primates such social relationships are fully developed, and as a result, most conflict over sexual access can be resolved by threats and in minor skirmishes rather than through injurious battles. Sex-related fighting is thus highly dependent on the degree of social organization. The social solutions to sexual affiliation are significant in that they effect a variation in sexual access as "a valued commodity." Other things equal, the more that members of one sex are monopolized in consort relationships and the longer the duration of these relationships in reproductive periods, the greater will be the commodity value of access to the monopolized sex and the probability of conflict among the monopolizers. It should come as no surprise, therefore, that the incidence of fighting generally increases during sexual seasons. The indicated covariation between reproductive state and aggression has indeed been established for chimpanzees (Sugiyama, 1969), macaques (Wilson & Boelkins, 1970), for example, and for many nonprimate species as well (cf. Johnson, 1972). Such apparent sex-aggression linkage seems nonunique, however. It appears to be governed by mechanics similar to those that produce a covariation between aggressiveness and the scarcity of food and/or shelter (Southwick, 1966, 1969).

Sex-related aggression other than access fighting tends to be more specific and unique. Interestingly, it may result from advanced forms of social organization—those that, as has been discussed, tend to curtail and minimize access fighting. Nonhuman primates have been found to practice infanticide that is highly selective socially. In gorillas (Fossey, 1981), for example, family-type troops are led by dominant males. In case a leader dies (or is otherwise lost) members of his troop are likely to be taken over by the leaders of other troops. When such outside intervention occurs, the usurping leaders tend to kill the offspring that are still being nursed. Killing seems deliberate, with bites into the infants' head and groin. It meets with little, if any, resistance from the mother and other members of the usurped troop. Such killing appears to be sex-related in that, by terminating the mothers' lactation, the females will become receptive again sooner. It has also been suggested (e.g., Fossey, 1981) that the killing serves to discontinue the progeny of the departed leadership and enables the new leader to pass on his own genes. This view is at variance with two observations, however. First, the killing is specific to infants being nursed. Weaned progeny are spared. Second, the leader may entertain consort relationships and show little or no sexual interest in the usurped females. The females whose infants were killed may end up reproducing with inferior males, even males from the usurped troop. Similar infanticide has been recorded in Hanuman langurs (Sugiyama, 1967).

Complex social organization may also produce what could be considered sexually motivated "kidnapping" (cf. Beach, 1976). In Hamadryas baboons, for example, large troops of hundreds of animals are composed of small family-type units that usually comprise a male adult with one to three adult females and their young. The males copulate exclusively with their own females, and intermale competition for sexual access is thus virtually nonexistent. Furthermore, the incidence of fighting for access is minimized by the indicated practice of kidnapping. Sexually immature females are adopted from dissolving families or, at times, taken by force (i.e., kidnapped) from intact families. They are then socially integrated until they mature and become mates. Kidnapping is also conducted by young adult males. They carry off the immature daughters of dominant males and thereby reduce the likelihood of father-daughter incest (Kummer, 1971).

Before turning to further unique sex-aggression linkages, it should be mentioned that sexual access is not always a matter of competition. It has been observed that males occasionally cooperate to attract females. In species that maintain communal mating grounds, the males often join forces in calling and in vigorous displays so as to reach females over longer distances. For example, bullfrogs (Capranica, 1965) and grouse (Hyorth, 1970), respectively, practice such cooperation. The males of the black-and-white manakin (Snow, 1956) initially collaborate, but compete once a female has been attracted. Even mere gregariousness among males can serve to attract females. In the village weaver, for example, it has been observed (Collias & Collias, 1969) that more females per male nest were attracted to large colonies of males than to small ones. Observations such as these temper the generalization that in nature sexual access is necessarily competitive, if not combative.

The analysis of behavior reveals what appears to be a unique association between sex and aggression in the performance of sexual activity as such. Ford and Beach (1951), after a thorough, extensive review of the pertinent literature, concluded that "physically aggressive behavior forms an integral part of the sexual pattern for vertebrates of every major phyletic class [p. 57]," but they readily granted some exceptions. Their conclusion is based mainly on the observation that biting, even injurious biting, quite characteristically accompanies copulatory behavior in a large number of species. In numerous mammals, for instance, the males bite the females during copulation. This is the case with shrews, bats, and rabbits, to name a few species. In these species, the male—as he mounts the female from the rear—seizes the skin or fur of her neck or back with his teeth and thus holds her during coitus. Domestic cats and predators such as lions conduct themselves similarly.

Ford and Beach ascribe functional significance to the biting. The biting, they suggest, compels the female to assume the copulatory position (i.e., to lower her forequarters) and permits the male to make the bodily adjustments necessary to achieve intromission. They further note that biting is associated with erection and suspect that it may aid in producing erection.

In some species, biting seems to be an essential part of precoital rather than coital behavior. In sheep and horses, for example, the males may extensively bite the females. Such precopulatory biting may be mutual, however, as in the case of elephant seals. Biting seems ferocious in many fur-bearing cetaceans, and courtship and mating are invariably described as involving much "painful stimulation."

Biting may produce injury and be part of what appears to be intense fighting preliminary to mating. Ford and Beach (1951) describe the sexual behavior of minks, martens, and sables as follows:

> The normal mating pattern . . . begins when the male springs upon the female and seizes the skin of her neck in his mouth. His long, sharp canine teeth pass completely through her pelt and his jaws may remain locked for most of the copulatory period. The female's initial response consists of a vigorous attempt to escape, and for a considerable length of time the two animals engage in what appears to be a violent battle. The male is much larger than his mate and when her struggles grow less marked he gets into a position that will permit intromission. Eventually insertion is accomplished, and . . . it may be maintained for several hours. Only after he has penetrated the female is the male likely to relax his grip on her neck, and if she tries to terminate the mating before he is ready to do so, he promptly secures another neck-hold and prevents her from escaping [p. 59].

In view of the female's apparent efforts to avoid copulation, the mating behavior of these species may seem to qualify as rape. Such an interpretation is questionable, however, as the female is actually cooperating with the male to some degree. This is clear from the observation that only receptive females permit intromission. Nonestrous females simply cannot be mated. With the possible exception of some nonhuman primates, this seems to be true generally. In many mammalian species, in fact, the sexual approach of unreceptive females is dangerous to the male. It may result in serious injury to the male, even in death (cf. Hediger, 1965).

Matters are further complicated by the fact that the involvement of aggression in copulatory behavior may have reproductive significance. The described violent mating of minks, martens, and sables, for instance, seems to be necessary for the release of ripe eggs from the ovaries. For conception to occur, the female apparently must be put through the agony of the assault. Without this agony, coitus tends to be sterile. The reproductive significance of fighting is further attested to by the fact that mink females have been observed to ovulate, without copulation, after extensive conflict and struggle with males (cf. Ford & Beach, 1951).

A good deal of aggressiveness is also part and parcel of the mating behavior of many nonhuman primates. In macaques (e.g., Carpenter, 1942; Hamilton, 1914) and baboons (e.g., Zuckerman, 1932), for example, the male tends to chase the female about, alternatively biting her and copulating with her. Minor injury is inflicted quite commonly, almost always by the male upon the female. Interestingly, the injured females show no signs of avoiding further contact and seem particularly eager for copulation. Sex-linked injury can be rather extensive. In macaques (Carpenter, 1942), for example, the females tend to be covered by scars and wounds that were inflicted upon them by their various sexual partners during the 9- to 10-day estrous period.

Sex-linked aggression need not be severe, however. In chimpanzees, for example, there is some biting, but it is nonvigorous and unlikely to cause appreciable pain. Howlers and spider monkeys are equally nonaggressive. Sex-related injury is very rare in these species (cf. Ford & Beach, 1951).

The involvement of aggression in precoital and coital behavior has been viewed as an essential condition in the elicitation of sexual excitement. Ford and Beach (1951) contend that if pain is not excessive to the point where it inhibits the animals' sexual activity, its effect is likely to "summate with the effects of other stimuli to produce an increased sexual fervor [p. 64]."

Such facilitation of sexual excitement seems not limited to painful stimulation, however. There are observations on nonhuman primates suggesting that arousal from any intense emotion, whether hedonically positive or negative, is capable of facilitating sexual excitement and sexual behavior. The likelihood of sexual approaches and copulation is increased, for instance, when males are socially stimulated. In chimpanzees (cf. Jensen, 1973), the unexpected meeting of two groups or the encounter of a food source by hungry animals tends to spark much excitement. This excitement manifests itself in vigorous charging displays on the part of males. In these displays, erection is a common occurrence. Furthermore, if a receptive female is present in the excited group, copulations are very likely. Work with macaques (Alexander & Perachio, 1970) shows this type of facilitation to depend on the social relationship between the animals whose sexual behavior is being facilitated and those whose presence causes the facilitation. Compared to the copulatory activity of a male and a receptive female in seclusion, the addition of an inferior male was found to enhance that activity. In contrast, the addition of a male of superior rank not only failed to enhance sexual activity, but inhibited it. In Hanuman langurs (Sugiyama, 1967), social stimulation (e.g., intermale skirmishes and leadership changes) was found to promote the sexual behavior of females. Perhaps the most perplexing condition that proves to promote sexual fervor in females is that of particularly vicious attacks on troops—attacks that involve the killing of infants.

Diverse and incompatible with sexual behavior as these facilitative conditions may appear, it should be noticed that all are likely to generate much excitement that potentially enters into sexual activity. I give more attention to the apparent process of sexual facilitation in later chapters (especially in Chapter 6) where I attempt to specify its mechanics for human behavior as well as for that of nonhuman species.

An association between sex and aggression, finally, seems to exist in expressive behaviors or "displays." Specifically, sexual and aggressive displays may have similar manifestations, and many particular displays are common to both sexual and aggressive situations (cf. Hinde, 1970; Wickler, 1967).

Some aggressive and sexual displays are virtually indistinguishable in many of the lower vertebrates. In fish, for instance, the initial stages of courtship behavior may be identical with displays preliminary to actual fighting (Barlow, 1962). The same is true for many species of birds and lower mammals (cf. Eibl-Eibesfeldt, 1970; Ford & Beach, 1951; Marler & Hamilton, 1968).

Similarly, there is considerable overlap between sexual and aggressive displays in the nonhuman primates. In chimpanzees (Goodall, 1965; Jensen, 1973), for example, two displays—the so-called "beckoning" and "tree-leaping"—are distinct courtship behaviors. Two others, however, are employed in both sexual and aggressive contexts. The first one is the "swagger," a behavior sequence in which the displaying animal stands upright, shows pilo-erection, and directs ostentatious bravado toward the interactant. This swagger is a male sexual display toward a female *and* a general threat display in situations of conflict. The "glaring look" is the other sex-aggression display. High-ranking males cause females to present for copulation simply by glaring at them. With great consistency, these females crouch and await the approach of the male or actually approach the male to present to him. Again, in situations of conflict, such glaring is a threat without sexual implications.

The obtrusive display of penile erection in nonsexual contexts has been the subject of much speculation and controversy. Because such erection accompanies some aggressive displays, its occurrence in nonsexual situations was widely interpreted as a threat posture. Nonhuman primates, especially baboons, typically employ so-called "sentinels" (i.e., male guards that sit in a remote position and are thought to alert the troop to imminent dangers), and these sentinels were observed to display their colorful genitalia, exhibiting erection as a dangerous situation developed. This behavior was viewed as serving the deterrence of intraspecific and interspecific intrusion alike (Eibl-Eibesfeldt, 1974). A more careful analysis of the circumstances (Hall, 1960) leads to quite different conclusions, however. The animals in question, it appears, neither function as sentinels nor threaten antagonists with their display. Rather, the display may indicate a fright reaction to conspecific strangers as much as threat (Wickler, 1967) and trigger the emission of warning signals that seemed intended and planned. But whether the response concurrent with erection is threat, fear, or a mixture of both, it usually entails a state of intense excitedness.

Erection displays have also been linked to the urine marking of territories that is practiced by many mammalian species (Hediger, 1944). This marking is applied to sexual objects as well as to nonsexual, territorial entities, and it is often accompanied by erection. In fact, the urine is often sporadically squirted in such marking, a circumstance that has led to the suggestion that the ejaculatory mechanism is involved, at least in part (Wickler, 1972). The emission of urine, whether associated with erection (or semierection) or not, is also characteristic of fear, however. Dogs (e.g., Berg, 1944) and many other mammals are well known for their fear micturition. The emission of urine may accompany fright as well as threat and sexual excitement in nonhuman primates (e.g., Kirchshofer, 1963). Urine squirting has also been observed to precipitate penile display in what appears to be a transition from fear to threat. Squirrel monkeys, for example, when confronted with their mirror image, tend to emit urine first and then perform a penis display at their mirror image (MacLean, 1964b). The analysis of testicular retraction (i.e., the ascent of the testes into the inguinal canal), a reaction related to penile erection and ejaculation, further corroborates that erection is not specific to sexual situations. It is characteristic of threat and fear as well (Altmann, 1962; Backhouse, 1959; Ottow, 1955). But in some mammalian species (e.g., the guinea pig), the testes descend both during threat displays and initially during courtship (Kunkel & Kunkel, 1964). As a result, the behavioral significance of testicular displays is in doubt, and interpretations are controversial (cf. Schultz, 1951). It is of interest to note that penile displays not only have a concomitant in testicular movement, but also in the coloration of the sexual skin (Sade, 1964), even in the coloration of exposed facial areas (Hill, 1955; Wickler, 1967). The latter, in particular, would seem to suggest that erection displays are likely to occur when the animal is highly excited, regardless of the specific source of the excitement.

It has been proposed that the penile displays of the nonhuman primates are a remnant of urine marking (Wickler, 1967). The actual discharge of urine is lost and replaced by the visual conspicuousness of the genitalia. This interpretation accords well with the fact that some minor urine discharge during displays is retained in some of the lower primates (e.g., the squirrel monkey). In evolutionary terms, such primates are among the species that manifest the transition from olfactory to visual control of sociosexual behavior (MacLean, 1963; Ploog & MacLean, 1963), and the shift from olfactory stimuli (e.g., urine) to visually obtrusive ones (e.g., penile displays) can thus be understood. In fact, laboratory data on penile displays in squirrel monkeys (Ploog & MacLean, 1963) can be interpreted as confirming the implied functional equivalence of urine marking in infraprimate mammals and penile displays in infrahuman primates. Squirrel monkeys were found to display erection toward conspecifics outside their group (in so-called "distant" displays) and, in the communal setting, toward peers of lesser rank only. This resembles indeed the behavior of animals who mark with urine discharges the social and environmental entities they control or seek to control.

How can all this information on sex-aggression connections in subhuman species be summarized? What generalizations can be made? Clearly, the behavior in question is extremely variable across species and can be highly variable within species. All-encompassing statements are inadvisable, because exceptions to the rule seem to be the rule. Nonetheless, granted that exceptions are likely, numerous qualified generalizations can be made:

1. Intraspecific aggression in the service of sexual access is common in many species. It appears to be most pronounced in infraprimate mammals.
2. Aggression for sexual access is predominantly intermale, almost exclusively so.
3. Aggression for sexual access tends to be most severe in species in which the male–female distribution is balanced and the members of one sex monopolize several members of the other. Characteristically, males seek exclusive sexual access to several females. The reverse—the monopolization of several males by females—is extremely rare. Intermale access aggression tends to be more severe, the more females per male are being monopolized.
4. Aggression for sexual access tends to be minimal in species in which males establish territories to which females are attracted and in which male–female pairs are formed.
5. Aggression for sexual access tends to be minimal in species with promiscuous sexual practices, especially when social relations that determine privileges (i.e., social ranks) are developed.
6. Intraspecific aggression tends to be most pronounced during sexual seasons.
7. Aggression for sexual access can vary greatly within phylogenetic classes. Such aggression can differ substantially in closely related species, usually as a result of different social habits in reproductive arrangements.
8. In nonhuman primates, aggression for sexual access tends to be minimal because of: (1) a high degree of sexual promiscuity; (2) the associated practice of sexual solicitation by estrous females; and (3) well-established social relations that control conflict generally.
9. The formation of consort relationships (i.e., the formation of pairs seeking sexual exclusivity) is common in nonhuman primates. Such relationships arise in promiscuous as well as in nonpromiscuous contexts. Access aggression in these social situations is minimized by a tendency for the consorts to seek solitude or privacy.
10. In some nonhuman primates, sex-related infanticide has been observed. Such infanticide seems to serve sexual access in that it terminates prolonged lactation in the mothers and returns them to the pool of receptive females.
11. Precoital and coital aggression is common in many species. In nonvertebrate species (e.g., arthropods), copulation-related aggression of females against males can be severe and fatal. The same is true for postcopulatory aggression. In vertebrates, copulation-related aggression is predomi-

nantly male action against females. Pain-inflicting behavior such as clawing and biting, both prior to and during coitus, is common, especially in lower mammals. Coital aggression may be injurious (destruction of tissue, mainly as the result of biting) to females. However, such destructive aggression, although characteristic of mating in some species, is rather uncommon across species. Precoital and coital aggression seem to serve a dual function: (1) the subduing of the female to achieve intromission; (2) the production of a sufficient degree of mutual excitedness.

12. Although in some species the females appear to be motivated to avoid the aggression-laden sexual assault, aggressive coital behavior does not qualify as "rape" because female cooperation is required for successful intromission.

13. Excitedness from a variety of nonsexual sources is capable of facilitating sexual activities in nonhuman primates.

14. In many vertebrates, communicative sexual and aggressive behaviors (so-called displays) have common elements. Some sexual and aggressive displays are indistinguishable.

15. In nonhuman primates, some communicative displays are employed in both sexual and aggressive social situations. The display of penile erection may be common to sexual, aggressive, and fright-evoking situations.

II. HUMAN BEHAVIOR

The study of sexual behavior in preliterate societies (e.g., Ford & Beach, 1951; Marshall & Suggs, 1971) and in literate ones, both ancient (e.g., Bullough, 1976) and contemporary (e.g., Eysenck, 1976; Hunt, 1974), leaves no doubt about the fact that such behavior has been and is extremely variable. The comparative analysis of preliterate cultures, in particular, reveals no condition that could be construed as "the natural state" (the sexual *Urzustand,* so to speak) from which all later forms of human sexuality have evolved. Rather, the analysis discloses a seemingly unlimited variation of sociosexual behaviors. Mainly because substantial differences in the sexuality of genetically comparable peoples are in obtrusive evidence, the apparent plasticity of sociosexual behavior cannot be explained as the result of varying sexual dispositions that are genetically fixed. Genetic variation may well contribute to sociosexual plasticity (e.g., Ginsburg, 1965), but such possible contribution has generally been deemed negligible in comparison to the great and undeniable influence of enculturation. This point of view is vehemently expressed by Davenport (1976) who asserts: "In man, . . . the inherited aspects of sex seem to be nearly formless. Only by enculturation does sex assume form and meaning [p. 161]." Davenport further contends that there is not and cannot be a human society without rules for sexual conduct. Such rules govern the expression of sexuality for every member of any social grouping, and they are uniquely intertwined with the rules for social conduct generally. It is indeed a universal characteristic of all preliterate human cultures, whose sociosexual behavior has been recorded, that sexual behaviors are shaped through social training from infancy to adulthood and through adult life. This shaping is accomplished, in principle, by setting up contingencies of reward for consensually approved sociosexual behaviors and punishment for consensually disallowed and condemned sociosexual behaviors, by creating behavioral expectations that accord with these contingencies, and by consistently applying contingent reward and punishment whenever necessary. Consensual guidance and correction, along with entitling and punitive rites, were eventually formalized in legal prescriptions of and sanctions against sexual behaviors. Consistent with Davenport's contention that all human sexual behavior is governed by strict rules of conduct, no literate culture is known that is without such legal control of sociosexual behavior.

The rules that govern human sexual conduct apply, of course, to any and every aspect of sexuality in society. For instance, they regulate expectations concerning desirable and satisfactory precoital and coital experience (e.g., Ford & Beach, 1951). First and foremost, however, they regulate sexual access (cf. Bullough, 1976). They may allow sexual affiliations that can be characterized as promiscuous or limit such affiliations to socially recognized units, usually pairs. They may tolerate occasional sexual liaisons (premarital, extramarital) or treat them as criminal transgressions. Similarly, they may tolerate, even encourage, sexual intercourse among juveniles or limit it to those who by some accepted criteria are considered adults; in addition, they may accept or condemn homosexual affiliations (e.g., Davenport, 1965). Finally, they will stipulate the extent to which aggression is permissible in seeking sexual access—as well as prior to and during sexual union.

In whatever way such rules of sexual conduct may have emerged and regardless of the degree to which they may reflect a consensus or are created and enforced by a social minority, it is clear that they differ immensely across societies. The enormity of this variation is usually illustrated by the report of the sociosexual behavior of two vastly different cultures: Inis Beag, a model of "sexual repression," versus Mangaia, a prototype of "sexual freedom" (e.g., Janda & Klenke-Hamil, 1980; Luria & Rose, 1979).

Inis Beag is a pseudonym for an island of the Gaeltacht. Its small Irish population was studied by Messenger (1969, 1971) in the late 1950s and early 1960s. Sexual behavior was observed to be rather restricted on Inis Beag. There was little talk of sex altogether, and—presumably as a result—many misconceptions existed about such matters as menstruation, orgasm in women, and menopause. Premarital and extramarital intercourse were not in evidence. Marital sexuality seemed to serve mainly procreation, leading to seven children on the average. It is possible, of course, to consider such numbers evidence of active marital sexuality accompanied by a lack of preventive efforts. Be this as it may, there was little, if any, expression of affection between men and women. Sex segregation pervaded childhood and adult life alike. But perhaps most importantly, the expression of sexuality itself seemed severely curtailed. Messenger was unable to discover knowledge or usage of such practices as kissing the female breast, manipulation of the penis by women, cunnilingus, fellatio, anal coitus, fetishism, or sadomasochistic behavior. Masturbation, in contrast, seemed widespread among males.

The sexual practices of the Polynesian inhabitants of Mangaia, a southern Cook Island in central Polynesia, are in stark contrast to those on Inis Beag. The population of Mangaia was studied by Marshall (1961, 1971) during the 1950s. On Mangaia, boys and girls are segregated at the age of 3 to 5. They are informed about the particulars of human reproduction at the age of 8. Both boys and girls masturbate quite freely. Actually, the children's masturbatory activities are discouraged by parents, but rather laxly so. At 13 or 14, boys undergo superincision and are taught techniques for maximizing sexual pleasure. Girls are likewise instructed at that age. Mutual orgasm is stressed as the objective of coitus. Boys engage in sexual intercourse after superincision, girls after having begun to menstruate. Sexual behavior is private, but the discussion of sex per se and of liaisons in particular may be quite open. In fact, sex-related teasing seems common, and social pressures are often brought to bear on boys and—to a lesser degree—on girls to seek out sexual adventures. Courting is minimal and to the point. Liaisons do not require affective commitments. Foreplay is scarce. And although many coital positions are known, only a few are commonly employed. Ventral-ventral intercourse, with either the man or the woman atop, and rear entry, with the woman standing bent over, account for most sexual unions. Sexual "testing" for compatibility is a universal prerequisite for marriage. Women tend to maintain extramarital liaisons, especially with premarital sexual partners. Men likewise seek out extramarital sexual engagements. Adultery is not openly practiced, however. Sexual engagements are considered healthy. Hence, traveling married men are not condemned for taking up with women, especially with unmarried ones. Women's adultery meets with a bit more contempt and is only condoned when women are living alone for extended periods of time. Group intercourse is not in evidence on Mangaia.

Surely, the sociosexual behavior on Inis Beag is restricted compared to that on Mangaia. Whether or not sexuality is repressed in the sense that men and women suffer acutely from not having premarital and extramarital liaisons remains unclear, however. The verdict of "repressed sexuality" certainly does not follow from the ethnographic accounts as such. It is conceivable that in the catholic community on Inis Beag sexual conduct is in line with sexual expectations and that, as long as these expectations are not altered by outsiders' projections of greater happiness in different, more liberal sociosexual arrangements, these people are content and happy with their sex life. The detection of "sexual repression," in short, may reveal more about prevailing values among ethnographers, and especially the interpreters of their work, than about the people said to suffer from repression.

This assessment applies to the detection of "sexual freedom" as well. The textbooks on human sexuality tend to protray many Polynesian cultures as the ultimate sexual paradise. Men and women are said to be truly equal. Sexual access is sought by either gender, and in sexual union, the two parties actively cooperate to achieve a maximum of mutual sexual pleasure. Happiness abounds, and social friction and conflict are virtually nonexistent in these portrayals of paradise. But, of course, happiness has not really been documented. And there is indication of ample conflict, mainly as the result of dishonesty in connection with adultery. In fact, although sexual access is comparatively easy to achieve, forcible rape is not uncommon. Even gang rape is in evidence (Marshall, 1971). Paradise, then, seems to have its problems. Regulations that govern access do exist, and violations do produce conflict and discontent. But regardless of explicit regulation, "consorts" may seek mutually exclusive access, and as the incidence of rape suggests, some girls do say "no!"

Self-serving distortions of ethnographic accounts tend to project promiscuity as the ideal solution to the problem of sexual access and human sexuality altogether. Nonpromiscuous societies are invariably characterized as repressive, but such characterizations are only meaningful if it is assumed that modest and moderate sexual expression is "unnatural" and cannot be a desired state. This kind of assumption has been severely challenged recently.

In the mountains of west New Guinea, Heider (1976) explored the sociosexual behavior of the Grand Valley Dani. The Dani proved to be extremely unmotivated sexually. Premarital coitus is very rare, even among couples headed for marriage. Extramarital liaisons hardly exist. Married couples appear to engage in sexual intercourse only about 2 years after being wed. After the birth of a child, the couples observe a 4- to 5-year period of abstinence from sexual activity. There is no evidence of masturbation or any other sexual "outlet." In fact, there is no evidence that the Dani are stressed or strained by the practice of sexual abstinence. They are described as a healthy, vigorous, and strong people. The Dani are affectionate and nonviolent intracommunally. (They engage in seemingly never ending warfare with neighboring communities, however, and these hostilities tend to produce casualties; Heider, 1979; Sillitoe, 1978.) In intracommunal interactions, the overt expression of anger is rare; and when it occurs, it tends to be masked by the expression of disgust (Ekman, 1972). Intracommunal fighting is equally rare. Finally, the Dani bring up their children in a nurturant, nonpunitive environment. It is important to note that noncultural determinants of the apparent disinterest in sexual behavior have been sought, but could not be found.

In view of such sociosexual behavior it is difficult to maintain that, say, three coital episodes per day or night—a common occurrence among young people on Mangaia—constitute a "natural" condition and that anything less is indicative of repression. Sociosexual enculturation, it seems, can *create* high levels of sexual expression as much as it may modify the incidence of such expression through curtailment (cf. Beach, 1976). If so, the search for "natural" and "unrepressed" sexuality in preliterate or literate societies can only be futile.

The sociosexual behavior of the Dani makes it appear similarly futile to look for a prevalence of aggression in cultures that place little value on sexual activity. Clearly, low levels of sexual expression can coexist with low levels of interpersonal aggressiveness. The preponderance of Freudian theorizing concerning repression has led some, however, to propose a causal relation between sexual repression and societal hostility and aggression. Prescott (1977), for instance, asserted such a relationship, and he attempted to support this assertion with a cross-cultural analysis of sex and aggression. In comparing numerous preliterate cultures, he noted a correspondence between the punitive treatment of premarital and extramarital sexuality, on the one hand, and bellicosity and crime, on the other. In addition, the punitive treatment of extramarital sexuality tended to vary with incidents of killing, maiming, and torturing. Does this prove that these asocial behaviors were produced by the restriction of sexual promiscuity prior to and during marriage? Obviously not! Such a correspondence has any number of possible explanations. It can be argued, for example, that only aggressive peoples developed a sense for usurpation and coercion and that those in power did not hesitate to institute and enforce punitive sanctions to insure compliance with desirable, mostly consensually approved (but occasionally self-serving), rules of social conduct, rules of sociosexual conduct included. There is no contradiction in the suggestion that access-regulating, restrictive rules may actually have served the curtailment of aggression, especially among violently inclined people. "Repression," then, can be construed as the consequence of aggressiveness, rather than as its cause. In fact, Prescott (1977) has provided data that can be considered consistent with such an interpretation. Aggressiveness that corresponded with punitive sanctions against nonmarital sexual liaisons manifested itself, among other things, in a preference for aggressive gods, in military glory, and in narcissistic inclinations—rather than in eruptions triggered by the presumed suffering from sexual denial.

Nonetheless, the data are simply not specific enough to permit a meaningful evaluation of the merits of any particular proposal concerning the cultural interdependence of sex and aggression. It can be argued that proposals such as those under consideration are so roundabout and vague as to elude any attempt at falsification, rendering them unverifiable. The contentions regarding a relationship between sexual repression and aggression are particularly troublesome, as Freud (e.g., 1920/1940) provided for the possibility that aggression may become self-directed. Thus, if sexual repression does not foster an appreciable increase in overt aggression, such as transgressive interpersonal violence, it may be "detected" in increased self-torment, and if it fails to increase self-torment, it may be expected to surface—because of redirection in accord with Freudian mechanisms—in the striving for athletic excellence or in the love of painting. Whatever happens, those who vested trust in the relationship between sexual repression and aggression need not worry. Their beliefs are not in jeopardy. Their convictions cannot be substantiated, but they cannot be faulted either.

The demonstration of human sociosexual variation by selected examples of cultures tends to focus on extremes. Such a focus exhibits the range of variability, but it fails to inform about the commonness or uncommonness of particular forms of sociosexual conduct. To learn about what is characteristic and what is not, Ford and Beach (1951) conducted a cross-cultural analysis on a large sample of preliterate cultures in which traits of interest were meticulously enumerated. Their exemplary investigation confirmed that sexual access is always subject to regulation and that access rules differ enormously across cultures. Access may be granted to sexually immature children or be disallowed substantially beyond the achievement of sexual maturity. Postpubertal access is most common, however. Almost universally, adults eventually enter a socially sanctioned affiliation (i.e., a marital arrangement) in which sexual access is secured. Polygynous systems of this kind are common; polyandrous systems are very rare. The most common arrangement, however, is the heterosexual pair. Sexual contacts outside these sanctioned social arrangements almost universally produce conflict and tend to be met with punitive sanctions. But these punitive sanctions differ immensely across cultures.

Males are nearly always the active pursuers of sexual access; females are rarely such pursuers. Males nearly always dominate coital activity, whereas females rarely do. Group access is not common and is usually limited to special occasions.

Aggression to achieve sexual access (i.e., rape) is comparatively rare, though more or less universal culturally. A reliable relationship between forcible access and the difficulty (or ease) of sexual access within society is not apparent, however. Aggression to achieve sexual access is almost universally disapproved and characteristically punished. Furthermore, aggression is generally not a sanctioned means of gaining sexual partners for socially recognized affiliations.

As the records of literate societies show (cf. Bullough, 1976; Ellis & Abarbanel, 1961), the patterns of sociosexual behavior are essentially the same for these more highly developed cultures. A notable exception is the tendency for literate cultures to deny premarital access. Furthermore, it is noteworthy that the regulation of sexual access tends to become an integral part of religious belief systems. In the advancement of civilizations, it seems, access regulations have come increasingly under the control of religious institutions (cf. Bullough, 1976; Ullock & Wagner, 1980).

Forcible sexual access was commonplace in connection with intergroup and intercultural combat. Victorious males tended to violate the females of the defeated and conquered. Sexual exploitation could be prolonged, such as through the institution of slavery. However, the incidence of forcible sexual access in coherent social groupings must be considered low, especially in view of the fact that men tend to be physically stronger than women and also are likely to have developed superior fighting skills. It is astounding, in fact, that in a few cultures women manage to violate men sexually. Trobriand women, for example, on occasion engage in orgiastic sexual violence against men (Malinowski, 1929). Intracultural forcible sexual access may have been retained at comparatively low levels because of commercial or sacred prostitution that was common in many cultures (cf. Bullough, 1976). Such possibilities are entirely speculative, however.

There is some suggestion that punitive sanctions against adultery and rape may at times function to entice violations. Peoples of the eastern Solomon Islands of the southwest Pacific (cf. Davenport, 1976), for instance, treat both adultery and rape as serious offenses that call for strong punitive measures, even violent action. Men of social influence openly commit adultery and rape, however, in apparent efforts to display the powers inherent in their high social position. The behaviors in question are consensually deplored, but they lend themselves to the exhibition of power in that only ordinary men are likely to suffer the application of the stipulated punitive measures. It seems that sexual violations can serve this type of power demonstration more readily than purely violent acts, such as murder, because they place the perpetrator at less risk of injury and are usually not considered to inflict permanent functional impairment upon the victim.

Aggression for sexual access can furthermore be found in the intersocietal abduction of women for the specific purpose of sexual usage. Human communities of limited size frequently confronted acute shortages of eligible females because of incest restrictions. Quite commonly, the men of such communities resorted to the violent abduction of women from neighboring communities. The victimized groups waged armed retaliatory strikes and committed counterabductions. Intercommunal aggression thus took turns and tended to escalate. Such warfare instigated by sexual-access needs has been documented, for example, among several societies of highland Papua, New Guinea (cf. Davenport, 1976).

Within society, in contrast, the taking of women (or men) as sexual partners in enduring, socially sanctioned relationships is rarely, if ever, accomplished by violent means. To be sure, men, women, boys, and girls were commonly exploited, both heterosexually and homosexually (e.g., Bullough, 1976; De Riencourt, 1974; Flaceliere, 1962), but their concubinage was arranged by nonviolent coercive means, mainly economic dependence, rather than by intermale combat.

It appears that infanticide in humans is unrelated to fighting over sexual access. Infanticide is, however, related to sexual access. Specifically, it has been suggested that human hypersexuality, due in large measure to the unrestricted copulatory readiness of the female, fosters great reproductive efficiency (cf. Jensen, 1973). Continual sexual access and reproductive efficiency ultimately led to considerable competition for resources (i.e., food and shelter). Apparently, neither abstinence nor the various forms of prostitution (which accomplished the insemination of few women by many men), wherever instituted, proved effective means of curbing massive progeny. Humans thus resorted to infanticide quite commonly. This practice may initially have been a necessity in the fight for survival. Often, however, it became a form of convenience killing that served the maintenance of a standard of living or the securance of pure hereditary lines in privileged social minorities.

The analysis of skeletal remains of adult human fossils suggests that infanticide is an ancient practice, indeed. Although gender proved to be balanced in some groups (e.g., in the mesolithic humans of Europe), males tended to outnumber females with considerable consistency (Vallois, 1961). The gender ratio could be as high as 1.41 in favor of males (e.g., in the upper paleolithic humans of Eurasia). Across groups, the ratio is 1.25, that is, 125 males to 100 females (Vallois, 1961). Such gender imbalance is assumed to exceed natural variation in the gender distribution of populations, and as gender-segregated life styles (hunting vs. gathering) tended to place males rather than females at greater risk, deliberate discrimination against females—in form of infanticide—has been inferred. This likely selectivity in favor of males further suggests that utility criteria were employed, as males were presumably in great demand for hunting and warfare.

Selective infanticide in favor of males has also been directly observed in preliterate peoples (e.g., Neel, 1970). In more advanced civilizations, efforts to control surplus progeny—or simply unwanted offspring—through contraception and abortion are in evidence. Infanticide tended to persist, however (cf. Langer, 1972, 1974). In promiscuous Rome, for example, it was common for those who could not afford abortions to put unwanted offspring out with the garbage (Ullock & Wagner, 1980). In contrast to the poor, whose behavior was the likely result of economic pressures, those in positions of social power committed infanticide mainly to insure the continuation of their privileged status. On the Hawaiian Islands (cf. Davenport, 1976), for instance, the hereditary aristocrats (prior to the missionary reforms that started in 1820) practiced this type of infanticide. These aristocrats were highly promiscuous. The highly born ones, males and females alike, had unrestricted sexual access to persons of lower rank. Sexual relations with persons of lowest rank were, in fact, proscribed by religious doctrine. As a result, considerable offspring were produced that were noble only in part. Infanticide of such impure progeny was the rule, and only the offspring of "pure," especially arranged matings (mainly among close relatives) were permitted to survive.

Another form of postaccess aggression is the usually highly destructive fighting that is occasioned by the urging or granting of sexual access by an intimately affiliated person to a person outside the formal or informal sociosexual affiliation. It has been estimated (Etkin & Freedman, 1964) that such "romantic triangle" aggression has been and still is the most frequent cause of murder throughout the world. Invariably, the injurious fighting is instigated by the person whose partner sought or granted sexual access to an outside party. Destructive fighting of this kind, furthermore, almost always occurs among males, rarely among females. Intergender assaults are not uncommon, however. Such gender differences are presumably due to the greater combative experience of males and, perhaps more importantly, to the culturally quite universal, greater sociosexual restrictedness of females.

Finally, the cross-cultural analysis reveals that in numerous cultures, especially in preliterate ones, sexual behavior as such can be laden with elements of aggression (cf. Ford & Beach, 1951). Both precoital and coital activities may be intertwined with the scratching, biting, squeezing, pulling, and striking of body parts. These actions unquestionably produce sensations of pain; often they prove injurious. The painful stimulation invariably fosters excitement, and this excitement appears to be purposely created at times, but by no means always.

According to Ford and Beach, the infliction of pain prior to and during coitus is not the province of one gender. It is characteristic of both males and females, and often it is mutual. Ponapean men, for instance, tug at the women's eyebrows, yanking tufts of hair out on occasion. Among the Apinaye, on the other hand, women bite off the men's eyebrows. Trukese women, when sexually aroused, vigorously poke fingers into their partners' ears. The biting of necks and shoulders is popular in numerous societies. The Toda, for example, take pride in displaying the resulting marks of discolored, swollen, and inflamed skin.

Holmberg (1946) reported that the Siriono indulge in rather rugged foreplay. Couples scratch and pinch each other in various body areas, and they poke fingers in each others' eyes. Coitus is described as a violent and rapid affair. Lovers bite one another on the neck and chest. During peaks of excitement, they scratch each other on the neck, chest, and forehead. According to Holmberg (1946), biting and scratching is often so intense that the lovers "emerge wounded from the fray [p. 184]."

Malinowski (1929) observed a similar admixture of aggressive behavior in the precoital and coital activities among the Trobriand Islanders. Biting includes snapping at the nose and chin. Lovers engage in the mutual sucking of the lower lips. The sucking escalates into biting, and the biting is continued despite the drawing of blood. Also, the lovers grab each other by the hair (of the head) and tear it vigorously. According to Malinowski, the women are sexually more violent than the men. In fact, women are actually allowed to lacerate their lovers, making their backs a showcase of their amorous life.

The cultures of Romonum Island (cf. Davenport, 1976) also link painful sensations with sexual gratification. The mutual infliction of pain is regarded both as a demonstration of affection and as sexually arousing. The most gratifying form of coitus is referred to as "striking" and can be described as "clitoral roughhousing." It appears that through predominantly painful manual stimulation the woman is brought close to orgasm and that the actual coital experience is limited to a concluding, brief intromission for ejaculation.

The apparent relationship between painful stimulation and sexual gratification is not always so straightforward, however. Among the Gusii of southwestern Kenya (cf. Davenport, 1976), for instance, sexual inclinations seem to depend on truly hostile and aggressive dispositions. Women are expected to resist the sexual advances of men physically. Men, on the other hand, are supposed to overcome any resistance by employing brute force. Even in marital arrangements, men torment women physically and seek to humiliate them. Normal intercourse is described as a form of rape with many of the affective accompaniments of such an experience. Little is known about the consequences of these unique sexual practices for the women who serve as victims. The role of sexual aggression is apparently becoming to the men. Reportedly, they derive heightened sexual gratification from intercourse with women "who put up a good fight" and, especially, who cry during coitus.

In summarizing the cross-cultural evidence on the fusion of sexual and aggressive elements of behavior, Ford and Beach (1951) uncovered a strong relationship between such fusion and sexual permissiveness. Societies in which coitus is regularly accompanied by scratching, biting, and hair pulling "prove inevitably to be ones in which children and adolescents are allowed a great deal of sexual freedom [p. 64]." These investigators further note that in such societies the women tend to be active participants in sexual activities. They are accorded equal rights in initiating intercourse, and they are expected to derive orgasmic gratification from coitus. Ford and Beach emphasize that, nearly without exception, the involvement of elements of aggression in sexual behaviors is thoroughly accepted by the peoples who practice such fused sexuality and that sex-related painful sensations are generally construed by them as enjoyable and desirable.

In contemporary societies throughout the world, the principal forms of the sociosexual behaviors of earlier cultures have prevailed. The enormity of the variation in these behaviors has been maintained cross-culturally. Sociosexual behaviors and their reproductive consequences have remained to be regulated. If anything, such regulation has become more pronounced and formalized. Sociosexual regulation, in addition, is still deeply influenced by religious belief systems and institutions. Forcible sexual access, almost always with males as aggressors and females as victims, continues to be a significant social problem worldwide. The violent abduction of women for sexual usage, however, may have been eradicated, owing mainly to the intrusion of governments into the traditions of "primitive peoples." Aggression as a means of founding lasting and stable sociosexual arrangements continues to be disapproved. And aggressive-sexual practices of intercourse have probably undergone little change.

In contrast, sociosexual behaviors in the complex, technologically advanced Western civilizations appear to have changed considerably (e.g., Eysenck, 1976; Kinsey, Pomeroy, & Martin, 1948; Kinsey, Pomeroy, Martin, & Gebhard, 1953; Oaks, Melchiode, & Ficher, 1976; Sorenson, 1973; Wagner, 1974). The incidence of sexual engagements of any kind, it seems, has steadily increased in recent years. The variety of both sociosexual arrangements and sexual activities as such, according to the available surveys, has increased within societies. Affiliations formerly branded as "deviant" have become socially viable, if not sanctioned. And formerly uncommon sexual practices, such as fellatio and cunnilingus, have become commonplace. Sexual liaisons are more freely formed and broken off than ever before. Premarital and extramarital sexual contacts meet with increased tolerance. Parental control of sexual engagements by teenagers has been greatly relaxed, and the age at which boys and girls become sexually active has successively decreased as a consequence. Finally, group intercourse has also become less uncommon.

It has been suggested that contemporary Western sexuality has only one slogan: *freedom*—the unrestricted freedom to explore all facets of sexuality with any party reciprocating this desire (Ruitenbeek, 1974). The yearning for sexual access and sexual experience beyond marital life has been expressed before (e.g., Ellis, 1928, 1939; Hurst, 1929; Lindsey & Evans, 1927; Russell, 1929). Only recently, however, have such calls for sexual freedom shed the aura of deviancy and become widely endorsed and, in fact, enacted.

The seemingly dramatic change in Western attitudes toward human sexuality has been attributed to the decline of Christian morality in particular (e.g., Beljon, 1967). Control of sociosexual practices by the church seems to have been weakened, indeed. However, it would appear that another factor has exerted a far greater influence on dispositions toward sexuality (and may actually be largely responsible for the diminished control over sexuality by religious institutions). This factor is the enormous advancement of progeny-preventing techniques. The chemical and mechanical means of birth control (mainly ingestible pharmaceuticals, vaginal foams, condoms, diaphragms, and intrauterine devices) have enabled the population at large to abrogate any fears of possible reproductive consequences of sexual engagements. The sociosexual inhibition rule of earlier days (viz., that a person good enough for sexual intimacy ought to be good enough for marriage) has lost its motivational basis: apprehensions about reproductive repercussions.

The so-called "sexual revolution" in Western societies, it appears, has very much come on the coattails of progeny-preventing innovations. These innovations have made visions of unrestricted "recreational sex" possible. At the very least, they have made human sexuality devoid of anxieties and thus created the basis for unimpaired sexual gratification—regardless of the particular social circumstances.

Although sexual liaisons (i.e., comparatively short-lived sexual affiliations) have become readily available, mateship (i.e., the formation of lasting, stable, usually cohabitational sexual affiliations, cf. Ford & Beach, 1951) has not gone out of style. Women especially continue to insist that sex be associated with nontransitory mutual affection (e.g., Hunt, 1974; Mosher & Cross, 1971). Most sexual activities continue to take place among well-established pairs. Whatever other values such arrangements may entail, they make sexual access conveniently available. Problems arise, however, when the relationship is highly formal, such as in the marital situation, and one party employs the formal status of the affiliation to coerce the other party sexually. Coercion of this kind is apparently not uncommon (e.g., Chapman & Gates, 1978; Davidson, 1978; Straus, Gelles, & Steinmetz, 1980). As indicated earlier, it revolves around specific sexual performances rather than access per se. The denial of specific sexual expectations, regardless of how "reasonable" or "unreasonable" these expectations may be, is undoubtedly a source of considerable conjugal violence. It is difficult, however, to ascertain exactly the extent of such violence, as only a portion of it comes to light because the victims fear the social repercussions of reporting their malaise.

Rape has continued to plague the women of Western civilizations. The general facilitation of sexual access seems to have had little, if any, impact on the incidence of rape in society (e.g., Clark & Lewis, 1977; Gager & Schurr, 1976). Again, precise quantification is wanting because victims fear the likely ill effects of reporting assaults and disclosing assailants.

Violent sexual assaults are, for all practical purposes, an exclusive male province, and although such assaults may be directed at other males, they most commonly victimize females. As violent acts of violent men, rape might thus be expected to carry with it elements of destructive behaviors that bear little relationship to sexuality. This is indeed the case. Many sexual assaults go far beyond what would be necessary to achieve sexual access. Rape, then, often seems to be more than mere access fighting. Contentions that it always is remain popular, but are unwarranted.

Groth (1979) classified the extent to which rape entails destructive aggression in excess of coercive utility in order to determine likely motivational underpinnings. He distinguished between: (1) rape that merely serves to achieve access; (2) rape that mainly serves aggressive ends; (3) rape in which violent acts are sexually instrumental. If sexual conquest is the goal, verbal threats tend to be employed to accomplish the coercive objective. As threats of aggressive actions fail, the rapist is likely to resort to the actions themselves. However, the achievement of access usually terminates any violent acts. Rape in which aggressive goals are dominant, in contrast, are brutal physical assaults in which sexual activity seems secondary. Beating of the victim is the rule. In fact, accounts of convicted rapists suggest that sexual penetration tends to be regarded as the utmost in beating—the most demeaning and humiliating thing that can be done to the victim. Pleasure is apparently derived from "beating up on someone," and the sexual context seems rather coincidental. Sadistic rape differs in that the pleasures sought are sexual, but largely depend on the commission of destructive acts. Groth (1979) speaks of a "sexual transformation of anger and power so that aggression itself becomes eroticized [p. 44]." Characteristically, the victim's sex-related body parts (breasts, buttocks, labia) are targets of abuse and injury, being hit, torn, bitten, and burned. The rapist takes great pleasure in surveying his victim's torment. During such enjoyment, offenders tend to masturbate, often to orgasm. At times, organ penetration does not occur at all, and the rapist may instead penetrate the victim with sticks or bottles.

The quantification of a large number of rapes in terms of these manifestations (Groth, 1979) shows that rape in contemporary America is predominantly aggression for sexual access (55%). Primarily aggressive, demeaning rape is also rather frequent (40%). Sadistic rape, in contrast, is comparatively rare (5%). The dominance of rape for access is likely to be more pronounced, however, than these findings indicate. Groth correctly pointed out that the data, which reflect rape of convicted offenders, are strongly biased against access rape. Because access rape—notwithstanding the trauma it produces in the victim—is often nonviolent and does not result in demonstrable bodily injury, it is less likely to be reported than injurious forms of violent rape. Moreover, because the devastating consequences to the victim can be more readily documented for violent and sadistic rapes, the probability of conviction is substantially greater for these forms of rape than for access rape. It is likely, therefore, that the use of aggressive means merely to achieve sexual access outnumbers by a considerable margin all other forms of rape combined.

Necrophilia, the practice of seeking intercourse with corpses, is usually presented as a rape-related form of sexuality (e.g., Janda & Klenke-Hamel, 1980). Indeed, a few cases are known in which murder was committed in order to gain sexual access to the victim (DeRiver, 1956). Such cases, however, are so extremely rare as to render necrophilia an entry in complete listings of sexual aberrations that has little social significance—other than to serve as a topic of conversation for those attracted to macabre dramatics.

Postaccess rivalry has remained a significant source of violence in Western societies. Triangular arrangements of sexual access, with one party in jeopardy of losing valued access, is still a common condition for murder. Interestingly, such murder is usually far more gruesome than murders among persons who are not thus affiliated (Wolfgang, 1958; Zillmann, 1979).

Infanticide as such is rare, but has not been entirely eradicated (e.g., Vital Statistics of the United States, 1980). Western civilizations have made it largely unnecessary by instituting abortion. Abortion, which can, of course, be construed as a form of infanticide, is very common (e.g., Moore-Čavar, 1974; Saltman, 1973).

Finally, Western societies have not abandoned the practice of fusing sex and aggression. Although not condoned generally, elements of aggression are often involved in precoital and coital activities. The extent to which this involvement of aggressive acts is consciously employed to increase sexual excitement, especially through the infliction of pain, is quite unclear, however. Further, it is unclear exactly how widespread such practices are and to what degree they produce acute pain.

The original surveys of sexual behavior conducted between 1938 and 1963 by Kinsey and his associates entailed questions concerning sex-related biting. The findings, which were published only recently (Gebhard & Johnson, 1979), suggest that at the time of the surveys biting was not particularly popular in the United States. About two-thirds of the persons interviewed denied ever having bitten their partners. The remaining third acknowledged *gentle* biting, with less than 10% reporting frequent biting. Presumably because interviewees felt less constrained to admit to being bitten, reports of receiving bites were generally somewhat higher. But again, only about 10% of the persons interviewed reported being bitten frequently. Of those who were bitten either frequently or occasionally, about 60% said they were sexually excited by it. Of those bitten only rarely, only about one-third found it arousing. Gender differences proved negligible for both biting and being bitten.

Hunt (1974), in a more recent survey of sexual behaviors in the United States, explored the infliction of pain in connection with gratifying precoital and coital behavior specifically. The questions probed whether or not sexual pleasure had been obtained from either inflicting or receiving pain. In contrast to the earlier findings on biting, Hunt observed pronounced gender differences regarding the infliction versus the reception of pain. Men reported the sex-linked infliction of pain to be more gratifying than the reception of pain. Women exhibited the opposite preference: They reported the sex-linked reception of pain to be more gratifying than the infliction of pain. This transverse interaction was consistently obtained in various subgroupings. As can be seen from Fig. 2.1, it was observed in different age groups as well as in single and married persons. The figure also shows that there was a tendency for younger persons (under 35) to employ more pain-inflicting techniques than older persons (35 and over). Furthermore, as can be seen, the sex-linked infliction of pain proved infrequent in married persons and rather frequent in single persons. The fact that the employment of pain in sexual endeavors was acknowledged by a portion of singles as high as 10%, whereas in earlier surveys that portion was characteristic of only frequent, gentle

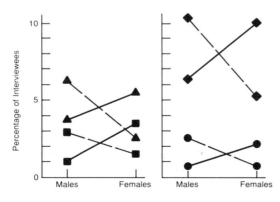

FIG. 2.1. Reports of both men and women of having derived sexual pleasure from inflicting and receiving pain, according to Hunt's (1974) survey of sexual behaviors in the United States. Broken lines denote pleasure from inflicting pain, solid ones from receiving pain; triangles denote young persons, squares older ones, diamonds single persons, and circles married ones.

(and presumably not painful) biting, is probably due to the greater degree of privacy and anonymity in the interview situation.

Despite valiant efforts to obtain random samples for their surveys, neither the Kinsey nor the Hunt samples are truly representative. Systematic bias in the estimation of population parameters cannot be ruled out, as particular groups of persons are known to decline interviews concerning sexual matters, whereas others eagerly respond to requests for such information. The possibility that reports are incorrect because of erroneous recall or distorted because of evaluation apprehension further compromises the validity of projections. Estimates of frequencies and ratios of specific behaviors in the population and in subpopulations are thus to be treated with due caution. The interrelationships that emerge between particular behaviors, however, are not directly subject to the problem of parameter estimation and tend to be reliable. This is to say that the interactions between gender, on the one hand, and the infliction and reception of pain, on the other, presented in Fig. 2.1 are more likely valid than the specific percentages associated with the various groups and the differences between the groups.

Granted the possibility of considerable estimation error, Hunt's (1974) findings concerning the involvement of pain in pleasurable sexual activities can nonetheless be taken to suggest that young persons tend to employ pain to a greater degree than older persons and that singles tend to employ pain to a markedly higher degree than married persons. These findings seem interdependent and can be explained in different ways.

First, it can be argued that, regarding sex, young persons have been brought up more liberally than older persons and that they have come to accept greater sexual variation, including the use of painful stimulation, as a result. Because the subpopulation of singles contains a larger portion of young people than that of married persons, the observation that singles involve pain in sexual activities more than do married persons can be considered explained. Second, it is conceivable that persons with sadomasochistic inclinations are less likely to get married than others. To the extent that persons with sadomasochistic inclinations are more strongly thus inclined when young than when older, the apparent age difference could be considered explained in turn.

Eysenck's (1976) work on sex and personality pertains to this issue and suggests yet another explanation. Eysenck employed a nonrepresentative British sample of adults, solicited a large number of responses concerning sexual attitudes and sexual behaviors, and subjected these responses to factor analysis in order to determine interrelations. He extracted 12 factors, among them one referred to as "aggressive sex." This factor entailed high loadings on items such as the urge to scratch and bite during coitus, hostile and aggressive sex-related feelings, the deemphasis on tenderness, and the desire to humiliate the sexual partner. For males, the only marked correlation with another factor proved to be with "impersonal sex." This factor was associated with high loadings on such items as the appeal of group sex, acceptability of wife-swapping, excitement from illicit relationships, enjoyment of watching the coital behavior of others, and satisfaction from "sex without love." An equally strong relationship between aggressive and impersonal sex emerged for females. "Aggressive sex" in women, however, also proved to be related to other factors, such as permissiveness, interest in pornography, and lack of sexual shyness.

On the basis of these findings it can be argued that, because the proportion of impersonal sexual contacts is likely to be substantially higher among single and young persons than among married and older persons, sexual activities that involve the infliction of pain will probably be higher in the former than in the latter groups. It should be noticed that this account parallels Ford and Beach's (1951) generalization about the relationship between promiscuity and violent sexuality in preliterate societies. Regardless of the degree of literacy and cultural advancement, it appears that promiscuous sexuality tends to promote impersonal sexual relationships and that such relationships, in turn, promote violent sexual inclinations. Affectionate, lasting sociosexual arrangements, on the other hand, seem to be associated with sexual activities that favor tenderness over wild and somewhat savage passion.

Although the transverse interactions between gender and the infliction versus reception of sex-related pain (displayed in Fig. 2.1) seem to agree with the contention that women's sexuality is "masochistic by nature" (e.g., Bardwick, 1971; Deutsch, 1944), it should be clear that a biological predisposition is in no way implicated. These interactions may merely reflect the fact that in Western cultures men have traditionally carried much of the coital action. Statistically speaking, men probably still outdo women as far as sex-related gross skeletal-motor activity is concerned. This action differential may simply carry over into the infliction of pain. Alternatively, it is conceivable that men's superior physical faculties for aggression, along with a greater emphasis on the development of these faculties, account for the preference for inflicting pain over receiving it. Women, on the other hand, may have come to accept their inferiority as aggressors and, in turn, their lot as recipients of sexual and violent action. This latter interpretation is at variance, however, with much experimental evidence on human aggression (cf. Zillmann, 1979), evidence that strongly challenges the portrayal of women as "masochistic." Women's apparent preference for receiving over inflicting pain in a sexual context appears to be restricted to that context.

Sadomasochistic sexual inclinations may surface occasionally, especially in connection with discontent, disrespect, or acute social conflict, or they may manifest themselves with regularity in a person's sexual behavior. The former, if rare enough, is likely to be absorbed without much adversity by sexual partners who neither appreciate nor reciprocate painful stimulation in connection with sex. Continued sadomasochistic action directed at or demanded from unappreciative parties, in contrast, is bound to produce irreconcilable conflict and lead to the abandonment of the sadomasochistically inclined person. Sadomasochists are thus confronted with a unique sexual-access problem. In contemporary Western societies this problem is resolved through informal groupings and quasi-formal clubs (e.g., Arnold, 1970; Dannecker & Reiche, 1974; Spengler, 1977). Interestingly, females are conspicuously absent in these subcultures. Even women who enjoy the application of moderate amounts of pain in connection with sexual activities avoid the affiliation with men who exhibit manifest sadomasochism, and they are exceedingly reluctant to join male clubs. Sadomasochistic men thus resort either to homosexual affiliations (e.g., Dannecker & Reiche, 1974) or to enlisting the collaboration of female prostitutes (e.g., Bornemann, 1974). Among prostitutes, female masochists seem widely available, but female sadists seem to be extremely rare and, according to Gebhard (1969), are "so highly prized that masochists will travel hundreds of miles to meet them [p. 77]." It has recently been proposed (Spengler, 1977) that the subculture media of sadomasochism (magazines, movies) flourish as they do because they fill a critical void, substituting fiction for reality. By portraying women in masochistic, and especially in sadistic roles, these media "are supposed to make the lack of like-minded and 'passionate' female partners bearable [p. 455]."

Manifest sadomasochism, then, is a more or less exclusively male phenomenon. Furthermore, as Gebhard (1969) notes, sexual sadomasochism "seems the monopoly of well-developed civilizations [p. 80]." As has been discussed already, the sex-related infliction of moderate amounts of pain is common in preliterate cultures. Sadomasochistic life styles, however, are not at all evident in these cultures.

The extent of manifest sadomasochism in contemporary Western societies has not been determined with any degree of accuracy. Such determinations face enormous difficulties, because sadomasochism is usually practiced in secrecy. Data provided by Spengler (1977) show that sadomasochists perceive their sexual preference as deviant and, presumably as a result, hide it from colleagues, friends, parents, brothers, and sisters. Even the wives of married masochists more often than not are unaware of their husbands' sexual preference. In this connection, it appears that reports on the counseling of "sadomasochistic marriages" (e.g., Kaunitz, 1977) are mostly based on a misclassification. Such marriages are more appropriately dealt with under the heading of "conjugal violence," as they characteristically entail an abusive, frequently intoxicated husband and a wife putting up with a seemingly intolerable amount of torment. The fact that sexual activities occur in this context—activities that might even be enjoyed by the wife because they tend to coincide with reconciliation (or, at least, with the termination of being beaten)—does not secure a deliberate sadomasochistic arrangement.

Although the extent of sadomasochism within societies is uncertain, recent studies have revealed aspects of the sadomasochistic sexual preference as such. It had been held, for instance, that manifest sadomasochism is a trait that dominates the sexual behavior of a person and that masochists are also sadists and vice versa (e.g., Luria & Rose, 1979). Such beliefs proved largely incorrect. Spengler (1977) observed that only a small minority (16%) of sadomasochistic men seeks exclusively sadomasochistic engagements. The majority of sadomasochistic men practices sadomasochism alongside more common sexual behaviors. This majority of occasionally to predominantly sadomasochistic men divides rather evenly into masochists, sadists, and true sadomasochists (i.e., persons indulging in the infliction as well as in the reception of sex-related pain). In sharp contrast, however, "exclusive" sadomasochists are rarely that—rendering the term a misnomer. Instead, they tend to be either sadists or masochists, mainly the latter. It has furthermore become clear that sadomasochistic men are often exclusively homosexual (38%). Nearly as often, however, they are not homosexually inclined (30%). The remaining sadomasochistic men are bisexual. Finally, sadomasochistic men can be found at all age levels. The age distribution roughly follows that of sexual activity, increasing to a peak between 31 and 40 and declining thereafter. Similarly, sadomasochistic men can be found at all levels of education. The largest portion, interestingly, comprises men with postgraduate academic training.

In summarizing the various forms of sex-aggression linkages in the behavior of humans, the following generalizations are possible:

1. Human sociosexual behavior is invariably subject to cultural rules of conduct. These rules of conduct are extremely variable across cultures, ranging from nearly unrestricted, promiscuous sexual access to the firm restriction of sexual access in permanent, socially recognized affiliations. Sex-related aggression is likewise regulated by conduct rules and is extremely variable.
2. Although it is conceivable that the cross-cultural variation in aggressive-sexual behaviors is in part genetically determined, enculturation appears to be the major force in the creation of this variation.
3. Formally sanctioned, potentially permanent sociosexual affiliations (e.g., the institution of marriage) can be found in practically all cultures. Pair affiliations are most characteristic. Polygyny is not uncommon, but polyandry is rare. Whatever the particular social arrangement, the attainment of affiliates from within the culture by violent means is generally disallowed.
4. The violent, extracultural abduction of women has been widely practiced in the past. This practice is near eradication, however.
5. The use of violent means to achieve sexual access is almost universally the province of males. Violent sexual access was common in connection with intercultural conflict. It is comparatively rare intraculturally. However, intracultural violent sexual access is common to all cultures.
6. Aggression for sexual access seems unrelated to the extent of sexual promiscuity or sexual restrictedness in society.
7. Infanticide has been common in many human societies.

8. Cross-culturally, infidelity among sexually affiliated parties has been a major cause for retributive violence.
9. In preliterate cultures elements of aggression commonly accompany precoital and coital activities. The infliction of pain and, occasionally, injury tends to be mutual. Painful stimulation seems limited to moderate levels, however, and dominantly sadomasochistic sexuality is not practiced.
10. Societies in which painful stimulation is commonly linked with sexual activities tend to be sexually permissive. Additionally, women tend to be highly assertive in these societies, especially with regard to sexual ventures.
11. In contemporary Western societies forcible sexual access constitutes a significant social problem. As a form of coercion, rape predominantly serves the achievement of sexual access. Violence-laden rape in which sexual objectives are secondary is common, however. Sadistic rape in which aggressive and sexual objectives are fused is comparatively rare.
12. Infanticide has become extremely rare. Abortion, which may be considered a form of infanticide, continues to be widely practiced, however.
13. Within contemporary Western societies a considerable portion of men and women exhibits a preference for an admixture of aggression in sexual activities. The use of moderately painful stimulation in precoital and coital behaviors is rather common. Males appear to favor the infliction of pain upon their sexual partners over the reception of pain. Females appear to favor the reverse. Young persons are more likely to involve painful stimulation than older persons. Similarly, singles are more likely to involve such stimulation than married persons.
14. The employment of moderately painful stimulation in connection with precoital and coital behavior appears to correspond with impersonal sexual dispositions.
15. In contemporary Western societies comparatively small minorities of men exhibit sadomasochistic sexual preferences. Women, other than prostitutes, rarely participate in truly sadomasochistic ventures. Sadomasochistic men are predominantly homosexually inclined. Sadomasochists with heterosexual preference are also quite common, however. Men with "exclusive" sadomasochistic inclinations are most commonly pure masochists, often sadists, but rarely both. Highly educated men more often exhibit sadomasochistic sexual preferences than less educated men.

III. EVOLUTION OF HUMAN SEX-AGGRESSION

The comparative analysis of sociosexual behaviors leaves no doubt about the fact that such behaviors are extremely variable. In infraprimates they vary enormously across species, but within species they are comparatively stable. In nonhuman primates they vary substantially both across and within species. Finally, in humans sociosexual behaviors vary greatly cross-culturally, and with increasing societal complexity they become highly variable within cultures. Sex-related aggression varies analogously.

In view of this overwhelming variation, it would seem inadvisable indeed to pretend that sociosexual and aggressive-sexual behaviors are genetically rather restrained, if not fixed, and can be unambiguously mapped onto an evolutionary chart that lays out the procession of life from the lower to the higher forms. Rather, it must be acknowledged that these behaviors are characterized by great plasticity in many species, especially in the nonhuman primates, so as to compromise any attempt at deriving the human behaviors on the basis of presumed inherited dispositions. Human sociosexual and aggressive-sexual behaviors, it appears, have evolved mainly as a function of prevailing ecological conditions and only secondarily as a consequence of a primate heritage (cf. Alcock, 1975). Pair bonding, for instance, may have been favored in humans because of a division of labor in hunting and gathering, a division that was dictated by bodily faculties (Trivers, 1972). The use of tools and weapons for predation and warfare, not to be found in other primates (Hall, 1968b), created other unique conditions that were likely to influence both sociosexual arrangements and sex-related aggression in humans (Washburn & Lancaster, 1968). Finally, it has been suggested that human cultures were deeply influenced by the need for male cooperation in both hunting ventures and warfare. It has been proposed that cooperation in such undertakings resulted in affiliative inclinations among males that ultimately produced gender-segregated cultures—and male-dominated cultures, in particular (Tiger, 1969; Tiger & Fox, 1971). If cultures indeed evolved from the hunting-and-gathering stage as suggested, much of the sexual-aggressive behaviors observed in various cultures could be understood without involving assumptions about behaviorally specific genetic endowments.

Given the extreme variation in sociosexual and aggressive-sexual behaviors across species and in humans specifically, any listing of behavioral similarities and differences, no matter how exhaustive, is unlikely to yield useful information concerning the aggressive-sexual ''nature'' of homo sapiens. Is intermale fighting for sexual access part of the ''human heritage''? Is the admixture of sex and aggression ''normal''? Is fighting for exclusive sexual access to a partner ''natural''? It is as easy to enumerate species on the ''yes'' side of the answer sheet as it is to list them on the ''no'' side. As long as this is recognized, grave misprojections are unlikely. Selective presentations of the evidence on nonhuman species are quite common, however, and those who resort to such selective practices to bolster their idiosyncratic convictions, whatever they might be, may believe their views supported. Sadomasochists, for instance, can point to the behavior of the mink and some other species, not to mention the Gusii of Kenya. Those who support abortion can cite infanticide in infrahuman primates and in humans through the millennia. Promiscuously inclined persons can stress the frictionless, nonaggressive sexuality of many primates. Men who forcefully pursue multiple partners can take comfort in knowing that deer and sea lions form harems. And those who seek nonaggressive sexual exclusivity in a pair can find the natural prototype in some eagles and other bird species. Such selective analogies, needless to say, prove absolutely nothing about "human nature."

The comparative analysis of sociosexual and aggressive-sexual behavior leaves the likely *Urzustand* (i.e., the original state) of human sexuality similarly unclear. What forms of sex-related aggression characterized early humans? We simply cannot tell from looking at the infrahuman primates, nor from inspecting present-day preliterate peoples or historical records of earlier civilizations. The popular projection of nonaggressive promiscuity is as much an unwarranted guess (cf. Davenport, 1976) as is the conjecture of the extremely violent domination of women by men—domination that permeated all facets of life, especially sexuality.

The most reasonable assumption to make, it seems, is that the sociosexual and aggressive-sexual behavior of early humans resembled that of the most advanced infrahuman primates. On the basis of this assumption, it can be projected that early humans were probably both nonaggressively promiscuous and aggressively protective of monopolized sexual consorts. It can be considered unlikely that fighting for sexual access specifically was pronounced, because the access problem was probably indirectly resolved through the fighting for social rank.

The possibility that affective bonding manifested itself in the inclination to monopolize a sexual partner is of interest because such inclination created access problems that, in turn, were likely to create social conflict and the propensity for aggressive behavior. In infrahuman primates a copulating pair is commonly harassed by sexually excited males in pursuit of access. Threat displays on the part of the sexually engaged male usually suffice to secure "privacy" for some time. Nonetheless, as has been reported earlier, consorts often seek seclusion for copulatory engagements. This apparent preference for "sexual privacy," which early humans may have shared with infrahuman primates, is significant in that it constitutes a means of reducing intraspecific and, especially, intermale aggression through the elimination of sexual stimulation under conditions in which sexual access is not immediately available. The account is, of course, entirely speculative. In fact, it can be considered compromised by the fact that in promiscuous situations the blockage of access is short-lived and that in many infrahuman primates males of high social rank "publicly" preoccupy receptive females without apparent aggressive disturbances by other mature males.

A somewhat more revealing approach in comparative analysis is the search for unique differences in the sociosexual and aggressive-sexual behaviors of humans and other species, especially other primates. Several distinctly human forms of such behaviors emerge from focusing the analysis in this way.

First, it becomes clear that stag fighting is only a remote analogue to human sociosexual behavior. In human society, as a rule, a mate is not gained through intraspecific combat, ritualistic or otherwise. Surely, some women may have been conquered by knocking out a rival or by pushing him over a cliff. But no human culture has generally condoned such practices. Many cultures provided women with the right to refuse particular mateships, but many more did not. In these latter cultures, women were mostly coerced into marital affiliations. It is important to recognize, however, that this coercion into mateship was not based on violence, but rather on the exploitation of social and economic dependence. Marriage, for males as well as for females, was commonly a controlled and arranged social undertaking linked with a complex trade of valued commodities. It rarely occurred after the successful, violent destruction of a competing party.

Interestingly, the stag-fight analogue persists in much of the ethological literature (e.g., Eibl-Eibesfeldt, 1970, 1973; Morris, 1968). It continues to serve as a model for seeking sexual access both in liaisons and in mateship. Men are seen as being engaged in never ceasing competition over women; women, by implication, are viewed as the fought-over creatures inclined to submit to the contestants that prove most impressive. Intermale combat over access, according to these views, takes place on the football field and the tennis court, in the mechanic's workshop, the executive's office, and the scientist's laboratory. Any assertive and competitive behavior, in short, presumably because it grants social status to the superior performer and used to be the province of men, has been likened to stag fighting. It has been recognized, of course, that such competition is devoid of actual aggression. Male assertiveness and intermale competition were consequently characterized as "ritualized aggression," a characterization implying that in earlier days such "fighting" was real.

Notwithstanding the doubtfulness of this premise, the characterization of intermale rivalry over the favor of women as a form of access *fighting* seems highly questionable. There can be little doubt that access rivalry exists. Sure-handed archers and skillful fencers in all likelihood gained favor with maidens and could more readily than more common men achieve sexual access. The same is probably true today for men who can toss the basketball with greater accuracy than others or run more elusively with the football. The analogy is wanting, however, as one looks for the presumed fighting over sexual access, especially for elements of hostility in such fighting. The gifted athlete—or for that matter, a talented musician—can hold great appeal to potential sexual partners without ever having attempted to ward off competitors. If one were to take the position that such sexually attractive persons commit an act of hostility to competing parties by the very fact that they are more appealing, one might as well consider the fact of a person's existence an "act of violence"—because any person, in the striving for sexual access, is likely to get in the way of a de facto competitor at one time or another.

The stag-fight model of sexual-access striving grossly misconstrues the complexity of human behavior. It implies that the determination of access, evolutionarily speaking, has changed very little: It is a tooth and claw type of conflict among males in which both teeth and claws have become somewhat defunct, with women still passively awaiting the outcome of skirmishes. It is difficult to see what usefulness this kind of model could have. Useful models of sexual access—models that can accommodate the complexity of human behavior— simply cannot be derived from the courtship rituals of selected ruminants or birds. Such models, it seems, need to acknowledge that women, in general, play an active part in the choice of sexual partners, that both men and women have an enormous arsenal of nonhostile and nonaggressive means at their disposal to make themselves sexually attractive, and that—to the extent that coercion is involved—compliance with sexual expectations is more likely to be sought and achieved through hostility or the threat of hostility (i.e., the infliction of harm other than bodily pain and injury or the threat thereof) than through aggression. Rather than to regard access rivalry as a remnant of presumed "primal violence," it would seem appropriate to consider humans to have developed specific means of handling the problem of sexual access. The fact that men or women can enhance their appeal and ultimately their chance of attaining a sexual partner by being knowledgeable about wine, by dancing smoothly, by using makeup skillfully, by not having forgotten to take a breath deodorant, or by any number of further distinctions, which bear no resemblance to "fighting" nor signal a reproductively commital rank, is certainly without precedence in other species. Likewise, the coercive, sexual exploitation of dependencies—regardless of how detestable it may seem—is a uniquely human form of access behavior.

Second, despite behaviors in other species that resemble rape, the achievement of sexual access by violent means, or by the threat of such means, is uniquely human.

Third, sadomasochism as a dominant sexual preference, although apparently limited to advanced civilizations, is a distinctly human form of aggressive-sexual behavior.

Finally, "triangle fighting" is unique to humans, because it tends to be retributive (i.e., a form of aggression that is based on moral considerations, cf. Zillmann, 1979). Aggression by abandoned persons against the sexual intimates who left them, or against those to whom these intimates were attracted and who are usually held responsible for the desertion, is punitive or retaliatory. Aggressors perceive themselves to have been wronged and seek "to put things right." The retaliatory status of violent action under these circumstances is indicated by the fact that such action is most likely after the aggressor realizes that reconciliation is not possible. Inasmuch as homo sapiens is the only known species that exhibits moral judgment, this type of violence obviously cannot be expected to manifest itself in other species.

Although these differences in the sociosexual and aggressive-sexual behaviors of humans and other species relate to superior human mental faculties, they are by no means apparent extensions on a phylogenetic map. The unique human behaviors do not emerge as "linear projections" from a hierarchical layout of species. Human sociosexual and aggressive-sexual behaviors do not follow from those of other species in any predictable fashion. They are in no recognizable way the culmination of an evolutionary progression in sexuality. They are very simply different from those of other species. Under these conditions it must appear futile, indeed, to search for clues of normalcy and naturalness of human sexual-aggressive behaviors by wallowing in data on analogous behaviors in other species.

But at the same time, it must be recognized that evolutionary progressions that powerfully influence the behaviors under consideration do exist. It is generally held, for instance, that the hormonal control of sexual behavior, which is rigid at lower levels of development, is greatly relaxed at higher levels. In higher mammals, especially in the primates, the control of sexual behavior successively shifts toward the central nervous system. The neocortex becomes increasingly involved, and because this structure is most highly developed in humans, it may be assumed that human sexuality is least controlled by hormonal processes—and more under "cognitive control" than in other species (e.g., Beach, 1956, 1958, 1969, 1976; MacLean, 1963; Whalen, 1976). This transition of control manifests itself, among other things, in the diminished function of olfaction and the increased significance of vision in human sexuality. Furthermore, there can be little doubt that human's special cognitive faculties have become increasingly involved in sociosexual and aggressive-sexual behaviors. The latter is a momentous event, because it sets humans apart from other species. The transition from strictly hormonal to hormonal-cortical control of sexual behavior, including the greater reliance on visual stimulation, is common (though different in degree) to all primates. Human cortical faculties, culminating in the ability to manipulate representations of reality seemingly at will, appear to be unique, however.

Regarding sexuality, the superior cortical faculties of humans manifest themselves in "sexual fantasies" (e.g., Byrne, 1977; Crépault, Abraham, Porto, & Couture, 1977; Money, 1977). Although similar cognitive activities may exist in other primates, humans are likely to be without equal in exploiting these activities in the maximization of pleasure. Through anticipatory imagery, humans can select courses of action that hold the greatest promise of providing pleasure, just as they can minimize aversion through the anticipation of outcomes that are to be avoided (cf. Zillmann, 1979). Anticipatory imagery, moreover, is not confined to probing the hedonic implications of actions and conditions that have been experienced already. Such imagery is capable of creating novel stimulus constellations that hold promise of yielding sexual gratification.

It is suggested, then, that humans are equipped with extraordinary anticipatory skills and that these skills, in the form of sexual imagery, serve the maximization of pleasure. Outside the realm of sexuality, these very skills account for human creativeness, innovativeness, and ingenuity. Within this realm, they continually project proven avenues toward sexual pleasure, and they point to novel, untried avenues as well.

All this is to say that human sexuality, evolutionarily speaking, is quite unique and nonhomologous to that of other species. Presumably, superior human anticipatory skills have served the maximization of sexual gratification better than any other system. In all likelihood, however, these skills are also responsible for suggesting visions of pleasure that cannot be converted into reality. Humans, on occasion at least, may thus have become the victims of their superior anticipatory skills, being thwarted in the pursuit of imaginable, yet unattainable, sexual gratifications. Likewise, excursions into the bizarre may at times be the result of exceedingly developed, yet malfunctioning, anticipatory skills.

As discussed earlier, Freud (1905/1942) suggested that the admixture of aggression and sex should not surprise anyone because persuasive skills are evolutionarily too vernal to be highly developed. He implied, of course, that in earlier days men had clubbed their rivals and forcibly taken the reluctant women. The view expounded here is very different in that it makes the relative infrequency of violent sexual access appear astonishing. Humans, much in contrast to other species and notwithstanding considerable cultural variation, are seen as being continually titillated by sexually salient stimuli. As sexual gratification is being anticipated, but access is thwarted, the use of violent means to achieve access must offer itself to the frustrated person. Yet the vast majority of men (and women) give no evidence of having even been tempted. The anticipation of aversive repercussions apparently dominates any such temptations (cf. Zillmann, 1979).

Thus, the entry of elements of aggression into precoital and coital behavior is not controlled by the anticipation of social reproach, and to the extent that this use of aggression is anticipated to be enjoyable, it may be expected to merge with pleasurable sexual practices.

In human society mating and reproduction have come to be segregated functions. Sexuality has become predominantly recreational. Particularly in contemporary Western cultures the sociosexual and aggressive-sexual probing for heightened sexual gratification is in obtrusive evidence. Inhibiting forces such as fear of venereal disease and concern about reproductive consequences have been largely eliminated. Additionally, religious doctrines have lost much of their sexuality-directing powers (presumably because they are increasingly perceived as humanly created). Under these conditions, one might indeed expect much sexual experimentation—experimentation that probes the fusion of sex and aggression specifically. Davenport's (1976) description of universally dominant sexuality, according to which "men take the initiative and, without extended foreplay, proceed vigorously toward climax without much regard for achieving synchrony with the women's orgasm [p. 149]," is unlikely to remain an accurate account of Western sexuality. And to the extent that Ford and Beach's (1951) discovery of a relationship between aggressive-sexual behavior, on the one hand, and promiscuity and assertiveness in women, on the other, applies to contemporary Western cultures, one might expect that aggression-laden sexuality will gain in popularity. Is such possible development "natural"? It all depends, of course, on the value premise one endorses. If, for instance, one regards as natural the uncompromised pursuit of imaginable sexual pleasures (i.e., of sexual pleasures the human organism is capable of providing, regardless of the particular ways in which their attainment is sought), the development would be natural. If one considers natural the sexuality that is specified in the precepts of Christianity and of other religious doctrines, it probably would not be natural. And if one deems natural only the sexual behavior of free-living animals, the verdict is definitely a split decision.

3 Connections in Neurophysiology

Perhaps the most intriguing connections between sex and aggression, and certainly the most fundamental and sweeping ones, have been made in neurophysiology. Research on the cerebral representation of erection, in particular, has led to proposals of specific, evolutionary, deep-rooted linkages. I first discuss these proposals, together with the evidence on which they are based. Thereafter, I consider differences and critical redundancies in the autonomic mediation of sexual and aggressive responses. This analysis includes a brief exploration of the hemodynamics of sexual and aggressive behaviors, especially of the tumescence of sexual organs.

I. CEREBRAL REPRESENTATION

MacLean (e.g., 1962, 1963, 1968a, 1968b, 1970, 1973) has pioneered the research on the cerebral representation of sexuality and has advanced profound and provocative hypotheses concerning the relationship between sexual and aggressive behaviors. His conception of a "triune brain" (e.g., 1970) and the delineation of specific lines of communication both within the so-called "limbic system" and between this system and other structures of the brain are essential to understanding his theorizing about sex-aggression linkages. I therefore briefly introduce these aspects of his reasoning.

MacLean (e.g., 1962, 1964a, 1967) distinguishes three basic structures in the mammalian brain: the reptilian, the paleomammalian, and the neomammalian. The reptilian division is phylogenetically the oldest and most archaic structure. It forms the matrix of the upper brain stem and is composed of much of the reticular system, the midbrain, and the basal ganglia. The actual reptilian brain, a structure distinguished by large basal ganglia that resemble the corpus striatum of mammals (cf. Papez, 1929, 1937), exhibits a rudimentary cortex only. Phylogenetically speaking, this rudimentary cortex is thought to have undergone substantial expansion and differentiation in animal forms that were antecedent to mammals. But as these presumed animal forms are not demonstrable, it is a matter of pure speculation to construct the shape and structure of the primitive cortex of the immediate predecessors of the known mammals. However, the fact that most of the cortex with primordial features can be found in all existing lower and higher mammals strongly supports the phylogenetic projection. Following Broca (1878), MacLean (e.g., 1952) refers to the convolutions that evolved around the brain stem as the "limbic lobe" (*limbic* means "to form a border around"). This limbic cortex constitutes the paleomammalian division of the brain. The term "limbic system," furthermore, designates the limbic cortex and structures of the brain stem with which it has primary connections. As the paleomammalian derivative, the limbic system is considered highly integrated anatomically and functionally. It is also considered to control sexual and aggressive behaviors (in fact, all conceivable emotions) in fundamental ways. Finally, the neomammalian division of the brain, the neocortex, evolved around the paleomammalian division, its development culminating in homo sapiens. Essentially, then, MacLean considers the reptilian brain an outgrowth of the brain stem, the paleomammalian brain to have evolved around that outgrowth, and the neomammalian brain to have evolved around the paleomammalian brain in turn. He believes these divisions of the mammalian brain to differ in chemistry and structure and to have a certain degree of functional autonomy. At the same time, however, he stresses the functional integration of these divisions in a truly triune brain.

It is significant in MacLean's theorizing on sex and aggression that the limbic lobe almost fully embraces the more archaic structures. As can be seen in Fig. 3.1, the lobe comes together around the olfactory bulb. Septum and amygdala constitute the lobe's extremities, the septum neighboring the bulb dorsally and the amygdala ventrally. Not only are septum and amygdala "next door" to one another (to use MacLean's characterization), they are also firmly interconnected. Furthermore, as can be seen from the figure, the medial forebrain bundle branches off to both the septum and the amygdala. For the consideration of sex-aggression linkages, however, it is also important that this major line of communication between the limbic lobe and the hypothalamus, the midbrain, and other structures of the brain stem additionally branches off to the anterior thalamic nuclei. This mammillothalamic pathway bypasses the olfactory apparatus. Through interconnections between the hypothalamus and the anterior and midline parts of the thalamus, it ultimately connects with the cingulate gyrus and the orbito-frontal cortex.

The described structures have been decisively implicated with sexual, aggres-

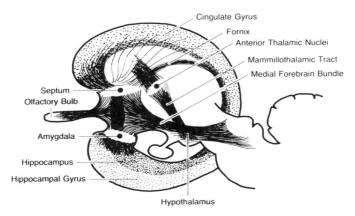

Cingulate Gyrus
Fornix
Anterior Thalamic Nuclei
Mammillothalamic Tract
Medial Forebrain Bundle
Septum
Olfactory Bulb
Amygdala
Hippocampus
Hippocampal Gyrus
Hypothalamus

FIG. 3.1.   Diagram of the limbic system and its interconnections, emphasizing structures thought to be significantly involved in the mediation of sexual and aggressive behaviors (circles). The stippled area constitutes the ring of the limbic cortex. The septum exerts control over sexual functions, the amygdala over oral and aggressive activities. The medial forebrain bundle, ascending from the central gray of the midbrain, branches off to both the septum and the amygdala. The diagonal band of Broca connects septum and amygdala. The mammillothalamic pathway, ascending from the hypothalamus to the anterior thalamus and bypassing the olfactory apparatus, comprises further important connections. (After Mac-Lean, 1962. Reprinted, with permission, from J. Zubin and J. Money (Eds.), *Contemporary sexual behavior.* Baltimore: Johns Hopkins University Press, 1973.)

sive, and sexual-aggressive functions in brain-stimulation studies on the male squirrel monkey (*Saimiri sciureus,* a small New World primate about the size of a guinea pig with a brain the size of a cat's) that were conducted by MacLean and Ploog (1962). In this research a stereotaxic platform with needle guides for the systematic intracerebral placement of electrodes was permanently attached to the animals' skulls. Subjects were stimulated while sitting in a chair. Penile erection responses were recorded. Several degrees of erection were distinguished in these recordings. In addition, subjects were monitored electroencephalographically. Explored were the midline cortical and subcortical structures between the gyrus rectus and a level immediately caudal to the mammillary bodies.

Positive loci for erection were found in three corticosubcortical areas of the limbic system: (1) the region of hippocampal projections to parts of the septum, the anterior and midline thalamic nuclei, and the hypothalamus; (2) the region comprising the mammillary bodies, the mammillothalamic tract, the anterior thalamus, and the cingulate gyrus; (3) the gyrus rectus, the medial part of the dorsal nucleus of the thalamus, and the regions of their interconnections. Stimulation in the septum and rostral diencephalon, after producing erection, led frequently to discharges in the hippocampus. Erections tended to be most pronounced and throbbing in nature during the hippocampal after-discharges. Following these discharges, erection tended to wax and wane for extended periods of time (up to 10 minutes). This period was followed, in turn, by unusual quietude, tractability, and somnolence on the part of the animals, an obtrusive mood change that tended to persist for several hours.

A momentous discovery regarding sexual-aggressive activities came with the stimulation of transitional zones for erection in the hypothalamus. In these regions, stimulation did not only elicit erection, but behavioral manifestations of fear and anger as well. Subjects exhibited cackling, piercing vocalizations, retraction of one or both corners of the mouth, and perhaps most importantly, displays of their fangs. According to MacLean and Ploog (1962), advancement of the electrodes by "a fraction of a millimeter [p. 54]" tended to produce the symptoms of fear and/or anger only. However, erection frequently occurred on the rebound after the cessation of fear- and anger-inducing stimulation. The loci for sexual and aggressive stimulation were thus in immediate proximity of one another.

In further research on the cerebral representation of genital tumescence in monkeys, MacLean and his collaborators (Dua & MacLean, 1964; MacLean, Denniston, & Dua, 1963; MacLean, Denniston, Dua, & Ploog, 1962) have traced the major effector pathway from the septal region downward to a position just lateral to the pyramidal tracts at the junction of the pons and medulla. Stimulation along the course of the medial forebrain bundle through the thalamus proved highly effective in eliciting erection. Starting at the level of the midbrain, the effective pathway led laterally into the substantia nigra, through the ventrolateral pons, and into the medulla just lateral to the exit of the sixth cranial nerve. The integration of all divisions of the triune brain in sexual functioning is indicated by the fact that the delineated "erection pathway" penetrates areas that entail limbic, extrapyramidal, and neocortical outflows.

MacLean and his associates have furthermore explored the area from the amygdala through the hippocampus. Stimulation in hippocampal regions was found to produce the previously described hippocampal after-discharges (resulting mainly from septal stimulation). Such after-discharges—rather than the initial charges—were characteristically associated with partial erection. In contrast, stimulation at positive loci in the septum and the anterior thalamus (MacLean et al., 1962; MacLean & Ploog, 1962), as well as in the medial frontal cortex (Dua & MacLean, 1964), had been found to produce erection and hippocampal after-discharges. As may be recalled, during these discharges erection tended to become throbbing. Despite this "orgastic appearance," however, ejaculation has never been observed under these circumstances. Seminal discharge occurred only when the stimulation involved loci that lie along the spinothalamic pathway and its medial ramifications into the caudal intralaminar region of the thalamus (MacLean, Dua, & Denniston, 1963).

A second momentous discovery regarding sexual-aggressive activities came with the stimulation of regions within the amygdala (e.g., MacLean, 1962, 1968b, 1973). Specific stimulation of parts of this structure was found to produce salivation and chewing immediately and penile erection after a characteristic delay (several seconds, up to nearly 1 minute). MacLean (1973) attributes the latency of the genital response to "the recruitment of neural activity in structures that are closely related to the amygdala, such as the nearby septopreoptic region [p. 61]." In establishing this orosexual connection, MacLean emphasizes the evolution of the primate brain: The olfactory sense is archaic and played a crucial part in both feeding and mating; this sense still holds oral and sexual functions together because the unique placement of the limbic lobe brings the representation of "head and tail" into close proximity with one another, as well as with olfaction (see Fig. 3.1). It should be noted that the neocortical representation of head and tail is well differentiated (paralleling the bodily layout, head and tail lie at opposite poles), making the representational arrangement of the limbic system unique indeed. Furthermore, it should be clear that oral functions are not limited to ingestion. Although in rodents the representation of feeding, on the one hand, and attack, defense, and flight, on the other, seems separated, the representation of feeding and attack largely overlaps in predators (cf. Ploog, 1975). In primates, as indicated by the previously reported findings on erection and defensive reactions (MacLean & Ploog, 1962), the representation of sexual functions and of biting and fighting is fused to a high degree. Thus, MacLean's (1963) proposal that "excitation in a region involved in oral mechanisms readily *spills over* into others concerned with genital function [p. 25, italics added]," and vice versa, should not be viewed as being limited to sexual linkages with the ingestion of food and with "ritualized" forms of devouring, such as kissing, licking, sucking, and mock biting. MacLean (e.g., 1973) explicitly incorporates angry and defensive behaviors under oral functions, and he regards their incorporation as essential to understanding aggressive and violent forms of sexual behavior.

Before summarizing MacLean's principal contentions regarding the neural linkage of sex and aggression, I briefly inspect immediately related evidence and assess its implications for his contentions.

Early indications of sexual-aggressive interdependencies owing to the limbic system came from ablation studies. Klüver and Bucy (1937) observed that bilateral anterior temporal lobectomy in monkeys produced extraordinary and "bizarre" behavioral changes. These changes were noted as early as 1888 by Brown and Schäfer, but they initially received little attention. Only later did they become widely known as the Klüver–Bucy syndrome. This syndrome entails: (1) a loss of fear and rage reactions; (2) hypersexuality (involving unusual activities that have been characterized as "perverted"); (3) indiscriminate ingestion of food; (4) visual agnosia (i.e., an inability to identify objects that are merely seen and to respond to them meaningfully); (5) a tendency to touch and examine by mouth all objects seen.

Subsequent research sought to determine more specifically which particular structures were responsible for the various symptoms of the syndrome. Mishkin (1954) and Mishkin and Pribram (1954) found that lesions in the ventrolateral portion of the temporal lobe tended to cause substantial impairment in visual discrimination, apparently without producing the other symptoms of the Klüver–Bucy syndrome. Additionally, Pribram and Bagshaw (1953) and Walker, Thomson, and McQueen (1953) observed that orbito-insulatemporal lesions and anteromedial lesions could produce both placidity and hypersexuality without impairing visual discrimination. Akert, Gruesen, Woolsey, and Meyer (1961), however, found that ablations to the neocortical gyri of the temporal lobe in which the rhinencephalic structures were only minimally disturbed produced all essential symptoms of the Klüver–Bucy syndrome, at least for some time. "Psychic blindness" was accompanied by placidity and uncommon oral behaviors, but only the loss of discrimination skills proved to be permanent.

The specific structure that seemed most critically involved in the mediation of the profound emotional changes that make up the Klüver–Bucy syndrome is the amygdala (cf. Deutsch & Deutsch, 1966; Tarpy, 1977; Thompson, 1967). Amygdalectomy has been found to produce docility in rats (Anand & Brobeck, 1952; Woods, 1956), cats (Schreiner & Kling, 1953, 1956), lynxes and agoutis (Schreiner & Kling, 1956), and monkeys (Rosvold, Mirsky & Pribram, 1954; Schreiner & Kling, 1956; Weiskrantz, 1956). But on occasion, amygdalectomy failed to produce notable behavioral changes (e.g., Hunsperger, 1959; King, 1958), and at times it resulted in drastically increased aggressiveness rather than in docility (e.g., Bard & Mountcastle, 1948; Spiegel, Miller, & Oppenheimer, 1940). Even discrete bilateral lesions in the basal and central nuclei of the amygdala, structures that produced fear and rage when stimulated, resulted— unaccountably—in increased aggressiveness (Wood, 1958). Furthermore, Ursin (1965) found some docility after bilateral lesions in the flight zone of the amygdala (as determined by stimulation studies); similar ablations in the defense zone occasioned little or no reduction in defense behavior, however.

Regarding sexuality, the effects of amygdalectomy are similarly inconsistent. Bard and Mountcastle (1948) found this procedure to produce rage linked with reduced sexuality in cats. Schreiner and Kling (1953), on the other hand, found it to instigate hypersexuality in this species, despite substantially reduced aggressiveness. Green, Clemente, and de Groot (1957), also working with cats, obtained entirely mixed results.

The amygdala has also been implicated with a social-dominance function. In primates, lesions in the amygdala have been found to promote submissiveness and docility in animals kept in their groups (Rosvold et al., 1954). These animals assume lower rank positions, presumably because of reduced assertiveness and inclination to fight. In contrast, the same lesions promoted irritability and aggressiveness in animals kept in individual cages. An investigation by Pribram (1962) established the dependence of the behavioral effects of amygdalectomy in primates more firmly. In an intact group of eight preadolescent male rhesus monkeys, the alpha animal was subjected to bilateral amygdalectomy. He became the omega animal. The beta animal advanced to the alpha position. After his rank was established, he was subjected to bilateral amygdalectomy. As with the original alpha animal, his rank dropped from top to bottom. He continued to express some aggression, however, and dominated the more timid original alpha animal. The gamma animal, meanwhile, had assumed the alpha position and was subjected to bilateral amygdalectomy. This animal, in stark contrast to his predecessors, not only maintained the alpha position, but exerted his dominance over the lower ranking animals with increased aggressiveness and furor. Apparently, the other high-ranking animals readily accommodated his assertiveness with submissive behavior. It should be remembered that these animals held intermediate ranks initially. Presumably because they had not developed dispositions to dominate others, they failed to challenge the position of the animal in charge. Pribram's findings, then, show that the behavioral effects of amygdalectomy very much depend on social dispositions and social circumstances, and they suggest that the amygdala is well integrated with structures that mediate social dispositions and the perception of behavioral contingencies.

Despite the inconsistencies in the behavioral consequences of lobectomy and, more specifically, of amygdalectomy in the research with nonhuman species, these procedures have been extensively applied to humans. The purpose of such psychosurgery is almost always the control of impulsive, aggressive behaviors, especially in episodically violent temporal lobe epileptics. Heimberger (1966), Narabayashi (1964), Narabayashi and Uno (1966), Sawa, Ueki, Arita, and Harada (1954), and Vaernet (cited in Mark & Ervin, 1970), for instance, report that amygdalectomy remedies violence more often than not. There are, however, frequent reports of no improvement, along with occasional reports of an increased propensity for violent behavior. Lesions in the temporal lobe (Mark, Sweet, & Ervin, 1975; Pool, 1954) have been reported to cure violent dispositions with some regularity. Lesions in the hypothalamus (Sano, 1962, 1975; Sano, Yoshioka, Ogashiwa, Ishijima, & Ohye, 1966), the thalamus (Spiegel & Wycis, 1952, 1962), and the cingulum (Le Beau, 1952; Tow & Whitty, 1953) have also been found effective techniques of ''sedative neurosurgery.'' Mark and Ervin (1970), finally, appear to have attempted lesions in more or less all limbic substructures in order to remedy excessive aggressiveness and epilepsy. Breggin (1972, 1975) has critically analyzed the behavioral implications of the various forms of lobotomy and found wanting their effectiveness as a cure for excessive aggressiveness as well as for epilepsy. He acknowledged as the only consistent effect of lobotomy the severe, nonspecific blunting of the patients' personality—a nearly complete loss of initiative, including that for hostile action.

The effects of lobotomy on sexual behaviors in humans also fail to be consistent. Temporal lobe lesions in men appear to cause loss of erectile ability without altering sexual desire (Weiss, 1972). At times, the loss of erectile ability is transient, however. Temporal lobe lesions have also been reported to restore normal sexual functioning in preoperatively hyposexual patients (Walker & Blumer, 1975). On the other hand, bilateral temporal lobectomy has been observed to produce hypersexuality, along with the other disorders characteristic of the Klüver–Bucy syndrome (Terzian & Ore, 1955).

Meyers (1962) reported that bilateral lesions in the ansa lenticularis, a procedure employed to remedy myoclonus, resulted in permanent impotence and loss of sexual desire. These findings are significant for the cerebral representation of erection in humans in that the lesions cross areas having analogues in the monkey brain that had been implicated with erection (e.g., MacLean & Ploog, 1962).

The work on brain stimulation seems to have yielded somewhat more consistent results than that on ablations, but there are also numerous inconsistencies.

The early research concentrated on rage and was usually conducted with cats. Stimulation of the brain stem (Hess, 1928), the hypothalamus (Masserman, 1941), and various hypothalamic substructures (Hess & Brügger, 1943; Hess, Brügger, & Bucher, 1945; Hunsperger, 1956; Ingram, 1952) was found to produce rage. Stimulation of the gray matter and adjacent regions yielded defensive responses (Hunsperger, 1956; Spiegel, Kletzkin, & Szekely, 1954). Stimulation of areas in the thalamus, however, evoked fear reactions (Delgado, Roberts, & Miller, 1954). Subsequent work implicated the anterior hypothalamus with the elicitation of rage and the posterior with that of flight (Hess, 1954). But aggressive responses were also associated with sites in the middle hypothalamus, and flight proved to be connected with rostral hypothalamic and preoptic sites (Nakao, 1958).

Later research probed the amygdala and related structures. Stimulation in various regions of the amygdala of cats proved to evoke both rage and fear (Kaada, Anderson, & Jansen, 1954; Magnus & Lammers, 1956; Shealy & Peele, 1957; Ursin & Kaada, 1960). De Molina and Hunsperger (1959) evoked these basic emotional responses by stimulation of the basal, central, and medial nuclei that are linked to the stria terminalis. Furthermore, these investigators traced the emotional reactivity along the pathway of the stria terminalis into the bed nucleus of this tract at the anterior commissure, at which point they found the effective loci to merge with those of hypothalamic and midbrain regions. A topographic separation of the amygdaloid loci associated with anger and fear was suggested by Ursin and Kaada (1960). It appears that anger is readily elicited from the ventromedial and caudal regions, whereas fear is linked to sites in the rostral part of the lateral nucleus and in the preamygdaloid region through the area of the central nucleus.

Amygdaloid stimulation, however, has also been found to produce the opposite effect in cats. It had a calming effect in some cases (Anand & Dua, 1956), and it promoted a friendly disposition and reduced aggressiveness in others

(Fonberg & Delgado, 1961). Egger and Flynn (1963) observed that in some cats it inhibited normal mousing.

Corroborating and expanding the previously described work of Pribram (1962) on the diverse consequences of amygdalectomy, stimulation research has furnished compelling evidence of the dependence of the behavioral effects of neural excitation on dispositional and social circumstances. Delgado (1967a, 1967b), in his pioneering work with radio-controlled electrical stimulation, demonstrated that identical charges to identical loci in the thalamus and the central gray could have entirely different consequences in rhesus monkeys, depending on whether the animals were restrained in a chair, free but alone in their colony cage, or free to interact with other colony members. In the restrained animals the stimulation produced staring, head movement, and low-pitched vocalizations. In the free but secluded animals it led to restlessness, pacing, and low-pitched vocalizations. In stark contrast, it produced profound changes in the aggressive behavior of the animals that were free in their colony. The specific effect of stimulation, however, was a function of social rank. Stimulation of the alpha animal of the group produced well-organized attacks upon subordinate animals, including chasing, striking, and biting. Attacks were primarily directed against animals that had been targets of aggressive action prior to the experimental treatment. Disposition toward particular individuals thus proved to be a significant factor in the aggressive reactions evoked by stimulation. Stimulation of the beta animal also produced well-organized attacks. These attacks were directed at all other animals in the group, including the alpha animal. Owing to repeated stimulations, the beta animal's hyperaggressiveness soon advanced him to the alpha position. Interestingly, analogous stimulation to low-ranking animals altogether failed to produce aggressive reactions. It merely induced restlessness.

In a follow-up investigation with rhesus monkeys (Delgado, 1967a, 1967b, 1969a), the dispositional dependence of the effect of neural excitation was demonstrated most rigorously by placing each subject into different social-dominance conditions and comparing the effects of identical stimulation within subjects across these conditions. The animals were stimulated when alone, in the company of a subordinate animal, and in the company of a dominant one. In isolated animals, stimulation to the right pedunculus cerebellaris medius close to the lateral lemniscus produced marked restlessness, but no behavior that could be construed as threat or aggression. The same stimulation produced threat displays and assaultive behavior when an animal of inferior rank was present, but it did not evoke any detectable signs of threat and aggressiveness when an animal of superior rank was present. In a further investigation different groups of four animals were uniquely composed to create systematic rank variations. It was found that identical stimulation produced negligible reactions when the stimulated animal was lowest in rank, that advancement in rank caused this stimulation to produce successively higher levels of aggressiveness, and that assaultive behavior was consistently directed toward animals of lower rank.

Stimulation of amygdaloid structures in humans has produced comparatively consistent results. King (1961), Delgado (1969b) and Sweet, Ervin, and Mark (1969) have found it to evoke reactions of anger that could lead to assaultive behavior. Kim and Umbach (1973), on the other hand, reported that stimulation of the amygdala produced aggressive reactions only in patients with a history of violent behavior; it had no appreciable effect on nonviolent patients. Furthermore, Valenstein (1976) observed that for those patients who are predisposed to respond violently to amygdaloid stimulation, it is of little moment exactly where, within the amygdala, they receive stimulation. These findings on humans, then, fail to confirm the topographic amygdaloid differentiation between anger and fear that was observed in other species (Ursin & Kaada, 1960), but strongly corroborate the dispositional dependence of stimulation effects.

The evidence regarding the functional significance of the septum and the hippocampus, structures connected by the supracallosal striae, is again rather inconsistent. In nonhuman species septal lesions have been found to produce increased emotionality (Brady & Nauta, 1953) or no appreciable change in affective behavior (Brady, 1958). They have not been found to promote irritability or to facilitate rage specifically (Bond, Randt, Bidder, & Rowland, 1957; Kling, Orbach, Schwartz, & Towne, 1960). Stimulation of the septum has been observed to produce both rage and fear (Hess & Brügger, 1943), and stimulation of the hippocampus produced similar results (MacLean & Delgado, 1953). Research on rewarding self-stimulation (Olds & Milner, 1954) initially focused on the septum and led to its projection as a major "pleasure center" (cf. Thompson, 1967). Later research yielded contradictory results, however, and showed the septum to be largely neutral (Olds, 1962).

More consistent findings have been reported in the research with humans. Septal stimulation has been observed to diminish violent behaviors (Heath, 1963). More generally, it was found to foster verbal reports of well-being and euphoria (Bishop, Elder, & Heath, 1963; Heath & Mickle, 1960; Sem-Jacobsen & Torkildsen, 1960). Such reports have often been rather vague, however (cf. Thompson, 1967). Additionally, their analysis tended to be highly informal and may have allowed considerable selectivity. Weiss (1972), finally, reports that septal stimulation in men not only produced reports of pleasurable sensations, but resulted in penile tumescence as well.

The search for the neural structures that control penile erection has involved nonhuman primates other than squirrel monkeys (e.g., MacLean & Ploog, 1962). Robinson and Mishkin (1968), Perachio, Alexander, and Robinson (1969), and Perachio, Alexander, and Marr (1973), for instance, explored various loci in the forebrain of rhesus monkeys. The results they obtained were generally compatible with those obtained with squirrel monkeys.

Much of the basic work on the neural control of sexual behavior, that of females as well as that of males, has been done with rats. In this research, different structures were implicated for males and females; consequently, I separate by gender the brief discussion of this research.

Both electrical and chemical stimulation studies have shown the medial preoptic area of the hypothalamus to be the critical sexuality-controlling region for male rats. Van Dis and Larsson (1971) observed that electrical stimulation in this region substantially promoted the copulatory behavior of castrated animals. Similarly, Davidson (1966) reported chemical stimulation (specifically, the implantation of small amounts of testosterone) to have the same effect on castrates. Sexual facilitation was obtained only when the androgen was deposited at the appropriate loci, not when it was placed at alternative sites.

In efforts to delineate the sexual control regions more precisely, Szechtman, Caggiula, and Wulkan (1978) recently employed minute knife cuts to sever the preoptic area of males in unique ways. Severing the lateral connections of the preoptic area, without destruction of the anterior, posterior, and dorsal ones, was found to impair sexual functioning profoundly. The incidence of copulation declined significantly. When copulation occurred, it was erratic. Ejaculation seemed unimpaired, however. Dorsal cuts produced entirely different results. Such cuts did not alter copulatory inclinations, but seemed to impair ejaculation. The animals spent more time and needed a greater number of intromissions to achieve ejaculation. Finally, anterior and posterior cuts were of little moment and did not appreciably alter sexual activities.

Szechtman et al. (1978) consider the connection of the medial preoptic area with the medial forebrain bundle essential. Only the lateral cuts severed this connection and created the copulatory impairment. The surgical disjunction appears to have disoriented the animals, rendering them unable to proceed from a state of sexual arousal to the appropriate motor reactions to receptive females. The disoriented males were obviously not deficient hormonally. Because they preferred the odors of estrous females over those of nonestrous ones, it also seems unlikely that their sexual incapacitation resulted from an olfactory deficit. Rather, it appears that they simply failed to respond to the visual and possibly tactile cues that guide the unimpaired males' sexual approach. In order to achieve copulation, the sexually disoriented males seemed to depend on the active sexual solicitation of females. The fully coordinated sexual response sequence apparently requires the intact linkage between the medial preoptic area and the medial forebrain bundle. This interpretation of the findings is quite consistent with MacLean's (e.g., 1973) contentions. MacLean has stressed the significance of the medial forebrain bundle in the instigation of sexual behavior. It should be recalled that stimulation along the course of this bundle proved highly effective in eliciting penile tumescence in squirrel monkeys.

In female rats the medial preoptic area controls the reproductively irrelevant male forms of sexual behavior, such as mounting. Lesions in this area greatly reduce mounting, but actually enhance lordosis, that is, the females' characteristic sexual posture that allows males to achieve intromission (Singer, 1968). In contrast, lesions of the anterior hypothalamus impair lordosis (Heimer & Larsson, 1967). Implants of small amounts of estrogen have further implicated the significance of this region for female sexual behavior. Lisk (1962) found that such implants in the medial hypothalamic area markedly facilitated lordosis. Additionally, implants of progesterone in the midbrain reticular formation proved to enhance lordosis in estrogen-primed females (Rose, Claybough, Clemens, & Gorski, 1971).

Sex-related gender differences have also been found in the neocortex. Larsson (1964), working with rats, observed that the sexual behavior of males was greatly impaired by neocortical lesions. In contrast, these lesions had no disruptive effect on the sexual behavior of females and actually facilitated lordosis.

The greater dependence on cortical tissue by males is usually explained as the result of the more elaborate and complex motor behavior required for successful mating. Generally speaking, the sexual response sequence of male mammals relies to a high degree on sight and smell, and any disturbance of these means of sexual access is likely to impair functional sexuality in males. Females perform a comparatively simple motor sequence and appear to respond mainly to tactile stimuli. In fact, sensitivity to touch seems greatly facilitated during estrus. Komisaruk, Larsson, and Cooper (1972), for instance, reported that upon elevation of the level of circulating estrogen the receptive fields of sensory neurons leaving the genital area of female rats are enlarged and highly responsive to touch. Interestingly, the estrus-linked heightened tactile sensitivity is not restricted to the female genitalia, but extends to other parts of the body surface. Bereiter and Barker (1975) observed that estrogen increased the size of the receptive fields of sensory neurons in facial regions as well.

It should be noted that the gender differences in the cerebral representation of sexual behavior are not limited to the differential localization of critical functions. These differences also manifest themselves in the differential size of particular structures and in their functional capacity. For instance, Gorski, Gordon, Shryne, and Southam (1978) found the medial preoptic nucleus to be more voluminous in male and androgenized female rats than in neonatally castrated males. Raisman (1974) detected sexual dimorphism in the position of synaptic terminals in the preoptic region of rats. Greenough, Carter, Steerman, and de Voogd (1977), moreover, compared the male and female preoptic area of the hamster brain and found differences in dendrite branching. A considerable amount of experimental evidence supports the view that gonadal hormones, secreted early in development, effect profound and permanent gender differences in the central nervous system and its functioning (cf. Goy & McEwen, 1980; MacLusky & Naftolin, 1981).

Taken together, the research seeking to determine the cerebral representation of sexual, aggressive, and sexual-aggressive behavior is plagued by considerable inconsistencies. These inconsistencies seem to result, for the most part, from imperfections in the experimental procedures employed. Ablation research, for instance, usually entails some damage to cerebral regions (in the immediate vicinity of the target organs) that ideally should not be disturbed. Electrical stimulation does not exactly reproduce the natural pattern of neural firing. And implanted chemicals tend to diffuse somewhat unpredictably from the point of origin. The situation is aggravated by the fact that the brain structures of interest (the limbic system and the hypothalamus, in particular) involve neural and glandular systems that operate in an integrated fashion. The hypothalamus is said (Thompson, 1967) to have been "designed in such a way as to frustrate experimental analysis of its physiological and behavioral functions [p. 537]." Notwithstanding these difficulties, reviews of large numbers of investigations that used different procedures (e.g., Goddard, 1964) tend to show that many investigations produce comparable, consistent results and that a small minority of studies makes for the overall inconsistencies. Giving credence to redundancy in experimentation, some cautious generalizations certainly can be made. The generalizations put forth by MacLean, to which I now turn, may seem somewhat daring, however. (It should also be mentioned that other investigators have interpreted the research evidence quite differently. Whalen, 1976, for instance, vehemently denied the existence of specific "sexual centers" after a thorough analysis of neurochemical brain mechanisms, insisting that all facets of sexual behavior are mediated by highly complex interactions of neuronal subsystems.)

MacLean (e.g., 1963, 1968b, 1973), relying mostly on the work of de Molina and Hunsperger (1957), considers the amygdaloid structures implicated with self-preservation functions: alimentation, predation, and defensive aggression. In contrast, the septal structures, along with the anatomically related hippocampal regions, are viewed as serving the sustenance of the species rather than of the self. Pleasurable social activities (e.g., grooming) and sexual behavior, including courtship, are considered linked to septal excitation. Individual survival functions and procreation are thus viewed as neatly separated. At the same time, however, they are seen to be interdependent. The previously described "evolutionary accident" that brought amygdala and septum into close proximity, along with strong structural interconnections and linkage to the anterior hypothalamus (see Fig. 3.1), are held responsible for this interdependence that results in the occasional fusion of sex and aggression.

The fusion (or confusion) of sex and aggression is said to be created in two principal ways:

1. Structural damage to amygdaloid regions *gives release* to septal excitation. Damage to septal regions likewise gives release to amygdaloid excitation. Thus, impairment of amygdaloid functioning should foster hypersexuality. The Klüver-Bucy syndrome can be taken as obtrusive evidence in support of this prediction. Analogously, impairment of septal and hippocampal functioning should produce hyperaggressiveness. Both dependencies have undoubtedly significant clinical implications.

2. In intact structures marked excitation in one structure *spills over* into another. Specifically, amygdaloid excitation recruits activity in the septum, and septal excitation recruits activity in the amygdala. Because both amygdaloid and

septal structures are immediately linked to the anterior hypothalamus, excitation originating in the amygdala may recruit septal excitation along the way. Likewise, excitation originating in the septum may recruit amygdaloid excitation on its path.

Figure 3.2 illustrates this generalization and shows its research basis in simplified form. The generalization concerning intact structures appears to explain the intimate linkage of oral activities with genital behaviors that has been observed in more or less all cultures. Almost universally, persons initiating or engaged in sexual behavior involve their mouth to "kiss" their partners on some parts of the body. The preferred parts are the mates' mouth, facial areas, neck, breasts, limbs, and—last but not least—genitals. Noninjurious biting is similarly widespread and also applies to practically all parts of the body. The behavioral tendency to lick, suck, and bite appears to have given rise to introspective accounts by sexually highly aroused persons of a "desire to devour" their partners, an insight that prompted much speculative interpretation in early psychology. MacLean's proposals seem to have overcome this stage of speculation and to have placed the orosexual connection on a solid biological and physiological foundation.

MacLean's proposals raise questions, however, when applied to pain-inflicting and injurious orosexual behaviors, to sadomasochistic activities, and to violent rape. Surely, it can be said (e.g., MacLean, 1973) that the disclosed functional relationships in the limbic brain are relevant to violent forms of sexual behavior. But exactly how relevant they are remains to be determined. It is

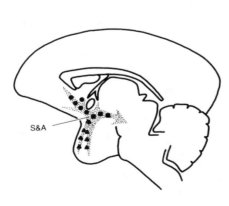

FIG. 3.2. Parasagittal diagram of the brain of the squirrel monkey, showing the anatomical affinity in the representation of sexual and oral-aggressive behaviors. Stimulation points in the medial septo-preoptic regions are associated with genital responses (circles), points in amygdaloid regions with oral responses (triangles), and points in the anterior hypothalamus with defense and aggressive reactions (squares). The stippled area indicates underlying pathways. The region in which the various functions are in immediate proximity (S&A) is thought to produce a fusion of sexual and aggressive responses. (After MacLean, 1964a. Reprinted, with permission, from J. Zubin and J. Money (Eds.),*Contemporary sexual behavior*. Baltimore: Johns Hopkins University Press, 1973.)

tempting to point to the close anatomical proximity between areas in the brain that have been implicated with the elicitation of aggressive and sexual behavior, respectively, and to functional interactions whenever violent sexual actions occur. But the explanatory value of proceeding in such a fashion is compromised by the fact that in contrast to a small, violent minority, the vast majority of people—both in Western and non-Western societies—fails to behave violently in their sexual endeavors despite the same anatomical and functional constitution of their brains. How can the discrepancy in behavior be explained? Can it be assumed that substantial individual variation exists in the proximity and in the degree of interrelatedness between the critical limbic structures, and as a result, some persons are prone to fuse sex and aggression, whereas others are not or are prone to a lesser degree? Such an assumption would salvage the proposals, but clearly, it is empirically unfounded at present. And in consideration of its social implications—namely, the absolution of responsibility to the sexually violent person (the behavior would, after all, be the result of a built-in condition)—it would seem inadvisable, if not irresponsible, to make this assumption.

Alternatively, it is conceivable that the impulsion to aggression, which in accord with the mechanics proposed by MacLean accompanies sexual arousal, is controlled and overpowered by mechanics of learning. Sex-related aggressive behavior would find release when it is not met with strong learned inhibition and/or when it is supported by acquired habits. In view of the fact that at this time virtually nothing is known about the relative motivational strength of limbically impelled versus mechanically learned or cognition-guided aggressive-sexual behavior and its interdependencies, it would seem premature to assume that critical differences in such behavior are the necessary consequence of differential control through learning. Additionally, this reasoning would endorse the unfounded projection that sexual arousal generally impels aggressive action, an impulsion that requires continual inhibition to prevent expression (see Chapter 5 for a detailed discussion of this issue).

MacLean's grand proposals, fascinating as they may be, thus seem to raise more questions than they answer. Does the millimeter proximity of aggression- and sex-eliciting regions in the brain of squirrel monkeys really mean that in this and other primates, humans included, sexual arousal generally impels oral and, especially, aggressive activities? Is environmentally induced excitation in the septum intense enough to diffuse into the amygdala, and vice versa? And is such possible spillover in man the principal source of violent sexual behavior? What about gender differences? Are women, despite likely structural and functional differences in the brain, as prone as men to fuse sex and aggression? The evidence at hand simply fails to provide definitive answers.

It is worthy of note that MacLean's proposals concerning the sex-aggression linkage also fail to explain the relative commonness of human masochistic inclinations. As should be remembered, masochistic sexual tendencies are more popular than sadistic ones, especially in women. The passive reception of pain in connection with sexual activities has, of course, little to do with oral impulses.

This passive behavior seems antithetical to aggression generally, in that the reception of pain is one of the most basic and strongest aggression-instigating conditions known (Hutchinson, 1972; Zillmann, 1979). MacLean's proposals cope only with the incorporation of sadistic elements in sexuality. To the extent that these elements encroach into the behavior of the various participants of sexual unions, masochistic experiences can be construed as part and parcel of sadistic action. As was pointed out earlier, however, masochistic inclinations often occur in pure form (i.e., devoid of sadistic elements), and in this pure form they seem to challenge the orosexual connection. Only through rather wild speculation could masochism be brought in line with MacLean's proposals of a sex-aggresion connection. It might be suggested, for instance, that the infliction of pain—as the major impetus for defensive fighting—occasions amygdaloid excitation that, when not finding release in defensive reactions, spills over into septal regions, thus facilitating purely sexual actions. Needless to say, this suggestion is without empirical support from stimulation studies and, hence, is entirely speculative.

Before leaving MacLean's innovative theorizing, a further proposal of his should be mentioned. MacLean (e.g., 1973) suggested that man was forced into "sexual modesty" (i.e., the concealment of the genitals by clothing) because of an evolutionarily deep-rooted tendency for males to use genital displays as threats. The suggestion is based on the observation of such displays in squirrel monkeys (MacLean, 1964b; Ploog, Hopf, & Winter, 1967; Ploog & MacLean, 1963). In some of the work, the subjects were exposed to their own image in a mirror and found to respond with erectile displays. The striatal complex was implicated in lesion studies as the neural repository for this type of behavior. Evolutionarily speaking, the squirrel monkey is one of the primate species that manifests the transition from olfactory to visual behavior control. MacLean draws upon this circumstance to argue that in the squirrel monkey the olfactory, urinary, territorial marking (see Chapter 2) of the osmatic infraprimate mammals was replaced by urogenital visual displays. Man, MacLean (1963) surmised, should have followed in this tradition of employing penile erection as threat, but he ultimately relied on superior intelligence and invented the fig leaf and the loincloth "to reduce the unpleasant social tension created by the show of these aggressive impulses [p. 30]." An element of sex (i.e., erection) is thus once more presumed to be closely allied with aggression.

The sex-aggression linkage in erectile displays is not, however, a unique erectile linkage. As MacLean (e.g., 1973) himself noted, in nonhuman primates erection accompanies nonaggressive social behaviors as well. Greeting is the foremost of these behaviors. Anthropological evidence further shows that in uncovered men penile displays accompany greeting, appeasement, anxiety, joy, elation, and surprise as much as anger and aggression (Gajdusek, 1970).

MacLean's suggestion also seems at variance with the fact that women, who have no penile threat to display, are generally compelled to cover their genitalia. Davenport (1976) stressed that in the few societies that fail to observe sexual modesty by covering their genitals, modesty is assured by strict behavioral rules. Among Australian aborigines, for example, it is deemed highly improper to stare at genital areas, and women, when seated, are expected to assume a modest posture such that their vaginal opening is hidden. The fact that women are expected to observe modesty is not only left unexplained by MacLean's speculation, but can be viewed as supporting alternative proposals that concern the origin of modesty. In accord with the reasoning on privacy presented earlier, it can be argued, for instance, that potentially aggressive rivalry for sexual access demanded modesty, especially on the part of women, in order to curb social conflict. It is also conceivable, however, that women sought to avoid harassment, owing to the indiscriminate sexual enticement of men, by observing genital modesty.

In summary, then, neurophysiological research has projected two related central linkages between sex and aggression:

1. In a sexual-aggressive connection, excitation associated with sexual stimulation is thought to spill over into areas controlling aggression and thus foster aggressive reactions alongside sexual ones; analogously, excitation deriving from instigation to aggression is thought to perfuse into areas controlling sexual responses and thereby feed sexual impulsion into aggressive actions. The neurophysiological evidence can be interpreted as suggestive of perfusion of excitation from sex to aggression, at least in mammals. In contrast, the neurophysiological evidence pertaining to the presumed perfusion of excitation from aggression to sex is quite inconsistent and inconclusive.

2. In an orosexual connection, mutual facilitation of specifically sexual responses, on the one hand, and oral activities such as licking, sucking, and biting, on the other, is projected from essentially the same neural mechanics of excitatory spillage. This proposal can be construed as being substantially narrower than that of the sex-aggression connection, as aggressive (or more probably, aggressionlike) activity is limited to oral manifestations. The neurophysiological evidence concerning the orosexual connection suggests that sexual stimulation promotes oral activity, at least in mammals. This evidence leaves unclear, however, to what extent, if at all, the reverse may occur.

Some data from the comparative analysis of sexual and aggressive behaviors (see Chapter 2) are consistent with the projection of a mutual facilitation between sex and aggression—and thus with the hypothesis of excitatory spillage in central structures. Other data, however, challenge mutual facilitation—and the spillage hypothesis along with it. Despite homology of neural structures, the behavioral consequences of presumed spillage are not only not universal, but they vary substantially. Such variation is most pronounced across species, but depending on numerous circumstances, it is evident within species as well. Notwithstanding these difficulties with universality, selected data from the comparative analysis of behavior seem obtrusively supportive of the spillage hypothesis, and that may explain why this hypothesis—in the face of inconsistent research findings, insufficient direct demonstrations, and challenges of its very assumptions—continues to attract considerable attention.

II. AUTONOMIC COMMONALITIES

Sexual behavior, it appears, is controlled in a dual fashion. Cerebral control is supplemented by spinal control manifest in reflex arcs. Both systems can function rather independently. At the same time, however, they are interdependent in critical ways.

According to the apparent locus of control of sexual reactions, environmental stimulation that induces genital tumescence and copulatory motions is usually classified as "psychogenic" versus "reflexogenic" (e.g., Weiss, 1972). Olfactory, gustatory, visual, auditory, and nongenital tactile stimulation, along with stimulation through imagination, that produce sexual reactions are considered psychogenic. Exteroceptive stimulation of the genital organs that results in sexual responses, and also interoceptive stimuli from the bladder and rectum that yield this effect, are considered reflexogenic.

Spinal sexual reflexes have been demonstrated in numerous mammalian species (Bard, 1940; Beach, 1967). Female cats, for instance, in whom the brain was surgically separated from the spinal cord, respond with characteristic sexual postures and body movements to the mechanical stimulation of their genitalia (Bard, 1940). Spinal rats behave similarly, although artificial stimulation proved somewhat unreliable in producing these reactions (Hart, 1969). The dispensability of the cortex as such for female sexual responsiveness (e.g., Beach, 1944; Clemens, Wallen, & Gorski, 1967) has already been mentioned. Hart (1967, 1978), in a meticulous investigation of sexual reflexes in male dogs, was able to elicit in spinal animals seemingly all facets of sexual behavior (e.g., erection, thrusting, leg kicking, and ejaculation) through mechanical stimulation of specific regions of the penis. The various reactions appeared to be organized in four distinct reflex arcs. However, Hart also noted that the intense ejaculatory reaction of intact dogs could not be produced by mechanical stimulation of the penis alone, but required the presence of a receptive female. Contributions from higher brain centers, then, seem necessary to produce the full-fledged, normal sexual reaction. Comparisons of the sexual behavior of spinal and intact male rats led to similar conclusions (Hart, 1968, 1978). Although many elemental sexual responses could be produced in spinal rats, their responses tended to be somewhat different from those of intact animals. Upon mechanical stimulation of the penile tip, for example, spinal animals exhibited a strong leg-kicking reflex uncharacteristic of intact animals. Again, higher centers appear to modify the spinally arranged elemental responses.

The sexual reflexes are organized in the inferior portion of the spinal cord and its afferent and efferent connections with the genital areas. Eckhardt (1863), through electrical stimulation of the parasympathetic branches of spinal nerves in dogs, implicated the sacral portion of the spinal cord with erective functions. Semans and Langworthy (1938) later confirmed these initial observations on the "nervi erigentes" in cats. However, stimulation of the pudendal nerve failed to produce erection. Its destruction, on the other hand, abolished erection in response to mechanical stimulation of the penis (Kuntz, 1953). The pudendal plexus is thus implicated with the transmission of afferent impulses in the sexual reflex arcs.

In man the efferent neural impulses that mediate penile tumescence are thought to arise from parasympathetic fibers in the sacral cord roots S2, S3, and S4. The involvement of S2 is somewhat uncertain, however (Pick, 1970). It should be noticed that these roots also supply the efferent, parasympathetic connections to the detrusor muscle of the urinary bladder and to the distal colon and rectum. The pelvic nerves from the sacral portion of the spinal cord thus control genital tumescence, micturition, and defecation. Although anatomically intertwined, the controlling pathways are not identical. Research on spinal cord injuries in men shows that erection, bladder, and bowel functions can be selectively impaired, and it suggests that bowel and bladder functions are more robust (i.e., less vulnerable to spinal injury) than genital tumescence (Bors & Comarr, 1971).

Sexual functioning (penile tumescence, in particular) does not entirely depend on sacral, parasympathetic outflow, however. It has become clear that pathways originating above the sacral plexus are also capable of producing erection. In a most revealing investigation, Root and Bard (1947) removed the entire sacral division of the spinal cord from male cats and observed unimpaired penile erection when estrous females were present. Mechanical stimulation of the penis, on the other hand, no longer produced erection. Subsequent transection of the spinal cord in the lower thoracic region abolished erection, but sexual excitement was still in evidence. Despite erective failure, the males mounted estrous females. The combination of the destruction of the sacral cord and complete thoracolumbar sympathectomy produced the same result: sexual excitement without erection. Provided, then, that communication with higher brain centers is intact, sympathetic spinal outflow can mediate penile tumescence without the aid of sacral, parasympathetic impulses. Because—with the destruction of the sacral plexus—the reflexogenic mechanism is defunct, the mediation of erection is obviously completely psychogenic.

Root and Bard also demonstrated that the bilateral severing of all sympathetic nerve chains below the diaphragm does not impair penile tumescence in male cats that are in the presence of estrous females. This procedure probably destroyed all efferent fibers from the thoracolumbar plexus that had been shown capable of mediating erection, and the findings thus suggest that in cats with intact spinal cords the sacral, parasympathetic outflow can mediate psychogenic sexual reactions as well as reflexogenic ones.

Observations on humans are consistent with those on subhuman species. Research with men who suffered spinal cord injuries (Bors & Comarr, 1960; Munro, Horne, & Paull, 1948; Talbot, 1955; Zeitlin, Cottrell, & Lloyd, 1957) shows that nearly all patients with complete spinal cord transections above the sacral cord level maintain the capacity for erection. However, penile tumescence occurs only after reflexogenic stimulation, not after psychogenic treatment. There is no question, then, that in the absence of suprasegmental connections erection is entirely under the control of the sacral reflex. It should be remembered that the pudendal nerve constitutes the afferent limb of the reflex arc. Destruction of this nerve should and indeed does produce impotence (Bors & Comarr, 1954). Patients who suffered complete bilateral motor neuron lesions of the sacral cord are also likely to lose erectile potency. Erection through psychogenic, but not through reflexogenic, stimulation may be maintained in a minority of cases only (Bors & Comarr, 1960). The capacity for ejaculation is nearly always lost (Hohmann, 1966; Lundberg, 1977). Patients with incomplete spinal cord lesions, however, tend to maintain the capacity for both psychogenic and reflexogenic erectile tumescence.

In patients who suffered complete destruction of the sacral cord, psychogenic erections appear to be mediated by outflow from the thoracolumbar cord—specifically by impulses from the adjacent twelfth thoracic and first lumbar nerves (Weiss, 1972). But it should be recognized that this sympathetic control of erection is largely dispensable in men with intact sacral structures. In support of this relative independence, Rose (1953) failed to detect erectile impairment after bilateral lumbar sympathectomy and after bilateral thoracolumbar sympathectomy. Whitelaw and Smithwick (1951), on the other hand, observed some degree of disturbance in erectile ability after bilateral thoracolumbar sympathectomy.

The research evidence on penile tumescence thus suggests the interrelated operation of two largely redundant systems of control. Sympathetic outflow from the thoracolumbar cord acts synergistically with parasympathetic outflow from the sacral cord in producing penile erection. Impulses from higher brain centers, but not from reflexogenic stimulation, mediate sexual arousal through the ''thoracolumbar erection centers.'' Simultaneously, the higher centers impact the ''sacral erection centers,'' and the sacral reflex arc, mainly via the pudendal nerves, receives input from mechanical stimulation. Clearly, these systems act in concert. The fact that in pathological cases each system is capable of substituting for the other to some degree (at least as far as penile erection is concerned) should not be interpreted as suggesting that the systems usually act autonomously.

It should be noted that the consequences of spinal cord injury for the sexual behavior of women are quite different from those for men. Women's capacity for sexual experience seems to suffer little, if at all, from spinal cord transections. Bregman (1973) and Fitting, Salisbury, Davis, and Mayclin (1978) reported more or less unimpaired sexual activity after injury. The women reported to be normally orgasmic. Menstruation, pregnancy, and delivery seemed unaffected. Impairment of genital sensation was a common complaint, however (Cole, 1975). On the other hand, orgasmic experiences were reported by women with complete denervation of all pelvic structures. Such reports, it seems, require cautious interpretation, because they might reveal more about the occasionally enormous ambiguity concerning self-reported orgasm than about physiological reality. But be this as it may, the data on the consequences of spinal injury for female sexuality project the female sexual response as being extremely robust— certainly as being substantially more robust than that of males.

Genital tumescence is, of course, a vascular phenomenon. Counter to earlier assumptions, the involvement of the ischio- and bulbo-cavernosus muscles is entirely negligible in penile erection (Weiss, 1972). Erection is the result of blood flooding: From the terminal branches of the internal pudendal arteries, blood inundates the corpora cavernosa and the corpus spongiosum (Henderson & Roepke, 1933; Newman, Northrup, & Devlin, 1964). Blood enters the collapsed vascular spaces of the flaccid penis at comparatively high pressure. Erection is maintained at considerably less pressure. Continuous high-volume flow of blood is essential, however, as mechanical constriction of the aorta is known to prompt rapid penile detumescence (Semans & Langworthy, 1938). More specifically, the distention of the penis with blood during erection is the result of the opening of anastomoses between the arterioles and the vascular spaces in the erectile tissue (Conti, 1952). So-called "polsters," structures that contain smooth muscle located at the anastomoses between the arterioles and the vascular spaces, function as valves. During flaccidity, they cause the blood to be shunted out of the erectile tissue into the veins. When impulses for erection are received, these polsters relax and thereby allow blood to inundate the erectile tissue. For the purpose of this discussion, it is most significant that the polsters are under the control of the autonomic nervous system through connections from both the thoracolumbar and the sacral erection centers (Newman et al., 1964). The floodgates to the penis, then, can be opened by sympathetic as well as by parasympathetic impulses. It is of further interest that the autonomic nerves from the sympathetic, thoracolumbar plexus contain both vasoconstrictor (adrenergic) and vasodilator (cholinergic) fibers. This fact might explain why the stimulation of these nerves (i.e., the simultaneous stimulation of antagonistic fibers) generally fails to produce erection. More importantly, however, the presence of both constrictor and dilator fibers in the thoracolumbar outflow allows selective, patterned effects. Psychogenic stimulation mediated by the thoracolumbar nerves thus can produce vasodilation in some structures and concurrent vasoconstriction in others.

Sexual arousal obviously manifests itself not only in genital tumescence. Penile and clitoral vasocongestion is characteristically accompanied by a host of autonomically mediated reactions. Masters and Johnson (1966), who distinguished excitement, plateau, orgasm, and resolution phases of sexual arousal, observed that during the excitement phase in human males penile tumescence is associated with vasocongestion of the scrotal integument, contraction of the smooth muscles of the dartos layer, elevation of the testes owing to tightening of the spermatic cord, and increase in testicle volume. Analogously, during the excitement phase in human females tumescence in the clitoral glans and shaft was found to be associated with elevation of the labia majora, thickening of the vaginal walls, expansion of the vaginal barrel, production of vaginal lubrication, and increase in breast size. Most significantly, however, genital tumescence in both males and females proves to be accompanied by pronounced sympathetic outflow in the apparent service of energy expenditure. Masters and Johnson recorded heart rates ranging from 110 to more than 180 beats per minute (bpm) for both males and females during coitus. Hyperventilation was evident in both genders, with respiration rates above 40 per minute. Blood pressure was found to undergo substantial changes. Systolic blood pressure increased between 40 and 100 millimeters of mercury (Hg) in males and between 30 and 80 mm Hg in females. Diastolic pressure also increased, but to a lesser degree: 20–50 mm Hg in males and 20–40 mm Hg in females. These and similar findings (e.g., Bartlett, 1956; Boas & Goldschmidt, 1932; Fox & Fox, 1969; Klumbies & Kleinsorge, 1950) are somewhat compromised, however, by the fact that some skeletal-motor activity contributed to the excitatory reaction. This is obviously the case for data deriving from coition, but it also applies to the automanipulative situations that have been employed. Nonetheless, the contention by Masters and Johnson (1966) that the exertion of intercourse is not sufficient to produce the observed cardiorespiratory concomitant of sexual activities seems well supported by findings of the excitatory effects of exposure to visual erotic stimuli (i.e., photographs and films of human sexual behavior). Such exposure is devoid of physical exertion, yet produces sympathetic, excitatory changes that, although altogether somewhat weaker, are comparable to those associated with precoital and coital behaviors (cf. Stern, Farr, & Ray, 1975; Zillmann, Bryant, Comisky, & Medoff, 1981).

In making a connection between sex and aggression on the basis of autonomic responses, these catabolic changes that produce the capacity for swift and vigorous skeletal-motor action are most important. Defensive fighting generally, experiences of anger, and annoyance-motivated hostile and aggressive behaviors in humans are characterized by these very changes (Zillmann, 1979, 1983a). In annoyance-motivated behaviors, whether fear and escape or anger and aggression are dominant response tendencies, the level of sympathetic excitation is generally greatly elevated. In experimental investigations, for instance, provocation through verbal insult has been observed to elevate systolic blood pressure by 20 mm Hg and accelerate heart rate by about 20 bpm (Zillmann & Sapolsky, 1977). Such laboratory provocation procedures are, of course, rather subdued owing to the necessity of safeguarding the welfare of the human subject. Provocations in real life are likely to be far more severe for the most part, and substantially stronger sympathetically mediated excitatory reactions should be expected. Generally speaking, it may be assumed that the sympathetic activity associated with aggressive instigation and sexual excitedness is commonly at similarly high levels.

Cannon's (1929) well-known fight-or-flight paradigm has been employed in the theory of annoyance-motivated hostility and aggression (Zillmann, 1979) to provide a functional account of the catabolic changes under consideration. According to this paradigm, the endangerment of the organism fosters an emergency reaction that primarily manifests itself in heightened activity in the autonomic nervous system and thus prepares the organism for the temporary engagement in vigorous motor activities, such as those needed for fight or flight. Inasmuch as sexual behavior also requires considerable skeletal-motor exertion, the paradigm may be applied to this fundamental form of behavior as well (cf. Zillmann, 1983b). The fact that the demands upon energy expenditure favor males (at least in nonhuman mammals) does not invalidate this application. It is conceivable, however, that the energizing, sympathetic component of sexual arousal might be somewhat stronger in males than in females. The data on systolic blood pressure during coition tend to suggest such a gender difference (Klumbies & Kleinsorge, 1950; Masters & Johnson, 1966). But the data from other indices fail to do so.

Regardless of considerations of function, utility, and purpose, the commonality of sympathetic excitation in aggressive and sexual behaviors is strongly suggested by the inspection of the autonomic structures involved in these behaviors. It should be recalled that thoracolumbar outflow, especially from the last thoracic and the first lumbar nerves, controls psychogenic sexual arousal. The same outflow impacts sympathetic excitation more generally through the control of numerous visceral structures (e.g., Crouch, 1978; Guyton, 1972). Most importantly, this outflow—through the lesser and least splanchnic nerves from the lower thoracic plexus—controls the adrenal medullae, the endocrine system so significantly involved in the production of sympathetic excitation. The adrenal medullae are directly innervated by sympathetic fibers whose stimulation prompts the release of the sympathomimetic catecholamines epinephrine and norepinephrine. Through the small splanchnic (and other connections), the release of these agents is thus under the immediate control of higher brain centers. It should be stressed that some sexual and aggressive impulses from higher centers travel through identical structures: From the last thoracic and first lumbar nerves, which constitute the essential part of the thoracolumbar erection center, sympathetic connections reach both the adrenal medullae and the sexual organs (e.g., Crosby, Humphrey, & Lauer, 1962). The critical interconnections are summarized in Fig. 3.3.

The described autonomic control of genital tumescence and sympathetic excitation via common pathways is certainly highly appropriate for sexual behavior as such. Impulses from higher brain centers simultaneously create coital readiness of the sexual organs and furnish the energy required for skeletal-motor exertion. (It can be speculated, of course, that insemination could be accom-

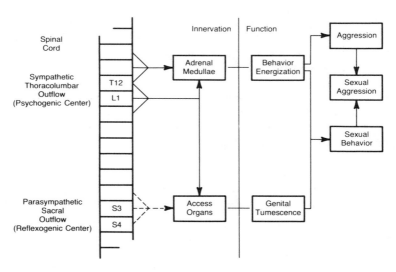

FIG. 3.3   Scheme of the spinal outflow common to sex and aggression. The sexual access organs are innervated by parasympathetic fibers from the sacral nerves. The nerves thought to constitute the reflexogenic sexual center are numbered (sacral 3 and 4). The access organs are furthermore innervated by sympathetic fibers from the thoracolumbar nerves. The nerves thought to constitute the psychogenic sexual center are numbered (thoracic 12 and lumbar 1). The adrenal medullae are innervated by sympathetic fibers of the same origin: the lower thoracic nerves, especially the least splanchnic nerve from T12. Genital tumescence is thus likely to be accompanied by increased diffuse sympathetic excitation, and vice versa. Provided appropriate environmental stimulation, this behavior-energizing excitation may facilitate sexual and aggressive behaviors, as well as any combination thereof.

plished without great energy expediture and that coition—especially human coition—tends to be vigorous only because of the presence of essentially excessive excitation that impels vigorous action. Indeed, the preparation for great energy expenditure that is associated with sexual arousal might be construed as quite inappropriate, and it could be conjectured that the sympathetic reaction accompanying genital tumescence is at least in part a remnant of earlier times when fighting for access and warding off harassment were frequently called upon. Irrespective of such possibilities, the fact remains that intense sympathetic activity and its behavioral implications are part and parcel of sexual arousal.) For aggression, as well as for other sympathetically intense emotions, the ''sharing'' of pathways seems to invite considerable confusion. The fight-or-flight reaction apparently carries with it a tendency toward genital blood flooding (cf. Gajdusek, 1970). The utility of this reaction for hostility and aggression is not immediately apparent. On the other hand, the reaction does not seem to impair fighting skills. Genital tumescence as such is apparently of little moment in aggression. The influence of sexual arousal on aggression comes, instead, through the accompaniment of high levels of sympathetic excitation. Intense excitedness impels action, and especially under conditions of annoyance, such impulsion can readily facilitate violent behaviors (Zillmann, 1979). The likely reverse facilitation of sex through aggression, in contrast, appears to come through contributions from both tumescence and excitation. Arguing and fighting have been said to increase genital blood flow, especially in women, and thereby to enhance sexual experience (Izard, 1977). But to the extent that sympathetic activity per se enhances the experiential quality of sexual behavior, excitation from aggressive instigation may also be expected to facilitate the experience (Zillmann, 1978, 1983b). Furthermore, the impulsion to vigorous action that derives from intense sympathetic excitation would seem to favor some roughhousing during sexual activities. Regardless of whether or not such action is deemed enjoyable, it has the potential for escalation. And if occasional ''sexual skirmishes'' should be perceived—probably accurately so—as heightening sexual enjoyment, the persons involved may come to employ aggressive behaviors in a sexual context on a more regular basis.

The sharing of autonomic pathways in sex and aggression, then, may indeed foster considerable interdependencies. I later (Chapter 6) develop a formal theoretical model from which the behavioral consequences of these interdependencies can be predicted. The purpose of the preceding discussion was to outline the autonomic basis for sex-aggression connections and, thereby, to lay the neurological foundation for this theoretical model.

Figure 3.3 summarizes much of the information on autonomic commonalities in sex and aggression. In recapitulating, the following additional statements can be made:

1. Sexual behavior is both psychogenically and reflexogenically controlled in many species, including humans. Cerebral and spinal control are functionally quite autonomous, but characteristically operate in a highly integrated fashion.
2. It appears that in human and nonhuman primates, and probably in mammals generally, the male's sexual behavior is more strongly controlled psychogenically .han that of the female—the greater reliance on reflexogenic control in the sexual behavior of the female apparently serving reproductive robustness.
3. Psychogenic control of sexual behavior is exerted through autonomic structures that are also involved in the control of aggressive behaviors. Specifically, both sexual and aggressive impulses from higher centers reach, through sympathetic thoracolumbar outflow (see Fig. 3.3), the sexual organs and the adrenal medullae. Owing to this insufficiently specific innervation, genital tumescence and sympathetic excitedness of the skeletal-motor system tend to covary—to some degree, at least—in both sexual and emotionally aggressive reactions (cf. Zillmann, 1979).

4
Connections in Endocrinology

It has long been conjectured that some sort of "male chemistry" is responsible for the obtrusive virile trait combination of sexual and aggressive eagerness. Once the androgens (i.e., the male sex hormones) had been identified and their behavioral implications were empirically explored, the apparent endocrine connection between sex and aggression seemed to grow stronger and beyond doubt. With the continued aggregation of research data it became clear, however, that the linkage is rather multifaceted and often sporadic. In this chapter, I discuss the principal aspects of this linkage and evaluate the validity of associations in light of the pertinent evidence. First, I explore the endocrine facets of sexual dimorphism and analyze their consequences for aggression. The discussion entails genetic considerations, because the analysis of endocrine processes across gender is confounded with—in fact, is based on—genetic differentiation. I trace the presumed sex-aggression connection in chromosomal aberrations that are characteristically associated with gross hormonal deviation. But I also investigate the consequences for sex and aggression of comparatively minor hormonal variation, such as during the female menstrual cycle. Finally, I specify endocrine commonalities in sexual arousal and aggressive instigation, commonalities capable of fostering a mutual facilitation of sexual and aggressive behaviors.

I. SEXUAL DIMORPHISM

Sexual dimorphism starts, of course, with the differences in the sex chromosomes: The 23rd chromosomal pair of females contains two X chromosomes, whereas that of males contains only one X chromosome linked with a much shorter Y chromosome. Although it is not yet fully understood in which ways these different "genetic codes" affect the ontogenesis of male versus female morphology and physiology, it is generally accepted that much of the gender-characteristic development is under the control of gonadal hormones. As the primary reproductive organs, the male gonads (i.e., the testes) produce sperm, and the female gonads (i.e., the ovaries) egg cells. In addition, however, the gonads produce sex hormones: The testes provide androgens, mainly testosterone, and the ovaries provide estrogen and progesterone. These gonadal hormones determine the accessory organs and other so-called secondary sex characteristics such as size and build of bodily structures, distribution of body fat and hair, and pitch of voice. (It should be noted that the hormonal differentiation is not a complete one. Males produce some estrogen and progesterone, and females analogously produce some androgen. The differentiation is thus quantitative rather than qualitative, with the ratio of androgen to estrogen-progesterone being substantially higher in males than in females.)

The presumed endocrine linkage between sex and aggression might be considered obtrusively exhibited by the gender differences in aggression that coincide with the genetically based sexual dimorphism. There can be little doubt that the males of the vast majority of mammalian species have been more aggressive intraspecifically than their female counterparts (cf. Gray, 1971). In the human species, males have carried the brunt of intergroup violence over the millennia, and they probably have outdone females in all domestic forms of fighting. Men in contemporary societies have not broken with tradition. They are still far more aggressive than women. Adult men commit more homicides than women, more violent assaults of any kind, and even more suicides. Aggression-laden delinquency is far more common in adolescent males than females. Strong gender differences in beating, pushing, and shoving extend down the age scale to 3-year-olds, always showing the male as being more active and aggressive. And this differentiation appears to be stable across cultures (cf. Maccoby, 1966; Maccoby & Jacklin, 1974; Sears, 1965).

Notwithstanding the apparent strength of the dimorphic sex-aggression connection, it should be clear that the gender differences in aggression cannot readily be attributed to genetic and/or hormonal distinctness. Males and females in human societies are brought up so as to conform to unique gender roles, and almost universally these roles favor aggression in males. The role division—in anthropological terms, the division of labor between hunting by men and gathering by women—may well reflect genetically and hormonally based differences (e.g., in the skeletal muscles) that foster superior fighting skills in males. Still, it is conceivable that the gender differences in human aggression are mostly, if not entirely, the result of enculturation (cf. Bandura, 1973). And it could similarly be claimed that in the nonhuman primates and most other mammals this difference in aggressive behavior derives in large measure from social learning. I avoid entering into a nature-nurture debate concerning the aggressive implications of sexual dimorphism simply by acknowledging the likely contributions of both genetic-hormonal factors and social learning or enculturation. However, although I regard gender differences in aggression as the result of the confounded operation of these forces, I concentrate on the consequences of genetic and hormonal variation and appraise the degree of control of this variation over sexual and aggressive behaviors.

The relative power of the genetic determination of gender differences in aggression is indicated by the findings of numerous studies on animals reared in isolation (cf. Johnson, 1972). Harlow (1965), for instance, observed that male rhesus monkeys that had been raised with inanimate surrogate mothers behaved significantly more aggressively than females raised under identical conditions. It is difficult, indeed, to see how—under these circumstances—the behavioral differentiation could be the result of nurture. On the other hand, such findings certainly do not implicate any genetic transmission of "innate aggressive dispositions." The observed behavioral differences are more likely the result of genetically determined skeletal and muscular differences, along with their neurological concomitants, that favor aggressiveness in the generally better endowed male (cf. Scott, 1958a; Zillmann, 1979).

The hormonal determination of the gender differences in aggression is suggested, in a general way, by the correspondence between hormonal changes and aggressive behavior during puberty. In humans, juvenile violence is an obtrusive, almost exclusively male phenomenon (Wolfgang & Ferracuti, 1967; Yablonsky, 1962). But the covariation of heightened androgen levels and increased aggressiveness can be found in numerous other species as well. In fact, it appears to occur universally in mammalian species. It has been observed, for example, that the pubertal rising of testosterone levels in male mice occasions increased fighting (Brain & Nowell, 1969a, 1969b; McKinney & Desjardins, 1973). Such observations do not decisively implicate the apparent correspondence between androgens and aggression, however, as the achievement of sexual maturity is usually associated with new sources of conflict. Thus, the greater incidence of skirmishes over access to vital commodities, rather than presumably aggression-facilitating androgens, might be responsible for increased fighting.

The same criticism obviously applies to the documentation of a seasonal covariation between androgen levels and intraspecific aggression in many vertebrate species. Such seasonal covariation has been observed, for instance, in birds (Crook & Butterfield, 1968), rodents (Healey, 1967; Sadleir, 1965), and nonhuman primates (Wilson & Boelkins, 1970).

Further correlational evidence of the covariation under consideration comes from comparisons across individuals. For species as diverse as mice (e.g., Lagerspetz, Tirri, & Lagerspetz, 1968) and rhesus monkeys (Rose, Holaday, & Bernstein, 1971), assertiveness and aggressiveness have been found to vary in proportion with the individuals' basal level of androgen. Such interindividual correlation between androgen and aggression is by no means universal, however.

For example, in the Japanese snow monkey—which like the rhesus monkey is a member of the genus *Macaca*—the correlation in question proved entirely negligible (Eaton & Resko, 1974).

The correspondence between androgens and aggression has been more compellingly demonstrated by investigations in which the production of gonadal hormones was either abolished by the removal of the gonads or mimicked by the administration of these hormones to intact or gonadectomized animals.

Administration of androgens (usually testosterone propionate) has been observed to increase aggressiveness in numerous species. It has been reported, for instance, that androgen treatments greatly increase aggressive behaviors in juvenile and adult male mice (e.g., Banarjee, 1971; Levy & King, 1953; Svare & Gandelman, 1975). Administration of androgen to adult female mice of particularly aggressive strains has also been observed to increase aggression, along with promoting male-type sexual reactions (e.g., Lagerspetz & Lagerspetz, 1975). Furthermore, experimentation has shown that castration tends to reduce aggressiveness markedly, but that the "lost aggressiveness" can readily be restored by the subsequent administration of androgen (e.g., Beeman, 1947; Tollman & King, 1956). The full spectrum of these effects has recently been demonstrated by Wagner, Beuving, and Hutchinson (1980). These investigators assessed aggressive biting in mice and found intact males to be far more aggressive than intact females. Castration reduced the biting rate by males to approximately the level of females. In contrast, ovariectomy had no appreciable effect on the female biting rate. The subsequent administration of androgen returned the biting rates by the castrated males to preoperative levels, but had only a negligible effect on intact males. Administration of androgen slightly increased the biting rates by females. Administration of estrogen, in contrast, had no appreciable effect on their aggressive behavior. Findings such as these leave little doubt that the male gonadal hormones can greatly facilitate aggressive behaviors. At the same time, they show that female gonadal hormones are of little consequence for aggression.

The influence of androgens on both sexual and aggressive behaviors has been most dramatically demonstrated by investigations in which androgens were administered early in the development of the organism as well as postpubertally (cf. Conner, 1972; Whalen, 1971). Early androgenization during species-specific critical periods (e.g., prenatal in primates; perinatal and postnatal in rodents) proved crucial in that it sensitizes the organism to the postpubertal exposure to androgen. Such early treatment produced profound effects on sexual development and, concomitantly, on the propensity for aggression.

The drastic sexual implications of early androgenization have been demonstrated, for instance, with rhesus monkeys. In an investigation by van Wagenen and Hamilton (1943), pregnant females were treated with synthetic testosterone. The genetically female offspring turned out to be pseudohermaphroditic (i.e., the females had developed penes, scrota, and other features of male build). The treatment had no appreciable effect on the male offspring, however, presumably because the androgen for male genital development was naturally produced in sufficient quantity. More recently, Goy, Wolf, and Eisele (1977) have systematically delineated the critical period for androgenization and the magnitude of the hormonal treatment that results in the pseudohermaphroditic development of genetically female rhesus monkeys (see also Goy, 1970; Young, Goy, & Phoenix, 1964). These investigators have further documented that prenatally treated females—both through administration of testosterone to the mother during gestation and through direct administration to the fetus, but especially the latter treatment—exhibit malelike sexual and aggressive behaviors.

This endocrine sex-aggression connection has been shown to be rather independent of female gonadal hormones. In an investigation by Eaton, Goy, and Phoenix (1973), prenatally androgenized female rhesus monkeys and untreated females were ovariectomized and later received androgen as adults. Only the prenatally treated animals were found to display the malelike sexual and aggressive behaviors, a finding that further supports the sensitizing and organizing function of androgen exposure during critical developmental periods.

It should be mentioned in this connection that in the nonhuman primates—and apparently also in humans—the females' sexual eagerness seems to be controlled by the male, rather than by the female, gonadal hormones. In an investigation by Trimble and Herbert (1968), it was observed that the administration of testosterone to ovariectomized female rhesus monkeys enhanced their assertiveness and made them more actively receptive sexually. These females pursued males and solicited mounting from them. The removal of all endogenous sources of testosterone through ovariectomy and bilateral adrenalectomy, in stark contrast, produced entirely unreceptive females (Everitt, Herbert, & Hamer, 1971). Furthermore, the administration of estrogen had no appreciable effect on the libidinal urges of ovariectomized females. These findings appear to agree with the scarce data on the libido of human females. Kinsey, Pomeroy, Martin, and Gebhard (1953) noted little change in sexual desire after ovariectomy or menopause. On the other hand, testosterone treatments have occasionally been observed to heighten the libidinal inclinations of women (e.g., Salmon & Geist, 1943). In primates, then, female sexual eagerness—and presumably assertiveness, if not aggressiveness, along with it—seems enhanced by androgens but unaltered by the females' own (dominant) sex hormones. The function of estrogen and progesterone in female sexuality of nonhuman primates has been explored by Herbert (1974, 1977, 1978). This investigator demonstrated that the ovarian hormones serve the females' sexual attractiveness to potential male partners. However, because this attraction seems mediated primarily by the hormonal effect on the swelling of the sexual skin and on vaginal odors, possible parallels in human sexual behavior are not immediately apparent.

The endocrine connection between sexual and aggressive behavior, furthermore, has been abundantly demonstrated in lower mammals, especially rodents (cf. Brown & Cooper, 1979; Hutchison, 1978; Levine, 1972). Phoenix, Goy, Gerall, and Young (1959) had shown that the treatment of pregnant guinea pigs with comparatively high doses of androgen resulted in pseudohermaphroditic female offspring. The external genitalia of this progeny were virtually indistinguishable from those of normal males. Harris and Levine (1962), in a similar vein, showed that postnatally androgenized female rats failed to exhibit sexual receptivity. This condition persisted even after their treatment with exogenous estrogen and progesterone. The administration of testosterone propionate, in contrast, fostered male-type sexual responses. Essentially the same pattern of effects was observed in female guinea pigs that were androgenized during gestation (Goy, Bridson, & Young, 1964) and in female mice that were neonatally androgenized (e.g., Edwards, 1971; Lagerspetz & Lagerspetz, 1975).

The relationship between sexual development and aggression has been well documented in the investigations on mice. Edwards (1971) demonstrated that the neonatal administration of various androgens produced profound effects on both sexual and aggressive behavior. Androgenized and control females (the controls received oil instead of androgen) were ovariectomized as adults and later treated with estrogen and progesterone. The thus treated neonatally androgenized females proved to be sexually unreceptive (and, prior to ovariectomy, were mostly anovulatory). Regarding aggression, the administration of androgens during adulthood proved to heighten the intraspecific fighting of neonatally androgenized females to levels substantially above those of the controls. Lagerspetz and Lagerspetz (1975) reported comparable effects, noting that the administration of testosterone propionate to neonatally androgenized females produced levels of aggression equivalent to those characteristic of normal males.

The sensitizing, organizing function of early androgenization in the effect of androgen during adulthood has been observed in numerous further investigations with rodents (e.g., Beach, Noble, & Orndoff, 1969; Brain & Evans, 1975; Feder & Whalen, 1965; Grady, Phoenix, & Young, 1965; Svare, Davis, & Gandelman, 1974; vom Saal, Gandelman, & Svare, 1976; vom Saal, Svare, & Gandelman, 1976; Whalen & Edwards, 1966). Nonandrogenized females and neonatally castrated males are quite insensitive to later androgen treatment. In order to induce any kind of fighting in these animals, it is necessary to administer massive doses of androgen over extended periods of time during adulthood. Androgenized females and normal males, in contrast, exhibit increased aggressiveness upon reception of comparatively small doses.

Taken together, these investigations leave little doubt that androgen is the critical defeminizing, virilizing agent that potentiates aggressive behavior. This aggression potentiation is not indiscriminate, however, and qualifications are indicated. Conner (1972) noted that the consequences of androgen treatments were different for specific aggression-eliciting laboratory procedures. Apparently, male gonadal hormones exert an unaccountably stronger degree of influence over isolation-induced than over shock-induced fighting. The distinction between intraspecific and predatory aggression is far more important, however, as the hormonal effects under consideration appear to be limited to intraspecific fighting. Predatory aggression has not been found to be critically affected by androgens.

The virilization of sexual behavior through androgen treatments appears to require some qualifications also. This virilization might be construed as an enhancement of specific sexual motivation, but such an interpretation seems at variance with findings from many investigations with rats (cf. Whalen, 1971). Whalen and Edwards (1967), for instance, gonadectomized male and female rats shortly after birth and treated them with testosterone propionate, estradiol benzoate, or oil (in the control condition). Upon maturation, all animals were treated with androgen. This treatment proved to be without effect on mounting. Males castrated at birth mounted as frequently as males castrated after maturation, and females, whether ovariectomized or not, mounted as frequently as females that had been androgenized perinatally. Further research (e.g., Beach et al., 1969; Grady et al., 1965; Whalen, Edwards, Luttge, & Robertson, 1969) corroborated that early androgenization was of little consequence to mounting. Despite clearly masculinized genitalia, for example, androgenized, pseudohermaphroditic females failed to exhibit more frequent mounting compared to control females. On the other hand, it has been observed in several investigations (e.g., Beach et al., 1969; Harris & Levine, 1965; Ward, 1969; Whalen & Edwards, 1967; Whalen et al., 1969; Whalen & Robertson, 1968) that neonatal androgenization increases the likelihood that adult animals will achieve intromission and display ejaculation-type responses. These sexual reactions, which are obviously crucial for reproductive success, are thus clearly influenced by androgenic sensitization (cf. Feder, 1978).

Whalen (1971), treating mounting as an index of sexual motivation and intromission and ejaculation as indices of sexual performance, concluded from the discrepant findings regarding these behavioral indices that early androgenization in rodents has profound effects on sexual consummation, but leaves sexual motivation unaffected. The extent to which such a conclusion applies to other mammals, especially to primates, remains unclear, however.

Furthermore, Whalen (1968, 1971) has thought to clarify the endocrine mechanics of the effect of androgen on consummatory sexual and potentially aggressive behaviors in rodents. Which structures are being masculinized by early androgenic stimulation? Many investigators were inclined to attribute behavioral virilization to the masculinization of central nervous system tissue. In fact, several investigations (e.g., Flerkó & Mess, 1968; Flerkó, Mess, & Illei-Donhoffer, 1969; Green, Luttge, & Whalen, 1969; McGuire & Lisk, 1969) seemed to lend support to such a view. In the investigation by Green et al., for instance, gonadectomized male, female, and neonatally androgenized female rats were administered radiolabeled estradiol. The animals were sacrificed at various times after administration and specific neural tissues were examined. These investigators argued that, if critical brain structures are dimorphic, the uptake and retention of the radioactive estrogen should be impaired in masculinized tissue. Consistent with this expectation, in the hypothalamus, in the preoptic area, and in the diagonal band region—all sites that have been implicated by lesion and stimulation research as critically involved in the sex-aggression linkage (see Chapter 3)—the levels of estradiol that were traced in the female tissue exceeded those traced in male tissue. Uptake and retention of estradiol in androgenized females assumed an intermediate level. However, these and similar findings cannot be regarded as providing compelling evidence for the proposal that behavioral dimorphism is primarily neurochemically mediated, as the observed uptake and retention of estradiol in brain tissue proved confounded with morphological differences outside the brain. Body weight varied with androgenization (i.e., males were heavier than androgenized females, which in turn were heavier than nonandrogenized females). The females, therefore, received an effectively smaller dose of estradiol than the males, with androgenized females assuming an intermediate position. It thus became necessary to control for this weight confounding statistically, and when this was done, the differentiation that would support dimorphic endocrine functioning in the critical brain regions was lost.

The implication of such dimorphism in the central nervous system is further complicated by the finding that sexual performance depends in large measure on the development of the genitals as such, rather than on neural tissue controlling genital responses. In several investigations on the consequences of the removal of endogenous androgen (e.g., Beach et al., 1969; Goldfoot, Feder, & Goy, 1969; Whalen, 1968), it was observed that early androgenization enhanced the size and the structural integrity of the phallus in male rats. Characteristically, male rats were castrated at different times after birth, tested for sexual behaviors following androgen administration during adulthood, and later sacrificed in order to assess phallic development. A high, positive correlation between penis weight and intromission emerged, suggesting that the peripheral genital development may have fostered the superior sexual performance of androgenized animals and impaired that of those animals whose early testosterone production had been curtailed. It is conceivable, then, that androgenization during critical developmental periods affects sexual behavior mainly through morphological changes in peripheral bodily structures. It is likely, of course, that such "peripheral virilization" has concomitants in tissue of the central nervous system, concomitants that should become demonstrable with the advancement of assessment procedures (cf. MacLusky & Naftolin, 1981).

It can only be speculated that the effect of androgenization on intraspecific aggressive behaviors is similarly mediated by peripheral bodily structures rather than the central nervous system. The well-established androgen effect on male build suggests superior muscular development. Such development translates into superior fighting skills, and these skills in turn make it likely that fights will be won and fighting reinforced (cf. Scott, 1958a; Zillmann, 1979). It is thus conceivable that the effect of androgenization on aggression manifests itself initially "in the muscles, not the mind" and that, ontogenetically speaking, aggressive dispositions follow rather than precipitate aggression in physically well-endowed fighters.

In humans the consequences of early androgenization are remarkably consistent with those ascertained for other mammalian species, especially for nonhuman primates. The prenatal androgenization of genetic females, in particular, has the masculinizing effect on the development of secondary sex characteristics and bodily build described earlier. The behavioral implications seem similar as well (cf. Money, 1973; Money & Schwartz, 1978).

Money and Ehrhardt (1972) studied girls whose mothers had received rather high doses of progestogens during pregnancy (in order to prevent spontaneous abortion) and girls who suffered from adrenogenital syndrome (an abnormal condition in which the adrenal gland of the fetus produces less corticosteroids and more androgens, resulting in the pseudohermaphroditic development of females). Exposure of the fetus to progestogens has an androgenizing effect that mimicks adrenogenital syndrome, but its consequences are usually substantially weaker. Money and Ehrhardt describe the behavior of androgenized girls as "tomboyish." The boylike behavior of these girls was characterized by high expenditure of kinetic energy, athletic ambitions, choice of male playmates, and the like. Sheer energy expenditure appears to be the behavioral characteristic that most strongly and most reliably distinguishes androgenized from normal girls (Ehrhardt, 1977). Cognitively mediated motivational differences seem to exist as well, however. During childhood, androgenized girls expressed less interest in romance, marriage, and babies than did normal girls (Ehrhardt & Baker, 1974). On the other hand, androgenized girls did not display lesbian inclinations, nor were they observed to initiate fights significantly more often than normal girls (Ehrhardt, 1977). Money and Schwartz (1976) also observed that adrogenital girls, despite their tomboyishness, do not exhibit an above-normal propensity for aggression and delinquency. In contrast, findings that might be taken as suggesting a greater propensity for aggression by androgenized than by normal girls have been reported recently (Reinisch, 1981). The behavior of girls who had been exposed to synthetic progestins during gestation, but who did not show any notable virilization of genitalia, was compared with that of unexposed siblings. The subjects were asked how they would resolve certain conflict situations, and the frequent choice of aggressive means was considered to indicate a high propensity for aggression. Androgenized girls displayed more aggression than normal ones on this measure. The construct validity of the measure can be challenged, however, as the projected response to a hypothetical situation does not necessarily assure that under similar circumstances the indicated response would be executed.

Early androgenization in humans, then, has profound effects on the development of the sexual access organs and other secondary sex characteristics such as muscular build. Its effect on related structures—larger heart and lung (Tanner, 1970), the latter enabling superior oxygen uptake per unit of body weight or muscular mass (Garn & Clark, 1953)—is similarly profound, and the implications of this effect (viz., a superior capacity for energy expenditure) appear to be robust. Further implications are rather fragile, however, presumably because potential endocrine influences are entirely confounded with sociocultural ones. The aggressive behavior of androgenized females seems to reflect this dual control: The superior propensity for fighting appears to be held in check by the adoption of female gender-role expectations. With regard to sexual behaviors, the ambiguity concerning the sexual access organs in females with adrenogenital syndrome (i.e., pseudohermaphroditic development) must be expected to lead to considerable gender-identity confusion, which in turn should eventually lead to somewhat uncommon sexual preferences (Ehrhardt, Epstein, & Money, 1968; Money & Schwartz, 1977).

Outside the realm of developmental consequences of early androgenization, the extent to which high levels of circulating androgen virilize sexual and aggressive behaviors in humans remains similarly unclear (cf. Bancroft, 1978). It appears that the sexual activity of men with abnormal testosterone production can readily be controlled and corrected through appropriate hormonal treatments. Administration of testosterone to hypogonadal men tends to promote erectile ability and coital behavior, along with enhancing secondary sex characteristics such as muscular build (e.g., Bancroft & Skakkebaek, 1979; Davidson, Camargo, & Smith, 1979). Administration of antiandrogenic agents (e.g., cyproterone, medroxyprogesterone) to hypergonadal men, in contrast, markedly reduces libidinal inclinations (e.g., Cooper, Ismail, Phanjoo, & Love, 1972; Money, Wiedeking, Walker, Migeon, Meyer, & Borgaonkar, 1975). Because the latter treatment also reduces aggressiveness, it seems that both sexual and aggressive urges might be curbed by a nonspecific reduction of energy levels and the propensity for taking vigorous action.

Little is known about normal fluctuations in androgen levels within men and the implications of these changes for sexual behavior. Fox, Ismail, Love, Kirkham, and Loraine (1972) traced such fluctuations over periods of several months and observed that testosterone levels consistently increased before and after coital behavior. The findings leave it unclear, however, whether precoital testosterone increases precipitated sexual desire or resulted from it. An investigation by Pirke, Kockott, and Dittmar (1974) showed that exposure to an erotic film occasioned elevated testosterone levels. This finding would seem to suggest that the psychogenic induction of sexual arousal causes increased testosterone production, rather than increased testosterone levels fostering sexual interest and sexual arousal. Bancroft (1978) discusses further findings that show the relationship between androgen levels and libidinal urges to be rather unreliable.

The corresponding relationship between androgen levels and aggression is similarly inconsistent. Persky, Smith, and Basu (1971) reported a positive correlation between testosterone levels and aggressive personality traits (Buss-Durkee hostility inventory) in young, but not in older, men. A similar investigation by Meyer-Bahlburg, Boon, Sharma, and Edwards (1974) largely failed to show similar correlations, however. Doering, Brodie, Kraemer, Becker, and Hamburg (1974) also failed in their attempt to replicate the earlier findings. These investigators assessed the relationship in question both within (over a 2-month period) and across individuals. They noted some within-subject correlations but were unable to detect any other consistencies.

The elusive androgen-aggression linkage was also explored in criminal populations. Kreuz and Rose (1972), who studied this linkage in male prison inmates, were unable to demonstrate a correlation. Levels of testosterone were found to be essentially the same in aggressive and nonaggressive individuals. Ehrenkranz, Bliss, and Sheard (1974), on the other hand, did observe a reliable relationship between circulating testosterone and aggressiveness in such a population.

Kreuz and Rose (1972), furthermore, classified their subjects on the basis of the extent to which the crimes that led to imprisonment entailed violence. Prisoners who had committed violent crimes proved to have higher testosterone levels than prisoners who had not employed violence during the commission of their crimes. Clearly, this finding is correlational and does not implicate a causal connection between testosterone level and the propensity for violent crime. It is conceivable, in fact, that the relatively higher androgen levels resulted from the special attention and corrective support that is usually afforded to prisoners with histories of violence. The finding is further compromised by the fact that violent inmates tended to be imprisoned earlier and longer than nonviolent ones. This again allows for the possibility that the differences in testosterone levels reflect differences in imprisonment, and it leaves open the possibility that at the time the crimes were committed, androgen levels may not have differed in violent and nonviolent offenders.

Rada, Laws, and Kellner (1976) conducted an investigation on imprisoned rapists in which subjects were similarly classified according to the degree of violence involved in their transgressions. The most violent men proved to have the highest levels of circulating testosterone. The correlation of androgen levels and violence employed was insignificant across rapists, however. The fact that especially violent rapists exhibited high androgen levels is again not conclusive, as it may result from special treatment during imprisonment, and the lack of reliable correlations further attests to the instability of the presumed correspondence between androgen and aggression—in this case, sexual aggression.

Despite such ambiguities in the research concerning the specific effects of androgen on sexual and aggressive behavior in men, the administration of anti-androgens to apparently hypergonadal men is commonly employed as a corrective for aberrant sexual behaviors, especially those entailing violent impulsion (e.g., Blumer & Migeon, 1975; Money et al., 1975; Rothschild, 1970). Anti-androgenic treatments are deemed clinically effective in reducing various transgressive actions in sex offenders (e.g., Laschet & Laschet, 1968; Walker, 1978). It is often acknowledged (Laschet, 1973) that antiandrogens "cannot alter the direction of sexual deviation [p. 317]" as such, and their effect is seen solely in the "reduction and inhibition" of the sexual or aggressive-sexual action to be corrected. According to clinical reports (cf. Laschet, 1973), administration of antiandrogens (e.g., cyproterone acetate) can be enormously effective in curtailing sexual-aggressive deviation. What remains in doubt is the specificity of such drastic effects. It is not only unclear whether the curtailing effect applies to sexual impulsion, aggressive impulsion, or both (and if the latter, to what degree to one or the other), but it seems unlikely that the effect is limited to these functions. If—as much of the pertinent research suggests—the virilization through androgen manifests itself mainly in peripheral structures, the compensatory action of antiandrogen should be similarly peripheral. And if—again as suggested by much of the research—these peripheral changes primarily serve the expenditure of kinetic energy, the administration of antiandrogen should eventually produce timidity and placidity. This "disposition" for action (or rather, inaction) might well take the impulsion out of sex and aggression. In all probability, however, it will do likewise to more or less all other active emotions (cf. Leventhal, 1974; Zillmann, 1983b).

In summarizing the information on the influence of gonadal hormones, the following generalizations are possible:

1. Gender differentiation is mediated in large measure by gonadal hormones. Early androgenization during species-specific critical periods, in particular, fosters the development of male accessory organs and male build, and it sensitizes the neural structures that control male sexual responses.
2. In nonprimate mammals early androgenization profoundly enhances sexual performance (i.e., reproductively effective consummatory behavior) in mature males. It seems to be without appreciable effect on sexual motivation (i.e., sexual approaches), however.
3. In nonhuman primates and in humans androgen appears to facilitate sexual interest and sexual behavior in both males and females. Estrogen appears to have little, if any, effect on sexual motivation in females. Antiandrogen curtails libidinal urges in men.
4. Androgen not only virilizes sexual behavior, but it potentiates aggressive behavior in both males and females as well. This potentiation does not seem to result from centrally organized motivational control, however. Rather, it appears to be mediated by a superior capacity for fighting that is the result of the androgen enhancement of masculine build (cf. Scott, 1958a; Zillmann, 1979). Androgen thus potentiates aggressive behavior in nonprimate mammals, in nonhuman primates, and in humans. Paralleling the effects on sexual behavior, estrogen seems of no consequence for aggression, and antiandrogen curtails aggressive impulsion in men.

5. Androgen (or antiandrogen) treatments that appreciably increase (or decrease) levels of sexual and aggressive behavior tend to be massive and prolonged. Variations in androgen levels that occur naturally have, for the most part, not been found to be associated with covarying levels of sexual and/or aggressive behavior.

6. As any effect of androgenization on aggressive behavior is probably mediated through secondary sex characteristics such as masculine build, androgenization is likely to affect a host of behaviors other than sex and aggression. Analogously, antiandrogen treatments are likely to have somewhat indiscriminate effects and remove the impulsion from behaviors that have little or no association with sex and aggression.

II. CHROMOSOMAL-ENDOCRINE ABERRATIONS

Ever since Jacobs, Brenton, Melville, Brittain, and McClemont (1965) observed that men with the chromosomal abnormality that is cytogenetically described as 47,XYY—the so-called double Y syndrome—were disproportionly frequent in maximum-security wards of state hospitals in Scotland and since other investigators (e.g., Court-Brown, 1967; Price & Whatmore, 1967; Welch, Borgaonkar, & Herr, 1967) who studied the inmates of prisons, mental institutions, and detention homes confirmed this overrepresentation of XYY males, the possibility that the surplus Y chromosome in some way promotes an aggressive, potentially criminal disposition has been pondered. The phenomenon has received much popular attention (e.g., Montagu, 1968), and at times, the "genetic determination of delinquency" seems to be considered well established.

Before I examine the reasoning that leads to the expectation that an additional Y chromosome should foster hyperaggressiveness and delinquency, I briefly describe the major sex-chromosome aberrations in order to provide the context needed for discussion.

Abnormal chromosomal conditions are defined by the absence of one of the two normal sex chromosomes (i.e., XX or XY, 46 chromosomes in all) and by the presence of additional ones (cf. Mittwoch, 1967; Valentine, 1969). The absence of an X chromosome in women (45,XO) is referred to as Turner's syndrome. Women with Turner's syndrome are without ovaries. Hence, they are sterile, do not menstruate, and remain of prepubertal build. Women with extra X chromosomes (47,XXX; 48,XXXX), sometimes referred to as "superwomen," exhibit little or no sexual abnormalities, but are often mentally retarded. Men with additional X chromosomes (47,XXY; 48,XXXY; 49,XXXXY), a condition referred to as Klinefelter's syndrome, are sterile. Their secondary sex characteristics are ambiguous (e.g., small, undescended testes, enlarged breasts). A considerable portion of these men are mentally retarded (Mertens, 1975). Additionally, considerable confusion regarding gender identity is common, and although libidinal inclinations seem subdued, homosexual and bisexual preference has been noted (Money & Pollitt, 1964). Men with double Y syndrome, finally, tend to be of tall build and low intelligence. Counter to what might be expected, their sperm production is subnormal, often to the point of actual sterility. Double Y men are not "superstuds" in continual pursuit of coital opportunities with women. Rather, they often favor homosexual relations and tend to exhibit a preference for more unusual sexual practices (Money, Gaskin, & Hull, 1970).

If it is assumed that in the development of a normal male the Y chromosome controls virilization in large measure through increased androgen production, it seems reasonable to expect that virilization of an individual might be intensified with additional Y chromosomes. If it is further assumed that X chromosomes somehow suppress androgen production, it could be expected that additional X chromosomes demasculinize (or feminize) individuals. Lastly, if it is assumed that Y chromosomes promote androgenization more strongly than X chromosomes are capable of suppressing it, the following ranking of genotypes from least to most masculine (or from most to least feminine) is feasible: XXXX, XXX, XX, XO, XXXY, XXY, XY, XYY. (Extremely rare karyotypes, such as penta-X syndrome and XYYY, cf. Grumbach & Conte, 1981, have been omitted from discussion. These conditions could be readily incorporated into the present scheme, however.)

The development of primary and secondary sex characteristics appears to accord reasonably well with such possible chromosomal-endocrine classification. Normally, female access organs develop only in the absence of a Y chromosome (the exception is a condition known as "complete androgen insensitivity," cf. Grumbach & Conte, 1981, in which genetic males—46,XY karyotype—exhibit female external genitalia, a vaginal pouch without uterus and tubes, and testes in the labial or inguinal region or in the abdomen), and ovarian development requires at least two X chromosomes. The contributions of additional X chromosomes to the female physique seem trivial, however. Other than its obtrusive effect on body height, the addition of a Y chromosome to the male genotype seems to have similarly negligible consequences for the male physique. In sharp contrast, the endocrine influences exerted by the X and Y chromosomes appear to collide in Klinefelter's syndrome. The additional X chromosome seems to compete with the Y chromosome for control over the development of sex characteristics, thus producing mixed, ambiguous structures. Additionally, it appears that the admixture of male and female gonadal hormone influences shifts toward female features with the further addition of X chromosomes (from 47,XXY through 48,XXXY to 49,XXXXY).

If the development of primary and secondary sex characteristics can be considered to agree with the discussed chromosomal-endocrine rationale, the propensity for sexual behavior cannot. The addition of a Y chromosome to the normal XY genotype obviously impairs rather than enhances reproductive efficiency, and it apparently also hampers rather than facilitates heterosexual engagements. Similarly, the addition of an X chromosome to the normal XX genotype fails to enhance the sexual propensity of women. Klinefelter's syndrome, presumably because of the acute gender-identity confusion associated with it, seems detrimental to sexuality altogether. As should be recalled, the genetic males suffering from it are sterile, and regarding nonreproductive sexual engagements, these men (or pseudowomen) tend to be faced with enormous difficulties.

In short, then, extra Y chromosomes do not enhance male sexuality; likewise, extra X chromosomes do not enhance female sexuality. Because additional sex chromosomes are frequently associated with retarded mental development, sociosexual and genital functioning tends to be further impaired. Mental retardation appears to increase with the number of surplus sex chromosomes, regardless of the particular syndrome (cf. Polani, 1969). Surplus sex chromosomes are thus truly detrimental to the development of satisfying sexual engagements and the social relationships in which they are likely to occur.

Given that reduced intelligence is often linked with genotypes XYY, XXY, XXX, and especially with XXXY, XXXXY, and XXXX, can aggressive behavior be expected to follow the ranking from minimal to maximal virilization?

As indicated earlier, attention was initially focused on the apparent connection between the double Y syndrome and violent crime. Jacobs and his associates had uncovered the overrepresentation of men with that syndrome in criminal populations. Studies of individual cases (e.g., Daly, 1969) and of very small samples (e.g., Price & Whatmore, 1967) disclosed histories of pronounced antisocial, aggressive tendencies in such men. And studies with inmates at institutions for the criminally insane led to the projection that potentially violent double Y men were up to 20 times overrepresented (e.g., Court-Brown, 1967). Other investigations lead to markedly lower estimates, however. According to chromosome surveys of newborns, XYY males constitute .1% to .4% of the male population (cf. Lubs & Ruddle, 1970). The presence of such males in prisons ranges from 1.0% to 2.9% (Casey, Segall, Street, & Blank, 1966). Overrepresentation, then, seems not to exceed a factor of 10.

Nonetheless, the fact that XYY men are considerably overrepresented in criminal populations remains and calls for an explanation. Could it be that the greater likelihood for double Y men to be involved in violent transgressions (cf. Conan, 1968) derives from hormonally mediated virilization? Are powerful build and sexual eagerness responsible? Or are alternative explanations more appropriate?

It has been speculated that the high levels of aggressiveness observed in XYY men derive from their obtrusive tallness—even that this tallness makes them appear dangerous and thus vulnerable to conviction by intimidated juries. It was observed (Hook & Kim, 1971), however, that the general physique of double Y offenders did not appreciably differ from that of other groups of offenders, an observation that would seem to invalidate such speculations.

Evidence that supports another alternative account—and at the same time rather decisively rules out the hypothesis that the aggressiveness of double Y men is the result of hypervirilization—comes from the study of imprisoned men with Kleinfelter's syndrome. Chromosome surveys of newborns show this abnormality to befall .1% to .2% of the male population (cf. Lubs & Ruddle, 1970). XXY men were found to constitute 1.0% to 1.3% of convicted offenders, however (Bartlett, Hurley, Brand, & Poole, 1968; Casey et al., 1966). The degree of overrepresentation of XXY men in criminal populations (i.e., up to a factor of 10) is thus virtually identical with that of XYY men.

This finding demands the rejection of any simplistic chromosomal-endocrine proposal such as that the presence of extra Y chromosomes masculinizes and promotes aggression and that the presence of extra X chromosomes has the opposite effects. According to this kind of reasoning, XXY males should have been particularly timid and, if anything, underrepresented in criminal populations. Quite obviously, other forces are more critically involved in the control of the development of hostile dispositions and aggressive habits in men with chromosomal aberrations. In one way or another, such men experienced being "social misfits" as boys. Cast out as peculiar and deviant, they were likely to suffer provocation continually and, because of this, to develop strong, hostile dispositions. And XYY boys, who were probably stronger than most of their peers, should have had occasion to learn that aggression has utility for them and, hence, to acquire violent habits. Likely mental deficiencies may have aided in this development.

There is ample reason, therefore, to believe that a host of "conventional" developmental influences are capable of producing the propensity for violence observed in XYY and XXY men. But whatever the specific constellation of social influences that produces this effect may be and however susceptible men with chromosomal aberrations—because of undeniable bodily manifestations—may be to these influences, it would be inappropriate to consider androgenization as a primary force in the mediation of aggression in chromosomally abnormal persons.

In summary, it seems that the implications of chromosomal-endocrine aberrations for sexual and aggressive behaviors have been misconstrued, at times grossly so. The sobering facts are as follows:

1. Surplus Y chromosomes do not enhance male sexuality.
2. Surplus X chromosomes, analogously, do not enhance female sexuality.
3. Abnormalities in the sex chromosomes tend to complicate and impair sexual functioning.
4. Criminal aggression in XYY men does not exceed that in XXY men. Surplus Y chromosomes thus do not seem to exert a direct influence on aggression through virilization. Analogously, surplus X chromosomes do not seem to exert a direct influence on aggression through feminization.

5. Chromosomal aberrations in men foster conditions that favor the development of aggressiveness, including that of a potentiality for criminal aggression. This development is mediated by a host of anatomical, dispositional, and social factors, such as the capacity for effective fighting (because of extreme tallness), mental retardation, realization of abnormalcy, feelings of inadequacy, and frequent provocation. It is not the immediate result of endocrine functioning or dysfunctioning.

III. MENSTRUAL CONCOMITANTS

In men, testosterone levels fluctuate, of course, but these fluctuations are comparatively minor and seem of little consequence to sex and aggression. It has been observed, for instance, that the stress of prolonged physical exertion (e.g., during military training programs) reduces both testosterone levels and sexual inclinations (Kreuz, Rose, & Jennings, 1972). The frequency of actual coital engagements by men enjoying unrestricted sexual access showed no appreciable covariation with testosterone levels, however (Kraemer, Becker, Brodie, Doering, Moos, & Hamburg, 1976). In women, testosterone levels are comparatively low, but also tend to be rather stable. The maintenance of these levels in women appears to be essential to sexual desire (cf. Rose, 1972), as adrenalectomy of ovariectomized women (i.e., the removal of the endogenous sources of testosterone) prompts a marked decline of sexual interest (Waxenberg, Drellich, & Sutherland, 1959; Waxenberg, Finkbeiner, Drellich, & Sutherland, 1960) and androgen treatment appears to restore sexual desire (Burdine, Shipley, & Papas, 1957; Salmon & Geist, 1943; Sopchak & Sutherland, 1960).

In sharp contrast, the levels of the female gonadal hormones estrogen and progesterone undergo considerable periodic changes in menstruating women (cf. Langley, 1971; Turner & Bagnara, 1971). During menses, both estrogen and progesterone levels are comparatively low. Estrogen secretion increases during the follicular phase and reaches a maximum at ovulation (i.e., near the end of the follicular phase at about midcycle). After some decline in the beginning of the luteal phase, estrogen secretion increases again and forms the so-called "luteal peak" (about day 21 of a normal 28-day cycle). It then drops off sharply during the premenstrual days and into the menses. Progesterone secretion begins to increase notably at about midcycle and reaches a peak during days 21 to 24 of the cycle. It drops sharply thereafter, paralleling the drop in estrogen levels. Estrogen, then, is secreted in higher concentration during both the follicular and the luteal phases, progesterone only during the latter. Estrogen thus dominates the follicular phase, whereas both estrogen and progesterone are equally involved in the luteal phase. In fact, both gonadal hormones peak at approximately the same time during this phase, and both hormones exhibit the same sharp premenstrual decline in their concentration.

What are the behavioral implications of such pronounced cyclic variation in the levels of female gonadal hormones? Does the prevalence of estrogen during the follicular phase alter sexuality and aggressiveness? Is the joint peaking of estrogen and progesterone midway through the luteal phase a significant factor? Or is the drop to low levels thereafter crucial?

Regarding sexual behavior, it might be expected that coital activities center around ovulation and thus coincide with the ovulation peak of estrogen (i.e., the first peak that is associated with a rather low progesterone level). Observations on nonhuman primates accord well with such expectations. Copulation tends to be most frequent at ovulation, but also occurs at other times (cf. Rowell, 1972). Grooming and similar sociosexual activities, furthermore, were observed to follow cyclic patterns. These patterns vanished after ovariectomy, suggesting a dependence on gonadal hormone secretion (Michael & Herbert, 1963). Additionally, the luteal phase is characterized by a general lack of sexual interest (Young & Orbison, 1944). This latter observation may seem to destroy a close correspondence of sexual receptivity with estrogen levels. It is conceivable, however, that progesterone counteracts the estrogen effect and that receptivity is low during the luteal phase because progesterone co-peaks with estrogen. There is, in fact, some indication that progesterone might depress estrogen-induced heat in nonhuman primates (Ball, 1941).

The research findings concerning human sexuality throughout the menstrual cycle are far less consistent. Benedek and Rubenstein (1939a, 1939b, 1942; see also Benedek, 1952) explored the psychodynamics of the menstrual cycle and concluded from their somewhat informal observations that: (1) the secretion of estrogen during the follicular phase corresponds with an impulsion toward extroverted heterosexual behavior; (2) ovulation is followed by a period of relaxation and relief from heterosexual impulsion; (3) secretion of progesterone during the luteal phase corresponds with the focus of attention to the woman's own body and to its welfare. In short, the women's behavioral efforts during the first half of the cycle serve insemination, and those of the second half prepare for the eventuality of a fertilized ovum (i.e., for pregnancy).

Surveys of the frequency of coital engagements during the cycle seemed for the most part to conform to such a functional, biological interpretation. Udry and Morris (1968, 1970) reported that frequency of coitus steadily increased to a maximum a few days prior to ovulation and declined thereafter to a minimum a few days before the onset of menses. In gross discord with hormonal distributions, however, these investigators also reported a sharp increase in coital behavior just prior to menstruation. James (1971), on the other hand, reported a maximum of coital behavior immediately after menstruation with no further meaningful changes throughout the cycle. Taken together, these findings fail to exhibit a unique correspondence between changes in the levels of female gonadal hormones and sexual behavior in humans. If hormonal effects exist, they are apparently overpowered by other influences. The most obvious one, it would seem, is that in human sexuality the male rather than the female determines when and how often intercourse is to take place. However, it is also possible that, consistent with considerations expressed earlier, the female gonadal hormones do not appreciably influence female sexuality and that the fluctuations in their secretion during the menstrual cycle are without consequence for women's sexual desire, in particular. The high frequency of intercourse following menstruation (James, 1971), for instance, might simply be the result of abstinence (in the sense of experiential deprivation or disruption of a habit rather than the buildup of a physical need) that sexually motivates women and men alike, though to different degrees.

Observations on nonsexual behaviors that nonetheless pertain to sexuality are also inconsistent with a strictly functional interpretation of hormonal processes during the cycle. There are, however, behavioral consistencies of great significance that closely correspond with hormonal changes toward the end of the cycle. These consistencies concern the premenstrual and menstrual periods (together spanning about 8 days—i.e., more than a quarter of the cycle) that are linked with the sharp joined drop in estrogen and progesterone levels and with the low levels of these hormones thereafter.

Benedek (1963) reported that during the days associated with high progesterone levels, women's dreams are laden with themes of pregnancy and mother-child interaction. Swanson and Foulkes (1968) failed, however, to confirm such reports. Instead, these investigators observed that sexual themes became prevalent in dreams during menses. To the extent that dreams about sex can be considered indicative of sexual desire, a functional view would, of course, lead one to expect the prevalence of sexual dream content during the follicular phase, especially around ovulation. Gottschalk, Kaplan, Gleser, and Winget (1962), on the other hand, found that around the time of ovulation women tend to report less anxiety and less "inwardly directed hostility." This finding has been interpreted as suggesting an opening up for social and, potentially, for sexual relations during this period. It might, of course, merely reflect well-being during this particular period.

Melges and Hamburg (1976) have reported mood changes during the menstrual cycle that closely correspond with hormonal changes. According to these investigators, the estrogen-dominated follicular phase of the cycle is characterized by a sense of well-being and alertness. Women's ratings of pleasantness, activation, and sexual excitedness were high during this period. The ratings of these experiential facets declined during the postovulation period associated with increased progesterone levels. A few days prior to the period of menstrual bleeding and concomitant with the drop of both estrogen and progesterone levels, irritability, anxiety, and pain were reported. These facets are, of course, the symptoms of the so-called "premenstrual syndrome" (cf. Parlee, 1973).

Other studies of the variation of mood during the menstrual cycle (cf. Smith, 1975) fail to show a reliable correspondence between the ovulation and luteal peaks of hormone secretion with affective behaviors. In contrast, profound changes in mood and emotional behaviors during the premenstrual period and during menses have been abundantly documented. Ivey and Bardwick (1968), for example, observed that women were more anxious and more depressed during the premenstrual period and during menses than during other phases of the cycle. Moos, Kopell, Melges, Yalom, Lunde, Clayton, and Hamburg (1969) similarly observed increased depression during the premenstrual period. In addition, these investigators recorded increased anxiety during menses. Marinari, Leshner, and Doyle (1976), furthermore, observed that during the menstrual phase women responded more strongly, in terms of andrenocortical reactions, to psychological stressors than at times when female gonadal hormones were at high levels.

It should be mentioned that oral contraceptives tend to attenuate mood variation during the cycle (e.g., Englander-Golden, Willis, & Dienstbier, 1977; Kutner & Brown, 1972; Paige, 1971). Interestingly, the so-called "combination pills" that regulate hormone titres in the same fashion across phases proved more effective in diminishing premenstrual symptoms than the so-called "sequential pills" that foster greater changes in hormone levels (e.g., Hamburg, Moos, & Yalom, 1968; Kutner & Brown, 1972). Such observations have been interpreted as suggesting that specific mood changes may indeed be controlled by variations in the secretion of female gonadal hormones throughout the menstrual cycle (e.g., Leshner, 1978). Findings presented by Beumont, Richards, and Gelder (1975) would seem to challenge such an interpretation, however. These investigators compared the premenstrual symptoms of normally menstruating women with those of women who cycled, but did not know when they cycled. Women in the latter condition had undergone hysterectomies; hence, they did not menstruate or know exactly when their cycles occurred. The women in this condition exhibited comparatively minor variations in mood across their cycles, a finding that can be taken as suggesting that hormonal changes may be less important than had been thought and that, more likely, the premenstrual syndrome may be the result of somatic changes and the experience thereof.

Further investigations (Englander-Golden, Whitmore, & Dienstbier, 1978) also suggest that the mood variation across the menstrual cycle may have been overestimated. It was found that only when the cycle was made salient (i.e., when attention was focused on experiences as a potential function of phases of the cycle) did women report appreciable cyclic variations in moods and affective behaviors. To the extent that requirements of daily or other frequent, evenly spaced mood reports, along with hints from questions concerning menstruation, fostered some awareness of the stage in the cycle associated with the report, women may have reported moods in conformity with their beliefs about phasic dependencies. Premenstrual complaints, for instance, may have been filed because they were believed to reflect a "normal" state. Or, at least, such complaints may have been exaggerated. These possibilities compromise much of the survey data that are based on repeated self-reports.

Such criticism cannot be levied against more behavioral assessments of experiential states and their consequences that vary with cyclic phases. Kopell, Lunde, Clayton, and Moos (1969), for instance, observed performance impairment in time estimates and in visual perception during the premenstrual phase. This impairment corresponded with reports of mild confusion. Dalton (1960a) observed similar impairments in the scholastic performance of premenstrual girls. Furthermore, Dalton (1960b) noted an increased proneness for bodily injury in premenstrual women.

It is difficult—and it certainly would be inconsiderate, if not outright cruel to women—to dismiss reports of premenstrual and menstrual discomfort and pain as a "self-fulfilling prophecy" based on folklore and the suggestive powers of mothers and peers. Women report apprehensions, inability to relax, depression, irritability, insomnia, and headaches during this critical period (cf. Hamburg, 1966; Rogers, 1963). These symptoms have a high prevalence in the general population (Kessel & Coppen, 1963) and must be considered to reflect intensely disagreeable somatic conditions. The apparent consequences of these conditions, furthermore, are obtrusively clear from unobtrusive assessments. Dalton (1964), for instance, reported that during the premenstrual and menstrual phases, compared to other phases, women employees call in sick more frequently, psychiatric admissions of women are up, and medical and surgical admissions similarly increase. During the critical phases, mothers appear to project their malaise into others as well. It has been observed, for example, that the majority of children attending clinics because of minor ailments (e.g., coughs or colds) was brought there by premenstrual and menstrual mothers. But perhaps the most telling evidence of menstruation-linked depression comes from reports of increased suicide attempts during the phases in question (Dalton, 1959; Torghele, 1957).

Destructive behavior, such as suicide, is not necessarily self-directed, however. It has been observed, for instance, that the frequency of assaultive behaviors in hospitalized psychiatric patients (MacKinnon & MacKinnon, 1956) and of crimes of violence generally (Morton, Addison, Hunt, & Sullivan, 1953) also increases in premenstrual and menstrual women. Such dramatic demonstrations are complemented by reports of feelings of increased aggressiveness during the critical phases (Ivey & Bardwick, 1968). The findings of increased hostility in the contents of dreams during menses (Swanson & Foulkes, 1968) might also be construed as corroborative. On the other hand, efforts to demonstrate variations in provoked and unprovoked aggressiveness as a function of cycle phases in more behavioral terms in laboratory experiments have not produced supportive data (Baron & Zillmann, 1981).

Given that aggressiveness in premenstrual and menstrual women appears to increase above levels associated with other phases of the cycle, what are the mechanics of this phenomenon? Is there a direct endocrine connection? Is the common decline of estrogen and progesterone secretion responsible? Or are there simpler, more parsimonious explanations?

A straightforward account could be offered on the basis of the consideration of the experience of somatic changes. Reports of premenstrual and menstrual discomfort and pain appear to be robust, and pain has been shown to facilitate aggressive reactions to provocation with great consistency (cf. Zillmann, 1979). The proposal that annoyance from an internal condition (i.e., menstrual pain) and an external condition (i.e., provocation) combines in some fashion to promote increased aggressiveness, even a propensity for violent reactions, seems parsimonious indeed. The relationship between hormonal changes and aggressiveness, in and of itself, does not provide a superior account. There are indications, however, that premenstrual and menstrual discomfort and pain are the direct result of hormonal changes, and to the extent that such a connection can be made, a more complete theoretical account can be developed.

Hamburg (1966) proposed that progesterone withdrawal is critically involved in creating the premenstrual syndrome. He pointed to the anesthetic properties of progesterone and likened the premenstrual drop in progesterone to the withdrawal of a potent sedative (Melges & Hamburg, 1976). Thus, premenstrual irritability and aggressiveness are viewed as withdrawal symptoms. Hamburg further proposed that essentially the same reactions to progesterone withdrawal make up the so-called "postpartum blues" and climacteric irritability in women.

The anesthetic effect of progesterone is not in doubt (e.g., Selye, 1941). It is also clear that progesterone enters the brain and has central effects (cf. Hamburg, 1966). In large doses, progesterone induces general anesthesia; in moderate doses, it is sedative. The anesthetic effect seems especially marked in females (Hamburg, 1966). Moreover, in studies with rats and dogs, progesterone proved to reduce the incidence of convulsion (Costa & Bonnycastle, 1952; Woolley & Timiras, 1962). In epileptic women, seizures were found to be relatively infrequent during the luteal phase of the cycle (i.e., when progesterone levels are high) and relatively frequent prior to, during, and just after menstruation (i.e., when progesterone levels are lowest); furthermore, premenstrual progesterone therapy proved effective in lowering the incidence of seizures (Laidlaw, 1956; Logothetis, Harner, Morrell, & Torres, 1959). The administration of estrogen, in contrast, was found to increase the likelihood of seizures. On the other hand, estrogen has some anesthetic properties also, and the premenstrual drop of estrogen levels might exacerbate the withdrawal reaction to the more potent anesthetic effect of progesterone.

There is some suggestive evidence, then, that appears to be consistent with Hamburg's proposal. The proposal's appeal, however, seems to stem mainly from the functional implication of progesterone that it entails. According to the proposal, progesterone serves gestation by aiding the childbearing woman to cope with a multitude of stress conditions to which she finds herself exposed. Delivery and climacteric make the continuance of such protection unnecessary. Similarly, during the menstrual cycle, the infertilized ovum is no longer afforded the protection that was prepared for it. The contingent removal of protective sedation then produces the various withdrawal syndromes. The premenstrual woman, for instance, suddenly suffers the brunt of obtrusive somatic changes. During this period of acute annoyance, she may be depressed or react somewhat overintensely to provocation.

However appealing such theorizing may be, the research evidence at hand does not decisively implicate it. The critical evidence is correlational and does not permit evaluation of causal hypotheses. Moreover, there are alternative explanations that cannot be ruled out entirely. Vogel, Broverman, and Klaiber (1971), for instance, have argued that estrogen exerts a central adrenergic effect and that progesterone counteracts the andrenergic impact. This reasoning projects that depression and related symptoms will follow the luteal peak of estrogen and progesterone secretion but leaves it unclear how premenstrual and menstrual aggressiveness could be enhanced. Reichlin (1968), on the other hand, considers estrogen withdrawal to be the crucial condition for premenstrual and menstrual symptoms. Recent investigations have not been able to clarify compellingly which of these possible mechanisms are operative. Bäckström and Carstensen (1974), for instance, assessed the time course of hormonal changes in the days preceding and during the premenstrual period in women experiencing either extreme or more moderate premenstrual irritability. Highly irritable women exhibited higher levels of estrogen, but lower levels of progesterone, than their less irritable counterparts. This particular finding would seem to support Hamburg's model, as irritable women did not enjoy the protection that elevated progesterone levels afforded the control women. It was also observed, however, that in normal women progesterone secretion declined at a faster rate than in irritable women. Normal women should thus have suffered more severely from progesterone withdrawal, because of the amount of change as well as because of the rate of change. This finding is in conflict with Hamburg's proposal. Moreover, it was observed that estrogen levels dropped off more rapidly from a higher point in irritable women than in normal women. This aspect of the findings supports Reichlin's position.

The situation is further complicated by the fact that numerous metabolites tend to covary with progesterone levels, leaving open the possibility that other hormones may critically impact the premenstrual syndrome. Be this as it may, it is clear that on the basis of endocrine processes theoretical connections between sex-related events and aggressive behaviors can be made. Specifically, premenstrual and menstrual discomfort and negative affect can be projected as a hormonal withdrawal reaction that potentiates aggression.

A comment on the automaticity of such possible potentiation of aggression seems in order. The consideration of hormonal processes tends to entail the view that, if certain hormones "motivate" sexual or aggressive behavior, little can be done—other than through endocrine counteraction—to prevent or alter the motivated "course of action." Such conceptualization grossly understates the complexity of human sexual and aggressive behaviors. Hormonal conditions may well favor and even invite sexual or aggressive action, but this action is not "automatically" taken. Particularly in humans, the impulsion to such action is subjected to considerable mediation by learning and cognition that readily prevents or alters a course of action, if the impulsion is ever action specific without the mediation in question. Regarding sociosexual and aggressive behaviors, dispositional control is likely to exert a strong influence, and it is conceivable that hostile reactions, despite highly favorable and appropriate hormonal conditions, will not manifest themselves. A recent investigation on premenstrual hostility (Baron & Zillmann, 1981) suggests that hormonal and somatic conditions may be prevalent and, presumably because of their salience, lead to reactions counter to those expected on the basis of hormonal considerations alone. It was observed that provoked premenstrual women, when provided with an opportunity to complain, expressed markedly *less* annoyance than equally provoked women in other phases, including women in the menstrual phase. How could this unexpected, counterintuitive finding be explained? One possibility is that premenstrual women, cognizant of the truism that women are irritable during this period, misconstrued their reaction of annoyance to the provocation as part of their premenstrual annoyance. Conceivably, then, premenstrual women might too readily blame a variety of annoyances on their obtrusive malaise and fail to assert themselves as they should and would, were they at other phases of the cycle. Cognizance of a bona fide malaise may thus occasion cognitive, attributional processes that lead to misconceptions about affective experiences and that prevent hostile reaction—all in the presence of hormonal conditions that might favor and impel hostile action.

Summarizing the data at hand makes it clear that the association between the sexual and aggressive behaviors of human females and particular hormonal conditions during the menstrual cycle is very limited:

1. The correspondence between changing levels of estrogen and/or progesterone, on the one hand, and changes in the strength of sexual interest and/or the frequency of sexual engagements, on the other, is poor.
2. Similarly, the propensity for aggression does not covary with levels of estrogen and/or progesterone during much of the cycle, nor does it covary with sexual behavior.
3. The propensity for hostile and aggressive behavior increases significantly, however, just prior to the onset of the menses and during menses. This potentiation of aggression corresponds with a sharp decline in levels of both estrogen and progesterone and with especially low levels of both following the decline. Premenstrual and menstrual irritability and aggressiveness appear to result—in part, at least—from acute estrogen and/or progesterone withdrawal that fosters a loss of protective sedation.

IV.   COMMONALITIES IN ADRENAL ACTIVITY

It should be remembered that the adrenals contribute to the production of androgens. Specifically, the *zona reticularis* of the adrenal cortex secretes adrenal sex hormones that resemble the gonadal sex hormones. To the extent that androgens potentiate sexual and aggressive behaviors, adrenal output thus may be expected to facilitate both types of behavior.

The fact that adrenalectomy of ovariectomized females diminishes or abolishes sexual desire and that administration of androgens restores sexual initiative in both nonhuman primates (e.g., Everitt et al., 1971) and humans (e.g., Salmon & Geist, 1943; Waxenberg et al., 1959; Waxenberg et al., 1960), together with the observation that ovariectomy alone (or menopause, for that matter) appears to have little effect on the libido of women (e.g., Kinsey et al., 1953), is often cited to implicate the function of adrenal androgens in sexual behavior (e.g., Brown & Wallace, 1980; Luria & Rose, 1979). It is conceivable that such modification of sexual interest in females is indeed the result of changes in androgen levels and that the sexual desire of males is analogously modified. It has been proposed, for instance, that androgen treatment fosters clitoral hypertrophy (or produces a similar penile effect) and that enhanced sexual interest is mediated by increased clitoral (or penile) sensitivity (Luttge, 1971). It seems more likely, however, that the effect of adrenal secretions on sexual behavior involves a variety of hormones rather than androgen alone. In fact, as Leshner (1978) pointed out, the libido-abolishing effect of adrenalectomy may well be due to the trauma created by such a procedure. Adrenalectomy has a host of significant metabolic consequences in addition to removing adrenal sex hormones. Most important here, this procedure deprives the organism of the glucocorticoids that derive from the *zona fasciculata* of the adrenal cortex and of the catecholamines that are produced in the adrenal medulla. Both the glucocorticoids and the catecholamines provide energy. The catecholamines, especially through the hyperglycemic effect of epinephrine, furnish the short-lived energy for emergency situations. The energizing effect of the glucocorticoids, in contrast, is long-term and may span considerable periods of time. Adrenalectomy, consequently, drains the organism's energy resources, and it should be no surprise to find that it causes a deterioration of sexual interest. The loss of initiative should not be specific to sexual behavior, however. It applies to all behaviors that require the expenditure of nontrivial amounts of energy.

It can be considered likely, then, that high levels of glucocorticoids promote sexual interest. There can be little doubt that high levels of these hormones facilitate aggressive behaviors. It has been shown, for instance, that the removal of the glucocorticoids from circulation decreases aggressiveness in mice (Brain, Nowell, & Wouters, 1971; Harding & Leshner, 1972; Sigg, 1969) and that replacement therapy with corticosterone restores the lost aggressiveness (Candland & Leshner, 1974). Furthermore, it has been observed that the administration of moderate doses of glucocorticoids facilitates aggressiveness in intact mice (Kostowski, Rewerski, & Piechocki, 1970) and that such administration can produce aggression in nonaggressive animals (Banarjee, 1971). A correspondence between adrenocortical activity and aggressiveness has also been ascertained in nonhuman primates. Levine, Gordon, Peterson, and Rose (1970) observed that highly aggressive rhesus monkeys have higher urinary 17-hydroxycorticosteroid levels than timid ones. These steroids are the metabolic end product of glucocorticoids and thus measure their secretion. In a similar investigation, Leshner and Candland (1972) found that squirrel monkeys with initially high urinary 17-hydroxycorticosteroid levels achieved higher ranks in the social dominance hierarchy, ultimately through fighting, than did their peers with lower levels. Moreover, after 4 years of group housing, the dominant animals exhibited higher levels of adrenocortical metabolites than the subordinate ones. The sexual privileges that accrue to dominance have been discussed earlier.

The joined involvement of adrenal androgens and glucocorticoids in the facilitation of both sexual and aggressive behaviors is further suggested by the humoral release mechanism that these hormones hold in common. As conditions for prolonged energy expenditure arise (so-called "stressful" situations), the hypothalamus emits a substance called corticotrophin releasing factor into the blood portal system that binds to reception in the anterior pituitary. The anterior pituitary, in turn, releases adrenocorticotrophic hormones into the bloodstream. As these hormones reach the adrenal cortex, they cause the release of the adrenocortical steroids. Specifically, they cause the release of both adrenal androgens and glucocorticoids, among other hormones. In view of these shared release mechanics, it appears that adrenal androgens and glucocorticoids indeed operate in a highly confounded fashion in their effect on sexual and aggressive behavior. Both of these adrenocortical steroids can be considered implicated with the facilitation of sexual and aggressive action. It remains unclear, however, to what degree the steroids act independently or interact in achieving their effect.

It is important to recognize that any facilitative effect that adrenocortical steroids may have on sexual and aggressive behaviors is comparatively stable over time, developing with appreciable latency and dissipating only after considerable periods of time. In short, it is *tonic* rather than *phasic*. These steroids, then, do not so much fuel individual sexual or aggressive episodes as they furnish a superior readiness for sexual and aggressive engagements. Heightened adrenocortical activity appears to place the organism in a condition of increased sexual and aggressive responsiveness. Whalen (1966), in dealing with sexual behavior specifically, referred to this tonic condition as "arousability," in contrast to phasic, episodic sexual arousal. The arousability concept can, of course, be applied to aggressive behavior as well. If sexual arousability is the organism's readiness for sexual engagements, aggressive arousability is its readiness for aggressive engagements. And if arousability in the sexual sphere is measured in the coital response rate to sexual stimulation, arousability in the domain of aggression can be measured analogously in the rate of attack upon provocation.

Provided that arousability conditions are such that sexual and aggressive engagements are possible, the energy for episodes of sex and aggression is furnished primarily by heightened activity in the adrenomedullary system. The adrenal medullae, as may be recalled, are sympathetically innervated. Thus, sympathetic stimulation prompts the immediate release of the catecholamines epinephrine and norepinephrine into the bloodstream, and the release of these sympathomimetic agents, after a brief latency period, fosters heightened activity in the sympathetic nervous system for a limited period of time (cf. Turner & Bagnara, 1971). Although the level of adrenomedullary activity may vary quasi-tonically throughout the day (rising during work periods and declining during recumbency, cf. Frankenhaeuser, 1979; Pátkai, 1971b), the energizing, hyper-glycemic effect of medullary secretion is essentially phasic. Generally speaking, the energy supplied is absorbed by one episode of vigorous, strenuous action, or by just a few such episodes at most.

Cannon (1929), in his fight-or-flight paradigm, has stressed the survival value of the discussed adrenomedullary provision of bursts of energy. With regard to sexual union, however, one might surmise that the energy required—for many mammalian species, at least—is of substantially less magnitude than the energy needed to cope with endangerments. It seems that the requirements for energy expenditure in sexual and aggressive behaviors can be viewed as comparable only if it is assumed that energy-consuming aggressive action is a significant element of successful reproductive efforts. In humans an intense adrenomedul-lary response to sexual stimulation might be considered an evolutionary rem-nant—a response that lost much, if not all, of its species-procuring utility. This situation would parallel the loss of adaptive value of heightened adrenomedullary activity during much interpersonal conflict in modern society (cf. Zillmann, 1979).

Regardless of evolutionary speculations, the issue of whether adrenomedul-lary responses to sexual and to aggressive stimulation are comparable or are critically different has been explored empirically.

It can be considered well established that stressful stimulation (e.g., acutely aversive treatments and the endangerment of the organism) causes the release of substantial amounts of catecholamines in both nonhuman primates (e.g., Brady, 1967, 1970) and humans (e.g., Elmadjian, 1963; Levi, 1972). There is some indication that the release of epinephrine is more closely associated with reac-tions of fear and escape than with reactions of annoyance and aggression and that the reverse is the case for the release of norepinephrine (e.g., Funkenstein, 1956; Mason, Mangan, Brady, Conrad, & Rioch, 1961). Other assessments, however, have failed to corroborate such a unique secretory pattern for a fear-anger dichot-omy and have yielded, instead, a rather stable pattern of catecholamine release for all aversion-related reactions (e.g., Euler, Gemzell, Levi, & Ström, 1959; Levi, 1963).

Catecholamine release in response to sexual stimulation has received comparatively little attention. Some data are available, however, and allow a tentative comparison of secretory response patterns to sexual and to aversive stimuli.

Levi (1967), in an initial study, exposed women to suggestive erotic films (i.e., films depicting precoital and coital behavior without showing genitals) and assessed urinary epinephrine and norepinephrine levels before, during, and after exposure. According to self-reports, the films induced moderately pleasant reactions. Excretion of catecholamines in response to such subdued sexual stimulation proved to be quite negligible, however. In a follow-up investigation, Levi (1969) employed four film segments that explicitly depicted the genital aspects of heterosexual intercourse. Both men and women were exposed to these erotic materials, and the excretion of catecholamines was traced—analogous to the procedure in the preceding study—in repeatedly taken urine samples. The excretion of epinephrine and of norepinephrine during exposure to erotica, as compared against pre- and postexposure levels of catecholamine excretion, increased significantly in both men and women. Both genders reported being sexually excited during exposure. Men, however, reported higher levels of excitement. The experience of excitement was construed as pleasurable, especially by men. A concomitant finding was that urinary epinephrine reached higher levels in men than in women. Overall, a close correspondence emerged between the intensity of the subjective assessments of sexual excitedness and levels of catecholamine excretion.

There can be little doubt, then, that the *pleasant* experience of intense sexual excitedness is accompanied by marked catecholamine release. However, sexual excitedness is not the only apparently nonaversive experience that is associated with increased adrenomedullary activity. Levi (1965) observed that gaiety, produced by exposure to comedy, is connected with increased catecholamine release. In fact, the epinephrine/norepinephrine ratio associated with mirth proved to be essentially the same as the ratios deriving from reactions of annoyance and empathetic fear in response to films featuring violent and anxiety-inducing events. Pátkai (1971a) has provided further evidence that the pattern of catecholamine excretion is not appreciably different during pleasant and unpleasant experiences of excitedness.

Taken together, the available research on catecholamine release in humans suggests that the secretory pattern of epinephrine and norepinephrine is independent of the particular hedonic valence of a behavioral situation and that it is essentially the same for states of sexual and aggressive excitedness. Whether or not unique quantities of catecholamines are released during these states (i.e., whether catecholamine release is more pronounced during sexual or aggressive engagement, or whether the reverse is the case) remains unclear, however, as the laboratory inductions of sexual excitedness and, especially, of aggressiveness may only approximate the release characteristic of sexual or aggressive behaviors that occur under normal circumstances.

I return to adrenomedullary commonalities in sexual and aggressive behaviors in discussing sex and aggression as emotions (Chapters 6 and 7, especially the latter). In much of the pertinent research on motivation and emotion, sympathetico-adrenomedullary activity is assessed in peripheral manifestations of sympathetic excitation. These manifestations largely reflect, of course, the release of catecholamines.

The essential information concerning commonalities in adrenal activity can be restated as follows:

1. Heightened adrenocortical activity fosters conditions of increased sexual and aggressive readiness and responsiveness. This effect is tonic (i.e., of comparatively long duration).
2. Heightened adrenomedullary activity similarly promotes both sexual and aggressive readiness and responsiveness. In contrast, however, this effect is phasic or episodic (i.e., of comparatively short duration). Essentially, the phasic effect furnishes the energy for the performance of just one sexual or/and aggressive engagement.
3. Adrenal activity serves both sexual and aggressive behaviors, potentially in a confounded fashion, because of highly similar mechanics in the release of adrenocortical and adrenomedullary hormones.

5 Connections in Motivation and Emotion

In the study of motivation and emotion it has been asserted frequently that sex and aggression have a propensity for mutual facilitation (cf. Cofer & Appley, 1964). Characteristically, the hypothetical construct of "drive" was employed to specify motivational forces, and these forces were considered to have great affinity in sexual and aggressive activities. Another hypothetical construct, "arousal," was used to define the magnitude of drive, and it was often assumed that sexual arousal could—without appreciable diminution—energize aggressive behavior and that arousal associated with aggressive action could likewise energize sexual behavior. Sexual drive and aggressive drive, then, were construed as readily interchangeable forces. The Hullian (1943, 1952) concepts of "generalized drive" and "irrelevant drive," probably in concert with related notions deriving from activation theory (e.g., Duffy, 1957, 1962; Lindsley, 1951, 1957; Malmo, 1959), promoted a widespread acceptance of this conceptualization. Generalized drive, a state of arousal that was regarded as nonspecific to particular behaviors, was viewed as capable of energizing sexual and aggressive reactions alike. Similarly, sexual drive was considered intensifiable by elements of irrelevant drive, such as arousal from the instigation to aggression; analogously, aggressive drive was deemed strengthenable by sexual arousal as irrelevant drive (cf. Zillmann, 1979). Moreover, Hull and others (e.g., Bindra, 1959; Brown, 1961) have emphasized that at high levels of arousal the organism exhibits a selective bias toward activities that are associated with high habit strength. If it is assumed that both sexual and aggressive responses tend to be well established in the mature individual and are likely to constitute strong, dominant habits, it may be expected that the interdependence between sex and aggression is not merely one of mutual intensification, but one of mutual elicitation as well (cf. Zillmann,

115

1983b). The possibility that the critical facilitative process is one of mutual disinhibition, rather than mutual instigation, has also received some attention (cf. Feshbach & Malamuth, 1978).

Recent theorizing on the sex-aggression connection in humans has taken its impetus from Schachter's (1964) two-factor theory of emotion. This theory emphasizes the cognitive appraisal of sensory feedback from excitatory reactions. More specifically, it posits that individuals, as they sense increasing arousal levels, construe the changes as responses to specific stimuli—usually stimuli in the individuals' environment. The causal attribution of the responses to stimuli may be erroneous, of course. In fact, in complex stimulus situations, the misattribution of at least some elements of the compounded excitatory reaction seems more likely than the entirely accurate attribution of the reaction to all its contributing sources. An excitatory reaction that confounds sexual and aggressive stimulation may be attributed, according to this reasoning, to the one or the other source in toto. Such proceeding entails a partial misattribution of arousal, and it is through this misattribution—or the "relabeling" of arousal—that an intensification of the experience to which the excitatory reaction is de facto attributed is expected. In the face of salient sexual stimulation, excitedness that actually derives from frustration, annoyance, and provocation thus may be misconstrued as sexual arousal and promote romantic inclinations. And alternatively, experiences of anger and aggressiveness might be enhanced by misattributed sexual arousal.

In this chapter, I first survey the research evidence pertaining to the proposal that sexual and aggressive drive states have great affinity and that, because of this affinity, sexual and aggressive drive states tend to impel both sexual and aggressive behaviors. I discuss some of the representative work with subhuman species and then review investigations designed to assess and document the presumed motivational affinity between sex and aggression in humans. Thereafter, I turn to the more recent work on sex-aggression confusions—or more accurately, anxiety-sex confusions—in the context of love as an emotion.

I.   DRIVE DIFFUSION IN NONHUMAN SPECIES

The suggestion of a covariation between sexual and aggressive behaviors as a function of elevated levels of sexual or aggressive drive has been rather extensively explored in rodents. Initially, drive was viewed as a persisting trait, and it was accordingly manipulated through training. In later research, however, drive was conceived of as a state, and characteristically, an acute drive state was equated with heightened levels of activation or arousal.

The treatment of drive as a trait failed to produce consistent findings. King (1956), for instance, observed that in mice variations in sexual experience and eagerness were without consequence for aggressive behaviors. Kahn (1961), on the other hand, found that aggressiveness training had significant effects on the mating behavior of mice. Through the repeated experience of victory or defeat in intermale fights, males became either aggressive or submissive. Once this trait had been established, the males were confronted with a virgin female in estrus. Aggressive males proved to be initiative sexually. They chased the female about, seeking to accomplish copulation. The submissive males, in contrast, showed little sexual initiative and escaped from the female's advances.

Kahn's findings can be taken as indicating that aggressiveness fosters the "aggressive" pursuit of sex, but does not necessarily promote sexuality. Data reported by Lagerspetz and Hautojärvi (1967) and Hautojärvi and Lagerspetz (1968) lend further support to such an interpretation. These investigators observed that male mice that were previously highly aggressive toward other males exhibited reduced sexual drive toward an estrous female. Instead, the aggressive males displayed increased aggression toward the estrous female. Aggressiveness, then, did not convert into sexual drive, but tended to be maintained—even inappropriately so. The situation was similar regarding efforts to convert sexual drive into aggressiveness. Males that had been very active sexually and that were confronted with another male exhibited homosexual inclinations along with reduced aggressiveness. Moreover, submissiveness that was accomplished through repeated defeats in intermale skirmishes proved to be without consequence for the animals' sexual behavior, and aggressiveness that was analogously achieved through repeated victories actually decreased sexual activity. The latter findings are inconsistent with those reported by Kahn (1961). More importantly, however, the findings, taken together, challenge the view that in the presence of appropriate environmental stimulation sexual drive (as a trait) converts into aggressive drive (also as a trait) and vice versa.

In contrast, the treatment of sexual and aggressive drive as a transitory state of heightened activation occasioned by appropriate stimulation did generate research that produced highly consistent findings. A set of investigations showed convincingly that pain, a practically universal inducer of aggressive reactions (cf. Hutchinson, 1972), can significantly enhance sexual activity. And there is some evidence that sexual stimulation can temporarily instigate aggression.

In an investigation by Barfield and Sachs (1968), mildly painful electric shock was administered to the back of sexually experienced male rats that were in the presence of an estrous female. Administration of shock, compared against a control condition in which no shock was delivered, greatly facilitated sexual activity. Characteristically, sexual responses consistently occurred shortly after the reception of shock. Sexual drive, according to Barfield and Sachs, seemed augmented by aggressive drive—or rather, by the nonspecific arousal reaction associated with it.

Caggiula and Eibergen (1969) employed sexually naive rats in a similar investigation. Males, in the presence of an estrous female, received electric shock to the tail. This procedure produced copulatory behavior in nearly four times as many animals as in a no-shock control condition. Moreover, almost all control animals that failed to copulate in repeated trials without shock did copulate after receiving shock. Shock also induced copulatory behavior toward other males and toward stuffed toy animals. In male-male situations, however, tail shock typically produced aggressive behavior. Finally, behaviors such as feeding, drinking, gnawing, or nest building were neither elicited nor enhanced by tail shock. This latter finding is of interest in that it suggests that the facilitative effect of pain-induced arousal is limited to behavior—such as sexual activity—that is associated with high levels of activation.

Further corroborating evidence comes from a study by Crowley, Popolow, and Ward (1973). These investigators conditioned sexually inactive male rats (so-called noncopulators) to associate tones with electric shock to the flanks and then presented the tones when the males were in the presence of an estrous female. The tones induced copulation with extreme regularity, a dud-to-stud conversion (to use the investigators' nomenclature) that was attributed to an arousal augmentation by the anticipation of pain.

The reverse facilitation, namely, that of aggressive behavior by elements of sexual drive, was explored by first exposing males to estrous females and by providing aggression opportunities thereafter.

Calhoun (1962) had observed that in colonies of rats in a quasi-natural habitat intermale aggression sharply increased as females came into estrus. Barnett, Evans, and Stoddart (1968) manipulated social events under less natural conditions and ascertained the consequences of such changes for aggression. Specifically, these investigators placed male interlopers into a resident animal's cage and recorded aggression against the intruder. In some instances, two females were placed into the cage along with the interloper. Levels of aggression against the interloper increased significantly when this was done. Unfortunately, however, the estrous status of these females was not established; hence it remains unclear whether the facilitation of aggression was due to increased sexual drive or resulted from other aspects of the social confrontation.

An investigation that rules out such alternative accounts has been conducted by Taylor (1975). For a period of 1 minute, male rats were exposed to either an estrous or a diestrous inaccessible female (i.e., the female was separated from the males by a wire mesh screen) and, immediately after this confrontation, provided with a choice between an empty compartment or a compartment containing a submissive male as a potential target for aggression. The encounter with the estrous female, compared to that with the diestrous one, fostered a strong preference for the submissive male over the nonsocial condition and led to sharply increased aggression against this submissive animal. The evocation of sexual arousal, then, promoted aggressiveness, and sexual drive—or at least, elements thereof—can be considered to have found expression in aggressive behavior.

In summing up, the following statements regarding drive diffusion in nonhuman species are possible:

1. Sexual drive and aggressive drive, conceived of and operationalized as comparatively long-lasting traits of individuals, have not been shown—in the research with rodents—to facilitate one another in any consistent fashion.
2. In contrast, the conceptualization and operationalization of sexual and aggressive drive as transitory states associated with heightened activation levels has led to research that shows a mutual facilitation of sex and aggression. Stimulation that commonly instigates aggression has been shown to enhance sexual behavior. Analogously, sexual stimulation has been shown to enhance aggressive behavior. It appears that elements of arousal from the one type of behavior potentiate the other type of behavior whenever the latter type defines the appropriate response to environmental stimuli and the former type does not.

However, although the capacity for mutual facilitation of sexual and aggressive behaviors is not in doubt, the mechanics of this facilitation remain unclear. Drive and arousal have remained rather roundabout hypothetical constructs in the research that has been discussed. Are drive and arousal states identical or different but similar in sexual and in aggressive behaviors? Exactly how nonspecific is arousal? In the absence of more specific conceptualizations and direct measurements, questions such as these cannot be answered.

II. DRIVE DIFFUSION IN HUMANS

In humans the presumed affinity between sexual and aggressive motivational states initially has been explored in terms of fantasies occasioned by the one or the other state.

Barclay and Haber (1965) conducted an investigation in which male and female students were provoked or not provoked and then asked to write stories in response to pictorial stimuli that were similar to those of the Thematic Apperception Test (TAT). Subjects were treated rudely by an experimenter and insulted by their instructor, both persons being male. The TAT-type stimuli depicted events such as a male and a female engaged in a chess game or one person sitting and the other staring lovingly at that person. Male and female roles were alternated in all these activities. In the latter scene, for example, a male would stare at a female in half of the cases, and in the remaining cases, a female would stare at a male. The stories were analyzed for contents pertaining to sex and aggression, the main measures being sexual and aggressive imagery. Self-reports of anger were also obtained in order to ascertain the effectiveness of the provocation treatment.

According to the self-reports, the provocation treatment increased levels of anger over those in the control condition in females, but not in males. Despite the latter, both females and males exhibited increased aggressive imagery in the provocation condition. But more importantly, this increased aggressive imagery corresponded to increased sexual imagery. Aggressive instigation produced a significant increase in sexual imagery in both males and females. Females were altogether somewhat less expressive sexually than were males, however.

Barclay (1969) conducted a follow-up investigation in which essentially the same procedures were employed. An extension was the use of urinary acid phosphatase as a measure of sexual arousal in men (cf. Clark & Treichler, 1950). In this investigation, both males and females responded similarly, with increased anger, to the provocation treatment. The treatment fostered increased aggressive imagery in males only, however. It had no discernible effect on the aggressive imagery of females. The crucial effects on sexual imagery were identical. Again, the treatment produced an appreciable increase in such imagery in males only.

There was a tendency toward higher acid-phosphatase levels in provoked men, as compared to unprovoked ones. Barclay (1969) interpreted this tendency as demonstrating sexual responsiveness and, therefore, as supporting the hypothesis that ''anger and sexuality are linked [p. 660].'' Such an interpretation appears to be premature, however, as the possibility that prostatic secretion may increase during acute annoyance and anger as well as in states of sexual excitedness cannot be ruled out on the basis of available data (e.g., Barclay, 1970b; Barclay & Little, 1972; Gustafson, Winokur, & Reichlin, 1963). It is conceivable, then, that the somewhat increased levels of urinary acid phosphatase merely reflected an annoyance response to the provocation treatment and were not a concomitant of sexual imagery. The possibility that prostatic secretion is not specific to sexual excitedness, but occurs in states of aggressiveness as well as in sexual ones, can be construed as a sex-aggression connection in itself. However, this possibility has not been exploited by Barclay, as urinary acid-phosphatase levels are treated as a unique, specific measure of sexual arousal (cf. Zuckerman, 1971).

In a further study, Barclay (1970a) sought to clarify the females' failure in the 1969 investigation to respond to provocation with increased aggressive and sexual imagery. He speculated that, because the provocation came from a male in a position of authority and because women have learned to inhibit hostile reactions toward such men, the females' imagery response may have been impaired. The possibility of this type of impairment was consequently removed by employing a female experimenter to administer the provocation treatment. Other aspects of procedure were as in the earlier studies.

It was found that both males and females responded with comparable increases in anger to the provocation treatment. However, neither provoked males nor provoked females exhibited reliably increased aggressive imagery. Sexual imagery, in contrast, was markedly increased by provocation in both males and females. Despite the change of the provoker's gender, women were altogether somewhat less expressive aggressively and sexually than were men.

Although the findings of the three investigations are not entirely concordant, they are rather consistent in showing that provocation tends to foster increased sexual imagery, especially in men. What does such an enhancement of fantasy mean? Does it mean, as Barclay (1970a) concluded, that "increased aggressive motivation leads to increases in sexual *motivation* [p. 25; italics added]?" Or does the enhancement merely reflect that in fantasy sexual and aggressive themes tend to covary, possibly because of the linguistic practice of expressing annoyance in four-letter words (cf. Zillmann, Bryant, Cantor, & Day, 1975)— words that could serve as cues for erotic themes? There is some indication of such a covariation of sexual and aggressive themes in the fantasies of men (Gelles, 1975). Additionally, it is known that aggressive themes are quite common in sexual fantasies (Hariton & Singer, 1974). But whatever the mechanics of the emergence of sexual themes in the stories told by provoked persons may be, the treatment of fantasies about third parties ("I think these people are doing this and that" in response to a somewhat ambiguous picture) as a measure of the motivation for overt action is highly questionable. Furthermore, generalizations about sexual motivation that are based on such measurement are obviously very tentative, if acceptable at all.

Kelley, Miller, Byrne, and Bell (1983) (see also Miller, Byrne, & Bell, 1977) took issue with Barclay's reliance on the imagery procedure and sought to demonstrate the apparent enhancement of sexual interest by provocation with quite different procedures. Additionally, these investigators attempted to expand Barclay's findings by assessing the consequences for sexual interest of having persons behave aggressively as well as having them merely provoked.

In a first investigation, Kelley et al. factorially varied a provocation treatment with the opportunity to aggress against the annoyer and had subjects report their sexual arousal in response to a series of nonerotic and erotic slides. Both males and females received either a positive or an arbitrarily negative evaluation of themselves. This evaluation was made, ostensibly, by another subject. Under the guise of a stress test, subjects then were provided or not provided with an opportunity to deliver electric shock to their evaluator. Exposure to the slides followed. A first set showed such nonerotic items as furniture and paintings. A second set depicted a male and a female kissing and undressing. The third and final set explicitly presented heterosexual intercourse.

The provocation treatment proved highly effective for both males and females. Provoked subjects reported more anger and also delivered shock of higher intensities to the evaluator than did nonprovoked ones. However, there was no discernible effect of this treatment on reports of sexual excitedness. The effect of having behaved aggressively was trivial, also. Neither anger nor aggression, then, had any appreciable impact on the sexual arousal reported in response to nonerotic and erotic stimuli. The only effect of interest was that men perceived themselves to be more sexually aroused by exposure to the erotic slides than did women.

Kelley et al. speculated that their failure to replicate Barclay's findings may have resulted from two aspects of their procedure that differed sharply from that employed by Barclay: the positive evaluation and the self-report of arousal. The positive evaluation, according to these investigators, may have fostered positive affect that enhanced perceptions of sexual excitedness because of its affinity with it. Both the positive and the negative evaluation thus may have promoted sexual arousal, and a differentiation could not materialize. The requirement to report sexual arousal may have further impaired a differentiation because subjects, unlike in the projective test employed by Barclay, were made cognizant of their arousal, may have felt embarrassed, and hence may have reported less arousal than they experienced. These possible sources of distortion consequently were removed in a follow-up study. Subjects were negatively evaluated, positively evaluated, or not evaluated at all, and they were not asked to report their own reactions of sexual excitedness, but to assess the sexuality of the person of opposite gender depicted in the slides. The latter assessment was deemed to approximate closely the technique employed by Barclay, as both procedures are assumed to reflect the subjects' own state and to measure it indirectly.

Sexuality was rated on a battery of scales (e.g., sensual, physically attractive, loving, intelligent, mature). Perceived sexuality was measured in the composite score from the ratings on five scales: sensual, sexually aroused, promiscuous, aggressive, and desires sex. These scales had emerged as a factor from the factor analysis of the battery of scales.

As in the initial experiment, the provocation treatment proved highly effective. Despite this, no appreciable effect was observed on the measure of perceived sexuality. The instigation of annoyance and anger again had failed to enhance sexual excitedness.

In a final effort at replicating, Kelley et al. approximated Barclay's procedures even more closely. Barclay's original nonerotic stimuli were employed, and ratings of the sexuality of both persons in the stimulus pictures were obtained. The analysis of the data was essentially the same as in the second study; the findings were also the same. The provocation treatment again had no appreciable effect on perceptions of sexuality and, to the extent that such perceptions measure sexual excitedness, on sexual arousal.

Taken together, the findings reported by Kelley et al. fail to replicate and expand those of Barclay. They challenge the view that aggressive drive readily converts to sexual drive or that elements of the response to provocation are sexual in nature. Moreover, these findings suggest that the sex-aggression affinity observed in Barclay's studies is limited to the storytelling technique and possibly results from a covariation of somewhat sexual and aggressive themes.

Using the discussed projective technique, Clark (1952) had reported data in support of a sex-aggression connection in the reverse direction: Sexually aroused persons exhibited more aggressiveness in their stories than did nonaroused persons. Barclay (1971) replicated this finding in an investigation in which subjects were exposed to different films and then asked to write stories about TAT-type pictures. The films featured heterosexual kissing and petting, verbal abuse in an interracial setting, a shaving-cream fight, and the production of paper airplanes. They were expected to induce sexual arousal, anxiety, amusement, and no affect, respectively. A control condition in which subjects folded paper airplanes, instead of being exposed to a film, was employed in addition. Aggressive and sexual imagery was found to be increased, relative to the controls, by exposure to the sexually arousing film only. Because the subjects considered themselves to be similarly aroused by the sexual, the anxiety-evoking, and the amusing film, Barclay thought he had implicated the increase in aggressive drive with the increase in sexual drive specifically. He also thought he had ruled out the alternative explanation that generalized drive or nonspecific arousal could have mediated the effect on aggressive imagery. However, Barclay's reliance on the storytelling technique renders these findings again open to the argument that the effect is simply due to a covariation in sexual and aggressive themes that is without necessary consequences for overt sexual or aggressive action. As may be remembered, elements of aggressiveness permeate sexual fantasies (cf. Byrne, 1977; Hariton & Singer, 1974); consequently, it should be no surprise to find such elements encroach into the stories produced by sexually stimulated persons.

The elusive affinity between sexual and aggressive drive has been further explored in a series of investigations conducted by Feshbach and his associates (cf. Malamuth, Feshbach, & Jaffe, 1977). In these investigations, aggressive actions and reactions in response to sexual stimulation were assessed in more behavioral terms.

Jaffe, Malamuth, Feingold, and Feshbach (1974) exposed unprovoked males and females to sexually arousing, erotic literature or to science-fiction readings devoid of sex and aggression. Subjects then performed a task in which they had to administer electric shock to another person in response to errors made by that person. Subjects were free to choose the intensity of the shock, and the choice of high intensities was viewed as reflective of punitive intentions and, therefore, as measuring aggressiveness.

Subjects exposed to the erotic materials considered themselves sexually aroused, and they construed their excitement as pleasant. Presumably because of this prevalence of positive affect in the experimental group, subjects in the control condition actually reported being more frustrated. Despite the latter, however, the evocation of sexual drive fostered increased punitive behavior. Following sexual stimulation, the intensity of shocks employed was found to be significantly higher than that exhibited in the control condition. This effect, moreover, proved robust in that it carried across variations in the gender of the subject, the experimenter, and the punished person.

A related investigation was conducted by Fisher and Harris (1976). Both males and females read erotic or nonerotic literature as part of an error-detection test and thereafter evaluated the research project. Sexually aroused subjects reported being more annoyed with the test than did control subjects. This increase in annoyance may, of course, result simply from the frustration created by distracting the subjects—through the signal-detection requirement—from potentially pleasant affective reactions to the erotic fare. Such an account does not apply to the earlier study by Jaffe et al. (1974), as subjects reported pleasant excitement after sexual stimulation. However, it is conceivable that the effects of both studies merely reflect the behavior energization of diffuse arousal that accrues to sexual excitement, not of specific sexual drive per se.

The results of an investigation by Jaffe (1974) have been interpreted (e.g., Malamuth et al., 1977) as evidence against the possibility that generalized drive, rather than specific sexual drive, is responsible for the observed facilitation of punitive behavior. The procedure employed in this investigation was essentially that of the study by Jaffe et al. described earlier. Unprovoked subjects were exposed to erotic or nonerotic materials and then engaged in a task requiring the administration of electric shock as punishment for errors, shock intensity being employed as a measure of punitiveness. Only males served as subjects this time. The critical, novel feature of the investigation was a time variation: Subjects performed the punishment task immediately after exposure to erotic or nonerotic stimuli, or they performed this task following a delay of about 15 minutes after exposure. It was argued that diffuse arousal from sexual stimulation would have dissipated in the delay condition; therefore, any facilitation of aggression that might be observed in this condition could not be ascribed to the action of such arousal.

Jaffe ascertained the arousal properties of two erotic and two nonerotic stimuli in a pretest. The erotic materials were a passage from erotic literature describing heterosexual intercourse and a film depicting a nude female in sexually provocative and seductive poses. The nonerotic materials were a film showing people shooting the rapids of the Colorado River and a film of scenic and historic places in Norway. Subjects reported themselves to be most aroused by the rapids film and least aroused by the Norway travelogue. Both erotic stimuli assumed intermediate positions on this measure. Arousal in response to the films was also assessed in blood pressure changes. On systolic blood pressure, the girlie film proved more arousing than the nonerotic stimuli; the latter stimuli did not appreciably differ from one another. Exposure to the individual stimuli in the main experiment did not produce reliable differences in punitive behavior either immediately following exposure or after the delay. However, when both erotica and both nonerotica conditions were pooled, exposure to erotica was found to produce a facilitation of punitiveness overall. The facilitative effect was most pronounced in the delay conditions. In contrast, it was minimal and unreliable immediately after exposure.

If it is assumed that diffuse arousal from exposure to erotica dissipated and arousal dropped to low levels in the delay condition, the findings indeed seem in conflict with a generalized-arousal explanation. Such an assumption is not necessarily reasonable, however. During the delay, it turns out, subjects solved (or attempted to solve) difficult choice dilemmas. The performance of tasks of this type is known to be arousing (e.g., Kahneman, Tursky, Shapiro, & Crider, 1969), and if it is assumed that these assignments maintained arousal of initially sexually stimulated men at high levels or even increased arousal levels, the findings are actually consistent with a generalized-arousal explanation. But be this as it may, the findings cannot be considered to refute the arousal explanation in any decisive way under these circumstances.

On the other hand, Jaffe's findings obviously are at variance with the view that specific sexual drive readily converts to aggressive drive and promotes punitiveness in a nonsexual context. Sexual drive, whether conceived of as a hypothetical motivational force or a uniquely sexual arousal state characterized by physical manifestations such as penile erection, must be assumed to have been at higher levels immediately after exposure to erotica than after the performance of distracting choice problems. Accordingly, punitive behavior should have been more pronounced immediately after exposure than following the intervening nonsensual activities.

Confronted with this dilemma, Feshbach and his associates (Feshbach & Malamuth, 1978; Malamuth et al., 1977) thought cognitive mechanics implicated and offered a new account for the presumed connection between sex and aggression. These investigators followed Freudian thought in proposing that human society tends to place strong taboos on the behavioral expression of many sexual and aggressive impulses, and they went on to suggest that the reduction or the removal of inhibitions concerning the one type of behavior will generalize to the other type of behavior, thereby facilitating the expression of the latter. According to Feshbach and Malamuth (1978): "Sexual arousal is not a stimulus for aggression [p. 114]," but increased aggression is expected to follow sexual stimulation because "a reduction in sexual inhibition will generalize to aggressive behavior where there are *common taboos affecting sex and aggression* [p. 114]." A reduction in aggressive inhibitions, due to frustration or provocation, analogously should generalize to sexual behavior and promote its expression.

Feshbach and his associates consider this reasoning to explain Jaffe's finding of delayed aggression-facilitation after sexual stimulation. Furthermore, these investigators reported additional observations (cf. Malamuth et al., 1977) that seem supportive of the proposed mutual disinhibition in sexual and aggressive behaviors.

Most to the point is an earlier study conducted by Feshbach, Malamuth, and Drapkin (1974). Male subjects first "loosened up" in a mock fight with soft bats and then performed the task in which electric shock had to be delivered in response to another person's apparent errors. Just prior to delivering shock, subjects were given disinhibiting, inhibiting, or no additional instructions. In the disinhibition condition, subjects were told that the use of high shock intensities is essential to the experiment and that they should not hesitate to choose such levels. Subjects in the inhibition condition, in contrast, were cautioned not to get carried away and act out personal hostility. Upon completion of the task, subjects read passages from erotic literature and thereafter rated their mood state on a checklist.

Subjects complied with the order to use high shock intensities. Intensity levels were reliably higher in this condition than in the other two. Compared to the no-instruction control, the caution to hold off personally hostile inclinations had no appreciable effect on the use of shock intensity, however. Sexual excitedness after exposure to the erotic materials, measured in the composite score of subjects' ratings of feeling "sensuous" and "sexually aroused," proved to be similarly differentiated. The highest scores were obtained in the disinhibition condition; the lowest in the inhibition condition. In the no-instruction control condition, the scores assumed an intermediate position and were not significantly different from those of the disinhibition or inhibition condition.

The study thus demonstrates that encouraging punitive behavior, as compared to discouraging it, can foster reports of increased sexual excitement in response to erotica. But is this effect due to mutual disinhibition? Did, as Feshbach and Malamuth (1978) have suggested, the subjects think something like: "Taboo behavior, like aggression, is okay. So I can drop the barriers to sex as well and let it all hang out." Or are there plausible alternative and possibly more parsimonious explanations?

An alternative account can be constructed, in fact, on the basis of the mechanism the study was designed to help discredit: generalized drive. If it is assumed that in the disinhibition condition subjects had misgivings about the delivery of intense electric shock that the procedure required and got irritated with the assignment, it can be argued that diffuse arousal from this experience facilitated the subsequent reaction to the erotica (cf. Tannenbaum & Zillmann, 1975). A more direct and parsimonious explanation is that the aggression-encouraging treatment relaxed the subjects' evaluation apprehensions, the aggression-discouraging treatment augmented them (cf. Rosenthal, 1966), and subjects were consequently freer or less free in reporting their private reactions of sexual excitedness. The observed difference in self-reported excitedness thus does not necessarily reflect an experiential difference, but simply may be the result of differential reporting of essentially identical reactions. It is conceivable, however, that the relaxation of apprehensions about being evaluated permitted more intense reactions to erotica and that the self-reports reflect differential responding as well as differential reporting.

The proposal that sex and aggression, because of their common taboo status, are mutually inhibitory is not only without acceptable support, but is severely challenged by a large number of experimental investigations in which effects opposite to expectations from this proposal have been reported. Feshbach and Malamuth (1978) themselves obtained contradictory findings. In one of their investigations, male subjects were exposed either to a film depicting a nude female in sexually provocative poses or to nonerotic materials. In the erotica condition, postexposure punitive behavior proved to be at a level signifcantly below that of the control condition. It was speculated that subjects may have been embarrassed in this study and that, hence, their aggressiveness was inhibited. This speculation does not apply to many other studies (e.g., Baron, 1974a; Zillmann, Bryant, Comisky, & Medoff, 1981), however, as subjects reported unperturbed, pleasant excitement after exposure to erotica.

Baron (cf. 1977) conducted a series of investigations in which sexually stimulating materials consistently were found to diminish aggressive behavior. In a first experiment (Baron, 1974a), male subjects were provoked by receiving from a confederate an arbitrarily high number of electric shocks in evaluation of their performance on a task. Other subjects were treated in a neutral manner. The subjects were then exposed to erotica or to bland, nonerotic materials. Photographs of nude females in sexually provocative poses, taken from girlie magazines, served as erotic stimuli. Photographs of scenery, furniture, and paintings constituted the control stimuli. After exposure, subjects were provided with an opportunity to administer electric shock to the confederate in response to errors made on a task. The intensity of these shocks served as the main measure of aggressiveness.

In provoked males, aggressiveness after exposure to erotica was found to be at significantly lower levels than after exposure to neutral materials. In unprovoked males, however, exposure had no appreciable effect. These findings were interpreted as showing a reduction of aggressiveness as the result of sexual enticement. Sexual drive apparently failed to mingle with and augment previously evoked aggressive drive. Stimulated sexual appetite, instead, proved incompatible with aggressive inclinations and antithetical to aggressive drive (cf. Bandura, 1973; Baron, 1977; Fromm, 1973).

In a very similar investigation (Baron, 1974b), photographs of large-bosomed females in tight sweaters and the like (so-called "cheesecake") were employed as stimuli in addition to the materials used earlier. Although the male subjects did not consider themselves sexually aroused by the seminudes, the aggression-modifying effect of exposure to these stimuli proved to parallel that of exposure to photographs of nudes in sexually provocative poses—exposure that, in contrast, was deemed sexually arousing. After exposure to either type of erotic material, punitive behavior was at a level significantly below that of the non-erotica control condition. This effect was observed in both provoked and unprovoked males. However, because no reliable effect on punitiveness of the provocation treatment was obtained, the effectiveness of that treatment—a derogatory evaluation—may be called into question.

Baron and Bell (1973) established that the aggression-diminishing effect of exposure to photographs of nude females is not specific to the gender of the victim. Unprovoked, sexually stimulated males, although altogether less punitive toward women than toward men, exhibited less punitiveness toward both males and females after exposure to such mild erotica than after exposure to neutral fare. Baron (1979), moreover, demonstrated that the effect of mild erotica on women parallels that on men. Female subjects were provoked or not provoked by a female confederate, exposed to photographs of seminude and nude males or to bland, nonerotic materials, and then provided with an opportunity to behave punitively toward the confederate. Exposure to the mild erotica was found to diminish aggressiveness in provoked females. In unprovoked females, however, it was of little consequence.

In a further investigation by Baron and Bell (1977), provoked and unprovoked male subjects were exposed to photographs of heterosexual intercourse as well as to the mildly erotic and nonerotic stimuli employed earlier. Exposure to photographs of coitus resulted in a sharp reduction of punitive behavior. This effect was independent of prior provocation. Exposure to photographs of seminude and nude females also reduced punitiveness, but less dramatically so. Prior provocation was again of little moment. Inasmuch as the effectiveness of the provocation treatment was documented in subjects' ratings of anger toward the confederate, the results suggest that the effects of erotica of the type employed are rather independent of initial feelings of annoyance and anger.

Other investigators have, generally speaking, corroborated Baron's findings of diminished aggressiveness after exposure to mild erotica (e.g., Ramirez, Bryant, & Zillmann, 1982). But some inconsistencies, especially in the findings concerning the role of prior instigation to aggression, have persisted.

Donnerstein, Donnerstein, and Evans (1975) conducted an investigation in which males were provoked through insult or not provoked, exposed to nonerotic stimuli, photographs of nude females in sexually provocative poses, or photographs of heterosexual intercourse, and then provided with an opportunity to behave punitively. Exposure to the various stimuli had no appreciable effect on the punitive behavior of unprovoked men. Provoked men behaved significantly more punitively after exposure to nonerotic fare and to the photographs of coitus. The difference between these two stimulus conditions proved negligible. In contrast, punitive behavior was at a markedly lower level after exposure to photographs of nude females. In fact, punitive behavior in this condition sank to the level of unprovoked men. Comparatively mild sexual titillation, then, was again found to reduce motivated aggressiveness.

Interestingly, Donnerstein et al. (1975) included in their study a condition in which subjects were first exposed to the erotic and nonerotic stimuli, provoked after exposure, and then provided with punitive opportunities. No reduction of punitiveness after exposure to erotic materials was observed under these conditions. After exposure to photographs of coitus, aggressiveness was actually enhanced.

The different findings resulting from the change in the sequence provocation/sexual stimulation/retaliation to the sequence sexual stimulation/provocation/retaliation further challenge a simple drive explanation. If sexual drive would readily mingle with aggressive drive, exposure to erotica should have facilitated aggressiveness regardless of the specific sequence of events. If anything, sexual titillation just prior to retaliation could have entered into aggression most directly and, hence, should have facilitated this behavior most strongly. The findings are, of course, inconsistent with such projections.

Donnerstein et al. attempted to explain the pattern of findings they had obtained by proposing that the aggression-mediating effect of exposure to erotica is a joined function of distraction from anger and diffuse arousal from sexual stimulation. The capacity for such distraction was assumed to be far superior for erotica than for nonerotica. Opposite-gender nudity was deemed capable of distracting while being rather nonarousing. Coital scenes were thought to produce stronger arousal reactions while being similarly distracting. Distraction effects were expected to manifest themselves most strongly in the condition in which exposure to erotica is interpolated between provocation and retaliation. Photographs of women in sexually provocative poses thus should distract from anger and thereby mitigate punitiveness more strongly when viewed after provocation. Moreover, according to this reasoning, the same effect of photographs of coitus is compromised by their being too arousing. Arousal is viewed as counteracting the distraction effect, leading to a negligible overall impact of exposure. In the sequence sexual stimulation/provocation/retaliation, arousal is less or not at all counteracted and thus can enhance aggressiveness.

Zillmann and Sapolsky (1977) tested this proposal and found it wanting. Specifically, the capacity to distract was determined empirically for the stimuli in question, and no appreciable differences in this capacity could be detected between the erotic and nonerotic materials that had been employed. Additionally, the erotic materials (i.e., photographs of nude females in sexually provocative poses and of heterosexual intercourse) proved similarly arousing—or more accurately, nonarousing. Effects of exposure to such erotica on aggressiveness thus cannot readily be attributed to distraction, arousal, or the joined operation of these variables.

The investigation by Zillmann and Sapolsky supported another explanation, instead. These investigators also assessed the hedonic valence of the various stimuli and observed that the expression of annoyance was significantly reduced by exposure to erotica that were perceived as very pleasant while being rather nonarousing. More specifically, provoked males expressed less annoyance about a mistreatment after exposure to pleasant erotica (both nudity and coital scenes) than after exposure to neutral, less pleasant fare. No corresponding reduction in punitive behavior was observed, however. Exposure to the erotica, furthermore, was without consequence for unprovoked men. Taken together, these findings suggest that sexual stimulation, when construed as pleasant and when not associated with marked arousal increases, can effectively intervene in acute states of annoyance and mitigate both the experience of annoyance and the hostile reactions motivated by it. Thus, sexual titillation, but not necessarily strong sexual instigation, seems antithetical to aggressive drive indeed.

Zillmann, Bryant, Comisky, and Medoff (1981) further implicated the hedonic valence of rather nonarousing erotica with the observed annoyance- and aggression-reducing effect. In their investigation, male subjects were provoked by a male confederate, exposed to a variety of stimuli or not exposed to stimuli, and provided with an opportunity to retaliate against their annoyer. In the context of a competitive task, subjects administered noxious noise to the confederate. Frequency and accumulated intensity of the noise served as measures of aggressive behavior.

In a pretest, the hedonic valence and the excitatory potential (sympathetic activity measured in peripheral manifestations) of erotic and nonerotic materials were assessed. Hedonically positive and negative erotica and nonerotica were distinguished. The materials were further subdivided into highly arousing and rather nonarousing stimuli. Finally, nonerotic stimuli were matched with erotic stimuli in terms of both hedonic and excitatory properties.

Erotica with positive hedonic valence and low excitatory potential, compared to erotica with negative hedonic valence and low excitatory potential and arousing erotica of either positive or negative valence, exhibited the aggression-reducing tendency (see also Zillmann, Bryant, & Carveth, 1981). This effect of positive hedonic valence was in evidence for highly arousing erotica as well. But perhaps most significantly, exposure to nonerotic stimuli that were hedonically and excitationally matched with the erotic stimuli produced effects that were virtually identical to those produced by the erotica.

These findings suggest that the aggression-reducing effect of exposure to genuinely pleasant but rather nonarousing erotic fare is due to their pleasantness, not to their sexual themes per se. Sexual themes may be predominantly pleasant, but they need not be, for whatever intrinsic or subjective reason. And when they are not, exposure to such themes is likely to annoy already annoyed persons further and thereby increase the propensity for hostile and aggressive action. This type of aggression-enhancement has been observed in several other recent investigations as well (e.g., Sapolsky & Zillmann, 1982; White, 1979; Zillmann, Bryant, & Carveth, 1981).

Clearly, if the observed aggression-reducing effect of exposure to pleasant but nonarousing erotica is due to their pleasantness rather than to their specific themes, the proposal that sexual drive is antithetical to aggressive drive cannot be considered directly supported. Only to the extent that positive affect liberated by exposure to pleasant erotica is deemed an integral part of sexual excitedness could the evidence at hand be construed as supportive of the view that sexual excitedness and aggressive drive are incompatible. Therefore, in building an accurate, predictive model of exposure effects, it would seem more productive to focus on hedonic valence as a stimulus condition that is potentially independent of sexual themes. After all, sexual and nonsexual pleasant stimuli proved equally effective in lowering the propensity for hostility and aggression (cf. Zillmann, Bryant, Comisky, & Medoff, 1981). *Hedonic incompatibility*, then, not an incompatibility between sexual and aggressive drives, explains the findings of reduced aggressiveness after sexual titillation.

Finally, an investigation by Jaffe (1974, 1981) provides strong evidence against a sex-aggression drive affinity. Unprovoked male subjects were exposed to the erotic and nonerotic stimuli described earlier in connection with Jaffe's first experiment of 1974 (i.e., a film of a nude female in seductive poses and written descriptions of intercourse serving as erotica; an adventure film and a travelogue serving as nonerotica). After exposure, subjects were placed in a supervisory role, giving feedback to a confederate for errors made on a task. Unlike in other procedures, however, subjects were not forced into an aggressive mode of responding by the requirement to administer electric shock to the other person, but were given a choice between behaving punitively or prosocially. Specifically, subjects could administer a shock for an error committed or, by pushing appropriate buttons on an apparatus, inform the confederate as to which response would have been the correct one to make. Under these novel conditions, the majority of subjects elected to behave prosocially over behaving punitively. Most importantly, however, the sexually stimulated subjects behaved significantly more prosocially than the control subjects. The stimulation of sexual appetite thus not only failed to promote an appetite for aggressive action, but actually dampened punitive and whetted prosocial inclinations. Needless to say, Jaffe's findings oppose with equal strength the proposal that any disinhibition of sexual drive generalizes to aggressive drive.

The experimental evidence concerning the effects of stimulating sexual appetite—without eliciting acute sexual needs associated with strongly increased activity in the sympathetic nervous system—in persons who have been instigated to aggression is impressively consistent. The investigations show, without exception, that exposure to mild erotica (e.g., opposite-gender nudes in seductive poses) diminishes annoyance and punitive inclinations in initially provoked persons. In sharp contrast, the effect of exposure to mild erotica on unprovoked persons is quite inconsistent. Reports of increased aggressiveness (Jaffe, 1974; Jaffe et al., 1974) are countered by reports of decreased aggressiveness (Baron, 1974b; Baron & Bell, 1973, 1977; Jaffe, 1974, 1981). In further studies, no appreciable effect emerged (Baron, 1974a, 1979; Donnerstein et al., 1975). It is conceivable that reading erotic passages embarrassed and annoyed some subjects and thereby fostered punitive inclinations. Other subjects may have had a hard time with the control stimuli (e.g., furniture, scenery) and suffered hostility-potentiating annoyance. Whatever the explanation for the discrepancy in these findings may be, in no way do they suggest that whetting an unperturbed person's sexual appetite will stir up aggressive urges in the sense of a desire to hurt and harm someone.

Up to this point I have dealt with the effects of what could be considered minor sexual stimulation. What about severe sexual instigation? What about the effects of exposure to highly arousing, "graphic" erotic fare, pleasant or unpleasant, on motivated and unmotivated aggressive behavior?

The effects of arousing stimuli, such as motion pictures that explicitly depict coital behavior in all imaginable variations, are dramatically different, indeed. Research findings concerning the immediate consequences of exposure to these more powerful erotica show with great consistency that: (1) punitive behavior of unprovoked persons is not appreciably altered; (2) hostile and aggressive retaliatory action of provoked persons is greatly facilitated (cf. Tannenbaum & Zillmann, 1975; Zillmann, 1979, 1983a). The former finding further challenges the contention that the evocation of sexual drive fosters aggressive inclinations. The latter finding, however, could be construed as supportive of the proclaimed affinity between sexual and aggressive drives. Sexual arousal, after all, appears to mix well with aggressive drive in facilitating aggressive reactions.

The research evidence alluded to is presented and scrutinized later (Chapter 6) in connection with a theoretical paradigm that projects specific mutual dependencies of sex- and aggression-linked arousal. Suffice it here to point out that the data, taken together, do not support a simple drive-affinity explanation and to discuss the findings that prove most damaging to such an explanation.

The investigation by Zillmann, Bryant, Comisky, and Medoff (1981) explored the effects of highly arousing materials in addition to those of the comparatively nonarousing stimuli already discussed. Analogous to the treatment of the nonarousing stimuli, the highly arousing materials were subdivided into those of positive valence and those of negative valence. Moreover, all erotic materials were again matched, both hedonically and excitationally, against nonerotic materials. Provoked males exhibited more aggressiveness after exposure to highly arousing erotica than after exposure to rather nonarousing erotica. They also exhibited more aggressiveness after exposure to unpleasant erotica than after exposure to pleasant erotica. Both the magnitude of excitatory reactions and the negativeness of affect facilitated motivated aggression, and they did so in an additive fashion. Most significantly, however, excitationally and hedonically matched nonerotica had effects that were virtually identical with those of the erotica. As can be seen from Fig. 5.1, the effects of all erotica and nonerotica were entirely parallel. Exposure to explicit coital scenes, for instance, had the same effect as exposure to equally exciting and equally pleasant scenes from a rock concert. And exposure to a film featuring bestiality had the same effect as exposure to an equally exciting and equally unpleasant film featuring an eye operation. The specific sexual theme thus was of little moment other than in producing pronounced excitatory reactions of positive or negative valence. It is the very fact, of course, that sexual stimulation can produce both positive and negative affect of varying intensities, affect which modifies hostile and aggres-

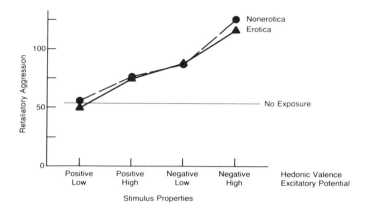

FIG. 5.1.   Parallelity of the effect of exposure to hedonically and excitationally matched erotica (triangles, solid lines) and nonerotica (circles, broken lines) on motivated aggressive behavior. Retaliatory aggression was measured in the delivery of noxious noise to the annoyer. Stimulus properties were determined in a pretest. Hedonic valence was ascertained through ratings; excitatory potential was measured in peripheral manifestations of sympathetic activity, such as increased blood pressure. (Adapted from Zillmann, Bryant, Comisky, & Medoff, 1981. Reprinted by permission of John Wiley & Sons.)

sive inclinations, that compromises the usefulness of the drive-affinity approach. Sexual drive evidently does not have a uniform effect on aggressive behavior, and the diversity of modifications that sexual stimulation can produce consequently cannot be accurately predicted from the mere fact of sexual stimulation.

The various findings concerning drive diffusion in humans may be summarized as follows:

1. Sexual stimulation does not generally facilitate aggressiveness, and instigation to aggression does not generally enhance sexual inclinations. Initial demonstrations of a drive affinity between sex and aggression seem artificial and unreliable, as they are bound to the use of projective techniques. Later efforts to establish the presumed affinity in more behavioral terms have failed to produce supportive evidence.

2. The view that an affinity between sexual and aggressive drives results from mutual disinhibition is not supported by the research findings at hand.

3. Exposure to sexual stimuli generally does not promote aggressiveness in persons who have not been aggressively instigated.

4. Exposure to pleasant and nonarousing sexual stimuli not only does not enhance, but consistently reduces, aggressive behavior in aggressively instigated persons. To the extent that exposure to such sexual stimuli is

considered to activate sexual drive and the instigation to aggression is deemed to activate aggressive drive, these findings constitute a major challenge to the proposal of drive diffusion in sex and aggression.

5. Exposure to highly arousing sexual stimuli (i.e., sexual stimuli that evoke strong reactions in the autonomic nervous system), in contrast, tends to facilitate aggressive behavior in aggressively instigated persons. However, this facilitation has been shown to be independent of the sexual theme as such. The diffusion of sexual and aggressive drives is thus ruled out as an explanatory mechanism for the facilitation of aggression through sexual stimulation.

III. MISATTRIBUTION IN ROMANTIC LOVE

Love has been characterized as a "tissue of paradoxes" (Finck, 1891, p. 244). In fact, early explorers of the phenomenon thought it to be so multifaceted and contradictory that it could not be comprehended in its entirety. Finck (1891), for instance, made this point in a peculiar way by asserting: "you may say almost anything about it you please [about love, that is], and it is likely to be correct [p. 244]." And one of the things he said about it—though through the words of Horwicz, a German contemporary of his—was that "love can only be excited by strong and vivid emotion, and it is almost immaterial whether these emotions are agreeable or disagreeable [p. 240]." Horwicz (quoted in Finck, 1891) had observed: "our aversion is most likely to be bestowed on individuals who, as the phrase goes, are neither 'warm' nor 'cold'; whereas impulsive, choleric people, though they may readily offend us, are just as capable of making us warmly attached to them [p. 240]." Negative emotions, it seemed to him, can enhance, if not incite, the positive emotion of love.

Freud (e.g., 1912/1943) similarly contended that aversive experiences associated with denial, frustration, and repression are prerequisites to romantic passions: "It takes an obstacle to drive the libido to great heights [p. 88; author's translation]." And he went on to assert that whenever in the history of humankind the thwarting of sexual satisfaction by natural barriers was insufficient, cultural barriers were erected in order for people to enjoy love. Without such barriers, he contended, love becomes worthless and life becomes empty. Fromm (1956), whose view on the matter has been discussed earlier, echoed both Finck's and Freud's contentions.

More recently, Walster and her associates (e.g., Berscheid & Walster, 1974; Walster, 1971; Walster & Berscheid, 1971; Walster & Walster, 1978) have promoted the idea that much negative affect may find its way into sexual attraction. In speaking of "passionate love," a romantic inclination defined as "unusually intense *liking* between two persons," Walster (1971) proposed the following:

Perhaps it does not really matter how one produces an agitated state in an individual. Stimuli that usually produce sexual arousal, gratitude, anxiety, guilt, loneliness, hatred, jealousy, or confusion may all increase one's physiological arousal, and thus increase the intensity of his emotional experience. As long as one attributes his agitated state to passion, he should experience true passionate love. As soon as he ceases to attribute his tumultuous feelings to passion, love should die [pp. 90–91].

It is contended, then, that intense romantic inclinations can be fueled by arousal from potentially any source. Negative affect, however, appears to be the dominant love enhancer. The listing of sources of arousal is biased in this direction. And so is the aggregation of illustrations by Walster and her associates (e.g., Walster & Walster, 1978). Although it is acknowledged that positive affect (e.g., feelings of gratitude) may on occasion foster unusually intense attraction, it is apparently considered much more likely that romantic passions are set into motion by frustration, rejection, mistreatment, and even humiliation. Anger and fear, it seems, are regarded as essential precursors of passionate love.

Obviously, Walster's suggestions are at variance with more conventional views of liking and loving (e.g., Byrne, 1971; Clore & Byrne, 1974; Homans, 1950; Newcomb, 1961; Rubin, 1974). These views project interpersonal and sexual attraction mainly on the basis of past experiences of gratification and aversion in the interaction with the liked or loved one. The more that gratifying experiences dominate over aversive ones, the greater is the attraction to the persons accountable for this mixture of past reactions. Romantic passions, in such a model, should arise from the dominance of exciting, gratifying sexual experiences over drab happenings, as well as from the expectation of further excitement and gratification occasioned by the experiences in question. These experiences should also give rise to intense romantic inclinations in encounters with strangers "who fit the bill"—that is, who are similar enough to known gratifiers to warrant the expectation of gratification. Even if the experience of passion and sexual gratification was with an imagined other only, a person who fits the bill might be encountered and stir up passionate sexual attraction because of the anticipation of great gratification—erroneous as this anticipation may be. But regardless of the specific formula one might choose to integrate the effects of gratification and aversion on the attraction to the apparent causal agent and regardless of the role one might assign to imagination and fantasy, as long as it is assumed that gratification and aversion have opposite effects on attraction, it cannot be predicted that aversive experiences will facilitate liking and loving.

The two approaches to love are actually less in conflict than might appear at first glance. Different forms of love have been distinguished, and the one or the other approach was deemed more applicable to certain forms and inappropriate for others. Walster and her associates (e.g., Walster & Walster, 1978), for instance, distinguished between "passionate" and "compassionate" love. They conceived of passionate love as a highly emotional state in which feelings of tenderness, pain, relief, anxiety, elation, jealousy, altruism, and sexuality are liberally confused. In contrast, they conceived of compassionate love as a friendly affection for and a deep attachment to the loved one. In this scheme of things, they readily accepted what I have called "conventional approaches" as explanations for compassionate love. For passionate love, however, they rejected these approaches as inadequate and thought their own model more appropriate.

I follow this distinction in disregarding the formation and maintenance of love of the compassionate variety and in concentrating on seemingly impulsive and irrational passions. The issue, then, is this: Can such passions, as contended, derive from and thrive on negative affect?

The two-component theory of passionate love (e.g., Berscheid & Walster, 1974) applies the two-factor theory of emotion (Schachter, 1964) to romantic inclinations in a most straightforward fashion. The generation of physiological arousal is considered the first step in the genesis of passionate love. Feedback from the arousal state is thought to occasion an epistemic search that results in the attribution of the state to an inducer. This process of causal attribution is referred to as "labeling," and this labeling is regarded as the critical second step in the genesis of passionate love (see Zillmann, 1978, for a detailed discussion of attributional processes thought to be involved).

In these terms, an example of passionate love proper would be a man's encounter with a superbly proportioned, scantily dressed young lady who prompts appreciable arousal increments that, once noticed, are labeled sexual attraction or passionate love. The theory was proposed chiefly to explain love paradoxes, however, because competing views can explain the intensification of sexual attraction through sexual arousal more parsimoniously (cf. Zillmann, 1978). As a result, the theory seems to project misconceptions in labeling as the rule rather than the exception. The misconceptions in question are, of course, erroneous causal attributions of arousal. For example, a male parachutist preparing for the jump might find himself strangely attracted to a nearby beautiful female parachutist. According to theory, he should have been unaware of the fact that he was aroused because of fear, and he should have thought himself excited by his female colleague. Analogously, a woman who has been belittled and insulted by a man she just met is considered capable of misattributing her arousal reaction to the mistreatment as being actually induced by the male as an object of affection, and if the arousal reaction is strong enough to make her wonder, it might be expected that she falls in passionate love with him.

Careful inspection of these illustrations ought to make it clear that Walster's (e.g., 1971) proposal is far less sweeping than it appears. It may well be that arousal from any source is capable of facilitating passionate love, as claimed, but the conditions under which such possible facilitation can occur appear to be very limited. The crux of the proposition is that passionate love is said to depend on the attribution of an agitated state to the loved one as the source. If the loved one *is* the source, and especially if alternative sources are not apparent, such attribution—and, for that matter, passionate love—is likely. On the other hand, in view of the fact that more parsimonious theoretical explanations are available for these situations, this condition does not require or justify the application of the two-component theory of passionate love. Yet where the theory would be useful, there seem to be problems. For instance, if a person *is not* the actual source of an agitated state, if sources other than this person are plausible, and perhaps most importantly, if in the agitated individual's mind this person is an unlikely source, it is difficult to see how anyone could misconstrue an agitated state and fall passionately in love because of fear, anger, or any other negative emotion. If the attribution of arousal is critically involved in passionate love at all, gross attributional errors seem extremely unlikely indeed. It appears, then, that paradoxical passionate love is restricted to attributional conditions of the following sort: (1) the loved one must be a credible source of an agitated state that can be construed as due to attraction, particularly to sexual attraction; (2) the actual source of the agitated state must be vague and go unrecognized; (3) the loved one must be the most plausible source of all possible sources of the agitated state.

The genesis of passionate love thus seems to depend in large measure on the immediate presence of a person who is deemed lovable for reasons other than arousal from ulterior sources. Furthermore, the mere facilitation of passionate love by arousal from such ulterior sources seems to favor minute and, at best, moderate arousal reactions that are unlikely to enhance any passions greatly, as strong arousal reactions tend to be recognized as caused by their actual sources and therefore cannot readily be misconstrued as reflective of romantic passions.

The requirement that the potential object for passionate love be attractive in the first place and that sexuality be salient in this attraction invites alternative explanations to romantic passions of the paradoxical variety. An aggressively abused woman, for example, may continue to love her abusive partner passionately—even love him more intensely than before—not so much because the abuse fosters love-enhancing arousal, but because the pains suffered seem bearable in view of gratifications that the relationship regularly provides and also because of compensatory actions that often follow abusive outbursts. What appears to be paradoxical love thus may not be all that paradoxical and, hence, not demand extraordinary explanations. However, the fact remains that a wealth of anecdotal evidence (e.g., Walster & Walster, 1978) suggests that passionate love can be utterly irrational in the sense that aversions of seemingly any kind are converted into sexual longing and that arousal is the critical driving force. But the two-component theory of passionate love is not based on anecdotal evidence alone. It has, in fact, generated a flurry of experimental investigations. I discuss the representative research now in order to determine to what extent romantic inclinations have been shown to be paradoxical in origin and/or intensity and to what extent the paradox is a paradox.

There is, first of all, some correlational evidence in support of the view that romantic love benefits from barriers and frustrations. Driscoll, Davis, and Lipetz (1972) observed a positive relationship between the extent of parental interference and the reported depth of romantic bonds that were formed despite this interference. The relationship is limited to unmarried dating couples, however. Parental interference is of little moment to romantic attraction in married couples, especially when the hostilities develop during the marriage.

This ''Romeo and Juliet'' effect of romantic love in youngsters with denying parents has been ascribed to frustration-induced autonomic arousal (cf. Kenrick & Cialdini, 1977), but direct assessments of such arousal mediation are not available. Surely, parental interference may constitute a stress condition that prompts increased adrenocortical activity for some time. Together with occasional bursts of adrenomedullary action, these hormonal changes may indeed elevate levels of autonomic arousal and thereby intensify emotional reactions of liking and loving. It is unclear, however, how arousal could be maintained at high levels for extended periods of time. Eventually, in the so-called resistance stage of the general adaptation syndrome (Selye, 1976), arousal must return to normal levels, and to the extent that romantic love depends on high levels of arousal, love should die. It seems unlikely that the high-arousal exhaustion stage of the syndrome, a stage associated with severe bodily illness, is ever reached by loving couples, as prolonged parental hostilities seem without consequence for love in married couples.

In view of all these possible and likely arousal changes over the time course of a romantic relationship, it would appear that a general reference to ''autonomic arousal'' as an explanatory mechanism does not do justice to the complexity of the situation. In particular, the supposition that arousal levels, once elevated by frustration, will remain elevated for indefinite periods of time—and enhance romantic love during that time—is at variance with the physiological facts. There must be ups and downs in arousal during romantic attachments. And if unusually intense liking were a simple function of level of arousal, as Walster implied (e.g., 1971), such liking should exhibit corresponding ups and downs. Romantic love is generally presumed to be more stable than that, however.

Regardless of these conceptual and factual difficulties with the arousal-love relationship, the observed correlation between parental interference and romantic love does not implicate the proposed mediating function of arousal in any acceptable way, because heightened arousal was assumed rather than empirically ascertained. Moreover, the finding can be alternatively explained in a more parsimonious fashion. It can be argued, for instance, that young persons who pursue an attractive partner despite parental harassment may come to overestimate their feelings of being attracted to their partner because they obviously are willing to put up with considerable torment to get what they desire. The investment of unusual efforts should convince these persons of unusually intense liking (Bem,

1972; Festinger, 1957, 1964). It is also conceivable that parents, through their opposition to a relationship, make themselves "the enemy" to be fought by the couple in love. The need to join forces in a common cause and the shared experience of resistance and defiance should foster feelings of closeness in which passions can flourish.

In the initial experimental research, arousal remained a rather nonspecific hypothetical construct, and the involvement of arousal in romantic love remained quite uncertain as a result. Stephan, Berscheid, and Walster (1971) conducted an investigation in which male undergraduates were exposed to materials considered sexually arousing or not arousing. They were then made to evaluate the photograph of a pretty blond female student who had described herself as active, fairly intelligent, easygoing, and moderately liberal. Prior to this evaluation, subjects were either assigned a date with her or led to believe that they would never meet her. It was found that subjects who had read about an amorous seduction and who considered themselves to be somewhat desirous of engaging in sexual behavior, compared against subjects who had read about reproduction in herring gulls and who reported little sexual enticement, deemed the female significantly more attractive, regardless of whether or not they would meet her. Accessibility proved critical, however, for the perception of sexual receptivity. Sexually enticed men found only the accessible girl more receptive (i.e., more amorous, uninhibited, promiscuous, etc.) than did men in a neutral state. When the girl was inaccessible, she was actually deemed less receptive by men with acute sexual interest than by more disinterested men.

The investigation thus shows that exposure to erotic materials can enhance the attractiveness of a viable and potentially accessible sexual partner. It remains unclear, however, whether this enhancement is due to increased arousal or simply results from the salience of seducing and lovemaking in the "arousal" condition. It can be argued, for instance, that the subjects who read about seduction still had "seduction" on their mind as they evaluated their date and that this cognitive preoccupation colored their perception of the female student (cf. Wyer & Srull, 1980a, 1980b).

The possible facilitation of heterosexual attraction through preceding negative emotional states was explored in a much cited unpublished investigation by Brehm, Gatz, Goethals, McCrimmon, and Ward (1967) (e.g., Kenrick & Cialdini, 1977; Walster, 1971). Male subjects either were led to expect the reception of a series of rather strong electric shocks, were led to expect the shock treatment but were then informed that they had been erroneously assigned to the shock condition, or were not led to expect the reception of shocks. After the fear, fear-relief, or control treatment was administered, they met with a female confederate and reported the extent to which they felt attracted to her. Attraction was found to be higher in the fear and fear-relief conditions than in the control condition. Relief was of no consequence, however, as attraction did not appreciably differ in the fear conditions. Although arousal was not measured, Brehm et al. interpreted these findings as supportive of the view that arousal from negative affect enhances the positive affective reaction of liking.

Dutton and Aron (1974) pursued the fear-attraction relationship further in a most imaginative series of studies. In a field experiment, unaccompanied males crossing one of two bridges in Vancouver, British Columbia, were approached by an attractive female experimenter and asked to fill in a questionnaire. One bridge was a narrow suspension bridge across a deep canyon with roaring rapids. Dutton and Aron (1974) described it as having "a tendency to tilt, sway, and wobble, creating the impression that one is about to fall over the side [p. 511]." The other bridge was a solid wooden one of low build, crossing the quiet waters of a tributary of the main river. Passage of the suspension bridge was considered to evoke fear; passage of the solid one no such reaction. The questionnaire to be completed by the subject was a Thematic Apperception Test on which sexual imagery could be assessed, a procedure adopted from Barclay's work (e.g., Barclay & Haber, 1965) which has been discussed earlier. Upon completion of the test, the experimenter gave her name and phone number to the subject and invited him to call if he wanted to talk to her further. A male served as the experimenter in a control condition, making the same requests as his female counterpart.

The Thematic Apperception Test, when taken in the presence of the attractive female experimenter, indicated more pronounced sexual imagery for subjects on the suspension bridge than for subjects on the solid one. Moreover, a significantly greater portion of men interviewed on the suspension bridge later phoned the experimenter, compared to men interviewed on firmer grounds. When the test was taken in the presence of the male experimenter, however, the bridges failed to influence sexual imagery or later calls.

Dutton and Aron thought they provided evidence for a linkage between anxiety and sexual attraction, but they also considered alternative accounts. One of them was the possibility that the bridges might attract different populations. The suspension bridge, they speculated, might have attracted a disproportionally large number of thrill seekers, whose greater sexual expressiveness and willingness to try their luck with a woman whom they encountered only briefly might account for the findings.

The entire selectivity issue was consequently avoided in a follow-up study. Subjects were approached on the suspension bridge as before or they were approached 10 minutes after crossing this bridge, at some distance from it, where any arousal reaction from fear, from elation, or from both presumably had dissipated. The findings of the initial study were fully replicated under these conditions.

Still, Dutton and Aron speculated that the female interviewer at the suspension bridge might have been perceived as especially helpless and frightened and that the enhancement of attraction might be a sympathy response to "a lady in distress.'' This kind of argument motivated a third and final study: a laboratory experiment in which the lady's apparent distress was manipulated. Male subjects were led to expect painful or weak electric shocks. They were further led to believe that an attractive female cosubject, actually a confederate, also would receive painful or weak shocks. While apprehensive about the shocks, subjects completed the Thematic Apperception Test ascertaining sexual imagery. In addition, they rated how much they would like to ask the pretty confederate out for a date and how much they would like to kiss her. The combined scores served as a measure of sexual attraction.

Subjects who presumably were in acute fear because of the threat of painful stimulation exhibited more sexual imagery and increased sexual attraction to the female confederate than did less apprehensive subjects. This effect was independent of whether or not the female was believed to be in distress. The distress treatment was without consequence altogether. Again, the findings are consistent with an arousal explanation. For lack of direct measurement, they do not convincingly implicate arousal with a mediating function, however.

Kenrick and Cialdini (1977) have taken issue with the research that purports to have established a link between anxiety and romantic love via the relabeling of aversive arousal. They concede that, on occasion, such arousal may be associated with amorous passions but argue that, more characteristically, romantic love is intensified because arousal is reduced rather than increased in the interaction with a loved one. Drive *reduction,* they feel, should be rewarding and should strengthen affective bonds. In this view, it is not the excitedness of sexual desire or the ecstasy of sexual action but the tranquility after the storm that fosters attraction. And if the excitement is of an aversive sort, it is the escape from it that fosters attraction—especially when this escape is accomplished through joint action. Fighting a common cause successfully should convert turmoil into serenity and thus forge love. But simply seeing turmoil come to an end seems to suffice as a condition in which love can prosper. Kenrick and Cialdini use the proverbial lovers' quarrel as an illustration: Making up after the experience of acutely aversive arousal tends to provide much satisfaction and usually enhances mutual affection greatly.

Applied to the enhancement of attraction through fear specifically, the argument runs as follows: The acutely fearful person finds comfort in the presence of an attractive other (cf. Schachter, 1959); the aversive excitedness construed as fear diminishes; and this negative reinforcement fosters and facilitates attraction to the instrumental other. In short, gains in liking come from the dissipation of aversive arousal, not from increases.

The tendency to seek comfort in affiliating with others under conditions of noxious excitedness is not in doubt (e.g., Mills & Mintz, 1972). And in view of the fact that arousal was not measured in the research under consideration and indeed may have dropped in the presence of pleasant company, Kenrick and Cialdini's alternative explanation to the findings of Brehm et al. and Dutton and

Aron cannot readily be dismissed. (It could be argued, of course, that in the Dutton and Aron study negative reinforcement should have promoted attraction to the male confederate as well as to the female. Why did the male fail to function as a source of comfort? Possibly because he was less pleasant in his appearance and manners than the female. The fact that more than two-thirds of the men that were approached at the bridges agreed to be interviewed by the female experimenter, whereas less than half of them elected to cooperate with the male, supports this speculation.)

The contention that romantic love grows on mislabeled noxious arousal confronts further difficulties. In a series of studies designed to clarify attributional processes presumed to create the phenomenon in question, Kenrick, Cialdini, and Linder (1979) failed to replicate the earlier findings. More specifically, these investigators employed variations of the design and the laboratory procedure devised by Dutton and Aron. Distracting tones replaced mild electric shocks in some instances, and the female interactant was an assistant rather than a fellow subject in one of the studies. Four experiments were conducted, all with male subjects. The later experiments replicated the procedures used by Dutton and Aron more closely than the earlier ones. In addition to assessing attraction, however, causal attributions of excitement and relaxation to the female companion and to the experimental situation were recorded in all studies.

Consistent across all experiments, Kenrick et al. failed to obtain any fear enhancement of attraction. The threat of painful electric shocks did not lead to ratings of increased attraction or to a heightened desire to date or kiss the attractive female confederate. Equally consistent across the experiments, subjects attributed their excitedness (or the lack of calmness) to the experimental circumstances—the threat of shock, in particular—and not to the presence of the female companion. Subjects, then, failed to misconstrue the sources of their arousal states, and love enhancements could not materialize because of attributional misconceptions. Kenrick et al. (1979) conclude that "arousal produced by unambiguous threatening stimuli is unlikely to be mislabelled as attraction [p. 332]." The findings thus not only compromise earlier demonstrations of love enhancement through fear, but undermine Walster's theory of passionate love by challenging the proposal that excitement from aversive stimulation can readily be dissociated from its source and misconstrued as loving passion.

Not all research efforts resulted in failures to replicate, however. Dienstbier (1979) has employed a novel procedure and succeeded, for the most part, in demonstrating that aversive arousal can foster increased liking. Subjects were seated in a dentist's chair, blindfolded, and moved about, ostensibly as part of a test of vestibular and balance functions. In the arousal condition, a startle reaction was elicited by a sudden backward tilt of the chair and exposure to loud noise during the tilt. Male subjects interacted with an attractive female experimenter in a first study. The subjects evaluated the experiment and rated both the appearance of the experimenter and their attraction to her. Both appearance and attraction were found to be higher in the arousal condition than in the control condition.

In an effort to discredit the reinforcement interpretation of this effect, Dienstbier conducted a follow-up study with a male experimenter. Arousal failed to alter ratings of appearance, but it affected liking. The male subjects liked the male experimenter less, rather than more, after startle than after the nonarousing treatment. Dienstbier interpreted this finding as evidence against the reinforcement account of passionate love. But could it not be argued that disturbed men have learned to reject being comforted by other men, and rather express hostility toward men associated with their malaise? Less liking may simply reflect greater annoyance. Women, in contrast, are less appropriate targets for hostile reactions, according to prevailing social norms, and thus are more readily accepted as comforting agents.

Dienstbier, in a third study, expanded the research on love enhancement through aversive arousal to females as respondents. Female subjects interacted with an attractive male experimenter and rated his appearance and their attraction to him. Startle-induced arousal enhanced the man's appearance, but it failed to make the women like him more.

In a fourth study, the reverse pattern was obtained for male subjects. Aroused men found themselves more attracted to a pretty woman than nonaroused men, but failed to consider her appearance superior. This study entailed a placebo-misattribution condition, but the variation was of no consequence. A fifth study employed a similar manipulation and failed altogether to produce significant results.

In a sixth and final investigation, Dienstbier employed in the laboratory setting the time variation of Dutton and Aron's second bridge study. A 10-minute rest period either preceded or followed the startle treatment. Males served as subjects, and attraction to a pretty female experimenter was assessed either immediately after the startle treatment or immediately after the rest period that followed the startle treatment. Arousal was expected to enhance attraction in the former condition only; in the latter, it was presumed to have dissipated. As expected, the female was deemed prettier by men who had been startled recently than by men who had rested for a while. The time variation had no appreciable effect on liking, however.

Dienstbier interpreted these findings as evidence against Kenrick and Cialdini's reinforcement explanation of romantic love. Obviously, if the dissipation of noxious arousal is crucial in the formation of affective bonds, attraction should, if anything, have grown in the rest period. Such an interpretation seems unwarranted, however, as the experimental procedure was biased against the facilitation of love by relief. During the rest period, the blindfolded subject was left alone in the laboratory and exposed to calming music. Any relief that may have been experienced thus was likely to be associated with the music, because the music was the only obtrusive stimulus condition accompanying relief. Had the pretty experimenter been present and visible during the recovery period, a reinforcement effect would have been given a better chance to manifest itself.

Taken together, the findings presented by Dienstbier, although not entirely consistent, lend further support to the proposal that noxious arousal is capable of facilitating attraction to attractive others. They do not implicate a specific mechanism with such a facilitative effect, however. In particular, and notwithstanding claims to the contrary, they do not rule out the possibility that it is the experience of relief from noxious arousal that makes the heart grow fonder.

A recent investigation by White, Fishbein, and Rutstein (1981) not only produced more consistent findings than the earlier research, but also provides stronger data against the relief explanation of love. In a first experiment, strenuous physical exercise was used to arouse male subjects. Nonstrenuous exercise was employed in the control condition. Arousal was assessed in self-reports and in increased heart rate. Exertion did not affect mood, however. Arousal thus may be considered to have been neither aversive nor pleasant. Subjects then were exposed to a video-taped self-disclosure statement by a female they thought they would meet later. The female was either attractive or unattractive. Following exposure, the subjects evaluated various traits of the female, judged her appearance, and recorded their feelings of being attracted to her. These feelings were measured in the combined ratings of physical attractiveness, sexiness, and the desire to date and kiss her.

Exertion-induced arousal was found to enhance the desirability of the attractive female generally. Aroused men considered her to be of superior character and appearance, and they thought themselves more attracted to her than did nonaroused men. With equal consistency, however, such arousal proved detrimental to the desirability of the unattractive female. Aroused men judged the unattractive women to be inferior in character and appearance, and they thought themselves less attracted to her than did nonaroused men. The effect of arousal, then, was a function of a person's initial, "intrinsic" attractiveness. It was in opposite directions and equally strongly so. Arousal enhanced the appeal of the pretty girl as much as it impaired the appeal of the homely one.

White et al. conducted a second experiment in which arousal derived from a noxious or a pleasant state. Male subjects either heard a grisly account of a mob killing and a mutilation, selections from the album of a popular comedian, or a description of the circulatory system in frogs (control condition). A pretest showed reactions to the violence to be negative, to the comedy to be positive, and to the biological item to be neutral, hedonically speaking. It also showed both affect-inducing materials to be more arousing than the neutral fare. Arousal was measured in increased heart rate as well as in self-reports. Attractiveness of the female was varied as before. The assessment of traits, appearance, and appeal was likewise taken from the first study.

The findings show the effects of arousal from a noxious experience and from a pleasant one to be entirely parallel. Relative to the no-arousal control condition, both arousal treatments enhanced valued traits, physical appearance, and sexual appeal of the pretty girl; they had the opposite effect of comparable strength for the homely one. Thus, the findings fully replicate the earlier ones and expand the effect of arousal from a neutral source to arousal from negative and positive affect. They document once again that the facilitation of romantic inclinations through arousal from ulterior sources presupposes a lovable target person and that, if the target person is repulsive, repulsion rather than attraction is likely to be enhanced. More importantly, however, the data of the second study by White et al. furnished compelling evidence against the love-by-relief argument. The parallelism of the effect of arousal from hedonically opposite experiences constitutes the damaging finding. Obviously, the opportunity for the enhancement of the appeal of an attractive person through relief from aversion is provided only in the negative-affect condition. Such enhancement should not have occurred after exposure to comedy, as there was no occasion for relief. The fact that it did occur implicates increased sympathetic activity with a mediating function instead.

The dependence of attraction-facilitating effects of arousal on "intrinsic" appeal is further evident from studies on the consequences of sexual excitedness. Even sexual arousal, it turns out, does not necessarily make unattractive persons of the opposite sex more desirable. To the contrary, it makes them less appealing.

In an investigation by Istvan, Griffitt, and Weidner (1982), male subjects were sexually aroused by exposure to visual depictions of heterosexual activities or were exposed to nonarousing, neutral fare. They then evaluated the appeal of attractive and unattractive females. Analogous to arousal from nonsexual sources, sexual arousal enhanced the sexual appeal of pretty girls but impaired that of homely ones. A parallel investigation with female subjects yielded the same pattern of results. Sexually aroused women detected greater sexual appeal in handsome men and less in unattractive ones than did nonaroused women.

The fact that interpersonal attraction and sexual appeal are critically controlled by cognitive processes that are not inspired by arousal states is also attested to by contrast effects on judgments of appeal. Carducci and Cozby (1974), for instance, observed that sexually aroused males found rather attractive female students less appealing than nonaroused males did. Because this was counter to the earlier findings by Stephan et al., (1971), procedural differences were held accountable for the failure to replicate. Specifically, it was speculated that, because sexual arousal was induced by visual stimuli that featured highly attractive women, the female students were perceived as less attractive than they otherwise would have been—even as unattractive by virtue of contrast. Carducci, Cozby, and Ward (1978) subjected this possibility to systematic testing by varying the attractiveness of a female to whom the subjects were exposed during the sexually arousing and nonarousing treatments, as well as the attractiveness of the female the subjects were to evaluate. Sexual arousal consistently facilitated the appeal of girls of average appearance when they were presented after exposure to girls of similarly average looks. Sexual arousal likewise enhanced the appeal of highly attractive girls that were presented after exposure to equally attractive girls. When girls of average looks were evaluated after exposure to very pretty girls, however, sexual arousal consistently prompted a decline in attraction. But inexplicably, arousal fostered a similar decline in the attraction of pretty girls when their evaluation followed exposure to girls of average appeal. The contrast reasoning, then, is only supported in part, and it appears to be the switching of women from one beauty standard to another that is not conducive to sexually aroused men's imagination and dependent verdicts of sexiness. Whatever the proper explanation of all these observations may be, the findings further document how fragile the arousal facilitation of interpersonal attraction is, and how strongly it depends on appropriate cognitive preconditions.

In summing up, it can be said that the research on interpersonal attraction and sexual appeal does not support the view that arousal from ulterior sources generally creates or enhances attraction to persons encountered. Such arousal, instead, tends to facilitate attraction only to persons deemed attractive initially and only if the source of extraneous arousal is not apparent. Analogously, such arousal tends to reduce the appeal of initially disfavored persons. The findings thus confirm an old truism: Looks are everything! Romantic love and passions, it seems, are not likely to be sparked or fueled by unrelated excitedness if the encountered person's looks aren't right. Descriptive accounts of falling in love—or of getting romantically involved—corroborate the significance of the physical appearance of the loved one in the initial, usually incidental, encounter (e.g., Averill & Boothroyd, 1977).

Perhaps the most intriguing suggestion in Walster's theory of passionate love is that arousal from aversion can spur romantic passions. What is the status of the evidence on that count? As evident from the preceding review, most laboratory or field procedures employed fear as the arousal-inducing aversion. Most of the demonstrations of increased attraction through "aversive arousal" consequently were vulnerable to the love-by-relief explanation. Evidence against the latter account comes from one study only (White et al., 1981). In this study, arousal derived from empathic distress (and in a critical, parallel condition, from gaiety). The investigations that employed the startle procedure (Dienstbier, 1979) to arouse subjects may have come closest to annoying and provoking people, but there is no evidence that reactions of this kind occurred. The research, then, has failed to simulate and employ arousing aversions that hold a central position in Walster's theory of passionate love: acute conflict, frustration, anger, and rage. As a result, nothing—beyond the commonplace— is known about the proposed effects of quarrels on love and lovemaking. The conditions under which a couple's fighting leads to further fighting, to irreconcilable dispositions, and to separation, or to resolution, feelings of greater closeness, and bursts of romantic passions instead remain to be uncovered. Meanwhile, it must be considered daring, if not reckless, to project that when bewildering excitement from potentially any source befalls someone, it is likely to be misconstrued as romantic love for someone in the vicinity.

6 The Excitation-Transfer Connection

A paradigm for the transfer of elements of sexual excitedness into aggressive behavior and, conversely, of elements of excitedness associated with annoyance, anger, and aggressiveness into sexual behavior is developed in this chapter. Research pertinent to the paradigm is then presented. After the review of numerous demonstrations of excitation transfer from sexual arousal states into aggressive actions, the scarce reliable data on transfer from aggression into sexual activities are discussed. Finally, much attention is given to excitatory habituation to nontactile sexual stimuli and its consequences for sex-aggression linkages. Sexual hyper- and hyporesponsiveness to such stimuli, primarily visual stimuli, is considered, and conditions under which hyporesponsiveness—through the involvement of stimulation associated with aggression—converts into adequate responsiveness, if not into hyperresponsiveness, are detailed. The consequences of the involvement of pain in sexual endeavors receive special consideration.

I. THE TRANSFER PARADIGM

The excitation-transfer paradigm is the application of the three-factor theory of emotion (Zillmann, 1978, 1979) to potentially unrelated successive emotional reactions and to emotional reactions elicited by simultaneously present, yet potentially unrelated, stimuli. In the former case, the paradigm projects the intensification of any emotional reaction that is evoked during the presence of residual sympathetic excitation from antecedent reactions—with some specifiable exceptions. In the latter, it projects the intensification of any emotional reaction by sympathetic excitation due to stimuli other than those that elicited the emotional

147

reaction proper. The paradigm is applicable to all emotional reactions associated with sympathetic dominance in their excitatory component. In this outline of the paradigm, however, attention is focused on sexual, aggressive, and sexual-aggressive human behavior. I first present the essentials of three-factor theory, then some of the assumptions on which the transfer paradigm is founded, and finally the paradigm as it applies to sex-aggression connections.

Three-factor theory distinguishes between the dispositional, excitatory, and experiential components of emotional behavior:

The *dispositional* component is conceived of as a response-guiding mechanism, with motoric reactions largely under stimulus and reinforcement control. The initial skeletal-motor behavior associated with emotions is thus seen as a direct response to emotion-inducing stimuli that can be made without the considerable latency characteristic of complex cognitive mediation.

The *excitatory* component is conceived of as a response-energizing mechanism. Excitatory reactions, analogous to skeletal-motor reactions, are also assumed to be largely under stimulus and reinforcement control, again without the necessary involvement of complex cognitive mediation. In accordance with Cannon's (1929) proposal of the "emergency" nature of emotional behavior, the excitatory reaction associated with emotional states is viewed as heightened activity in the sympathetic nervous system, primarily, that prepares the organism for the temporary engagement in vigorous action such as that needed for fight or flight. Sexual excitedness is viewed analogously as an emergency reaction that prepares the organism for vigorous action. The provision of energy for vigorous skeletal-motor behavior can be seen as motivating the organism to perform such behavior. It is not assumed, however, that any impulsion to act vigorously has specific appetitive properties. This is to say that, unlike in deprivation-based behaviors (e.g., hunger and thirst), the excitatory emergency reaction per se is impartial to specific emotions and relies on independent means for response guidance.

The *experiential* component of emotional behavior is conceptualized as the conscious experience of the skeletal-motor and/or the excitatory reaction to a stimulus condition. It is thus assumed that exteroceptive and/or interoceptive information about any facet of an immediate emotional reaction may reach the awareness level, enabling the individual to appraise the precipitating and experiential circumstances. Such continual monitoring allows the individual to assess the utility and appropriateness of emotional reactions and actions and, within limits, to modify and correct behavioral efforts. The experiential component of emotions, then, is viewed as a corrective that can substantially alter unfolding emotional behavior. It may be considered a cognitive means of influence capable of overriding the more archaic, basic mechanics of stimulus and reinforcement control.

Applied to emotional reactions in succession and those in response to complex stimulus conditions, three-factor theory projects excitatory reactions that are unlearned (e.g., responses to pain or to tactile stimulation of genital regions) or learned (e.g., responses to stimuli signaling the forthcoming experience of pain, responses to stimuli triggering the anticipation of pleasurable stimulation, responses to sexual fetishes). However, although the initial reactions, especially their magnitude, are assumed to elude voluntary control, the dissipation of excitation or the maintenance of high levels of excitation, respectively, may be greatly influenced by appraisal and monitoring. Analogously, initial skeletal-motor reactions, including reactions in the facial muscles, are unlearned or learned. As such reactions are being monitored, however, they are likely to be modified or inhibited. Because skeletal-motor activities are largely under voluntary control, the inhibition of incipient responses may be complete and comparatively fast. Taken together, the organism seems capable of rapid adjustment to stimulus changes only with regard to skeletal-motor behavior. Excitatory adjustment, in contrast, is rather inefficient and tends to be incomplete for extended periods of time. This imperfection of excitatory adjustment constitutes the basis of transfer theory: Residues of excitation from a preceding emotional reaction enter into and intensify (i.e., are *transferred* into) a subsequent state that is the result of appropriate dispositional and experiential assimilation of a change in the stimulus condition. Analogously, elements of excitation from stimulation other than the concurrent stimulation that produces specific emotional reactions will enter into and intensify (i.e., are transferred into) these reactions.

The assumptions underlying the transfer paradigm, along with the research evidence pertaining to them, have been discussed in considerable detail elsewhere (Zillmann, 1983b). Suffice it here to consider in brief only those that apply most directly to excitation transfer from sexual to aggressive and from aggressive to sexual behavior.

1. The excitatory activity of emotions that are characterized by sympathetic dominance in the autonomic nervous system is largely nonspecific.

Across these so-called "active emotions" (Leventhal, 1979), there is considerable redundancy in the pattern of excitatory reactions. It is, obviously, the sympathetic component itself that is responsible for much of this redundancy. The nonspecificity thus might be more appropriately referred to as "sympathetic commonality."

Sympathetic commonality in sexual and aggressive behaviors has been detailed already. Its neurophysiological foundation has been presented in Section II of Chapter 3 under the heading "Autonomic Commonalities." Its endocrinological basis, especially that regarding adrenomedullary functioning, has been developed in Section IV of Chapter 4 under "Commonalities in Adrenal Activity." There can be no doubt, according to the various physiological mechanisms that were discussed, that both sexual and aggressive behaviors share sympathetic excitedness. Both types of behavior, as should be recalled, are characterized by markedly elevated levels of sympathetic excitation—excitation assumed to be impartial in its energization of sexual, aggressive, and sexual-aggressive behaviors.

A significant aspect of sympathetic commonality and its behavioral consequences is its independence from the hedonic quality of the emotional experiences involved. Counter to earlier contentions in which hedonically negative emotions were thought to be accompanied by a general decrease in physiological functioning (e.g., Wenger, Jones, & Jones, 1956), hedonically positive and negative emotions have been shown to hold similar sympathetic charges. Mirth and sadness (e.g., Averill, 1969) and pleasure and distress (e.g., Levi, 1965; Pátkai, 1971a), for instance, have been found to be sympathetically comparable. Sympathetic excitation associated with reactions to conflict, provocation, and physical pain, then, is commensurate with sympathetic excitation fueling sexual desire and consummatory action.

In this connection, it is worthy of note that what might be considered the unique feature of sexual arousal (viz., vasocongestion in the access organs) is by no means a specific response capable of unambiguously differentiating states of sexual and nonsexual excitedness. Research discussed under ''Cerebral Representation'' (Chapter 3, Section I) leaves no doubt about the fact that in many mammals, including nonhuman primates, penile erection may accompany numerous aggressive and nonaggressive actions in nonsexual contexts (e.g., MacLean, 1973). Uncovered men similarly exhibit erection in a variety of emotional reactions devoid of sexual connotations (e.g., Gajdusek, 1970). Erection has been observed during anxiety, surprise, appeasement, anger, and aggressive behavior as well as during greeting, joy, and elation. One might assume that female primates experience clitoral tumescence in similar emotion-evoking situations. However, because this reaction is less obtrusive than penile erection, confirming or disconfirming data are not available.

2. Interoception of activity in the autonomic nervous system is highly nonspecific to emotion. Exteroceptive feedback is similarly nonspecific.

Interoceptive and exteroceptive nonspecificity is largely due to the high degree of nonspecificity of the autonomic activity itself. In addition, however, both interoception and exteroception are poorly developed and fail to provide accurate representations of any patterned states of excitation. The perception of specific autonomic changes is usually unreliable. Only gross overall changes are discernible with reliability. Mandler (1975) summarized this state of affairs by stating that, for all practical purposes, feedback of potentially specific autonomic reactions signifies ''general autonomic arousal [that varies] in degree but not in discriminable pattern [p. 128].'' This is not to say, however, that autonomic perception is inaccurate by necessity. Rather, it appears that the mammalian organism is endowed with the capacity for considerable interoceptive sensitivity (Ádám, 1967; Chernigovskiy, 1967) and that humans, if properly trained, are capable of discriminating comparatively small autonomic changes (Brener, 1974, 1977; Schwartz, 1976, 1977). The commonly observed imprecision of autonomic perception (e.g., Mandler & Kahn, 1960; Mandler & Kremen, 1958; Mandler, Mandler, Kremen, & Sholiton, 1961; Thayer, 1967, 1970) seems to be the consequence of a lack of utilization of an existing capability. Presumably, interoceptive feedback of autonomic activity has less adaptive utility than response feedback from more sensitive structures (e.g., the facial and skeletal muscles) and is being neglected as a result.

Consideration of feedback from general somatic activity, especially from activity in the muscles, further suggests that information about autonomic processes is nonspecific. Gellhorn (e.g., 1964) has stressed the close correspondence between autonomic and somatic activity. Apparently, sympathetic excitation and muscle tone undergo parallel changes. "Upward" discharges from the posterior hypothalamus to the cerebral cortex are associated with sympathetic-somatic "downward" discharges of proportional intensity. Proprioceptive impulses from the muscles reach the cerebellum and the motor cortex, and collaterals from the specific afferent systems feed into the reticular formation and the hypothalamus. The involvement of these structures fosters diffuse excitation, and proprioception is likely to reflect this diffuseness. Somatic feedback, then, appears to parallel autonomic feedback in that it represents a variation in intensity, not in patterned specificity.

Regarding states of sexual excitedness, the situation may appear to be quite different. Males, at least, seem to have reliable feedback of genital vasocongestion. Full-fledged erection is obtrusive, and the individual probably becomes aware of his reaction. Men thus might be considered to be provided with highly reliable feedback of states of sexual excitedness. The problem here is with the nonuniqueness of the response rather than with feedback. In addition, it may be speculated that many penile blood-volume changes below the level of acute erection go unnoticed. Discernment of genital vasocongestion in females might be similarly poor, even for pronounced congestion. Notwithstanding these difficulties, genital vasocongestion—especially in males—is likely to be a response that the individual construes as a reliable indicator of sexual excitedness specifically.

3. Individuals do not partition excitation compounded from reactions to different inducing conditions. Autonomic and/or somatic feedback permits neither the isolation of all factors that contribute to a state of excitation nor the apportionment of excitation to the various contributing factors. As a result, individuals tend to ascribe their excitatory reaction in toto to one specific, though potentially complex, inducing condition.

Based on the nonspecificity assumptions, this assumption implies that, in general, individuals are not continually engaged in a careful accounting of their excitatory activity and that, in fact, they are not capable of monitoring the independent time courses of concurrent excitatory reactions with any degree of precision. Confounded excitation cannot be accurately partitioned into components and portions attributable to particular inducers. Likely misconceptions concern both simultaneously induced reactions and reactions elicited in succession.

Individuals who construe a state of excitedness as sexual arousal may, according to this assumption, be partly excited because they are afraid, angry, or in pain. Likewise, individuals in a hostile confrontation may consider themselves to be genuinely angry, although much of the excitement experienced may derive from sexual stimuli. It is conceivable that—at times, at least—states of excitation are suspected to derive from different and potentially incompatible sources. Yet, even in such cases, individuals will not be able to partition their excitatory state and accurately link portions to inducers.

4. Excitatory activity, especially autonomic activity, does not terminate abruptly. Because of the involvement of humoral processes, sympathetic excitation dissipates comparatively slowly. Residues of this slowly decaying sympathetic excitation may thus enter into subsequent, potentially independent emotional reactions and emotional experiences.

The endocrine mechanics of the sympathetic-adrenal medullary system that mediate phasic excitatory reactions have been detailed earlier (Section IV, Chapter 4). As should be recalled, the emotional emergency reaction is produced by the release of the catecholamines epinephrine and norepinephrine (cf. Smith, 1973; Turner & Bagnara, 1971). The circulating amines mediate excitation, of course, until they are chemically converted to a nonsympathomimetic agent (Axelrod, 1959, 1971). The peripheral concomitant of this conversion is the slow, steady decline of blood pressure, among numerous parallel autonomic reactions (cf. Grings & Dawson, 1978). Emotional behavior is also associated with increased activity in the pituitary-adrenal cortical system, where the release of corticosteroids is likely to produce elevated levels of excitation that extend far beyond the time course of emergency reactions (cf. Conner, 1972; Hennessy & Levine, 1979).

The transfer paradigm was initially developed to explain dependencies in successive emotional reactions, specifically, the dependence of emotional reactions on preceding emotional states. I first present this paradigm for emotion sequences. Thereafter, I simplify it in order to deal with emotional responses in which quasi-simultaneously elicited excitatory reactions are compounded. The latter is necessary because this condition for transfer seems to be particularly significant in the consideration of sex-aggression linkages.

Transfer in Successive Excitatory Reactions

1. Given a situation in which: (1) individuals respond to emotion-inducing stimuli and assess their responses; (2) levels of sympathetic excitation are

still elevated from prior, potentially unrelated stimulation; and (3) individuals are not provided with obtrusive intero- and/or exteroceptive cues that link their excitatory state to prior stimulation, residues of excitation from prior stimulation will inseparably combine with the excitatory reaction to the present stimuli and thereby intensify both emotional behavior and emotional experience.

2. Emotional behavior and/or emotional experience will be enhanced in proportion to the magnitude of transferred residual excitation.

3. Both the period of time during which transfer can occur and the magnitude of residues for transfer are a function of: (1) the magnitude of the preceding excitatory reaction and/or (2) the rate of recovery from the excitatory state.

4. Individuals' potential for transfer is: (1) proportional to their excitatory responsiveness and (2) inversely proportional to their proficiency to recover from excitatory states.

Transfer in Concurrent Excitatory Reactions

1. Given a situation in which: (1) individuals respond to emotion-inducing stimuli and assess their responses and (2) levels of sympathetic excitation are heightened by responses to secondary stimuli that are potentially unrelated to the primary ones that direct emotional behavior, the compounded excitatory reaction will intensify both emotional behavior and emotional experience.

2. Emotional behavior and/or emotional experience will be enhanced in proportion to the magnitude of transferred secondary excitation (i.e., excitation not elicited by the behavior-guiding stimuli).

3. Individuals' potential for transfer is: (1) proportional to their excitatory responsiveness and (2) inversely proportional to their proficiency to recover from excitatory states.

It is assumed that alien (i.e., residual or secondary) excitation and emotion-specific, primary excitation combine in a summative fashion. Figures 6.1 and 6.2 display additive models of excitation transfer for successive and concurrent reactions, respectively. The additivity assumption is parsimonious and has proved useful in that it satisfactorily accommodates pertinent research findings (cf. Zillmann, 1979). It should be clear, however, that accurate predictions of transfer effects cannot be based on the additive combination of two or more excitatory reactions that, in a hypothetical fashion, are assessed against basal levels. Such a procedure would violate the law of initial values (cf. Sternbach, 1966; Wilder, 1957). It must be taken into consideration that the magnitude of excitatory reactions is a function of prevailing levels of excitation (i.e., pre-

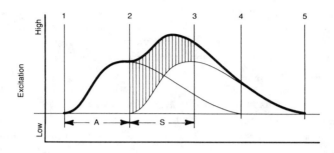

Time of Activity

FIG. 6.1. A model of excitation transfer in which residual excitation from a preceding excitatory reaction combines additively with the excitatory reaction to current stimulation. An antecedent stimulus condition (A), persisting from time 1 to time 2, is assumed to produce excitatory activity that has entirely decayed only at time 4. Similarly, a subsequent stimulus condition (S), persisting from time 2 to time 3, is assumed to produce excitatory activity that has entirely decayed only at time 5. Residual excitation from condition A and excitation specific to condition S combine from time 2 to time 4. The extent to which the transfer of residues from condition A increases the excitatory activity associated with condition S is shown in the shaded area. (Reprinted, with permission, from D. Zillmann, *Hostility and aggression*. Hillsdale, N.J.: Lawrence Erlbaum Associates, 1979.)

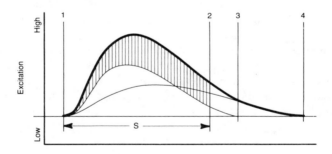

Time of Activity

FIG. 6.2. A model of excitation transfer in which excitation from a secondary excitatory reaction combines additively with the excitatory reaction to the primary, behavior-directing stimulation. The stimuli for the primary (PR) and secondary reaction (SR) concur from time 1 to time 2. It is assumed that the excitatory activity of PR has entirely decayed at time 3 and that decay of the activity of SR is complete at time 4. Behavior directed by the primary stimulation (S) is associated with the combined excitatory activity of PR and SR. The extent to which the transfer of secondary excitation increases excitation specific to the primary stimulation is shown in the shaded area.

stimulus levels). Specifically, excitatory reactions are likely to be inversely proportional to prestimulus levels of excitation. Qualifications are necessary, consequently, if only to prevent the prediction of excitatory intensity above maximally possible levels.

In case of transfer of residual excitation, a modification can be readily expressed as a correction to be applied to the prediction of the intensity of the subsequent excitatory response. A linear correction, for example, would take the form $\alpha = 1 - (p - b)/(m - b)$, where p is the prestimulus, b the basal, and m the maximal level of excitation. The factor α would modify the "normal" intensity of the subsequent excitatory response (i.e., its intensity assessed against basal levels). This intensity, clearly, would not be affected if $p = b$. If $p = m$, in contrast, it is reduced to O. Nonlinear corrections may prove to be more appropriate but are certainly not demanded by the scarce data at hand.

As an approximation, the suggested modification can be applied to the summation of simultaneously elicited excitatory reactions as well. The intensity of the primary excitatory response replaces the prestimulus level p, and α corrects the intensity of the secondary instead of the subsequent excitatory reaction.

II.   TRANSFER PROJECTIONS

Although for reasons quite different than those of other theories concerning connections between sex and aggression, the excitation-transfer paradigm projects the mutual facilitation of sexual and aggressive behavior under a great variety of circumstances. The fact that limiting conditions for transfer have been specified should not be interpreted as meaning that alternative views are more inclusive. If anything, transfer projections are broader in scope, as any specific affinity between sexual and aggressive motivation—a critical condition in most alternative theories—is deemed immaterial.

First, excitation transfer may be expected to facilitate aggression that follows sexual enticements. Residual sexual arousal (or more accurately, the sympathetic component of this arousal) should intensify aggressive behavior in response to annoyance. This annoyance may be devoid of sexual elements. Alternatively, however, it may be laden with sexual elements, "sexual frustration" being a case in point. Aggressive behavior analogously may be pure or contaminated with sexual elements. If—for whatever particular reason—sexual-aggressive behavior is performed after pronounced sexual excitedness, this type of behavior should be intensified by prevailing residual excitation.

Second, excitation transfer may be expected to enhance both the sexual behavior and sexual experience that follow conflict, aggravation, provocation, and assault. Residual excitation should enter into and thereby intensify sexual action.

In order for transfer to occur, the sex-aggression or aggression-sex sequence must be contiguous or, at least, proximal. The likelihood of transfer-facilitation decreases, of course, as the time separation between antecedent and subsequent reactions increases. On the other hand, any abrupt change from sexual to aggressive or from aggressive to sexual instigation may jeopardize transfer. Such "nontransition" might make the individual cognizant of his or her still being excited from the preceding stimulation, and this awareness might prevent any "overreaction" because the experienced excitatory state cannot be ascribed to prevailing stimulation and corrective action is likely.

Third, excitation transfer may be expected to intensify either sexual or aggressive behavior and experience, but foremost both sexual and aggressive behaviors in a confounded fashion, in any situation that concurrently entails both sexual and aggressive stimulation and action. However, the fusion of sexual and aggressive behaviors should not be considered limited to situations in which both onset and termination of sexual and aggressive stimulation coincide perfectly. In fact, sex-aggression fusion is much more likely in situations in which brief episodes of aggression are interspersed or "superimposed" in sexual activities. Sex-aggression fusion, furthermore, is characteristic of situations in which brief periods of sexual and aggressive stimulation alternate in rapid succession. The condition that defines sex-aggression fusion is thus not so much the specific onset/offset pattern for sexual and aggressive stimulation as it is the occurrence of aggressive action in a sexual context or of sexual action in an aggressive context. Whatever the primary reaction to such stimulus admixtures may be, the transfer paradigm projects that it is this reaction, along with its experiential component, that will be enhanced and intensified by excitation from any preceding or secondary reaction. If the primary reaction is one of annoyance, anger, aggressiveness, or rage, excitation liberated by sexual cues will fuel these responses. If this reaction is one of sexual eagerness, excitation deriving from conflict, annoyance, provocation, or pain will enhance sexual behavior and experience. Surely, under the circumstances that produce sex-aggression fusion, considerable ambiguity may exist—at times, at least—as to what emotional reaction is the primary one. It is conceivable that the dominance of sexual and aggressive responses (the latter entailing the reception of pain as well as the infliction of pain) vacillates depending on the strength of the respective stimulation and that individuals have to integrate several dominance changes and reconcile to themselves whether a particular behavioral episode, taken together, was sexual, or aggressive, or both. As a rule, however, ambiguity is limited, and individuals can readily ascertain the dominant emotion.

In practical terms, the transfer paradigm projects the intensification of aggression that follows sexual stimulation without much delay. Sexual arousal may be produced by any person or thing, confronted directly, or represented in any fashion (e.g., movies, photographs, books). But because sexual arousal is considered nonappetitive with regard to aggression, aggressive action must be independently evoked. Facilitation, then, is rather universal and not restricted by stipulations such as that the target for aggression need be the agent of sexual enticement. On the other hand, it should be clear that the potentiality for facilitation is short-lived; it vanishes with the dissipation of residual sympathetic excitation.

The facilitation of aggression through excitation from sexual stimulation in fusion situations differs in that the entity responsible for sexual excitedness is the likely target for aggression, and the decay of excitation is of little moment because of the intertwining of sexual and aggressive stimulation. Conflict in sexual contexts that escalates into aggression should consequently produce vicious, potentially destructive fighting. Fighting in romantic triangles occasionally might be fueled by sexual excitedness and become devastating (cf. Wolfgang, 1958; Zillmann, 1979). The thwarting of sexual intentions is another fusion condition in which aggressiveness may become dominant. Sexual eagerness may turn to hostile action as a person realizes that access is being denied. Similarly, the denial of specific sexual services (Russell, 1980a) may spark hostilities both prior to or midway through sexual engagements. In the latter case, sexual action may become aggressive, and the infliction of pain—rather than the provision of gratification to self and other—may become the dominant objective. Finally, violent rape may be regarded as the most extreme form of sex-aggression fusion in which sexual excitedness intensifies aggressive action. The violence in both "anger rape" and "sadistic rape" (cf. Groth, 1979) seems powered by sexual arousal. The infliction of pain through aggressive action is clearly the purpose of the former type of rape. The latter type is characterized by considerable ambiguity. Sexual gratification may appear to be the goal, with the attainment of this goal depending on aggressive action. Aggression thus can be considered to have sexual utility. Alternatively, however, sadistic rape can be viewed as a pure act of violence, though an act of violence that in large measure may be sexually motivated.

Regarding the facilitation of sexual behavior and sexual experience, the transfer paradigm analogously projects the intensification of any such behavior or experience that follows aggressive action without appreciable delay. It is immaterial whether residual excitation derives from perpetrating hostile or aggressive actions, from being victimized by such actions, or from confrontation, acute conflict, or fighting that produced neither a victorious party nor a victim. Again, it is not necessary that the entities associated with conflict, hostility, and aggression be the targets of sexual attraction and action. Residual excitation from an argument with the boss, if maintained at high levels through rehearsal, should enhance sexual activity with a lover as much as comparable residues from a quarrel with that lover. The likely dissipation of residual excitation favors, of course, the induction of aggression-linked excitation just prior to the performance of sexual activities. This condition, in turn, would seem to favor the facilitation of sexual activities through residual excitation from hostile and aggressive action among intimates—the proverbial "making up" following lovers' quarrels.

As with the facilitation of aggression through sex-linked excitation, the facilitation of sexual behavior through excitation deriving from hostile and aggressive action is most direct in fusion situations. Excitatory decay is not an issue, as any excitation from secondary reactions connected with aggressive behavior more or less immediately enters into and thus intensifies sexual behavior and experience. The only critical condition that need be met is that sexuality be dominant over aggression. In violent rape, for instance, hostile and aggressive action is likely to dominate the rapist's experience so strongly that aggression rather than sexuality may be expected to be enhanced by prevailing excitation—at least, most of the time during sexual assault. The experience of the victim of violent rape is even more likely to be dominated by aggression. To the extent that aversive stimulation—the suffering of acute pain, in particular—is dominant, a facilitation of sexual behavior and experience cannot possibly be expected. Aggression-linked excitation, in such a case, is expected to intensify whatever emotion the victim arrives at: disgust, rage, shame, terror, sadness, fury, degradation, any combination thereof, or yet other reactions.

The consequences of rape that mainly serves sexual access (so-called "power rape"; cf. Groth, 1979) are less clear. The rapist's sexual experience is probably facilitated by any nonsexual action that contributes excitation: the transgressive nature of the action (involving fear of detection and punitive repercussions), the employment of threat to well-being or life, and the infliction of pain and injury. Aggression in access rape thus may be most facilitative of the rapist's sexual experience. In sharp contrast, the involvement of overt aggression in access rape probably assures the dominance of pain and terror in the victim. Sexual arousal that is being liberated by the mechanics of sexual stimulation can only intensify this aversive experience. If the so-called rape myth (i.e., the assertion that rape victims will come to enjoy being sexually stimulated, even come to enjoy it to an extraordinary degree) has any basis at all, it can only be in nonviolent access rape. A victim who readily yields to threat to well-being might nonetheless be excited by the hostile circumstances and the xenophobia created. Such a victim might habitually respond to sexual stimulation and construe the experience as one of sexual excitement. That experience should, of course, be enhanced by transferable excitation. This myth-conforming outcome seems quite unlikely, however, as it presupposes an enormous degree of callousness on the part of the victim. Victims of access rape, even if the rape is nonviolent in the sense that the infliction of pain is threatened only and does not actually occur, are likely to experience acute fear. This fear may be expected to dominate sexual experience despite the possibility of sexual excitedness, even orgasmic responses, due to mechanical sexual stimulation. Most importantly, perhaps, the victim of a sexual assault will probably not be able to construe, especially in the assessment of the experience after the assault, any aspect of it as having been truly euphoric. It is significant that this postassault appraisal is made at a time when excitation from fear, terror, and possibly pain, and from sexual stimulation on the other hand, is still at extremely high levels. Maybe some callous persons could be found who would, under these circumstances, revel in the memory of the sexual experience and benefit from excitation transfer. As a rule, however, the victim's experience of terror and of having been violated should persist for some time and be intensified by residual excitation from sexual stimulation.

The sex-aggression fusion in which aggression in a rather controlled fashion is exploited for the benefit of sex is not rape but sadomasochistic behavior. Inasmuch as the parties involved in sadomasochistic ventures have to consent to the happenings, many arousing events are compromised. Threats of destructive, violent abuse (e.g., bodily mutilation or death) lack credibility. The suddenness of an assault and the uncertainty of the outcome are similarly lost. Despite efforts to maintain a scenario threatening mutilation and death in sadomasochistic practices, the remaining principal arousers are the infliction and the reception of pain—especially the latter. These arousers can be exploited to the fullest, however, as consenting parties can agree to limits in the employment of pain and paining; these limits insure that sexual experience remains dominant over aggression. As excitedness associated with sexual activities is supplemented through the infliction and/or the reception of pain, one party can signal to the other to stop this stimulation before it assumes primacy and possibly gets out of hand. Additionally, should the aversion threshold have been crossed, a party can express distress and thereby signal a desire to return to sexual stimulation as the primary mode. The comparatively common use of aversive stimuli during precoital and coital behavior (e.g., painful pinching, scratching, and biting) conforms to the same model.

It must be emphasized again that all these interdependencies between sexual and aggressive behaviors are projected without assuming any motivational affinity between sex and aggression. The capacity for mutual facilitation is not derived from peculiarities in the evolution of the central nervous system (e.g., MacLean, 1963). The elicitation of behavior of the one kind is not assumed to trigger—by spillage of excitation in central connections—behavior of the other kind. Rather, the capacity for mutual facilitation is viewed as the result of poor sympathetic differentiation between sex and aggression. Poorness of endowment seems exacerbated by poorness of interoception. The latter appears to result in large measure from neglect. This neglect of the development of sympathetic and, more generally, autonomic sensitivity would seem to suggest that the autonomic differentiation of sex and aggression has had little adaptive utility. Evolutionarily speaking, the misreactions in sexual, aggressive, and sexual-aggressive behaviors that the transfer paradigm projects on the basis of sympathetic commonality apparently did not place the organism at a disadvantage. If anything, these "confusions" aided reproductive success by enhancing the capacity for fighting in sexual situations and for sexual engagements in aggressive contexts. There is reason, then, to believe that the transfer connection between sex and aggression is archaic indeed. Despite the likelihood of frequent fusion of sex and aggression throughout evolution, however, and notwithstanding assertions to the contrary (e.g., Freud, 1912/1943), the transfer connection appears to be one of mutual facilitation devoid of appetitive influences.

In considering the role of sympathetic excitation in the evolution of sex-aggression linkages, it must be acknowledged that excitation at "emergency" levels (cf. Cannon, 1929) is by no means a precondition for the successful performance of reproductive behavior per se. Surely, the males of many mammalian species were placed into behavioral emergencies by having to fight off rivals and in seeking the females' submission in order to achieve access (see Section I of Chapter 2). The females of these species generally were not placed into such a situation, however. In many species of nonhuman primates, for instance, the solicitation of sexual engagements by estrous females would seem to have made any emergency reaction inappropriate, even counterproductive. Sexual activities, especially in pairs that sought and accomplished privacy, could take place under serene circumstances. High levels of excitedness, then, are often not required—especially in females, if it is accepted that the males' energy expenditure in coital locomotion tends to exceed that of females. Similar conditions prevailed and prevail for humans in numerous cultures (see Sections II and III of Chapter 2). Interestingly, however, it is the sexual behavior and the sexual experience that is linked with pronounced excitatory activity and, hence, associated with "strong emotion" that is treasured in a large majority of cultures. Contemporary Western cultures are no exception. A strong preference for excitement-laden sex is undeniable (e.g., Eysenck, 1976; Hunt, 1974; Walster & Walster, 1978). As there is no compelling biological reason for such a preference, the peoples' desire to engage in emotionally charged sexual ventures, rather than in placid and tranquil ones, seems best explained as conformance with culturally defined sexual scripts (e.g., Gagnon, 1973; Simon, 1973; Simon & Gagnon, 1969). Excitement has become an integral part of valued experience generally. Consequently, it should be no surprise to find that excitement-laden sexual experiences are assigned great value, whereas tranquil sexual engagements are not—owing to their drabness and proximity to boredom. But whatever the particular reason for the preference for "exciting sex," it should be clear that such a preference burdens the sexually active: They must find means to get and keep themselves excited for sexual engagements, especially when sexual stimulation alone fails them. The transfer connection between sex and aggression suggests, of course, that sexual excitedness can be supplemented and lost sexual responsiveness can be revived and replenished by excitation from aggressive action.

The previously discussed imprecision in the penile response in emotion is of interest in this connection. Specifically, if erection is not unique to sexual stimulation and also occurs during aggressive action, men should be prone to misconstruing their inclinations and "detect" sexual impulses in purely aggressive actions. This, for one thing, might explain the male tendency to express violent intentions with sexual verbiage. The nonspecificity of the vasocongestive genital response may be comparable in females (e.g., Heiman, 1977); however, feedback of this response is not obtrusive, as in the male, and misconceptions about sexual responsiveness are less likely as a result.

III. TRANSFER FROM SEX TO AGGRESSION

The possibility of excitation transfer from sexual excitedness to aggressive behavior has been explored in an investigation by Zillmann (1971). Male subjects were aggressively instigated, sexually stimulated or not, and then provided with an opportunity to retaliate against their annoyer. Sexual stimulation was accomplished by exposure to a clip from an erotic film that depicted a young couple engaged in precoital behavior. In the control or "neutral" condition, a clip from an innocuous educational film devoid of sexual or aggressive references was employed. A clip from an aggressive film, depicting a prizefight, was used in addition. All films were identical in length to assure equal time separation between provocation and retaliation.

The excitatory capacity of these stimuli was determined in a pretest. Sympathetic reactions were assessed in peripheral manifestations. Specifically, systolic and diastolic blood pressures, heart rate, and vasoconstriction were measured prior to, during, and after exposure. The analysis of these indices of excitation and of various composites of them (e.g., sympathetic activation, an index combining blood pressures and heart rate) showed the excitatory potential of the erotic stimulus to be consistently higher than that of the neutral stimulus. The potential of the aggressive film assumed an intermediate position. On the basis of this information, it was expected that excitatory residues from exposure should be the strongest after the erotic film, intermediate after the aggressive film, and minimal after the neutral film and that aggressive actions taken during this period should be intensified accordingly. The findings fully confirmed these expectations. Aggressive behavior, measured in the intensity of electric shock delivered to the annoyer, proved most pronounced after sexual stimulation. Compared to the control, exposure to the aggressive film facilitated aggressiveness also, but to a lesser degree. This facilitation, it should be noticed, is readily explained as the result of excitation transfer and corroborates the paradigm as well. The close correspondence between magnitude of residual sympathetic excitation and aggression facilitation is exhibited in Fig. 6.3.

The demonstration that exposure to sexually arousing materials is capable of intensifying motivated aggression was soon repeated by Rosene (1971) and Meyer (1972). Rosene exposed provoked males to a sexually enticing film, a sexually enticing film that involved fighting, a film of a prizefight, or a film about breaking in horses. These films were classified as sexual, violent-sexual,

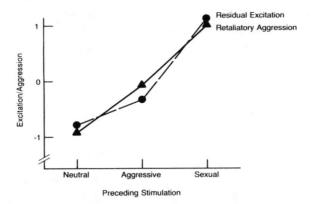

FIG. 6.3.   Facilitation of aggressive behavior by excitation transfer from sexual stimulation. Residual excitation from exposure to communication was assessed in a composite measure, sympathetic activation, involving systolic and diastolic blood pressures and heart rate (circles, broken line). Retaliatory aggression was assessed in the intensity of electric shock delivered to the annoyer (triangles, solid line). Residual excitation and aggression are expressed in z scores for ease of comparison. (Adapted from Zillmann, 1971. Reprinted by permission of Academic Press.)

violent, and neutral, respectively. Retaliatory behavior was measured in the delivery of electric shocks to the annoyer. Following sexual stimulation, aggressive behavior was found to be at significantly higher levels than after exposure to neutral fare. This effect was observed for both purely sexual and violent-sexual stimulation, without appreciable differences between these two conditions. Exposure to purely violent materials was also found to elevate aggressiveness to levels above those of the control. Meyer, employing essentially the same procedures, compared the impact of a stag film with that of an aggressive and a nonaggressive film. Facilitation of motivated male aggressiveness after exposure to erotic and violent materials was again in evidence. Meyer's investigation involved a condition in which subjects were not exposed to any film. The aggression-facilitating effects reported were obtained relative to this no-exposure control as well. Such comparison rules out the possibility that the facilitation of aggression is illusory, as ''facilitation'' effects relative to neutral films might actually have been due to the possible aggression-reducing impact of these films.

The short-lived nature of the facilitation of motivated aggression that the transfer paradigm projects was explored by Zillmann, Hoyt, and Day (1974). The prediction that the facilitation diminishes and vanishes with the dissipation of excitatory residues from preceding sexual as well as nonsexual stimulation was tested by delaying retaliatory opportunities. Male subjects were provoked and then exposed to a neutral film, an aggressive film that featured a prizefight, a violent western film that featured a blood bath, or an erotic film depicting precoital and coital behavior. During the delay period after exposure, subjects viewed a neutral documentary on the formation of rivers. They retaliated thereafter by administering noxious noise to the annoyer. Various measures of sympathetic excitation were taken intermittently. It was found that after only 1 minute of presumably calming, intervening stimulation, the residues from exposure to both the aggressive and the violent film had dissipated. Levels of excitation in these two film conditions were no longer appreciably above those in the control (i.e., the neutral-film condition). Residual excitation from exposure to the sexual materials, in contrast, was still substantial at this time. However, after 2 minutes of intervening stimulation, these residues had decayed also. At this time, excitation was at comparable levels in all exposure conditions. The facilitation of aggression was found to be in full accord with residual excitation during retaliation. As sexual stimulation was the only kind that produced excitatory reactions strong enough to outlast the short period of intervention, aggression-facilitation could and did occur only in this situation. After continued intervention, the facilitative effect predictably vanished. These findings not only implicate residual sympathetic excitation from preceding stimulation with the facilitation of motivated aggression, but also suggest that any aggression-promoting effect of exposure to erotic fare—and to violent fare, for that matter—is extremely short-lived.

Donnerstein, Donnerstein, and Evans (1975) reported findings that further highlight the importance of the proximity between sexual stimulation and enhanced reactions. Perhaps more importantly, however, they show that aggression can be facilitated through the transfer-enhancement of annoyance and aggression-precipitating anger. These investigators altered the commonly employed experimental sequence of provocation/exposure/retaliation to exposure/provocation/retaliation and compared the effects of both sequences. In one of the two orders, male subjects were provoked and exposed to photographs depicting coital activities or neutral events. All were thereafter provided with an opportunity to retaliate by administering electric shock to the annoyer. In the conventional sequence, sexual stimulation first intervenes in and potentially distracts from acute anger; anger is then reinstated by the reconfrontation with the annoyer, and the revived anger can be facilitated by residual excitation from sexual stimulation. In the new sequence, in contrast, residues from sexual stimulation can immediately enter into unmitigated, acute anger, and because the experience of anger is directly followed by aggression opportunities, facilitated anger can find immediate expression in facilitated aggression. Conditions characterized by immediacy between sexual stimulation and anger/aggression, then, should produce a higher degree of aggression facilitation than any situation that relies on the cognitive reinstatement of annoyance, especially when the emotional intensity of the initial reaction has faded. The findings support this expectation. Sexual stimulation facilitated aggressive behavior in the exposure/provocation/retaliation sequence significantly more than in the provocation/exposure/retaliation sequence. Compared with the effects of exposure to neutral materials, sexual stimulation facilitated aggression in the former sequence. It actually failed to do so in the latter. This failure is the likely result of the rather modest excitatory capacity of the particular stimuli employed (cf. Zillmann, Bryant, Comisky, & Medoff, 1981; Zillmann & Sapolsky, 1977).

The early investigations on sex-aggression transfer involved only male subjects. Restriction to males may have been ethically inspired or resulted from the special gravity of male and intermale aggression. It also may have resulted—in part, at least—from early reports of strong gender differences in the excitatory response to erotic materials. Kinsey, Pomeroy, Martin, and Gebhard (1953), for instance, reported that females exhibit far less sexual excitedness in response to exposure to such materials than do males. More recent investigations show this excitatory response in men and women to be quite comparable, however (e.g., Schmidt, 1975; Schmidt & Sigusch, 1970; Sigusch, Schmidt, Reinfeld, & Wiedemann-Sutor, 1970). Assessments of autonomic reactions, in particular, demonstrate essentially the same excitatory responsiveness in men and women (e.g., Hare, Wood, Britain, & Frazelle, 1971; Heiman, 1977). To the extent that females respond excitedly to sexual stimulation and then are provoked into aggression, aggressive behavior should, of course, be facilitated just as strongly as in males.

The expected sex-aggression transfer in females has been demonstrated in experiments by Cantor, Zillmann, and Einsiedel (1978) and Baron (1979). In the former investigation, subjects were exposed to an erotic film depicting coition or a neutral film, provoked or not provoked by a peer whose gender was not revealed, and immediately thereafter provided with the opportunity to behave aggressively by delivering noxious noise to their peer. Strong excitatory responses to sexual stimulation were in evidence. Residual excitation, as predicted from the transfer paradigm, intensified aggressive behavior under conditions of provocation only. The residues had no effect on aggression when aggressive reactions were not motivated by provocation. In this situation, anger could not be felt, and aggression was inappropriate; hence, neither anger nor aggression could be facilitated by prevailing residual excitation from sexual stimulation. Baron's study fully corroborated these findings. Females were provoked or not provoked by a female peer, exposed to sexual and nonsexual stimuli, and provided with retaliatory opportunities (i.e., the opportunity to deliver electric shocks to their peer). Compared to exposure to neutral materials, exposure to photographs of coital activities fostered increased aggression in provoked females. It not only failed to have this effect in unprovoked females, but actually led to reduced aggressiveness. The latter finding gives further evidence to the contention that sexual excitedness is devoid of appetitive properties as far as aggression is concerned.

Although variations in the target of aggressive assaults are not particularly relevant to the transfer paradigm proper, excitation transfer from sexual stimulation into the aggressive behavior of men against women has attracted considerable attention. Research on violence among intimates, especially on marital violence (e.g., Gelles, 1979; Steinmetz & Straus, 1974), certainly suggests that sexual enticements and intentions can readily get entangled with conflict and then escalate into violent action. Could it be that such action is intensified above and beyond the levels that could be expected on the basis of transfer from residual and secondary sexual excitedness alone? It is conceivable, for instance, that heterosexually inclined, sexually enticed men maintain their state of sexual excitedness to a higher degree in hostile interactions with women than with men. Transferable excitation, then, would be of greater magnitude, and aggressive behavior, once it becomes dominant, would be more intense toward female than male targets. But it may be argued alternatively that in acute conflict situations—regardless of the gender of the parties involved—excitation is near maximum levels and transfer of alien excitation is of little moment. (See the discussion of the law of initial values in connection with the transfer paradigm.) It could further be argued that sexual excitedness is behaviorally incompatible with arousal states linked with acute conflict (e.g., Baron, 1977) and that this incompatibility impairs the development of arousal and intense anger. Male aggression might thus be less pronounced when directed at female targets compared to male targets. It is, of course, also conceivable that the fate of aggression-energizing excitatory reactions is not appreciably influenced by the gender of the potential target of aggression, but that the gender of the target nonetheless exerts a certain degree of influence over aggressive reactions. Women might simply draw stronger assaults than men because they are comparatively "safe" targets in the sense that men usually need not fear violent counterassaults. Moreover, and presumably because of a history of minimal repercussions, men may have developed strong habits of forcing women into compliance through violent action (cf. Zillmann, 1979). Especially among intimates with extensive experiences of conflict, women might be ready targets for male aggression. On the other hand, one might expect a certain degree of courtship and chauvinism in the male treatment of females, especially among persons of limited acquaintance, and aggression directed at female targets might be subdued in comparison to that directed at men under similar circumstances. In the face of all these possibilities, what does the research tell us?

The previously discussed study by Rosene (1971) involved both male and female targets for male aggression. Sexual stimulation was found to facilitate aggression toward both targets. Additionally, however, aggressive behavior directed at female annoyers proved to be significantly more intense overall than did that directed at male annoyers. This tendency seemed particularly strong after exposure to sexual and violent-sexual materials, in contrast to exposure to purely violent ones. It appears that women were indeed perceived as "easy victims" and that, after witnessing sexually and aggressively engaged women, men were less inhibited in their aggressive action than after not bearing such witness (cf. Leonard & Taylor, 1983; Zillmann & Bryant, 1983).

In a similar investigation, Donnerstein and Barrett (1978) did not observe such gender differences regarding the target of aggression, however. Male subjects in their experiment were provoked or not provoked by a male or a female interactant. Aggression opportunities were provided after exposure to a neutral or a stag film, the latter featuring a variety of heterosexual and homosexual behaviors. Aggression was measured in the delivery of electric shock. Measures of peripheral sympathetic activity were taken intermittently. Confirming earlier observations, sexual stimulation was found to be without consequence for the aggressive behavior of unprovoked males. Provoked males, in sharp contrast, exhibited the expected transfer facilitation of aggression. This facilitation was in evidence for aggression against both male and female targets. Independent of film exposure and transfer, however, provoked males directed stronger retaliatory attacks against men than against women. This outcome is opposite to that reported by Rosene, and it is in line with "chauvinistic" precepts rather than with the easy-target notion.

Donnerstein and Hallam (1978) conducted a follow-up experiment in which repeated opportunities for aggression were provided. Male subjects were provoked by a male or female peer, exposed to an explicitly sexual film, a neutral film, or no film, and allowed to retaliate immediately thereafter and once more after a waiting period of 10 minutes. In other regards, the procedure was identical with that employed by Donnerstein and Barrett. It was found that motivated aggression toward both male and female targets was at higher levels immediately after sexual stimulation than immediately after the no-film treatment. As substantial excitatory reactions to the erotic stimulus were recorded, this facilitation of aggressive behavior is entirely consistent with excitation-transfer projections. Aggression directed at female targets was somewhat stronger than that directed at male targets, however. This observation agrees with Rosene's findings, but conflicts with those reported by Donnerstein and Barrett. When aggression opportunities were provided for the second time, aggressiveness increased to levels above those initially recorded. This outcome accords with earlier findings of increased use of intense shock over extended trial periods (e.g., Zillmann, 1971; Zillmann, Katcher, & Milavsky, 1972) and generally has been explained as the result of the overcoming of initial inhibitions in delivering painful electric shock to others (cf. Zillmann, 1979). But unexpectedly, aggression directed at female targets increased much more sharply over initial levels in the erotic-film condition than in the other conditions. Inasmuch as excitatory residues from sexual stimulation in this condition did not appreciably differ from those recorded in the other conditions, it cannot be argued that sexually aroused men maintain their state of excitedness to a higher degree in hostile interactions with women than with men. Also, as a differential maintenance of levels of excitation was not in evidence, the pronounced facilitation of continued, delayed male aggression directed at female targets cannot be explained as transfer. Other mechanics must be invoked. An explanation suggested by recent findings on perceptual and dispositional changes occasioned by exposure to erotica (Zillmann & Bryant, 1983) is that the erotic film may have promoted callousness toward women. Although also transitory, the callous dispositions may have outlasted residual excitation and mediated the stronger aggressive reactions toward the female targets. If so, the effect reported by Donnerstein and Hallam is specific to sexual stimulation induced by exposure to erotica capable of promoting callousness toward women. It would not apply, for instance, to situations in which the person toward whom aggression is directed is also the source of sexual stimulation.

Investigations by Donnerstein (1980) and Donnerstein and Berkowitz (1981) further attest to the fragility of the gender-of-target effect in the facilitation of aggression after purely sexual stimulation. Following exposure to a film depicting a variety of coital activities, male aggression toward female annoyers tended to be at levels below those associated with aggression toward male annoyers. However, these investigations helped to clarify the target issue by involving violent erotica and by assessing their impact relative to that of merely sexually enticing erotica.

In Donnerstein's (1980) experiment, males were provoked or not provoked by a male or female peer, exposed to a neutral, an erotic, or an aggressive-erotic film, and then given the opportunity to aggress against the peer by delivering electric shock to him or her. The aggressive-erotic film featured an armed man entering the home of a woman and forcing her into sexual intercourse. Although excitatory residues from exposure to this and the purely erotic film were comparable in magnitude, motivated aggressive behavior was significantly more intense after the rape film than after the film depicting coitus among consenting parties. This difference resulted from pronounced aggressive action directed at the female annoyer specifically. Clearly, this target effect goes beyond the transfer facilitation of aggression. Could it again be explained as the result of callousness that is made salient by the film? It could, but only if it is assumed that the rape film conformed to the "rape myth" and thus did not evoke reactions of sympathy with a victim—an assumption that has considerable credibility, as pornographic productions characteristically dwell on joy rather than on genuine suffering. Donnerstein's experiment, furthermore, showed that after exposure to the rape film, even unprovoked males tended to behave more aggressively toward female than male targets. This observation, it should be noticed, is in full accord with the proposal that certain erotica promote callousness toward women and thereby encourage hostilities.

The follow-up experiment by Donnerstein and Berkowitz (1981) generated data that can be interpreted as providing further evidence in support of the proposed mediating role of callousness. Two versions of an aggressive-erotic film were created and employed in addition to a neutral and an aggressive film. One version incarnated the rape myth, featuring two men who, after getting a girl drunk, tied her up, stripped her, slapped her, and assaulted her sexually; the girl exhibited no resistance and expressed enjoyment in the end. The other version was parallel, but all expressions of enjoyment were omitted; additionally, a preamble to the film asserted that the girl responded with disgust and humiliation to the treatment she received. It was found that after exposure to either one of the aggressive-erotic films, provoked males directed stronger assaults at female than at male targets. This outcome confirms the earlier finding. More importantly, however, the assaults on female targets were most pronounced after exposure to the rape-myth film. To the extent that it can be accepted that the portrayal of a woman's euphoric response to aggressive-sexual abuse fostered callousness that generalized to another woman, this outcome can be considered explained. The callousness argument gains additional support by the finding that unprovoked males behaved significantly more punitively toward females after the rape-myth film than after the rape film. The rape-myth film was, in fact, the only film that facilitated unprovoked aggression against women.

These investigations suggest that it is not the erotic exploitation of aggressive themes per se that promotes aggression against women. Rather, it is the popular, demeaning portrayal of women as creatures capable of converting any aggressive and sexual assault into pleasure. Rosene's (1971) findings presented earlier are consistent with such an interpretation. In his investigation, the erotic film that involved "playful" fighting among mutually consenting females had the same effect on motivated aggression directed at female (and male) targets as had the erotic film devoid of aggressive action. This is not to say, however, that aggressive contents are necessarily without effect on aggression. Tannenbaum (cf. Tannenbaum & Zillmann, 1975), for instance, has demonstrated that the involvement of aggressive motives in erotic fare is capable of increasing motivated intermale aggression.

Recent research on erotica effects has shown that the hedonic valence of the stimulus materials constitutes yet another condition that modifies the effect of excitation transfer. Findings of an investigation conducted by Sapolsky and Zillmann (1981) indicated strong gender differences in the valuative, hedonic response to particular erotica (cf. Izard & Caplan, 1974) and suggested an aggression-promoting effect of negative affective reactions. The experiment by Zillmann, Bryant, Comisky, and Medoff (1981) detailed in Section II of Chapter 5 was designed to explore this suggestion further and to determine the degree to which transfer and hedonic responses combine in the facilitation of motivated aggression. As may be recalled, various materials were pretested to accomplish a factorial stimulus variation in excitatory potential (low vs. high), hedonic valence (negative vs. positive), and sexual theme (erotica vs. nonerotica). A no-exposure control condition was incorporated in the design as well in order to assess the direction of effects (i.e., facilitation vs. reduction of aggression). As expected, the aggression-facilitating effect of residual excitation (under high excitatory potential) combined with that of negative hedonic reactions. Aggression facilitation was most pronounced in the conditions that exhibited arousing, repulsive erotica (e.g., films featuring sadomasochistic actions and bestiality) and nonerotica (e.g., films featuring eye operations and the slaughter of baby seals). Annoyance during exposure apparently summed with annoyance in response to provocation. By the same token, hedonically positive reactions (in response to the appropriate stimuli) summed with annoyance from provocation in diminishing the strength of this aggression-mediating response (cf. Baron, 1977). The findings proved the effects of transfer and of annoyance summation to be independent and additive. The resulting model for the effects of erotica on motivated aggression (Zillmann & Bryant, 1983) is displayed in Fig. 6.4 (left side).

The reported aggression-facilitating effect of arousing, displeasing erotica resulted from stimuli that entailed aggressive action. The effect, consequently, could be ascribed—in part, at least—to the exhibition of aggressive behavior (cf. Berkowitz, 1974). But such a possibility was ruled out by the findings of a follow-up study (Zillmann, Bryant, & Carveth, 1981). In this study, males were provoked by another male, exposed to equally arousing and equally displeasing stimuli that entailed or did not entail aggressive action, and provided with opportunities to retaliate by exerting painful pressure on the annoyer's arm. The aggressive-sexual film featured flagellation in conjunction with various sexual

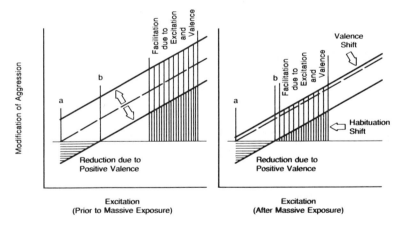

FIG. 6.4.   A two-component model of the effect of erotica on postexposure aggression. The broken line projects aggression-facilitation as a linear function of excitation. The upper solid line defines the added effect of negative hedonic valence. The lower solid line defines the counterfacilitative effect of positive hedonic valence. The horizontally shaded area specifies the effect of pleasing but nonarousing erotica (point a) and of pleasing and somewhat arousing erotica. At point b, the aggression-facilitating effect of excitation is nullified by the aggression-reducing effect of positive valence. The vertically shaded areas specify the effect of arousing erotica of negative valence (light plus dark) and of positive valence (dark only) prior to (graph at left) and after (graph at right) excitatory habituation and valence changes from massive exposure. Effects of massive exposure are discussed in Section VI of this chapter. (After Zillmann and Bryant, 1983. Reprinted, with permission, from N. M. Malamuth and E. Donnerstein (Eds.), *Pornography and sexual aggression.* New York: Academic Press, 1983.)

activities. The matched, purely sexual film showed various acts of bestiality. Compared against retaliatory behavior in a control condition without exposure to a film, aggression facilitation was evident after exposure to either erotic stimulus. There was no appreciable difference between the two stimuli, however. Consistent with an earlier conclusion, then, aggressiveness per se (i.e., irrespective of valuative and hedonic considerations) is of little moment in the effect of erotica.

The determination of the effect of the hedonic valence of stimulation on motivated aggressive behavior is not only important in its own right, but furnishes evidence for the dismissal of an old speculation that has plagued the theorizing on sex-aggression transfer. Following Freudian thought, it has been argued that any facilitation of aggression after exposure to erotica is simply due to the fact that sexual stimulation is discontinued. Essentially, it is due to "sexual frustration." The enormous popularity of erotic fare has, of course, always been at variance with such a frustration argument. Are people seeking exposure time and time again in order to frustrate themselves? Nevertheless, reliable assessments of hedonic reactions to erotica and of affect after exposure have only now become available. Recent research (cf. Zillmann & Bryant, 1983) leaves no doubt about the fact that persons, especially men (e.g., Sapolsky & Zillmann, 1981), enjoy seeing others perform precoital and coital activites. And although they are likely to be sexually enticed by the exposure, there is no indication of frustration after exposure. The experience is apparently one of pleasant entertainment. But facilitative effects on motivated aggressive behavior are being recorded right after such genuinely pleasant reactions (e.g., Ramirez, Bryant, & Zillmann, 1982). Surely, if any kind of frustration is incurred during or after exposure to erotica, facilitative effects may be expected to gain in strength. Frustration, especially sexual frustration, thus can be regarded as a contributing factor, but it should not be considered a necessary or sufficient condition for the facilitation of aggression.

A look back at Fig. 5.1, which summarizes the findings of the investigation by Zillmann, Bryant, Comisky, and Medoff (1981), further establishes the independence of aggression facilitation after sexual stimulation from the sexual theme as such. The fact that the effects of excitationally and hedonically matched erotica and nonerotica were entirely parallel implicates the generality of sympathetic excitation and hedonic valence as factors in the facilitation of motivated aggression. Sexual stimulation promotes such aggression to the extent that it produces excitation and elicits displeasure and annoyance. To the extent that nonsexual stimuli liberate these reactions, these stimuli should have the same effects on aggression. Music, for instance, should be expected to modify aggressiveness in accordance with the two-component model of erotica effects presented in Fig. 6.4. Such expectations actually have been confirmed in recent research (Day, 1980). Excitatory residues from hedonically neutral treatments (e.g., physical exercise) also have been found capable of intensifying aggression (e.g., Zillmann et al., 1972). All these findings corroborate the proposal that sex-aggression transfer is not the result of uniquely sexual excitedness, but rather derives from the sympathetic concomitants of this excitedness.

In summing up the research findings concerning transfer from sex to aggression, the following statements can be made:

1. Provoked aggressive behavior, as a rule, is intensified by residual excitation from preceding sexual stimulation. This facilitation of motivated aggression occurs in both males and females.
2. The described facilitation of aggression is short-lived. It diminishes and vanishes with the dissipation of residual excitation.
3. The described facilitation of aggression is not specific to sexual stimulation. It is the sympathetic component of sexual excitedness that appears to mediate the effect on aggression.
4. Residual excitation from sexual stimulation does not appreciably influence unprovoked aggressiveness in males or females.
5. The intensification of provoked aggressive reactions through excitation transfer may be complemented by other factors. Negative affect associated with sexual stimulation increases the transfer facilitation of motivated aggression. (Positive affect associated with sexual stimulation, on the other hand, tends to counteract and reduce it.)
6. Sexual stimulation that promotes callousness toward women may facilitate both provoked and unprovoked male aggression directed at female targets. Under other circumstances, however, the provoked or unprovoked aggressive behavior of sexually excited males appears not to favor a particular gender as target.
7. The transfer-complementing influences presumably are also limited in time, but the time course of these influences is not known at present.

It should be recognized that all generalizations about sexual excitedness pertain to arousal during the so-called "excitement phase" (Masters & Johnson, 1966). Experimental demonstrations of sex-aggression transfer during other phases do not exist. Consequently, it is unknown whether or not aggressive activities might be intensified by residual arousal in the resolution phase (i.e., after orgasm). It can only be speculated that, as conditions for hostility arise during that period, residues for transfer will be of trivial magnitude as sex-linked excitation is rapidly dissipating. Analogously, it would seem that transfer is of little moment for aggressive behavior during refractory periods. During these periods, men exhibit a lack of sexual responsiveness by definition. This lack of responsiveness is, of course, characterized by minimal excitedness—a condition that fails to provide the very basis for excitation transfer from sex to aggression.

IV. TRANSFER FROM AGGRESSION TO SEX

As indicated earlier, research on excitation transfer from aggression into sexual behavior is scarce. Direct demonstrations of the predicted transfer facilitation of sexual behavior and sexual experience do not exist, in fact. There are, however, several investigations that pertain to aggression-sex transfer which have produced findings that are highly suggestive of this type of transfer.

The animal studies that were reported in Section I of Chapter 5, for instance, can be considered suggestive of transfer. As may be recalled, Barfield and Sachs (1968) observed that sexual behavior was greatly facilitated by the infliction of pain on male rats in the company of estrous females. Caggiula and Eibergen (1969) similarly observed the infliction of pain to produce a dramatic facilitation of sexual behavior. Crowley, Popolow, and Ward (1973), moreover, demonstrated that the anticipation of painful stimulation alone produced powerful sex facilitation. To the extent that the reception of electric shock or the anticipation thereof simulates salient features of fighting, aggressive behavior can be considered to have enhanced sexual action. However, in the absence of any measurement of activity level and of autonomic activity specifically, it can only be speculated that the facilitation was mediated—in a critical way, at least—by sympathetic activity resulting from pain or "fear" of pain.

The necessary concern for the welfare of human subjects prevents, of course, direct demonstrations of transfer from aggression to sex. Human subjects can neither be attacked nor be made to attack others in a realistic fashion. The employment of pain-inflicting procedures is severely limited, as is the employment of fear-inducing procedures. Finally, immediate access to the sexual behavior of others is restricted also. Compelling experimental demonstrations of aggression-sex transfer thus cannot and should not be expected—now or in the foreseeable future. Instead, the likelihood of such transfer will have to be established through the integration of demonstrations of specific facets of the proposed process.

Perhaps the closest approximation to a direct demonstration of aggression-sex transfer has been accomplished in an investigation by Hoon, Wincze, and Hoon (1977). These investigators induced or did not induce distress in female subjects and immediately thereafter exposed them to sexually enticing stimuli. Vaginal blood volume was monitored throughout these treatments, increased volume being taken as a measure of sexual excitedness. It was found that females became more rapidly and more intensely aroused sexually after distress than following an affectively neutral state.

The finding that distress facilitates capillary engorgement in the vagina during subsequent sexual stimulation seems to confirm the popular beliefs about enhanced sexual behavior and sexual experience after a quarrel or fight. Actually, it can also be taken as suggesting that rape creates superior physiological conditions for coition. Only the rapist, needless to say, is likely to benefit experientially from this situation. Furthermore, to the extent that the investigation by Hoon et al. assessed the effect of acute distress, which constitutes the essential emotional reaction that mediates sexual excitedness in women, the infliction of pain in sadomasochistic behaviors should also be expected to enhance sexual behavior and ultimately sexual experience. This facilitation of sex would seem to benefit men more than initially threatened and assaulted women.

As all these extensions and speculations hinge on distress, a convincing operationalization of this reaction in the study by Hoon et al. would seem vital. The operationalization (Hoon et al. actually attempted to operationalize anxiety), unfortunately, can be questioned on several counts. Analogous to sexual stimulation, which was accomplished by exposure to a film depicting a couple engaged in precoital behavior, and to the creation of a neutral state by exposure to a travelogue, the elicitation of distress reactions (or of anxiety) was attempted through exposure to film. The film in question showed the aftermath of tragic automobile accidents in vivid detail and included occupants' death cries. Subjects, then, witnessed the effects of destructive events on others, but did not experience pain or anticipate experiencing pain themselves. The kind of emotional reaction elicited under these circumstances is usually classified as "empathetic distress" (cf. Zillmann, 1980). Such distress is characteristically less intense than distress from actual pain or fear of painful stimulation (cf. Sternbach, 1968), and it can be argued that any effects of empathetic distress are not representative of effects of distress from immediate threats to a person's own well-being. On the other hand, the effects of empathetic distress may be similar to the effects of distress from threat to self or pain to self, and projections may be conservative rather than exaggerated. This is to say that the facilitation of sexual excitedness observed by Hoon et al. might have been more pronounced had distress been stronger and more convincingly manipulated. Still, the experimentally created state might be considered too remote from the infliction of pain through deliberate violent action and the actual suffering of pain, or to the imminence of either, to allow any responsible generalizations of the effects of acute distress on sexual excitedness.

An investigation by Wolchik, Beggs, Wincze, Sakheim, Barlow, and Mavissakalian (1980) suggests, in fact, that the facilitation of genital vasocongestion by preceding distress depends in large measure on the kind and/or the intensity of the distressing experience. This investigation sought to extend the findings reported by Hoon et al. to males, and it succeeded only in part. The experimental procedure employed was essentially that of the earlier study with women, except that penile tumescence was measured and a somewhat different type of distressing film was used in addition to the types of material previously used. The added film featured the anxieties of persons threatened with amputation of limbs. A pretest showed it to elicit stronger anxiety reactions than a film featuring fatal and near fatal car accidents. The accidents film was very similar to the distressing film employed by Hoon et al. The control film, a travelogue describing life in Finland, and the erotic stimulus were also very similar to the respective films of the earlier study.

Wolchik et al. found that all three nonerotic films had an entirely negligible effect on erection. Subsequent exposure to the erotic stimulus produced significantly different degrees of penile tumescence, however. Preexposure to the most distressing (i.e., anxiety-inducing) film, presumably because it evoked the strongest reactions of sympathetic excitation, resulted in greater tumescence than preexposure to the control film. Up to this point, the findings appear to support the view that prearousal, even if brought on by noxious stimulation, facilitates specifically sexual excitedness. Indeed, they seem to show that anxiety may enhance sexual excitedness in men as much as in women. Such an interpretation is compromised, however, by the finding that preexposure to the accidents film produced less penile tumescence than preexposure to the possibly less arousing control film.

As a pretest had shown the accidents film to be depressing rather than anxiety inducing, Wolchik et al. thought the quality of emotion preceding sexual stimulation to be implicated in causing the effect on sexual arousal. Specifically, these investigators concluded that anxiety, if not overly intense, facilitates subsequent sexual responses; depression, in contrast, impairs and decreases these responses. This interpretation is certainly consistent with their data, but it raises the question why women in the study by Hoon et al. responded so differently to such a similar film. Why should men be depressed and women be scared by films featuring violent car accidents? Additionally, why should men respond with depression to depictions of car accidents and with anxiety to depictions of amputation threats to others? On the other hand, if one simply accepts the pretest data concerning anxiety and depression, one might speculate that depression had a suppressing effect on subsequent sexual arousal because of the especially low levels of sympathetic excitation commonly associated with depression. Only the direct assessment of excitatory responses in these stimulation transitions will eventually clarify which mechanisms are involved. But until such assessments become available it would seem prudent to acknowledge that different affective states (i.e., states that differ in kind) may differentially affect subsequent sexual arousal and that only distress that respondents can construe as a form of anxiety has been shown to facilitate subsequent genital vasocongestion in both men and women.

A further objection to the interpretation of the findings by Hoon et al. and Wolchik et al. as evidence for a connection between anxiety-distress and sexual behavior can be based on the fact that only vaginal capillary engorgement or penile tumescence, respectively, were assessed. Although genital vasocongestion undoubtedly is an essential part of sexual behavior, pronounced congestion, in and of itself, may be of little consequence for sexual behavior as such and for sexual experience in particular. It could be argued that only to the extent that genital vasocongestion is accompanied by strong excitatory activity can it be expected that sexual activities will be intensified and sexual experience enhanced. Such accompaniment is suggested by findings reported by Hare et al. (1971). These investigators assessed autonomic reactions to materials very similar to those employed by Hoon et al. and Wolchik et al. (viz., slides of homicide scenes). Distress in response to these stimuli was associated with intense excitatory reactions in both male and female subjects. Compared to a control condition in which innocuous stimuli were presented, strong vasomotor and electrodermal responses were in evidence. A similar investiation by Craig and Wood (1971) with male subjects only produced corroborating findings. It also showed that the peripheral manifestations of autonomic arousal associated with distress tend to be indistinguishable from those associated with states of sexual excitedness. It must be considered likely, then, that genital vasocongestion in response to distress will be accompanied by behavior-energizing excitatory responses that favor vigorous sexual action and that foster intense emotional experience.

Considered in isolation, the investigations by Hoon et al. and Wolchik et al. obviously do not implicate excitation transfer with the facilitation of sexual excitedness. In combination with the observations reported by Hare et al. and Craig and Wood, however, this research may be regarded as highly suggestive of transfer facilitation. Yet, evidence proving a facilitation of sexual responsiveness and experience as a result of residual sympathetic excitation specifically was still lacking.

Cantor, Zillmann, and Bryant (1975) conducted an experiment that filled this void. Affectively neutral, strenuous physical exercise was employed to produce sympathetic excitation for transfer into males' responses to sexual stimulation. It was predicted that such residues, if not properly ascribed to exertion, would enhance sexual responsiveness and experience. The risk of accurate attribution was considered acute immediately following exertion, but not after the disappearance of obtrusive cues such as heavy breathing and trembling hands. Awareness of excitedness from preceding, unrelated stimulation had been shown to inhibit transfer (e.g., Geen, Rakosky, & Pigg, 1972; Reisenzein & Gattinger, 1982).

Three theoretically significant phases of the dissipation of exertion-induced excitation were determined in a pretest: a first period in which subjects were still aroused from exertion (as measured in peripheral manifestations of sympathetic excitation) and perceived themselves as being still aroused from exertion; a second period in which subjects perceived themselves as having recovered but actually were still aroused from exertion; and a third period in which subjects perceived themselves as having recovered and actually had recovered. Excitation transfer should occur, of course, during the second phase. The third phase constitutes a control condition devoid of transferable residues. In the first phase, transfer is likely to be compromised by the person's inability to misconstrue his excitedness as deriving from sexual stimulation, in full or in part (cf. Zillmann, 1978, 1983b). Subjects in the main experiment again performed strenuous exer-

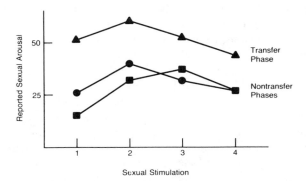

FIG. 6.5.   Facilitation of sexual excitedness by excitation transfer from exertion. Sexual stimulation occurred immediately following strenuous physical exercise when subjects perceived themselves as being aroused from the exercise (squares), in the transfer phase when subjects were still aroused from exercise but failed to recognize it (triangles), or after further delay when subjects had actually recovered and believed themselves to have recovered (circles). Only residual excitation that was not correctly attributed to its inducing condition facilitated sexual excitedness. (Adapted from Cantor, Zillmann, & Bryant, 1975. Reprinted by permission of the American Psychological Association.)

cise and then were placed into one of the three predetermined phases for sexual stimulation. A film featuring coition served as the stimulus. It was halted at different times to allow subjects to record the degree to which they perceived themselves to be sexually excited. After exposure to the entire film, subjects evaluated various aspects of the film.

It was found that sexual excitedness was significantly enhanced during the transfer phase (i.e., the second period). Despite higher levels of residual excitation in the first period, sexual excitedness was particularly low. Figure 6.5 shows that the initial suppression of reports of sexual excitedness eventually vanished, and reports became comparable with the control. Nonetheless, the data leave no doubt that obtrusive feedback from the response to exertion prevented subjects from construing their excitedness as deriving from exposure to the erotic film. Finally, the enhancement of sexual excitedness in the transfer phase was complemented by a facilitation in the perception of valued properties of the film. The stimulus was deemed more exciting, more involving, more entertaining, and of greater aesthetic quality in the transfer condition than in the other two conditions, the latter exhibiting no appreciable differences in these evaluations. Taken together, then, the findings lend strong support to the transfer paradigm. Residual sympathetic excitation, pure and untempered by emotion, produced the predicted facilitation of sexual responsiveness and sexual experience. As quarreling and fighting, being threatened, being scared, and being beaten constitute behavioral emergencies that entail increased sympathetic activity, all these activities should be capable of enhancing sexual behaviors that emerge in the aftermath.

The recent investigation by White, Fishbein, and Rutstein (1981), discussed in Section III of Chapter 5 in connection with romantic love, may be cited as further corroboration that residual sympathetic excitation can facilitate sexually salient experiences. These investigators, it may be remembered, ascertained that residual arousal from physical exercise enhanced the sexual appeal of attractive members of the other gender. Residues from exposure to gruesome accounts of killings and maimings—and for that matter, from exposure to hilarious comedy—did likewise. To the extent that the assessment of sexual appeal (which involved the measurement of the desire to date and to kiss the person under consideration) can be considered to have tapped sexual desire and eagerness, these findings demonstrate the transfer facilitation of sexual inclinations. The findings are of further relevance to transfer theory in that they highlight once again the sexually nonappetitive nature of autonomic arousal. Residual sympathetic excitation proved to enhance repulsion of the potential sexual accommodator when repulsion was the immediate reaction to a nonattractive target.

In summing up, the following statements are possible:

1. Distress that respondents can construe as a form of anxiety is likely to facilitate sexual responses to immediately subsequent sexual stimulation. Specifically, it is likely to enhance genital vasocongestion, that is, vaginal capillary engorgement in women and penile erection in men. Acutely aversive experience prior to sexual engagements, then, seems capable of enhancing sexual behavior and sexual experience.
2. Depressive reactions may impair penile erection in response to immediately subsequent sexual stimulation.
3. Residual sympathetic excitation from affectively neutral, nonsexual stimulation, if not recognized as such, is likely to enhance sexual excitedness in response to sexual stimulation in men.
4. Similarly, residual sympathetic excitation from hedonically neutral, positive, or negative nonsexual stimulation is likely to enhance men's sexual attraction to sexually appealing women.
5. Although it has been demonstrated that residual sympathetic excitation from unrelated prior affective reactions (or their excitatory component alone) tends to enhance both sexual attraction to sexually appealing persons and experiences of sexual excitedness in response to sexual stimulation, the extent to which such residual excitation mediates the recorded facilitation of genital vasocongestion after acute distress remains to be determined.
6. Similarly, the extent to which prior distress and its excitatory component are, through the facilitation of genital vasocongestion, capable of enhancing sexual motivation, sexual performance, and sexual experience in humans has not been ascertained. Direct demonstrations of distress-enhanced sexual motivation and sexual performance are limited to rodents.

V.   TRANSFER IN SEX-AGGRESSION FUSION

As pointed out earlier, sex-aggression fusion occurs under conditions in which sexual and aggressive stimulation and/or responses alternate in rapid succession. Residual excitation thus can facilitate sexual and aggressive actions in chains of alternating actions and also in actions in which sexual and aggressive responses are inextricably merged. However, sex-aggression fusion often results from stimulation that confounds sexual and aggressive enticements and from "misreactions" to particular stimuli, most significantly from reactions of sexual excitedness to aggressive stimuli.

The latter type of sex-aggression fusion has been explored in the work with sexual deviants by Abel and his associates (e.g., Abel, Blanchard, & Becker, 1976) and in its extension to normals by Malamuth and his co-workers (e.g., Malamuth, 1981b).

Abel, Barlow, Blanchard, and Guild (1977) assessed sexual excitedness in response to sexual, aggressive-sexual, and aggressive stimuli in both rapists and nonrapists. Sexual excitedness was measured in penile tumescence (specifically, in the greatest percentage of full erection during stimulation) and in self-reports. The experimental stimuli were auditorily presented verbal accounts that simulated the subjects' stream of thought preceding and during: (1) intercourse with a consenting woman; (2) rape of a woman; and (3) nonsexual assault of a woman. The sexual action was parallel in the intercourse and rape accounts, as was the aggressive action in the rape and assault conditions.

In a first study, the reactions of rapists and nonrapists to the intercourse and rape stimuli were compared. Both rapists and nonrapists exhibited strong erection responses to the account of intercourse with a consenting partner, differences between the two groups being insignificant. Rapists thought themselves significantly less sexually aroused than nonrapists, however. These observations confirm earlier findings. Kercher and Walker (1973), for instance, had exposed rapists and nonrapists to a variety of sexual stimuli and found that, although penile responses were comparable in both groups, subjective assessments of sexual excitedness were lower in rapists. This was the case despite a tendency for rapists to respond to the stimuli with greater excitedness generally (reactions assessed in electrodermal changes). More significantly, however, the data presented by Abel et al. (1977) revealed strong differences in the penile responses of rapists and nonrapists to the rape account. The penile response of rapists to this account did, in fact, not appreciably differ from the responses to the account of intercourse devoid of coercion. In sharp contrast, penile responses of nonrapists to the rape account were minimal. Subjective assessments of sexual excitedness were in accord with measured penile responses for nonrapists. For rapists, these assessments again underrepresented their bodily reaction. Essentially, then, the findings show that in their penile reactions rapists fail to differentiate between sexual situations that entail threats of violence and violent actions and sexual situations devoid of coercion and aggressive behaviors. Nonrapists, on the other hand, are acutely sensitive to coercion and victimization. Presumably as the result of witnessing a person suffer from fear and physical abuse, erection is severely inhibited. Finally, subjective appraisals of sexual excitedness correspond very closely with penile responses in nonrapists. Rapists consistently underestimate their actual sexual excitedness.

In an extension of the initial study, Abel et al. (1977) involved the account of the purely aggressive assault and compared the reactions of rapists to the intercourse, rape, and assault stimuli. Penile responses to the intercourse and the rape accounts proved to be strong and comparable, as in the first study. Responses to the assault account were substantially weaker (about one quarter of full erection, compared to above half for the responses in the intercourse and rape conditions). Notwithstanding the fact that the magnitude of the penile responses to the assault account was somewhat less than half that of the responses to the rape account, Abel et al. (1977) detected an extremely close correspondence in a rapist's sexual excitedness from exposure to pure violence and sexual violence. The correlation of penile responses to these two types of stimuli proved to be practically perfect. Moreover, Abel et al. observed that sadistically inclined rapists responded with strong erection to pure violence and to rape. Their response to coital behavior devoid of violent action tended to be quite weak. In an extreme case, the penile response to pure violence proved to be markedly stronger than that to rape, and the penile response to sex devoid of aggression proved to be negligible. Taken together, these findings would seem to suggest that nonsadistic rapists, irrespective of the facts, tend to experience themselves as being insufficiently aroused by sexual stimuli. Sadistic rapists experience the same and actually are insufficiently aroused. Both groups of rapists, then, but especially the latter, potentially can complement their sexual excitedness by exposure to stimuli to which they are excitationally responsive: the violent achievement of sexual access. The findings leave it unclear, however, to what extent penile reactions covary with sympathetic excitation in its peripheral manifestations and to what extent peripherally manifest excitation influences the subjective assessment of sexual excitedness. Needless to say, the findings also leave uncertain the degree to which the actual commission of violent and violent-sexual acts might promote sensations of specifically sexual and more general states of excitedness. It can only be speculated that the commision of violent acts would facilitate feelings of sexual excitedness more than their contemplation does.

The findings of Abel et al. (1977) have been successfully replicated by Barbaree, Marshall, and Lanthier (1979). In several recent investigations, however, individuals from the general population were found to be as strongly excited sexually by portrayals of rape as by depictions of coital activities among consenting partners (e.g., Farkas, 1979; Malamuth, 1981a). It appears that the excitatory response of exposure to sexual activities entailing coercion and the infliction of pain depends in large measure on the specific reactions of the victims. Malamuth and Check (1980b), for instance, had observed that nondeviant males and females reported similar degrees of sexual excitedness in response to accounts of coition among consenting partners and to accounts of rape. However, independent of the involvement of coercion and pain in the depicted sexual endeavors, reported sexual excitedness declined when disgust was an element of the response to sexual stimulation. Malamuth, Heim, and Feshbach (1980), in contrast, found that nondeviant males and females reported less sexual excitedness in response to the portrayal of rape than to the depiction of coition among consenting partners. Subjects apparently assumed disgust and abhorrence in the rape victim. When this impression was eliminated by depicting the rape victim as being sexually responsive (i.e., as being involuntarily orgasmic), subjects reported sexual excitedness comparable to that from coition with consent. Disgust and abhorrence in response to sexual stimulation, then, seem to be the reactions that impair sexual excitedness in the onlooker. Witness of pain reactions does not necessarily have this consequence. In fact, Malamuth, Heim, and Feshbach (1980) observed that males reported the highest degree of sexual excitedness when the orgasmic rape victim experienced pain. Females, on the other hand, reported greater excitedness when the orgasmic victim did not experience pain. The tacit acceptance of the rape myth that is manifest in these reactions has been ascertained more firmly by Malamuth, Haber, and Feshbach (1980). Men and women alike were found to believe that women tend to enjoy sexual assaults that entail the infliction of pain. But few female subjects believed that they themselves could derive pleasure from being victimized.

An investigation by Malamuth and Check (1980a) went beyond self-reports of sexual excitedness and determined the apparent consequences of the victim's response to sexual assault in more behavioral terms. Nondeviant men were exposed to accounts of: (1) coition with a consenting woman; (2) rape of a woman abhoring the experience throughout the assault; and (3) rape of a woman becoming sexually responsive during the assault. Sexual arousal responses were measured in penile tumescence. As expected, it was found that sexual excitedness was impaired only by the portrayal of abhorrence in rape. Excitedness in response to the depiction conforming with the rape myth was most pronounced and exceeded that in response to the account of coition among consenting partners. The findings appear to reconcile discrepancies in earlier observations (cf. Malamuth, 1981b). More importantly here, they confirm that neither the use of coercion in gaining sexual access nor the infliction and/or reception of pain per se are detrimental to sexual excitedness. If anything, coercion and pain facilitate sexual arousal. Only the evocation of aversive reactions devoid of sexual qualities (e.g., pure disgust, abhorrence, terror, and shock) seems to impair sexual excitedness in nondeviant men.

The work of Malamuth and his associates (e.g., Malamuth, 1981b) clarified which aspects of the victim's response to sexual assault deter sexual arousal, and perhaps more importantly, it extended the reasoning on the rapist–nonrapist dichotomy (cf. Abel et al., 1977) to a graduation applicable to normals. Specifically, these investigators developed means to assess, through ratings, the degree to which a male is accepting of force in the sexual conquest of a woman. The index revealed a proclivity for rape—or somewhat less extremely, a high degree of callousness in the pursuit of sexual access—in large segments of the male population (see also Tieger, 1981). Most significantly, however, the index was found to correlate positively with both penile tumescence and reports of sexual excitedness in response to accounts of sexual assaults and rape, but did not correlate with such responses to accounts of coital behavior among consenting parties (Malamuth & Check, 1980a; Malamuth, Heim, & Feshbach, 1980). Callous normal men, then, did not differ from noncallous normal men in their sexual response to sexual themes devoid of coercion and aggression, but with increasing callousness, normal men became increasingly responsive to violent sexual happenings. This tendency might be attributed to a lack of inhibition due to insensitivity concerning another person's welfare, to an excitatory reaction to dominance and power (cf. Miller, Byrne, & Bell, 1977), or to both. However, as penile reactions to accounts of rape in accordance with the rape myth tended to be more pronounced than to depictions of noncoercive sexual activities (Malamuth & Check, 1980a), lack of empathy with the victim seems to be an insufficient explanation. Exposure to dominance, power, force, and violent action apparently complements sexual excitedness in callous men, and this complementing excitedness consequently must be considered elicited by the stimuli that convey these themes.

How can specifically sexual responses, such as penile tumescence, come to be elicited by witnessing coercive and potentially injurious action? Or, for that matter, how can they be elicited by contemplating or performing such action? Constitutional reasons, which to be sure are not yet fully understood, have often been invoked. In a similar vein, psychoanalytically oriented writers have held the deviant's personality development at large accountable (e.g., Karpman, 1954; Rado, 1949; Salzman, 1972). But the elicitation of sexual responses by seemingly nonsexual stimuli has also been considered the result of learning, although learning under somewhat peculiar circumstances. As early as 1888, Binet promoted the view that the stimulus–response connections in question were established, largely by accident, in critical early sexual experiences. Learning tended to be expected to take place in a one-trial fashion. Characteristically, the environmental stimuli that happened to be around during initial experiences of sexual excitedness were thought to assume the power to evoke such excitedness at later times. The process thus was viewed as one analogous to imprinting in lower vertebrates (e.g., Hess, 1959). Such learning interpretations have come under criticism (e.g., Jaspers, 1963), as they would seem to predict peculiar and bizarre sexual fixations as the rule rather than the exception.

The view that the learning of sexual responses to "nonsexual" stimuli is gradual like any other learning process, although the building of some connections may be constitutionally advantaged (cf. Seligman, 1970), has gained acceptance only rather recently (e.g., Barlow, 1974; Marshall, 1973; Rachman, 1961). McGuire, Carlisle, and Young (1965) proposed a conditioning theory for sexual deviations that proved particularly influential. These investigators argued that in accordance with the classical conditioning paradigm: "any stimulus which regularly precedes ejaculation by the correct time interval should become more and more sexually exciting [p. 186]." The stimuli that thus gradually assume the power of eliciting sexual excitedness may, of course, be circumstantial or deliberately arranged. McGuire et al. have shown that they tend to be circumstantial at first but later are employed deliberately. A rejected male, for instance, might masturbate while imagining forcibly seducing the person who rejected him. Thoughts of aggression may well be spontaneous in such fantasies. However, if this experience is repeated and the "aggressive fantasy" comes to trigger sexual excitedness, thoughts of rape should become deliberate. Exposure to accounts of sexual assault generally should become exciting and attractive.

The conditioning theory of sexual deviations applies to fetishism and transvestism as well as to sadomasochism and rape. In nonassaultive deviations, sexual excitedness is primarily conditioned to environmental stimuli (e.g., particular apparels). Covert accompaniments of exposure—be they the imagination of actions by self and/or actions and reactions by others in whatever form—are also likely to become arousing stimuli. Assaultive deviations, presumably because the approximate external stimuli are difficult to arrange during masturbation, appear to depend more on covert than on overt stimuli. But common to all deviations, according to McGuire et al., is that elements of the climactic experience of ejaculation are conditioned to some aggregate of overt and covert stimuli that preceded the climactic experience. McGuire et al. point out that men masturbate to climax very liberally (e.g., Hunt, 1974), making them particularly susceptible—in contrast to women—to developing deviations in the proposed piecemeal fashion.

The conditioning theory of sexual deviations, it should be noticed, is entirely consistent with the three-factor theory of emotion. Three-factor theory stresses the stimulus control of excitatory reactions. This control, usually applied to sympathetic activity only, is readily extended to the combination of locomotion-energizing arousal and genital vasocongestion (cf. DiCara, 1970; Kimmel, 1974). The total reliance on classical conditioning by McGuire et al. would seem to be limiting, however. Stimulus control may also be established through operant learning (Skinner, 1969). Ejaculation can be treated as a reinforcer for the patterned arousal reaction preceding it, and it is conceivable that sexual excitedness prior to climax functions as a reinforcer as well. But regardless of the specific learning paradigms that might be invoked or considered implicated, it is clear that the acquisition of general excitatory and specific sexual responses to initially neutral stimuli is mediated by well-established learning principles. It appears, moreover, that the learning in question is constitutionally advantaged by the confounded mechanics of the reflexogenic and psychogenic control of sexual excitedness that have been detailed earlier (Section II of Chapter 3 and Section IV of Chapter 4; see also Fig. 3.3). The tactile stimulation of masturbation, according to these mechanics, will initially involve the reflexogenic center and produce genital vasocongestion through parasympathetic sacral outflow. Genital vasocongestion, via stimulation of the adrenal medullae, will eventually foster sympathetic thoracolumbar outflow and involve the psychogenic center. Reflex action thus is directly linked to higher central functions. Specific connections between external stimuli and their internal representations, on the one hand, and genital tumescence and peripheral excitatory responses, on the other, should be readily established as a consequence.

The conditioning of sexual excitedness has been convincingly demonstrated in the research on sexual deviations. Rachman (1966), for instance, classically conditioned penile reactions to a fetish. Extinction and spontaneous recovery of these reactions were demonstrated in addition to response acquisition. Most of the research, as might be expected, served therapeutic objectives and concentrated on aggressive deviations. In this realm, "masturbatory conditioning" and "fading" are techniques that proved effective in shifting stimulus control away from the objectionable conditions toward more appropriate substitutes (cf. Abel & Blanchard, 1974; Abel et al., 1976). Abel, Barlow, and Blanchard (1973) and Abel, Blanchard, Barlow, and Flanagan (1975) reported that sexual aggressives who were made to masturbate to depictions of nonaggressive, mutually enjoyable intercourse not only became sexually responsive to such depictions, but also exhibited a reduction of sexual arousal in response to the portrayal of aggressive-sexual behaviors. Marshall (1973) and Marshall and Williams (1975) achieved similar results with rapists and pedophiliacs. Davison (1968, 1977) succeeded in eliminating sadistic inclinations. In fading, the objectionable stimuli are more gradually replaced by acceptable ones. Images of young children, for example, are in a step-by-step fashion replaced by images of adult women. Barlow and Agras (1973) and Laws (1974) reported successful applications of this technique. On occasion, coition has been substituted for masturbation in the conditioning of appropriate sexual responses (e.g., LoPiccolo, Stewart, & Watkins, 1972). Finally, masturbatory conditioning techniques also proved useful in the treatment of such matters as voyeurism (e.g., Jackson, 1977) and homosexuality (e.g., Barlow & Agras, 1973; Thorpe, Schmidt, & Castell, 1963).

The therapy-inspired research, then, leaves no doubt about the fact that sexual excitedness can be produced and complemented by responses to stimuli that are initially devoid of sexual connotations. All conceivable aggressive behaviors—whether executed, suffered, or witnessed—and any pictorial and/or verbal representation thereof—whether seen and heard in movies, learned from books, or merely imagined—constitute stimuli that can assume control over sexual excitedness. Sex-aggression fusion (and confusion), in other words, is readily learned.

In summing up, the following conclusions can be drawn:

1. Sex-aggression fusion derives, in large measure, from reactions of sexual excitedness to aggressive stimuli. Sexual excitedness is likely to be accompanied by elevated sympathetic activity. Both components of the excitatory reaction to aggressive stimuli are in all probability acquired.

2. Men who have a high proclivity for rape and men who are approving of the use of coercive means in gaining sexual access exhibit similar degrees of penile tumescence in response to coital depictions involving violent, coercive action and to coital depictions devoid of such action. Men who are disapproving of coercion as a means of achieving sexual access, on the other hand, exhibit less penile tumescence in response to coital scenes involving violent, coercive action—especially when the victim responds with disgust, abhorrence, and terror—than to coital scenes enacted by mutually consenting parties.

3. In depictions of coercive coition, reactions of pure abhorrence on the part of the victim generally tend to inhibit penile tumescence. Erection does not suffer impairment, however, regardless of the fact of coercion and the possible infliction of pain upon the victim, when indications of grave anguish are absent—and especially, when indications of acceptance, even enjoyment, are present. Under the latter conditions, the use of force and the infliction of pain tend to facilitate sexual excitedness.

4. The tendency to respond with sexual excitedness to aggressive stimuli can be acquired through classical and/or operant conditioning. In the application of these paradigms, preclimactic excitedness and ejaculation—induced by masturbation or coition—are treated as unconditioned responses or reinforcers, respectively. Learning appears to be constitutionally advantaged by the confounded mechanics of reflexogenic and psychogenic control of sexual excitedness.

VI.   HABITUATION AND ITS CONSEQUENCES

The elicitation of sexual excitedness by "nonsexual" stimuli might be considered sexual hyperresponsiveness. Sexuality-enhancing as these stimuli may be, such hyperresponsiveness usually is thought to be in need of correction—especially when it is associated with transgressive violence (as in rape), but also when it is deemed "inappropriate," "deviant," or "stigmatizing" despite innocuousness (e.g., as in fetishism). Sexual hyporesponsiveness (i.e., subnormal to minimal sexual responsiveness to sexual stimulation), in contrast, has hardly ever been branded as deviant. With the exception of acute impotence, it tends to be viewed as the normal decline of libido that comes with failing health and with age (cf. Kinsey, Pomeroy, & Martin, 1948; Kinsey et al., 1953). As a result, it tends to be treated chemically with androgens and related drugs, if not with unproven exotic aphrodisiacs.

Sexual hyporesponsiveness often is not a function of bodily deficiency, however, but results from predictable changes in the capacity of stimuli to evoke particular excitatory reactions. Excitatory reactions to essentially all stimulus conditions diminish with repeated exposure (cf. Grings & Dawson, 1978; Tighe & Leaton, 1976). This phenomenon is commonly referred to as "habituation." It should be expected, then, that specific sexual stimuli also lose some of their power to elicit sexual responses and/or the more general excitedness that is usually associated with them. Habituation of these responses causes grave problems, of course, to the individual who deems intense reactions of sexual excitedness highly desirable. Therapeutic guidance lacking, the hyporesponsive individual tends to enhance his or her excitedness in a trial-and-error fashion. Such random probing probably accounts for the development of sexual techniques that exploit excitation transfer. Before discussing these likely developments, however, I inspect the scarce data on the habituation of excitatory reactions to sexual stimuli. There are two relevant lines of research. The first explores habituation of sexual excitedness in response to repeated and potentially massive exposure to erotica. The second deals with habituation indirectly through the exploration of the obtrusive revival of lost libido that is occasioned by the exchange of sexual targets.

Although research on the excitatory consequences of exposure to erotica may seem abundant (cf. Zillmann, Bryant, Comisky, & Medoff, 1981), only a few studies address habituation of libido and sexual excitedness. The obvious reason for this is the requirement to assess the subjects' behavior repeatedly over extended periods of time.

Mann, Sidman, and Starr (1971; see also Mann, Berkowitz, Sidman, Starr, & West, 1974) exposed married couples to sexually explicit or nonerotic films in four consecutive weekly sessions. During the treatment period, subjects recorded their sexual activities in diaries. Exposure to erotica was found to stimulate libido only temporarily. Sexual activities were more frequent on exposure days than on the days thereafter. Most importantly, however, this transitory enhancement of libido grew weaker over the weeks and became trivial in the last week. The sex-inspiring effect of exposure to explicit depictions of sexual behavior apparently underwent rapid habituation.

An investigation by Howard, Reifler, and Liptzin (1971; see also Reifler, Howard, Lipton, Liptzin, & Widmann, 1971) assessed the habituation of sexual excitedness more directly. On 15 days distributed over a 3-week period, male college students were given access to pornographic films, photographs, and readings or were not given such access in a control condition. Subjects in the exposure condition were free to choose from among these materials and from among nonerotic ones in the initial ten sessions. In the following three sessions, the original pornographic materials were replaced by new ones, and in the final two sessions, the nonerotic materials were removed. Subjects recorded their activities intermittantly during all these sessions. Prior to and following the extended treatment period, subjects in both the exposure and the control condition were shown an explicitly sexual film. Eight weeks after the treatment, the subjects in the exposure condition were once more shown such a film. Numerous measures of sexual excitedness were taken during and after exposure to these erotic films, and a battery of perceptual and dispositional measures was recorded after exposure.

The findings show that the young men initially had a strong interest in erotic materials. But with repeated exposure, this interest faded rapidly. Even the introduction of novel materials failed to restore initial levels of interest. Liberal access to pornography ultimately led subjects to appraise their reactions to coital scenes as boredom. Although interest in erotica was maintained to some degree, the findings give no indication that pornography was or could ever become enjoyable.

The analysis of penile tumescence and associated excitatory reactions revealed a loss of responsiveness that can be considered consistent with the loss of interest in exposure to erotica. Compared with responses to the pretreatment film, exposure to an explicitly sexual film immediately after the conclusion of the longitudinal treatment produced diminished reactions on measures of both sexual and general excitedness. The tumescence recordings showed that erections were less pronounced and more poorly maintained than prior to frequent exposure to erotica. Release of acid phosphatase, a prostatic secretion, indicated redundant changes. Concomitant sympathetic excitation underwent parallel changes. Heart rate, respiration rate, and skin temperature (measured from the earlobe) exhibited diminished responsiveness. The loss of specifically sexual responsiveness appeared to be stronger than that of its sympathetic accompaniment, however. The remeasurement of reactions to explicit erotica after a period of 8 weeks during which subjects were not treated in any particular way (i.e., during which they presumably had little exposure to erotica) revealed some degree of recovery from the loss in responsiveness. Both sexual and excitatory reactions assumed levels intermediate to the initial ones and those immediately after conclusion of the exposure treatment.

This demonstration of habituation of sexual and autonomic arousal to erotica is somewhat compromised by the fact that the longitudinal treatment served as both an independent and a dependent variable. Exposure was first a measured effect and later the causal condition for habituation. As exposure was free to vary, it was by no means massive throughout. Had exposure been more consistent and more pronounced, stronger and longer lasting habituation effects might have been attained. On the other hand, effects might have been weaker had the subjects been provided with a larger supply of erotic materials such that exposure could always have been to novel stimuli. The fact that the supply of materials was rather limited during the initial ten sessions might actually explain why the subjects developed boredom with erotica. Kelley (1982) has observed that repeated exposure to identical erotic stimuli leads to rapid satiation and loss of sexual excitedness. Notwithstanding these ambiguities, the research by Howard et al. and Reifler et al. convincingly shows that even limited exposure to erotica is capable of habituating sexual and excitatory responses for extended periods of time.

With regard to habituation, the discussed findings accord well with the fate of excitatory responsiveness in emotional behavior generally (cf. Bandura, 1969). The finding of growing boredom, in contrast, seems in conflict not only with the increasing commercial success of pornography (a success attesting to insatiable interest) but with theoretical considerations also. Byrne (1977; see also Byrne & Byrne, 1977), for instance, projected increased enjoyment of and interest in erotica as the result of massive exposure. He assumed that exposure to pornographic materials initially may offend and disturb some and produce apprehensions in others. He went on to propose, based on Zajonc's (1968) empirical generalization that repeated exposure to any stimulus results in more favorable evaluations of the particular stimulus, that frequent exposure to erotica diminishes negative reactions and negative appraisals of these reactions—in part because of excitatory habituation. Once individuals have thus grown more tolerant of erotic fare, Byrne continues to argue, the stimuli are more likely to entice them to engage uninhibitedly in pleasurable sexual fantasies. In fact, he suggested that after repeatedly witnessing sexual practices associated with apprehensions and disapproval, people will eventually be inspired to perform the behaviors in question because of the promise of joy from erotica-induced imaginative rehearsals. But whether or not these rehearsals are followed up by action, the consumption of erotica should become increasingly enjoyable.

Excitatory habituation to erotica and associated perceptual and dispositional changes have been reexamined recently by Zillmann and Bryant (1983). Both males and females were exposed to different amounts of erotic materials in a strictly controlled fashion. Subjects watched thirty-six films in six consecutive weekly sessions, six films per session. In a massive-exposure condition, all films were erotic ones. All were standard pornographic fare, explicitly depicting fellatio, cunnilingus, and coital behavior in all conceivable positions. In a control condition, all films were nonerotic, innocuous ones. In addition, an intermediate-exposure condition was employed in which subjects saw three erotic and three nonerotic films per session. Exposure to erotica thus was half that in the massive-exposure condition.

One week after the conclusion of the longitudinal exposure treatment, subjects were exposed to three erotic films. Ample time for excitatory recovery was allowed between exposure. The first film depicted heterosexual petting and precoital activities in a nonexplicit, suggestive fashion. The second one was of the kind employed in the longitudinal treatment (i.e., it explicitly depicted heterosexual intercourse and associated activities). The third film explicitly portrayed sadomasochistic action and acts of bestiality. The first and third stimuli were included to learn about the extent to which habituation might generalize to sexual stimuli other than those that produced habituation. Excitatory responses to the films were assessed in peripheral manifestations. Affective reactions were recorded in ratings.

Figure 6.6 summarizes the findings concerning habituation. Strong type-specific habituation of excitatory reactions is clearly evident. Massive exposure to explicit erotica not only reduced excitatory responses to such fare, but virtually eliminated them. Heart rate and systolic blood pressure, for instance, showed average changes of less than 1 beat per minute or 1 millimeter of mercury, respectively. The findings suggest some degree of generalization to the nonexplicit depiction of sexual activities, presumably because of great stimulus similarity resulting from redundancies in the actions. There is no indication, however, that excitatory habituation generalizes to depictions of substantially different forms of sexual behaviors. All these effects were parallel for males and females.

The analysis of associated reactions of repulsion and enjoyment confirmed Byrne's projections: Repulsion diminished and enjoyment increased with the amount of exposure. These effects, again parallel for males and females, proved strong and clear-cut. They obviously challenge the contention that frequent exposure promotes boredom with erotica (e.g., Howard et al., 1971). The findings on repulsion and enjoyment further showed that massive exposure to standard

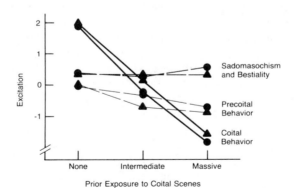

FIG. 6.6.   Excitatory habituation to coital scenes by prior massive exposure to coital scenes (solid lines). Habituation did not generalize to scenes of uncommon sexual practices, such as sadomasochism and bestiality (thick broken lines). Generalization to scenes of precoital behavior was poor (thin broken lines). Heart rate (triangles) and systolic blood pressure (circles) are presented in *z* scores for ease of comparison. (Adapted from Zillmann & Bryant, 1983. Reprinted by permission of Academic Press.)

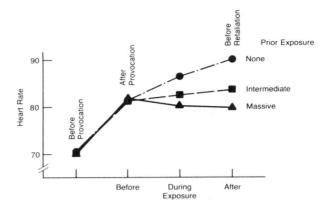

FIG. 6.7.   Excitatory habituation to erotica 2 weeks after conclusion of the habituating treatment. (After Zillmann & Bryant, 1983. Reprinted, with permission,
from N. M. Malamuth and E. Donnerstein (Eds.), *Pornography and sexual aggression.* New York: Academic Press, 1983.)

erotic fare fosters acceptance of not-so-standard forms of pornography. Massive
exposure to coital scenes led to diminished reactions of repulsion to sadomasochistic activities and acts of bestiality. And although both males and females
reported little enjoyment from exposure to the less common sexual practices,
heavily exposed subjects exhibited a higher degree of enjoyment than subjects in
the control condition. Unlike excitatory habituation, then, the effect of massive
exposure to common sexual activities on repulsion and enjoyment did generalize
to portrayals of comparatively uncommon sexual behaviors.

The investigation by Zillmann and Bryant involved the assessment of the
consequences of excitatory habituation for aggressive behavior. Two weeks after
the conclusion of the longitudinal exposure treatment, subjects in all three treatment conditions were provoked, exposed to no film, a film depicting coition, a
film featuring sadomasochism, or a film featuring bestiality, and provided with
an opportunity to retaliate against their annoyer. Retaliatory aggression was
measured in the transgressive infliction of pain (i.e., in the deliberate administration of excessive pressure to the arm; cf. Zillmann, Bryant, & Carveth, 1981).
Excitatory reactions were measured in heart-rate changes.

Figure 6.7 displays the time course of excitatory reactions across the three
erotic stimuli employed. While watching an erotic film, subjects with massive
prior exposure to erotica actually recovered from their provocation-induced excitatory reaction. Subjects without prior exposure, in contrast, advanced to increasingly higher levels of excitedness. Two weeks after the conclusion of the
massive-exposure treatment, excitatory habituation is thus still in evidence.

Retaliatory aggression varied with excitedness during and after exposure to
erotica. Massively exposed, excitationally habituated persons behaved least ag-

gressively. Nonhabituated persons behaved significantly more aggressively. Persons having undergone the intermediate exposure treatment exhibited intermediate levels of aggressiveness. There were no gender differences. Retaliatory aggression, then, proved to be a function of residual excitation from sexual stimulation. The magnitude of these residues, in turn, proved to be a function of the individual's history of exposure to the stimuli in question. All this is exactly as predicted from excitation transfer theory.

Independent of habituation, the three erotic films employed in the aggression experiment were equally arousing, but they differed in hedonic valence. The films featuring sadomasochism and bestiality were deemed repulsive. The film depicting heterosexual intercourse, in contrast, did not elicit such reactions. Enjoyment varied inversely. The two-component model of erotica effects (see Section III of this chapter, especially Fig. 6.4) thus projects that motivated aggression should be facilitated more strongly by the films depicting the uncommon sexual acts that were met with repulsion (as both are arousing and annoying) than by the film showing common coital activities (as it is arousing but not annoying). The findings support all these predictions. Retaliatory behavior after the coition film was at significantly higher levels than after no exposure. In turn, retaliatory behavior after exposure to either one of the repulsive erotic films was at significantly higher levels than after the coition film.

These findings seem to have straightforward practical implications: As the excitatory response to explicit erotica habituates with repeated exposure, the potential for the facilitation of motivated aggression diminishes. Massive exposure to such materials consequently can be viewed as a remedy to the undesirable effect of aggression facilitation that accrues to occasional exposure. The short-lived transfer facilitation of aggressive behavior should indeed become a trivial phenomenon. Recent reports of diminished excitatory reactions to erotica and of associated failures to observe transfer effects on aggression (e.g., Donnerstein & Berkowitz, 1981; Sapolsky & Zillmann, 1981) can be taken as an indication that this stage might have been reached already, as large segments of the population, through their own choice of exposure, may have undergone habituation. Although viable in themselves, such conclusions are somewhat misleading, however, because they ignore perceptual and dispositional changes regarding sexuality that result from massive exposure to erotic fare. These changes, which have only now been brought to light, pertain to aggressive and sexual-aggressive behaviors most directly.

In the longitudinal investigation by Zillmann and Bryant, subjects returned to the laboratory for a final session 3 weeks after the conclusion of the massive-exposure treatment. They estimated the use of specific sexual practices in the population of sexually active adults, dealt with the regulation of pornography in society, and after being exposed to a rape case, recommended appropriate punishment (i.e., in a mock-jury situation, they recommended a prison term in years and months). (The investigation involved additional assessments; see Zillmann & Bryant, 1982, 1983, for a more complete account.)

The projection of the usage of sexual practices revealed that massively exposed subjects, both males and females, grossly overestimated the popularity of sadomasochistic activities. Moreover, massively exposed subjects were more approving and supportive of pornography than were others. Massively exposed subjects saw little reason, for instance, to limit access to pornography for minors or to restrict the broadcast of pornography in any way. These effects of massive exposure were observed in both males and females. Females were altogether less approving of pornography, however. Such findings can be taken as suggesting that, along with all other elements of pornography, the exhibition of sexual-aggressive behaviors becomes more acceptable with excitatory habituation occasioned by massive exposure.

The findings regarding rape make this point more compellingly. Massively exposed subjects prescribed far less severe punishment for rape than did control subjects. Recommended time of incarceration was about half that in the control condition. This was the case for both males and females, but females recommended substantially greater punishment for rape overall. Massive exposure to erotic materials (i.e., materials that were actually devoid of sexual coercion and other sexual-aggressive activities) apparently trivialized rape as a criminal offense. Irrespective of excitatory habituation and diminished transfer facilitation, then, aggression against women seems to be promoted by rather persistent perceptual and dispositional changes from massive exposure to erotica. Data collected at the end of the final session from the male subjects confirm this generalization. The men who had been massively exposed to erotica had become highly callous toward women. As measured on a sex-callousness scale developed by Mosher (1971), massively exposed males exhibited significantly greater sexual callousness than did males in the control condition. The focal point of such callousness is, of course, the sexual conquest of the female at seemingly any cost and without regard for the woman's welfare. As a behavioral disposition, sexual callousness undoubtedly promotes the sexual harassment of women. But whether it can ever grow to a point where it becomes the driving force in the transgressive, violent seeking of sexual access may be questioned. If recent assessments of men's proclivity for rape (e.g., Malamuth, 1981b; Tieger, 1981) are any indication, a large proportion of males seem callous enough to contemplate rape occasionally and to shy away from the commission of sexual assaults only for fear of punitive consequences. Conservatively speaking, however, sexually callous men are likely to do "anything they can get away with"—that is, they are likely to resort to means of coercion whenever persuasion fails. And to the extent that massive exposure to pornography, as has been demonstrated, fosters lasting dispositions of sexual callousness, such exposure can be considered to promote hostile behavior in the long run.

It can only be speculated at this point that any hostile action against women that is mediated by men's callous dispositions ultimately derives from the pornographic portrayal of women as socially nondiscriminating and without personal involvement or attachment (cf. Zillmann & Bryant, 1983). Characteristically, the female in pornography yearns for sexual and pseudosexual stimulation from any male in the vicinity, responds euphorically to any stimulation from anybody, and shows no loyalties. Whether or not a valid representation of "female nature," such a portrayal makes women appear unworthy of trust and special attention. Callous attitudes, then, would seem appropriate in the sense that any investment into an extended relationship is misplaced. Caring for a woman and empathy with a woman's distress appear to be ventures without utility. The inhibition of hostile action that is usually mediated by protective reactions is jeopardized as a consequence. Potentially hostile sexual exploitation becomes intelligent defensive behavior, in fact, as it minimizes both the effort put into gaining sexual access and distress from the loss of a valued relationship.

Leonard and Taylor (1983) have reported recent findings that are highly consistent with the view that men become callous toward women who display great sexual desire and seem indiscriminately promiscuous. In their investigation, male subjects, one at a time, interacted with a female confederate. Each pair was exposed to a series of slides and then competed in a reaction-time task that was rigged to measure the male's aggressive reactions to provocation by the female. Specifically, at the hands of the female confederate, the male subject received electric shock that appeared to be set at unreasonably high intensity levels, and the shock intensities chosen by the subject in retaliation for this served as the measure of aggression. The preceding slide presentation featured heterosexual erotica (i.e., precoital and coital activities) vs. persons from magazine advertisements in a control condition. Most importantly, the erotica were presented in three different social situations: In a first condition, the female made ostensibly spontaneous comments such as "that looks like fun" and "I'd like to try that"; in a second condition she made disapproving remarks such as "oh, that's awful"; in the third condition, as in the control, she made no comment at all. Postexposure aggression against the female in the condition in which she appeared prudish was at the level of the control condition. When she gave no indication of her reaction to the erotica, aggressiveness increased with repeated provocation to levels above those associated with the control. This increase is readily explained as an excitation-transfer effect. The transfer effect was not observed in the condition in which the female appeared prudish, which indicates an aggression-reducing effect of such an appearance. But most significantly, in the condition in which the female gave the impression of sexual eagerness and promiscuity, aggression increased substantially. Throughout the exchange, the intensity of shock delivered was about twice that in the control condition. The expression of unqualified sexual eagerness on the part of the female, then, seems to have fostered male callousness that liberated particularly intense aggressive reactions toward her.

Returning to excitatory habituation to erotic stimuli, the question arises as to whether or not such habituation could generalize to "coital scenes" immediately witnessed by parties involved in them (i.e., by parties engaged in precoital and coital activities). The data at hand do not allow any definitive evaluation of this possibility. Although generalization from coital scenes to depictions of other sexual activities was nonexistent or poor, the stimulus similarity between coital scenes in erotica and coital scenes as witnessed by the sexually engaged parties themselves may be considered to be substantial (especially if it is assumed that in the exposure to erotica attention is focused, as in actual behavior, on persons of the sexual partner's gender), and generalization cannot be ruled out. On the other hand, it would seem unlikely that massive exposure to erotica could critically impair excitatory responsiveness in intimate encounters because any response deficiency should readily be compensated for and overpowered by excitatory reactions to tactile stimulation and to the complex stimulus situation that gains excitation-eliciting power through "coital conditioning" (see the discussion of stimulus control through masturbatory and coital conditioning in the preceding section). This is not to say, however, that habituation to the stimuli that produce sexual and autonomic arousal in intimate interpersonal situations does not occur. Clinical accounts are highly suggestive of a successive loss of excitatory reactions to the same sexual stimuli (e.g., Ard, 1977). After years of monogamy, for instance, it is not uncommon for men to develop acute sexual disinterest—even secondary impotence (cf. Masters & Johnson, 1966). Systematic demonstrations of excitatory habituation to sexual stimulation in humans do not exist, however.

In screening the research with subhuman species for pertinent data, it might appear that the evidence concerning the so-called "Coolidge effect" is supportive of habituation of the male sexual response. This effect—labeled to commemorate President and Mrs. Coolidge for making rather innocuous remarks about the virility and promiscuity of roosters—refers to the fact that in numerous species the sexually exhausted males' sexual activity can be revived quasi-instantaneously by the introduction of novel females. It has been observed in rodents (e.g., Fisher, 1962; Fowler & Whalen, 1961; Grunt & Young, 1952; Wilson, Kuehn, & Beach, 1963) and in farm animals (e.g., Hale & Almquist, 1960), for instance, that during the refractory period males will vigorously copulate with novel females, but exhibit no sexual interest in familiar ones. This much cited, obtrusive phenomenon certainly pertains to stimulus control. But whether the libidinal ebb during characteristic refractory periods in the interaction with familiar mates results from stimulus habituation and the virile response to novel mates from the lack thereof or whether alternative causes mediate the effect remains a matter of conjecture. Additionally, in the face of enormous differences in the control of sexual behavior in rodents and humans, it would seem a monumental jump indeed to base conclusions about libido enhancement in human males on the behavior of sexually exhausted rats and guinea pigs.

In their research with rhesus monkeys, Michael and Zumpe (1978) have approached much more closely the human condition under which habituation of sexual excitedness is likely to occur. These investigators have simulated the continual sexual receptivity of the human female by placing female monkeys into continual estrus. This was accomplished by daily injections of ovariectomized females with estradiol benzoate. The thus treated females were joined with males in daily test sessions over a period of 4 years. During these sessions, the sexual behavior of the couples was recorded in terms of latency of initial mounting and frequency of ejaculations. The experiment's crucial variation was the replacement of the females with which the males were familiar by identically treated novel females at the beginning of the 4th year and the restoration of the initial situation after a 4-week period of interaction with the novel females.

The findings show a dramatic habituation of the sexual response to familiar females. After 3 years, the latency of the first mount had doubled, and the frequency of ejaculations had dropped to approximately one third of the initial level. The introduction of the novel females at this time prompted both sexual eagerness and sexual performance to jump back to initial heights. These elevated activity levels were not sustained, however, when the novel females were removed and the familiar ones reintroduced. Sexual activity immediately dropped back to the habituation level. In fact, there was no indication of any carry-over from the resurgence of sexual action in the interim. Figure 6.8 gives an overview of these effects.

The findings implicate habituation more compellingly than the observations concerning the Coolidge effect because various alternative mechanisms could be ruled out. For instance, Michael and Zumpe monitored the vaginal secretions of all females for pheromone content and established that there were no appreciable differences between the familiar and novel females in that regard. Moreover, the frequency of sexual enticements and refusals by familiar and novel females was recorded and the absence of differences demonstrated. A further point of departure from Coolidge-type situations is the fact that in the investigation by Michael and Zumpe sexual exhaustion is not an issue. The males were potent throughout. The weekly assessment of plasma testosterone levels is of interest in this connection. The sexual resurgence in the interaction with the novel females led to a sharp increase in testosterone levels. Elevated levels were without consequence for sexual behavior, however, when the familiar females were reintroduced. As sexual behavior reassumed habituation levels, testosterone levels similarly fell quickly in place. Sexual behavior, then, appears to have been under stimulus control—at least, primarily so.

Michael and Zumpe contemplated the implications of their findings for human sexual behavior and arrived at intriguing proposals. They speculated that extended monogamy, especially if institutionalized as in most human societies,

FIG. 6.8.   Habituation of sexual behavior in rhesus monkeys. Long-term
interaction with the same continually
receptive females led to a deterioration of males' sexual response. Sexual activity underwent resurgence
when continually receptive novel
females were interposed, but prompt-
ly fell back to habituation levels
when the familiar females were reintroduced. Data on the latency of
mounting revealed the same pattern
of effects. (Adapted from Michael &
Zumpe, 1978. Reprinted by permission of the American Association for
the Advancement of Science.)

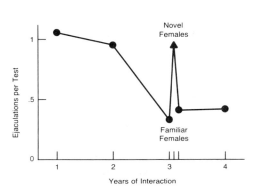

furnishes the very conditions that were created in their investigation and that monogamy consequently might produce similar effects. To the extent that the sexual response habituates, they argued, one should expect that human so-cieties—through customs, rites, and legal stipulation—sanction and encourage: (1) the discontinuation of consort bonds and the formation of new ones with other partners; (2) periodic changes of the stimulus properties of persons through fashions that govern clothing, adornments, coiffures, and odors; and (3) an imposition of periodicity on sexual activity with menstrual, pregnancy, and religious taboos. Finally, these investigators suggested that many of the societal precepts and prohibitions concerning sexual behavior have been instituted to sustain male potency rather than, as traditionally thought, to protect men and women from one another, especially women from the relentless sexual pursuit by men.

Surely, these suggestions have some degree of plausibility. One can readily cite fitting examples. Many cultures, after all, have instituted festivities and other special occasions and conditions that allow the disregard of monogamous ties with impunity (e.g., Marshall & Suggs, 1971). The contemporary use of erotic lingerie and other sexual paraphernalia seems to make the point rather compellingly that the stimulus properties of the nude body are often in need of enhancement through modification (e.g., Luria & Rose, 1979). The existence of more or less formalized periods of sexual abstention is evident from accounts of numerous cultures (e.g., Marshall & Suggs, 1971).

However, nonfitting examples can be cited just as readily. The very institu-tion of nontransitory monogamy, whether informally arranged and maintained or culturally prescribed and legally enforced (cf. Bullough, 1976), seems to chal-lenge the contention that sexual excitedness inevitably habituates and sexual interest diminishes or vanishes altogether. If the habituation of sexual arousal were a significant phenomenon, it could be argued, monogamy should not be as culturally ubiquitous as it is, and human civilizations should have more vigorously promoted promiscuity to protect male potency. In defense of the potency proposal it could be contended, however, that habituation is likely to produce acute problems only in cultures in which continual male potency is deemed desirable, if not imperative. Only to the extent that sexual behavior becomes a vital recreational endeavor and is practiced at frequencies that exceed any reproductive utility by an enormous margin—as it apparently is in contemporary Western cultures—might monogamy have outlived its status as *the* social condition in which sexual gratifications can be maximized. In this connection, it appears that the extensive recreational exploitation of sexual activities places great demands on women and that protective taboos (e.g., during menstruation or pregnancy) tend to be violated and abolished (e.g., Kinsey et al., 1953) rather than adhered to and expanded in the interest of male potency.

Even fashions generally do not conform to the proposed usage as habituation fighters. Traditionally, fashions served the differentiation of ethnic groups (cf. Hauser, 1958). They became "uniforms" that could span generations. Variations within a fashion covaried with religious and nonsexual social occasions rather than with the sexual enticement of males. Rapidly changing fashions characteristic of advanced industrial cultures—so-called "consumer societies"—may accommodate situational changes more effectively, but also have failed to provide publicly exhibited garments, coiffures, and fragrances that are uniquely associated with coitus. In sexually liberal cultures, most public garments and adornments may well be designed to enhance the sexual appeal of women, but they are displayed indiscriminately (i.e., on nonsexual as well as on sexual occasions). There may be great stimulus variety, but there is no consistency in the employment of the various stimuli that would permit a meaningful application of the reasoning on the stimulus control of sexual excitedness.

Habituation and the effects of inconsistent stimulus employment actually can be viewed as related phenomena. Specifically, in the stimulus control of sexual arousal and excitedness, habituation may result—in part, at least—from the nonspecific use of stimuli. Sexually arousing stimuli, if indiscriminately displayed in nonsexual and sexual situations, should lose their capacity because every nonsexual exhibition functions as an extinction trial. Exposure to the female breast, for instance, is likely to trigger sexual excitedness in men, if only because of coital conditioning (i.e., exposure to the breast regularly occurs during coition and climax, giving elicitation power to that stimulus). If exposure also occurs while respondents dine in restaurants, drink in bars, loaf at beaches, and shave in bathrooms, conditioning theory projects a deterioration of stimulus control. Coital conditioning (and potentially, masturbatory conditioning during exposure to the representations offered in girlie magazines as well) may eventually restore the initial capacity. However, many stimulus conditions cannot be controlled in this manner. Female faces, for example, may be part of the stimulus situation of coital conditioning, but a unique linkage with sexual events usually cannot be established or maintained. In terms of stimulus control, then, the optimal arrangement that prevents the habituation of sexual arousal and excitedness is not so much variation as the securement of uniquely sexual stimuli whose power is strengthened by consummatory behavior. This is the wisdom of sexual modesty. The breast is concealed to give it maximum stimulus power for sexual engagements when unveiled. The argument can be expanded, in fact, to include the concealment of genitals. In this form, it becomes an alternative to the "fig-leaf hypotheses" discussed earlier: Man resorted to sexual modesty in order to prevent the habituation of sexual excitedness, or in terms preferred by Michael and Zumpe, in order to sustain potency.

All this is theoretical conjecture, of course, as systematic observations on the habituation processes in question are not available. Nonetheless, the clinical literature, as mentioned earlier, leaves no doubt about the fact that habituation occurs rather frequently in monogamous couples. The research on nonhuman primates projects the exchange of sexual consorts, without return to the initial partners, as a solution. How long such solutions may last is entirely unclear, as it must be assumed that habituation will manifest itself in the newly formed relationships as well. Periods of nonhabituation might become shorter and shorter, in fact, and relationships entered into might have to be abandoned quickly in order to sustain sexual responding and excitedness. Eventually, habituation might take general form and apply across personal variations in appearance and expression.

It may seem ironic, but the characteristics of extended monogamous relationships that tend to be valued most highly (viz., being cared for, protected, and secure) are also those likely to foster drabness in sexual interaction. Interaction with a novel partner, in contrast, is laden with uncertainty, and this circumstance alone provides for much excitedness (cf. Leventhal, 1974). Strong excitatory reactions to novel sexual partners thus may be considered due to "minor xenophobia." A sense of danger—be it a husband's fear that his sidestep might be detected or a schoolgirl's fear of getting pregnant—should furnish further excitement. According to transfer theory, all this arousal from extrinsic sources should contribute to sexual excitedness and ultimately intensify sexual experience. If, then, sexual intercourse with novel partners turns out to be more exciting, more vigorous, and more enjoyable than with familiar ones, transfer may be considered as much implicated with the enhancement as with the absence of habituation.

It can be argued, of course, that in sexually permissive societies there is little occasion for the transfer exploitation of anxieties. In earlier times, forbidden love may have benefited from fear and guilt. It has been suggested, for instance, that in the days of American slavery black men and white women who joined in sexual ventures virtually did risk their lives and their social standing, respectively, and that the resulting intensity of sexual experience gave rise to notions of extreme black virility. In recent years, the changes in sexual mores have made such fear facilitation of sexual behavior unthinkable. The days of guilt-ridden lovers are numbered, it seems. "Safe" sexual access is readily granted, and transitory uncertainty about a partner and possible apprehension about the sexual performance of self might remain the only potential enhancers of sexual excitedness in the interaction with novel partners.

As the arousing capacity of novel partners is likely to fade and acute emotional reactions such as fear and guilt are improbable accompaniments of sexual activities, what can be done to combat the drabness of routine sexual engagements that is expected to result from excitatory habituation? Roughhousing, pinching, biting, and beating emerge as viable answers. In terms of theory, it is the controlled infliction of pain that holds promise of reliably producing excitatory reactions for transfer into sexual behavior and experience. The excitatory capacity of acute pain is not in doubt. Moreover, pain is extremely resistant to habituation (e.g., Casey, 1978; Chapman, 1978; Sternbach, 1968). Acute pain, then, always can be counted on to stir up excitement. It is the habituation fighter par excellence. However, its exploitation demands limited usage. Pain must be secondary to sexual excitedness. It must be dominated by sexual stimulation. Only when thus dominated can it be expected to enhance sexual excitedness. If aversion becomes dominant experientially, it will motivate avoidance reactions and impair sexual excitedness and consummatory behavior (e.g., Marshall & McKnight, 1975). Although it is conceivable that pain, which under different circumstances might be considered intense, if not unbearable, could be employed as a facilitator of sexual experience, pain thus sets its own limits for employment. But these safeguards against abuse operate only as long as the sexually engaged parties agree to honor them. Sadistic participants in sexual activities, for instance, are likely to disregard signals to limit the infliction of pain. Excessive infliction might serve their ends, but it certainly destroys any gratification for the suffering parties.

In summing up these theoretical projections it can be said that excitation transfer from the controlled use of pain into sexual behavior and sexual experience appears to be dependable. Misuses and abuses are likely, however, when callous parties are involved.

Is the widespread exploitation of pain for sexual excitedness a farfetched possibility? Not if one considers the use of scratching, biting, and beating through the ages, the popularity of these behaviors in promiscuous societies (Ford & Beach, 1951), and the fact that they tend to flourish in transitory relationships (Hunt, 1974) formed by comparatively callous persons (Eysenck, 1976). This consideration would seem to justify the expectation that in societies in which frequent transitional sexual relationships are common and in which emotionally intense sexual experiences are valued, excitatory habituation to sexual stimuli will be combated by biting and fighting. Because contemporary Western cultures meet both of these specifications, aggression-laden sexual behaviors might be on the rise. Then again, and unlikely as it may seem, sexual mores could change, and scripts of rather nonexcited, serene sexual behavior may become acceptable. Habituation might be countered with a more careful employment of potent sexual stimuli than characteristic of societies in which erotic stimulation is commercialized entertainment. Finally, excitatory habituation and the reduction in potency associated with it might become acceptable and be construed as adaptive. After all, it can be viewed as a gradual adjustment that frees men from the continual urge to seek sexual access and that protects women from constant sexual harassment—at least, in protective and secure social relationships.

The various findings and theoretical suggestions concerning habituation of sexual excitedness can be summarized as follows:

1. Exposure to coital scenes initially fosters strong reactions of sexual enticement, genital tumescence, and sympathetic excitation; reports of intensely felt sexual excitedness reflect these reactions. Repeated exposure, especially massive exposure, tends to diminish and remove the strength of each of these responses.
2. In many nonprimate mammals and in nonhuman primates, prolonged sexual consort relationships appear to reduce the females' capacity to evoke strong reactions of sexual excitedness in males. The males respond with considerably stronger sexual motivation and sexual performance to females outside these consort relationships. Analogous response tendencies are likely to exist in humans, but have not been reliably demonstrated.
3. Habituation of sexual excitedness to sexual stimuli appears to result largely from the inconsistent use of these stimuli—that is, from their frequent occurrence outside the coital context.
4. It seems likely that arbitrary stimulus modification will restore—in part, at least—the capacity of a stimulus condition for evoking sexual excitedness that was lost through habituation. Stimulus alterations that are consistently and exclusively employed in the context of coital behavior should, through coital conditioning, assume some degree of control in eliciting sexual excitedness.
5. The excitatory reaction associated with the infliction of bodily pain is highly resistant to habituation. It thus appears that the sympathetic component of sexual excitedness can be dependably complemented by sympathetic activity from pain. The likelihood for the employment of excitement-enhancing pain seems to increase, among other things, with the degree of habituation to purely sexual stimuli and the extent to which inhibiting concerns about the future of the sexual partnership are absent.

VII. TRANSFER IMPLICATIONS

As has been emphasized repeatedly, the excitation-transfer paradigm projects unique interdependencies between sexual and aggressive behaviors without assuming motivationally specific or appetitive mutual influences. The performance of activities of the one kind is not considered a condition that gives impetus to the simultaneous or subsequent performance of activities of the other kind. Nor is the enticement of actions in the one domain considered a stimulus condition for actions in the other domain as well. Sexual activities are not thought to carry with them an impulsion to engage in particular aggressive activities; analogously, aggressive activities are not thought to entail a component that impels the organism to engage in sexual activities specifically. Rather, the paradigm asserts that mutual facilitation between sexual and aggressive behaviors depends on numerous conditions outside the facilitating force proper. The occurrence of mutual behavioral facilitation is thus viewed as limited and by no means "automatic." More specifically, sympathetic excitation (i.e., the facilitating force proper) that derives from the one type of behavior, although it may well be partial to energetic action, is considered essentially appetitively blind toward the other type of behavior. For the facilitation of the one kind of behavior via excitation from the other kind to occur, the potentially facilitated behavior must first be evoked by means extrinsic to excitation. These means, generally speaking, are environmental stimuli that act on established response tendencies and ideational stimuli that tend to exploit established response tendencies for pleasure gain and/or aversion reduction. The facilitation of sexual behavior, then, relies on the concrete or ideational presence of stimuli that inspire sexual action, and the facilitation of aggressive behavior analogously presupposes the concrete or ideational presence of stimuli that evoke aggressive actions. In short, the paradigm denies mutual appetence enhancement and, instead, entrusts the determination of specific behavioral engagements to stimulus control, habit formation, and contemplation.

Such conceptualization contrasts sharply with interpretations of the research evidence aggregated in neurophysiology and endocrinology. Granted that many investigators have taken exception with the prevalent contentions in their respective areas of inquiry, the view that the apparent interdependencies between sexual and aggressive behaviors are the result of mutually appetitive influences has been explicitly promoted or, at least, implicitly endorsed in these disciplines, especially in neurophysiology. The neural-spillage hypothesis may be considered the purest incarnation of the proposal that sexual stimulation motivates aggression and that the instigation to aggression motivates sexual action. But the suggestion of mutually appetitive influence is also manifest in numerous endocrinological findings. It is implicit, for instance, in the motivational effects of androgens on both sexual and aggressive behaviors. In fact, the confounded action of androgens can be interpreted as suggestive of poorly differentiated central mechanics in the control of sexual and aggressive behaviors. This lack of functional differentiation in central structures is, of course, the cornerstone of the spillage hypothesis, as only such central nondifferentiation allows the prediction of sexual *and* aggressive *impulsion* on the basis of sexual *or* aggressive *instigation.* However, whereas in neurophysiology "impulsion" tends to be construed as behavior control and behavior determination, in endocrinology it is often assigned the status of an appetitively enhancing (rather than eliciting) condition.

But whatever interpretation of impulsion might be accepted, it should be clear that in much of neurophysiology and endocrinology some notion of confounded central control of sexual and aggressive behaviors ultimately has been adopted and that little attention has been given to the possibility of motivational influences from conditions outside the confounded control—especially the independent determination of the behavior to be facilitated. Such insistence on mutually *appetitive* influences between sex and aggression is not only at variance with the research evidence at large, but has implications for human behavior that—in the face of lacking research support—appear to be highly questionable.

The difficulties in explaining the facts at hand have already been detailed in the discussion of the neural-spillage hypothesis (see Chapter 3). Specifically, sexual, aggressive, and sexual-aggressive behaviors are enormously variable both across and within species (see Chapter 2), even within individuals over time (see Chapters 4 and 5), despite homology of neural structures. This variation is left entirely unexplained by the hypothesis. The assertion of appetitive influences, furthermore, is severely challenged by the research on motivation and emotion (see Chapter 5; also Chapter 6, Sections III, IV, and V). In general, the mutual facilitation of sexual and aggressive behaviors has been shown to depend on the presence of appropriate external stimulus conditions. The enhancement of sexual behavior through aggressive activities presupposes dominant sexual stimulation; analogously, the enhancement of aggressive behavior through sexual activities relies on the instigation to aggression. As may be recalled, sexual enticements failed to promote aggression when aggression was not motivated by provocation; similarly, annoyance and anger failed to promote sexual attraction when the stimulus condition failed to inspire such attraction. The research with nonhuman species underscores the dependence on external stimulation in the mutual facilitation of sexual and aggressive behaviors, and it further challenges the proposal that one type of stimulation motivates behaviors in both domains— whether situationally appropriate or not—because of central excitatory diffusion.

In light of the untenability of the proposal of mutual appetitive influence, the proposal's implications for human conduct are curious indeed. The adherence to appetence in sex-aggression connections, especially if combined with simplistic notions concerning the evocation of specific behaviors by particular neural events, invites highly deterministic visions in the "control" of sexual and aggressive behaviors. Individuals, it seems, are largely freed from assuming responsibility for actions that might be socially condemned. For example, the male who becomes violent upon sexual stimulation can point to neural spillage—or for that matter, to high levels of circulating androgen—and demand absolution from his destructive action. He could contend that he couldn't help it because of the way he's built. The individual seems at the mercy of connections as built-in, rigid, unalterable givens.

The excitation-transfer paradigm, in contrast, is not only in complete accord with the research evidence from the various disciplines cited, but projects connections between sexual and aggressive behaviors that are characterized by considerable *plasticity*. Connections can be formed and undone. They can be strengthened, weakened, or altered. In short, they are subject to change—and to control through manipulation. To the extent that individuals can influence and determine the arrangement of stimulus conditions that governs their sexual and aggressive behaviors (specifically, that forms, alters, or resolves particular sex-aggression connections), they can control these behaviors. As a result, they could be held accountable for their actions.

Clearly, it is not suggested that individuals control and, hence, ought to be held totally responsible for all sexual, aggressive, and sexual-aggressive acts that are somehow influenced by excitation transfer. This is the case for several reasons.

First of all, the transfer model entails processes of response acquisition that are quite independent of cognitive control. Excitatory reactions, in particular, can be reflexive, or their learning can be constitutionally advantaged (see Section V of this chapter). Deliberate efforts to influence these reactions tend to be ineffective. Limited influence can be attained through the ideational representation of arousing or unarousing stimuli (e.g., in sexual or aggressive fantasies or in the production of distracting images). Conscious efforts such as these, which actually underscore the stimulus dependence of excitatory reactions, require considerable discipline, and they often fail for this reason alone.

Furthermore, it is generally accepted that as sympathetic excitation rises to extreme levels behavior becomes increasingly impulsive (see Zillmann, 1979, for a formal model of this relationship). Cognitive influences, such as inhibitions based on the anticipation of social reproach, tend to become dysfunctional at these levels. As a result, socially disapproved sexual, aggressive, and sexual-aggressive actions that usually would not be taken might now be enacted. Individuals who have engaged in asocial, destructive actions under the extreme excitatory conditions considered tend to be granted mitigating circumstances in most human cultures. In some cultures, these individuals have been fully absolved, as they are deemed unable to control their behavior and declared "temporarily insane." More characteristically, however, some degree of control is assumed and, hence, some degree of responsibility is assessed.

Finally, and perhaps most importantly, it is difficult to see how individuals could control and be held fully accountable for the development of associations between sexual and aggressive inclinations that they fail to comprehend. How, for instance, could he who in total ignorance of the facts produces a fetish for himself through masturbatory conditioning be considered the intentional creator of it? Or how could he who, again ignorant of the facts, enhances his sexual experience through the infliction and suffering of pain be deemed accountable for "establishing a connection" that might not be entirely desirable?

These illustrations show that ignorance about connections between sexual and aggressive behaviors—in particular, about how such connections are formed, maintained, and dissolved—places the individual at the mercy of potentially incidental external and internal happenings. Comprehension of the specifics of these connections, on the other hand, affords the individual a degree of control over their development. Essentially, the development of connections that, for whatever reason, are deemed undesirable can be prevented by avoiding the stimulus conditions that produce them. Analogously, established undesirable connections can be weakened or abolished by avoiding stimulus conditions that maintain them and/or by arranging stimulus conditions that interfere with them. Counseling and therapy can aid in providing the requisite understanding of the mechanics of sex-aggression connections. The consequences of comprehension in the control of undesirable connections should not be overestimated, however. The utility of comprehending these connections lies in the ability to arrange stimulus conditions so as to reduce the likelihood of "self-entrapment." Counseling and therapy that simply concentrate on aiding the individual in arranging the stimulus conditions in question, devoid of efforts toward explaining the specific consequences of the arrangements, should be similarly effective.

Ignorance, then, might protect the individual from having to take full responsibility for behaviors that derive from *undesirable* connections. Enlightenment removes such protection by providing a degree of control over behavior and making correction possible. Ironically, being ignorant or informed has quite different consequences for *desirable* connections. Understanding the transfer mechanics of the facilitation of sexual behavior, in particular, tends to prevent the facilitation. Ignorance, it seems, is a welcome state of affairs in this context, and enlightenment fails to provide beneficial control over behavior. For instance, it has been shown that the appeal of potential sexual partners and sexual desire can be enhanced by excitation from unrelated arousing experiences. This enhancement relies on ignorance about the actual source of the "alien" excitement. A young man's strong romantic feelings for a young woman are likely to fade rapidly if he were shown that their intensity derives, for the most part, from the horror film they went to see. And, more generally speaking, the conscious production of excitedness (say, through the use of drugs) for transfer into specifically sexual excitedness is unlikely to do the trick. All this adds up to the colloquialism: You can't have it both ways! One cannot exploit ignorance about transfer to maximize sexual excitedness where and when it is wanted and, at the same time, benefit from understanding similar transfer connections by correcting unwanted influences wherever and whenever that seems opportune.

As this is not intended to be a treatise in morality, I do not pursue the question of what—under particular circumstances—might be deemed desirable or undesirable in the sense of being socially proper or condemnable, laudatory or punishable, or simply good or bad. Instead, I attempt to provide a final, simplified overview of the principal transfer influences between sexual and aggressive behaviors in humans. In so doing, however, I indicate implications likely to be of grave concern to most, and I point out means of behavior control and behavior correction.

The two basic aspects of stimulus arrangements that, according to the excitation-transfer paradigm, strongly influence the mutual facilitation between sexual and aggressive behaviors are: (1) sequence and (2) consistency. Sequential arrangements can be entirely discrete, with one type of behavior following the other without appreciable delay. They can also be mixed, however, in the sense that sexual and aggressive instigation alternate in rapid succession. Finally, sexual and aggressive behaviors may be simultaneously evoked by complex stimulus situations. I refer to these different arrangements as: (1) sequential; (2) mixed; and (3) simultaneous. The consistency of arrangements concerns the stimulus context of the elicitation of excitatory reactions. Excitatory responses can be consistently evoked in a context in which such responses are behaviorally appropriate or inappropriate. They also can be inconsistently evoked in a context in which they are behaviorally appropriate. (The possibility of inconsistent evocation in an inappropriate context is of no consequence for this discussion.) I refer to these arrangements as: (1) consistently appropriate; (2) consistently inappropriate; and (3) inconsistently appropriate. Clearly, the arrangements subsumed under "sequence" foster situational influences. Excitation transfer occurs between emotional states in great propinquity of time. The arrangements subsumed under "consistency," in contrast, manifest developmental conditions for the stimulus control of excitatory reactions that may be appropriate or inappropriate for either sexual or aggressive behavior. I now briefly review the principal transfer implications in the various, specified categories of stimulus arrangement.

Sequential stimulus arrangements can be construed as the prototypical conditions for behavioral facilitation through alien excitation. In this arrangement, residual excitation from sexual stimulation tends to facilitate provoked aggressive actions, and residual excitation from aggressive instigation tends to facilitate sexual behaviors. Subjective ignorance about the facilitating process seems imperative. Persons who are cognizant of still being aroused from preceding events are less likely to exhibit enhanced responses to later stimulation than persons who are not, because any overreaction is recognized as inappropriate and "artificial" under the circumstances. Cognizance of excitatory activity is more likely to prevent the transfer facilitation of subsequent behavior, the more obtrusive and proximal the preceding reaction of excitedness.

The facilitation of aggressive behavior through elements of sexual excitedness, then, could be curtailed, if not prevented, if respondents could be enlightened about the behavior-intensifying processes involved. However, such enlightenment seems of little moment for the behavior of highly aroused, acutely annoyed persons, because cognitive behavior correction is greatly impaired and tends to become defunct at extreme levels of excitedness. The provoked and enraged person's comprehension of the mechanics of excitation transfer thus is unlikely to protect against facilitated outbursts. The potential victim's understanding of these mechanics might prove more effective in curtailing aggressive reactions. Essentially, the informed person at risk can minimize an aggressor's overreactions by refraining from doing anything that would aggravate the situation and provoke violent action for the period of time during which residual sexual excitedness is thought to persist.

The facilitation of sexual behavior through excitedness from aggressive actions (including fear in response to the threat of violence, fear from the anticipation of being assaulted, fear in response to actual assault, acute anger, assaultive behavior, and the aversive stimulation associated with fighting) is similarly dependent on knowledge about transfer mechanics. It is difficult to see how informed persons could elect to fight deliberately in order to generate excitedness for transfer into subsequent sexual behavior. Such mock-fighting is unlikely to produce appreciable excitedness, as all threats are hollow. The production of appreciable amounts of excitation thus relies on the infliction and reception of pain, and being cognizant of the exploitation of aversive actions and reactions for pleasure should make these presexual activities seem counterproductive to the parties involved. Persons who are ignorant of the facilitating processes, on the other hand, should have no such qualms about fighting as a preliminary to sexual engagements. They can take advantage of the experiential enhancement because—as far as they are concerned—"it works." Needless to say, parties whose sexual activities are associated with extreme levels of excitedness could not benefit from transferred excitation and, hence, have no need for aversive preliminaries. Parties who have such a need might object to the kind of experiental enhancement in question on aesthetic grounds, or they might be unwilling to consider it because they abhor conflict and fighting generally. The avoidance of aversive stimulation, especially the reluctance to inflict pain upon a partner, should be particularly pronounced in parties who have formed lasting consort relationships. It should be minimal among parties who meet for singular sexual engagements. A particular situation of such a one-time sexual encounter is, of course, the case of rape. According to theory and research, the rapist is likely to benefit from transfer-enhanced sexual excitedness the more intensely the victim is scared, horrified, and pained. Unlike common beliefs about the rape victim's sexual experience, however, the theory also projects that, as a rule, the victim's reaction of abhorrence totally dominates any pleasure impulse that might come from the mechanics of sexual stimulation.

Mixed and *simultaneous* stimulus arrangements function much like the sequential ones. Generally speaking, cognizance of the behavior-facilitating processes also tends to impair and prevent transfer effects—a consequence that is usually desirable for aggression, but undesirable for sexual behavior. Subjective ignorance about these processes, then, is again a condition that makes the mutual facilitation between sexual and aggressive behaviors likely. However, there are also differences, which mainly concern the magnitude and duration of excitatory activity for transfer. In sequential arrangements, the facilitation of an entire episode of sexual or aggressive behavior relies on residual excitation from just one prior aggressive or sexual episode. Appreciable residues for transfer thus presuppose initial excitatory reactions of considerable magnitude. To complicate matters, such strong excitatory reactions place transfer in jeopardy because they tend to make the respondent cognizant of his or her excitedness. The conditions for excitation transfer are more unobtrusive in mixed and simultaneous stimulus arrangements. Excitatory reactions for transfer need not be extreme. They can be moderate, yet still have their behavior-intensifying effect because of the adjacency and concurrence that make excitatory decay an irrelevant consideration. Additionally, such moderate reactions can be repeatedly evoked and maintain the transfer facilitation of behavior over extended periods of time. Last but not least, the nonextreme alien excitatory reactivity is unlikely to draw attention to itself and thereby impair or prevent transfer.

In mixed and simultaneous stimulus arrangements, then, provoked aggressive behavior is enhanced by the interspersed or continual presence of sexual enticements. Sexual excitedness for transfer into aggression may be evoked by incidentally present stimuli as well as by deliberate action. The aggression-intensifying effect of incidental sexual stimulation is likely to go entirely unrecognized. Deliberate sexual enticements by parties toward whom anger is directed, on the other hand, are likely to be recognized as efforts at diffusing a hostile confrontation. If so, they are bound to aggravate the situation further and fuel violent action. Should such efforts succeed, however, sexual behavior—which under these circumstances may well become somewhat unbridled and riotous—would undergo intensification.

The facilitation of sexual engagements through the transfer of excitation from mixed-in or simultaneous aggression-related stimulation seems partial to the infliction of pain—in moderate doses, to be sure. It seems that sexual arousal (for transfer into aggression) can be produced most readily by exposure to visual stimuli. Appropriate tactile stimulation can complement the production, or it can function independently. The generation of aggression-linked excitation for transfer into sexual behaviors, in contrast, relies chiefly on tactile stimulation. It may appear that some groups were able to exploit "scenarios of violence" (i.e., images of whip-swinging barbarians and the like) for the evocation of reactions of fear and horror of great intensity. Such extreme reactions are not in evidence, however, and it seems more likely that the excitatory reactions evoked by the scenarios in question are byproducts of conditioned responses of sexual excitement—responses that may well be misconstrued as acute fear by the respondents themselves. It appears that there is no substitute for pain as a reliable standby for the creation of excitedness in case it is lacking. Pinching, scratching, sucking, biting, squeezing, pulling, shoving, and hitting constitute the bulk of the arsenal of aggression-related arousers that can be exploited for the enhancement of drab sexual endeavors. And in exploiting these means, receiving tends to work better than giving.

Paralleling what has been said about the possible exploitations of aggressive *pre*liminaries to sexual engagements, the exploitation of pain in mixed and simultaneous stimulus arrangements tends to be limited and kept under control in nontransitory consort relationships. The risk that the employment of pain as a sexual enhancer can escalate into truly aggressive and violent action may be substantial for parties who meet for singular sexual engagements—or for occasional ones in social arrangements characterized by the absence of concern for the sexual partners' welfare. Rape again constitutes the most extreme antisocial condition in which aggressive action—specifically, the infliction of acute pain—seems fully exploitable in enhancing the rapist's experience, but not the victim's.

Turning to the consistency with which particular stimulus arrangements occur in the context of sexual, aggressive, or sexual-aggressive behaviors, it appears that recognition or awareness of specific stimulus–response connections is of little moment in the control of excitatory activity. An individual may be fully cognizant, for instance, of his reaction of sexual excitedness to a rubber fetish but be utterly unable to prevent the reaction. Similarly, cognizance of a former stimulus–response connection cannot restore a stimulus' lost power to evoke an excitatory reaction. Nostalgia does not help a man whose excitatory reaction to, say, females in the nude has undergone complete extinction. The control of excitatory reactions, then, is quite independent of deliberate cognitive operations and may seem archaic indeed.

With cognitive influences thus limited, the conditions under which excitatory reactions to particular stimuli are acquired, modified, and extinguished would seem to be of critical importance. Ideally, sexual stimuli should be arranged in such a way that strong reactions of sexual excitedness are triggered only when behaviorally appropriate—that is, when they can be placed into the service of sexual engagements. And analogously, cues that signal danger should be allowed to trigger energizing, excitatory reactions only when these reactions are adaptive by aiding fight or flight. Such nonoverlapping, completely segregated stimulus arrangements for sexual and aggressive behaviors obviously cannot be created for any member of society. At best, persons can achieve a high degree of separation between stimuli that generate sexual arousal and stimuli that produce behavior-energizing arousal for aggressive action devoid of sexual elements.

Consistently appropriate stimulus arrangements define such a desirable state of affairs. Miselicitation of excitatory reactions (i.e., sexual excitedness in response to aggressive cues and excitedness not associated with genital vasocongestion in response to sexual cues) should be minimal under these conditions. The development of maladaptive behavioral confusions should be unlikely as a result. This does not mean, however, that consistently appropriate stimulus arrangements prevent or impair excitation transfer from sex to aggression or from aggression to sex. Entirely appropriately elicited sexual excitedness still can be sequentially arranged so as to facilitate subsequent aggressive behavior, and residues of entirely appropriately elicited excitation from hostile and aggressive encounters still can enter into subsequent sexual behaviors and intensify them. Moreover, even in mixed and simultaneous stimulus arrangements transfer is not in jeopardy. Entirely appropriate excitatory reactions to inappropriately present stimuli can come to enhance both sexual and aggressive behaviors. Excitation transfer as such, then, is independent of the degree to which reactions of sexual arousal are specific to stimuli with sexual connotations, and reactions of general excitedness are specific to cues linked to danger, fear, and aggression.

Consistently inappropriate stimulus arrangements are, of course, those developmental conditions that produce what has been labeled "miselicitations." Stimuli that are only marginally related to sexual behavior or that are devoid of sexual connotations come to evoke specifically sexual excitedness, and stimuli exhibiting blatantly sexual themes fail to do so. In the latter case, the sexual stimuli may or may not produce general excitedness.

The miselicitation of sexual arousal is not necessarily detrimental to sexual behaviors. On the contrary! It may be argued, first of all, that such arousal constitutes sexual behavior and, moreover, that it can have considerable experiential quality. Whether sexual excitedness is conditioned—as it readily can be, through masturbation and/or coition—to boot heels, rubber suits, pink candles, musky fragrances, woodsy incense, soft music generally, or Ravel's *Bolero* specifically, the experience may be deemed pleasurable in its own right. More importantly, however, such fetish-produced sexual excitedness can be exploited for coital behaviors. It can be used to complement sexual arousal in response to the coital conditions proper. Needless to say, this type of arousal complementation has been liberally practiced in many cultures.

The fetishlike exploitation of the so-called "scenarios of violence" may seem similarly innocuous. As long as whips and ropes merely replace candles and incense as "props," it certainly is. Characteristically, however, such scenarios entail the use of whips, ropes, and other instruments of torture. Sexual excitedness ultimately results not so much from the mere exhibition of these tools and weapons, as from their use in forcing slavish cooperation with all requests and from their impact on the victim—especially his or her expression of pain. Still, as long as the scenario is just that, the pleasure exploitation of fetishes of violence might be considered in extremely poor taste, but as it fails to produce a coerced victim, it cannot be condemned as asocial. The issue of concern is that sexual excitedness may become increasingly dependent on stimuli of torment and suffering and that the dependent individual will become increasingly tempted to produce the needed stimuli through his or her own action, especially in the absence of willing collaborators. But whether or not a dependence for sexual excitedness on violence fetishes eventually comes to motivate potentially sadistic rape, any consistently inappropriate stimulus arrangement that establishes images of coercion and instrumental aggression as elicitors of sexual excitedness is likely to produce asocial consequences. If the models of masturbatory conditioning have any validity at all, it should be expected that those who masturbate while engaged in aggressive fantasies are under way to motivating themselves to employ aggressive means to satisfy their sexual desires. Masturbation, in and of itself, might be of little moment in the development of sexual responsiveness. But as it occurs consistently in particular environments, especially "fantasy environments," peculiar stimulus conditions may assume the power to elicit sexual arousal. None of these conditions seems more troublesome than the sheer imagination of forcing another party into compliance with sexual requests.

Inconsistently appropriate stimulus arrangements are those that produce habituation and excitatory insensitivity. Stimuli lose their capacity to evoke strong excitatory reactions because they frequently occur in behavioral contexts in which such reactions are somewhat or entirely inappropriate. Characteristically, they have to be waited out; that is, the excited individual does nothing, or something irrelevant for distraction, until the inappropriately triggered excitatory reaction has dissipated. The excitatory reaction, thus deprived of behavioral utility, grows weaker with repeated "abuse."

In the realm of aggression, excitatory habituation is generally welcome. The likelihood of violent action is thought to decrease as the excitatory reaction to aggression-instigating targets diminishes. For instance, a person who, on several occasions, was forced to hold back angry actions toward an annoyer will, upon another encounter, respond less intensely than initially, feel less angry as a result, and be less prone to lash out. Such an effect of habituation will probably not be characterized as "increased aggression insensitivity." Even the soldier who experiences battle fatigue (i.e., excitatory habituation to seemingly continual endangerment) is rather safe from this kind of accusation. Only habituation to communication-mediated violence has been branded as insensitivity. For instance, the person who was initially scared out of his or her wits by the endangerments presented in horror movies, yet whose excitatory reactions to these endangerments have reached trivial magnitudes because of repeated exposure to such stimuli, is at risk of being considered callous for fear that he or she may have lost the capacity for empathy with victimized others.

Excitatory habituation to sexual stimuli, in contrast, is nearly universally construed as a deplorable loss of sensitivity. Ironically, the more valued the experience of sexual excitedness and the stronger the desire to exploit this excitedness, the more likely becomes the inconsistent use of stimulus arrangements that foster excitatory habituation. The indiscriminate display of the female breast, for instance, may pleasantly titillate men over extended periods of time, but it is bound to deprive this stimulus of the excitatory power it has when its revelation is limited to the coital context. As life in the office, in restaurants, on formal occasions, and around the house is turned into a continual jiggle show, and as the entertainment media provide further cheesecake and beefcake, one ought not expect a burst of sexual excitedness in response to visual manifestations of sexual partners. But the creation of intense sexual excitedness does not, of course, depend on visual enticements. It can be olfactory and, ultimately, tactile. And in these stimulus modalities, especially in the latter, the stimulus arrangements are typically not, or not yet, inconsistently appropriate. Excitatory habituation to particular stimuli, hence, is presently not an issue for those modalities.

Societies such as ours, in which—partly because of the commercialism involved—the visual modality of sexual stimulation is heavily used and abused, seem to violate standards of good excitatory housekeeping in the sexual domain. Surely, if the experience of great sexual excitedness is to be maximized, superior strategies for stimulus arrangements offer themselves. Yet it is conceivable that the kind of housekeeping of sexual stimuli that prevails in our society approximates the "best of all worlds" rather well. Strong excitatory reactions to visual sexual stimuli may be lost to habituation. But such sacrifice is compensated for by the practically continual exposure to sexual pleasantries. More frequent minor sexual enticements and experiences replace less frequent major ones. Yet the major ones are not lost. The elicitation of sexual arousal via nonvisual stimulation has remained largely unimpaired, and any deficit in sympathetic excitedness can be overcome by the many means of excitation transfer that have been discussed.

REFERENCES

Abel, G. G., Barlow, D. H., & Blanchard, E. B. *Developing heterosexual arousal by altering masturbatory fantasies: A controlled study.* Paper presented at the meeting of the Association for Advancement of Behavior Therapy, Miami Beach, December 1973.

Abel, G. G., Barlow, D. H., Blanchard, E. B., & Guild, D. The components of rapists' sexual arousal. *Archives of General Psychiatry,* 1977, *34,* 895–903.

Abel, G. G., & Blanchard, E. B. The role of fantasy in the treatment of sexual deviation. *Archives of General Psychiatry,* 1974, *30,* 467–475.

Abel, G. G., Blanchard, E. B., Barlow, D. H., & Flanagan, B. *A controlled behavioral treatment of a sadistic rapist.* Paper presented at the meeting of the Association for Advancement of Behavior Therapy, San Francisco, December 1975.

Abel, G. G., Blanchard, E. B., & Becker, J. V. Psychological treatment of rapists. In M. J. Walker & S. L. Brodsky (Eds.), *Sexual assault: The victim and the rapist.* Lexington, Mass.: Lexington Books, 1976.

Ádám, G. *Interoception and behavior: An experimental study.* Budapest: Publishing House of the Hungarian Academy of Sciences, 1967.

Adler, N. T. On the mechanisms of sexual behaviour and their evolutionary constraints. In J. B. Hutchison (Ed.), *Biological determinants of sexual behaviour.* Chichester: Wiley, 1978.

Akert, K., Gruesen, R. A., Woolsey, C. N., & Meyer, D. R. Klüver–Bucy syndromes in monkeys with neocortical ablations of temporal lobe. *Brain,* 1961, *84,* 480–498.

Alcock, J. *Animal behavior: An evolutionary approach.* Sunderland, Mass.: Sinauer, 1975.

Alexander, B. K. Parental behavior of adult male Japanese monkeys. *Behaviour,* 1970, *36,* 270–285.

Alexander, M., & Perachio, A. A. An influence of social dominance on sexual behavior in rhesus monkeys. *American Zoologist,* 1970, *10,* 294.

Altmann, S. A. Social behavior of anthropoid primates: Analysis of recent concepts. In E. L. Bliss (Ed.), *Roots of behavior.* New York: Harper, 1962.

Anand, B. K., & Brobeck, J. R. Food intake and spontaneous activity of rats with lesions in the amygdaloid nuclei. *Journal of Neurophysiology,* 1952, *15,* 421–430.

Anand, B. K., & Dua, S. Electrical stimulation of the limbic system of brain (''visceral brain'') in the waking animals. *Indian Journal of Medical Research,* 1956, *44,* 107–119.

Ard, B. N., Jr. Sex in lasting marriages: A longitudinal study. *Journal of Sex Research,* 1977, *13,* 274–285.

Arnold, D. O. *Subcultures.* Berkeley, Calif.: Glendessary Press, 1970.

Averill, J. R. Autonomic response patterns during sadness and mirth. *Psychophysiology,* 1969, *5,* 399–414.

Averill, J. R., & Boothroyd, P. On falling in love in conformance with the romantic ideal. *Motivation and Emotion,* 1977, *1,* 235–247.

Axelrod, J. Metabolism of epinephrine and other sympathomimetic amines. *Physiological Reviews,* 1959, *39,* 751–776.

Axelrod, J. Noradrenaline: Fate and control of its biosynthesis. *Science,* 1971, *173,* 598–606.

Backhouse, K. M. Testicular descent and ascent in mammals. *XVth International Congress of Zoology, London,* 1959, 413–415.

Bäckström, T., & Carstensen, H. Estrogen and progesterone in plasma in relation to premenstrual tension. *Journal of Steroid Biochemistry,* 1974, *5,* 257–260.

Ball, J. Effect of progesterone upon sexual excitability in the female monkey. *Psychological Bulletin,* 1941, *38,* 533.

Banarjee, U. The influence of some hormones and drugs on isolation-induced aggression in male mice. *Communications in Behavioral Biology,* 1971, *6,* 163–170.

Bancroft, J. The relationship between hormones and sexual behaviour in humans. In J. B. Hutchison (Ed.), *Biological determinants of sexual behaviour.* Chichester: Wiley, 1978.

Bancroft, J., & Skakkebaek, N. E. Androgens and human sexual behaviour. In *Sex, hormones, and behaviour: Ciba Foundation Symposium 62 (new series).* Amsterdam: Excerpta Medica, 1979.

Bandura, A. *Principles of behavior modification.* New York: Holt, Rinehart & Winston, 1969.

Bandura, A. *Aggression: A social learning analysis.* Englewood Cliffs, N.J.: Prentice-Hall, 1973.

Barbaree, H. E., Marshall, W. L., & Lanthier, R. D. Deviant sexual arousal in rapists. *Behaviour Research and Therapy,* 1979, *17,* 215–222.

Barclay, A. M. The effect of hostility on physiological and fantasy responses. *Journal of Personality,* 1969, *37,* 651–667.

Barclay, A. M. The effect of female aggressiveness on aggressive and sexual fantasies. *Journal of Projective Techniques and Personality Assessment,* 1970, *34,* 19–26. (a)

Barclay, A. M. Urinary acid phosphatase secretion in sexually aroused males. *Journal of Experimental Research in Personality,* 1970, *4,* 233–238. (b)

Barclay, A. M. Linking sexual and aggressive motives: Contributions of ''irrelevant'' arousals. *Journal of Personality,* 1971, *39,* 481–492.

Barclay, A. M., & Haber, R. N. The relation of aggressive to sexual motivation. *Journal of Personality,* 1965, *33,* 462–475.

Barclay, A. M., & Little, D. M. Urinary acid phosphatase secretion under different arousal conditions. *Psychophysiology,* 1972, *9,* 69–77.

Bard, P. The hypothalamus and sexual behavior. *Research Publications of the Association for Research in Nervous and Mental Diseases,* 1940, *20,* 551–579.

Bard, P., & Mountcastle, V. B. Some forebrain mechanisms involved in the expression of rage, with special reference to suppression of angry behavior. In J. F. Fulton (Ed.), *The frontal lobes.* Baltimore: Williams & Wilkins, 1948.

Bardwick, J. M. *Psychology of women: A study of bio-cultural conflicts.* New York: Harper & Row, 1971.

Barfield, R. J., & Sachs, B. D. Sexual behavior: Stimulation by painful electrical shock to skin in male rats. *Science,* 1968, *161,* 392–393.

Barlow, D. H. The treatment of sexual deviation: Toward a comprehensive behavioral approach. In K. S. Calhoun, H. E. Adams, & K. M. Mitchell (Eds.), *Innovative treatment methods in psychopathology.* New York: Wiley, 1974.

Barlow, D. H., & Agras, W. Fading to increase heterosexual responsiveness in homosexuals. *Journal of Applied Behavior Analysis,* 1973, *6,* 355–366.

Barlow, G. W. Ethology of the Asian teleost, *Badis badis.* IV. Sexual behavior. *Copeia,* 1962, *2,* 346–360.

Barnett, S. A., Evans, C. S., & Stoddart, R. C. Influence of females on conflict among wild rats. *Journal of Zoology,* 1968, *154,* 391–396.

Baron, R. A. The aggression-inhibiting influence of heightened sexual arousal. *Journal of Personality and Social Psychology,* 1974, *30,* 318–322. (a)

Baron, R. A. Sexual arousal and physical aggression: The inhibiting influence of "cheesecake" and nudes. *Bulletin of the Psychonomic Society,* 1974, *3,* 337–339. (b)

Baron, R. A. *Human aggression.* New York: Plenum Press, 1977.

Baron, R. A. Heightened sexual arousal and physical aggression: An extension to females. *Journal of Research in Personality,* 1979, *13,* 91–102.

Baron, R. A., & Bell, P. A. Effects of heightened sexual arousal on physical aggression. *Proceedings of the 81st Annual Convention of the American Psychological Association,* 1973, *8,* 171–172.

Baron, R. A., & Bell, P. A. Sexual arousal and aggression by males: Effects of type of erotic stimuli and prior provocation. *Journal of Personality and Social Psychology,* 1977, *35,* 79–87.

Baron, R. A., & Zillmann, D. Unpublished data. Purdue University, 1981.

Bartholomew, G. Reproductive and social behavior of the northern elephant seal. *University of California Publications in Zoology,* 1952, *47,* 369–471.

Bartlett, D. J., Hurley, W. P., Brand, C. R., & Poole, E. W. Chromosomes of male patients in a security prison. *Nature,* 1968, *219,* 351–354.

Bartlett, F. Physiologic responses during coitus. *Journal of Applied Physiology,* 1956, *9,* 469–472.

Beach, F. Effects of injury to the cerebral cortex upon sexually receptive behavior in the female rat. *Psychosomatic Medicine,* 1944, *6,* 40–55.

Beach, F. A. Characteristics of masculine "sex drive." In M. R. Jones (Ed.), *Nebraska Symposium on Motivation* (Vol. 4). Lincoln: University of Nebraska Press, 1956.

Beach, F. A. Neural and chemical regulation of behavior. In H. F. Harlow & C. N. Woolsey (Eds.), *Biological and biochemical bases of behavior.* Madison: University of Wisconsin Press, 1958.

Beach, F. Cerebral and hormonal control of reflexive mechanisms involved in copulatory behavior. *Physiological Reviews,* 1967, *47,* 289–316.

Beach, F. It's all in your mind. *Psychology Today,* July 1969, pp. 33–35; 60.

Beach, F. A. Cross-species comparisons and the human heritage. In F. A. Beach (Ed.), *Human sexuality in four perspectives.* Baltimore: Johns Hopkins University Press, 1976.

Beach, F. A., Noble, R. G., & Orndoff, R. K. Effects of perinatal androgen treatment on responses of male rats to gonadal hormones in adulthood. *Journal of Comparative and Physiological Psychology,* 1969, *68,* 490–497.

Beamer, W., Bermant, G., & Clegg, M. Copulatory behaviour of the ram, *Ovis aries.* II: Factors affecting copulatory satiation. *Animal Behaviour,* 1969, *17,* 706–711.

Beeman, E. A. The effect of male hormone on aggressive behavior in mice. *Physiological Zoology,* 1947, *20,* 373–405.

Beljon, J. J. *Waar je Kijkt . . . Erotiek.* Amsterdam: Wetenschappelijke Uitgeverij, 1967.

Bem, D. J. Self-perception theory. In L. Berkowitz (Ed.), *Advances in experimental social psychology* (Vol. 6). New York: Academic Press, 1972.

Benedek, T. *Psychosexual functions in women.* New York: Ronald Press, 1952.

Benedek, T. An investigation of the sexual cycle in women. *Archives of General Psychiatry,* 1963, *8,* 311–322.

Benedek, T., & Rubenstein, B. B. The correlations between ovarian activity and psychodynamic processes: I. The ovulative phase. *Psychosomatic Medicine,* 1939, *1,* 245–270. (a)

Benedek, T., & Rubenstein, B. B. The correlations between ovarian activity and psychodynamic processes: II. The menstrual phase. *Psychosomatic Medicine,* 1939, *1,* 461–485. (b)

Benedek, T., & Rubenstein, B. B. *The sexual cycle in women: The relation between ovarian function and psychodynamic processes.* Washington, D.C.: National Research Council, 1942.

Bereiter, D. A., & Barker, D. J. Facial receptive fields of trigeminal neurons: Increased size following estrogen treatment in female rats. *Neuroendocrinology,* 1975, *18,* 115–124.

Berg, I. A. Development of behavior: The micturition pattern in the dog. *Journal of Experimental Psychology,* 1944, *34,* 343–368.

Berkowitz, L. Some determinants of impulsive aggression: Role of mediated associations with reinforcement for aggression. *Psychological Review,* 1974, *81,* 165–176.

Berkson, G., Ross, B. A., & Jatinandana, S. The social behavior of gibbons in relation to a conservation program. In L. A. Rosenblum (Ed.), *Primate behavior: Developments in field and laboratory research* (Vol. 2). New York: Academic Press, 1971.

Berscheid, E., & Walster, E. A little bit about love. In T. L. Huston (Ed.), *Foundations of interpersonal attraction.* New York: Academic Press, 1974.

Beumont, P. J. V., Richards, D. H., & Gelder, M. G. A study of minor psychiatric and physical symptoms during the menstrual cycle. *British Journal of Psychiatry,* 1975, *126,* 431–434.

Bindra, D. *Motivation: A systematic reinterpretation.* New York: Ronald Press, 1959.

Binet, A. *Le Fetichisme dans l'Amour.* Paris: Doin, 1888.

Bishop, M. P., Elder, S. T., & Heath, R. G. Intracranial self-stimulation in man. *Science,* 1963, *140,* 394–396.

Blumer, D., & Migeon, C. Hormone and hormonal agents in the treatment of aggression. *Journal of Nervous and Mental Disease,* 1975, *160,* 127–137.

Boas, E. P., & Goldschmidt, E. F. *The heart rate.* Springfield, Ill.: Thomas, 1932.

Bond, D., Randt, C. T., Bidder, T. G., & Rowland, V. Posterior, septal, fornical, and anterior thalamic lesions in the cat. *AMA Archives of Neurology and Psychiatry,* 1957, *78,* 143–162.

Bornemann, E. *Sex im Volksmund* (Vols. 1 & 2). Reinbek/Hamburg: Rowohlt, 1974.

Bors, E., & Comarr, A. E. Effect of pudendal nerve operations on the neurologic bladder. *Journal of Urology,* 1954, *72,* 666–670.

Bors, E., & Comarr, A. E. Neurological disturbances of sexual function with special reference to 529 patients with spinal cord injury. *Urological Survey,* 1960, *10,* 191–222.

Bors, E., & Comarr, A. E. *Neurological urology.* Baltimore: University Park Press, 1971.

Bower, H. *Lecture presented to a short course in primate behavior.* University of California, Davis, June 26, 1971.

Brady, J. V. The paleocortex and behavioral motivation. In H. F. Harlow & C. N. Woolsey (Eds.), *Biological and biochemical bases of behavior.* Madison: University of Wisconsin Press, 1958.

Brady, J. V. Emotion and the sensitivity of psychoendocrine systems. In D. C. Glass (Ed.), *Neurophysiology and emotion.* New York: Rockefeller University Press, 1967.

Brady, J. V. Endocrine and autonomic correlates of emotional behavior. In P. Black (Ed.), *Physiological correlates of emotion.* New York: Academic Press, 1970.

Brady, J. V., & Nauta, W. J. H. Subcortical mechanisms in emotional behavior: Affective changes following septal forebrain lesions in the albino rat. *Journal of Comparative and Physiological Psychology,* 1953, *46,* 339–346.

Brain, P. F., & Evans, C. M. Attempts to influence fighting and threat behavior in adult isolated female CFW mice in standard opponent aggression tests using injected and subcutaneously implanted androgens. *Physiology and Behavior*, 1975, *14*, 551–556.

Brain, P. F., & Nowell, N. W. Some behavioral and endocrine relationships in adult male, laboratory mice subjected to open field and aggression tests. *Physiology and Behavior*, 1969, *4*, 945–947. (a)

Brain, P. F., & Nowell, N. W. Some endocrine and behavioral changes in the development of the albino laboratory mouse. *Communications in Behavioral Biology*, 1969, *4*, 203–220. (b)

Brain, P. F., Nowell, N. W., & Wouters, A. Some relationships between adrenal function and the effectiveness of a period of isolation in inducing intermale aggression in albino mice. *Physiology and Behavior*, 1971, *6*, 27–29.

Breggin, P. R. Lobotomies are still bad medicine. *Medical Opinion*, March 1972, pp. 32–36.

Breggin, P. R. Psychosurgery for the control of violence: A critical review. In W. S. Fields & W. H. Sweet (Eds.), *Neural bases of violence and aggression*. St. Louis: Green, 1975.

Bregman, S. *Behaviors relating to feminine attractiveness and sexual adjustment among women with spinal cord injuries*. Unpublished master's thesis, California State University, Los Angeles, 1973.

Brehm, J., Gatz, M., Goethals, G., McCrimmon, J., & Ward, L. *Psychological arousal and interpersonal attraction*. Unpublished manuscript, Duke University, 1967.

Brener, J. Learned control of cardiovascular processes: Feedback mechanisms and therapeutic applications. In K. S. Calhoun, H. E. Adams, & K. M. Mitchell (Eds.), *Innovative treatment methods in psychopathology*. New York: Wiley, 1974.

Brener, J. Sensory and perceptual determinants of voluntary visceral control. In G. E. Schwartz & J. Beatty (Eds.), *Biofeedback: Theory and research*. New York: Academic Press, 1977.

Broca, P. Anatomie comparée des circonvolutions cérébrales. Le grand lobe limbique et la scissure limbique dans la série des mammifères. *Revue Anthropologique*, 1878, *1*, 385–448.

Brodyaga, L., Gates, M., Singer, S., Tucker, M., & White, R. *Rape and its victims: A report for citizens, health facilities, and criminal justice agencies*. Washington, D.C.: U.S. Government Printing Office, 1975.

Brown, J. L. *The evolution of behavior*. New York: Norton, 1975.

Brown, J. S. *The motivation of behavior*. New York: McGraw-Hill, 1961.

Brown, K., & Cooper, S. J. (Eds.). *Chemical influences on behaviour*. London: Academic Press, 1979.

Brown, S., & Schäfer, E. A. An investigation into the functions of the occipital and temporal lobes of the monkey's brain. *Philosophical Transactions of the Royal Society of London*, 1888, *179*, 303–327.

Brown, T. S., & Wallace, P. M. *Physiological psychology*. New York: Academic Press, 1980.

Brownmiller, S. *Against our will: Men, women, and rape*. New York: Simon & Schuster, 1975.

Bullough, V. L. *Sexual variance in society and history*. New York: Wiley, 1976.

Burdine, W. E., Shipley, T. E., & Papas, A. T. Dalatestryl, a long-acting androgenic hormone: Its use as an adjunct in the treatment of women with sexual frigidity. *Fertility and Sterility*, 1957, *8*, 255–259.

Burgess, A. W., & Holmstrom, L. L. Rape trauma syndrome. *American Journal of Psychiatry*, 1974, *131*, 981–986.

Burgess, A. W., & Holmstrom, L. L. Coping behavior of the rape victim. *American Journal of Psychiatry*, 1976, *133*, 413–417.

Burt, M. R. Cultural myths and supports for rape. *Journal of Personality and Social Psychology*, 1980, *38*, 217–230.

Buss, A. H. *The psychology of aggression*. New York: Wiley, 1961.

Buss, A. H. Aggression pays. In J. L. Singer (Ed.), *The control of aggression and violence: Cognitive and physiological factors*. New York: Academic Press, 1971.

Butterfield, P. A. The pair bond in the zebra finch. In J. H. Crook (Ed.), *Social behaviour in birds and mammals.* New York: Academic Press, 1970.

Byrne, D. *The attraction paradigm.* New York: Academic Press, 1971.

Byrne, D. The imagery of sex. In J. Money & H. Musaph (Eds.), *Handbook of sexology.* Amsterdam: Elsevier/North-Holland Biomedical Press, 1977.

Byrne, D., & Byrne, L. A. *Exploring human sexuality.* New York: Crowell, 1977.

Caggiula, A. R., & Eibergen, R. Copulation of virgin male rats evoked by painful peripheral stimulation. *Journal of Comparative and Physiological Psychology,* 1969, *69,* 414–419.

Calhoun, J. B. *The ecology and sociology of the Norway rat* (U.S. Public Health Service No. 1008). Washington, D.C.: U.S. Government Printing Office, 1962.

Campbell, B. *Sexual selection and the descent of man.* Chicago: Aldine, 1972.

Candland, D. K., & Leshner, A. I. A model of agonistic behavior: Endocrine and autonomic correlates. In L. V. DiCara (Ed.), *Limbic and autonomic nervous systems research.* New York: Plenum Press, 1974.

Cannon, W. B. *Bodily changes in pain, hunger, fear and rage: An account of researches into the function of emotional excitement* (2nd ed.). New York: Appleton-Century, 1929.

Cantor, J. R., Zillmann, D., & Bryant, J. Enhancement of experienced sexual arousal in response to erotic stimuli through misattribution of unrelated residual excitation. *Journal of Personality and Social Psychology,* 1975, *32,* 69–75.

Cantor, J. R., Zillmann, D., & Einsiedel, E. F. Female responses to provocation after exposure to aggressive and erotic films. *Communication Research,* 1978, *5,* 395–411.

Capranica, R. R. *The evoked vocal response of the bullfrog.* Cambridge, Mass.: MIT Press, 1965.

Carducci, B. J., & Cozby, P. C. *Judgments of female attractiveness following exposure to erotic material.* Paper presented at the 54th Annual Meeting of the Western Psychological Association, San Francisco, April 1974.

Carducci, B. J., Cozby, P. C., & Ward, C. D. Sexual arousal and interpersonal evaluations. *Journal of Experimental Social Psychology,* 1978, *14,* 449–457.

Carpenter, C. R. Sexual behavior of free ranging rhesus monkeys *Macaca mulatta. Journal of Comparative Psychology,* 1942, *33,* 113–142.

Carpenter, C. R. The howlers of Barro Colorado Island. In I. DeVore (Ed.), *Primate behavior: Field studies of monkeys and apes.* New York: Holt, Rinehart & Winston, 1965.

Carthy, J. D., & Ebling, F. J. (Eds.). *The natural history of aggression.* London: Academic Press, 1964.

Casey, K. L. Neural mechanisms of pain. In E. C. Carterette & M. P. Friedman (Eds.), *Handbook of perception* (Vol. 6B). *Feeling and hurting.* New York: Academic Press, 1978.

Casey, M. D., Segall, L. J., Street, D. R. K., & Blank, C. E. Sex chromosome abnormalities in two state hospitals for patients requiring special security. *Nature,* 1966, *209,* 641–642.

Chapman, C. R. The hurtful world: Pathological pain and its control. In E. C. Carterette & M. P. Friedman (Eds.), *Handbook of perception* (Vol. 6B). *Feeling and hurting.* New York: Academic Press, 1978.

Chapman, J. R., & Gates, M. (Eds.). *The victimization of women.* Beverly Hills, Calif.: Sage Publications, 1978.

Chernigovskiy, V. N. *Interoceptors.* Washington, D.C.: American Psychological Association, 1967.

Clark, L. C., & Treichler, P. Psychic stimulation of prostatic secretion. *Psychosomatic Medicine,* 1950, *12,* 261–263.

Clark, L. M. G., & Lewis, D. J. *Rape: The price of coercive sexuality.* Toronto: Women's Press, 1977.

Clark, R. A. The projective measurement of experimentally induced levels of sexual motivation. *Journal of Experimental Psychology,* 1952, *44,* 391–399.

Clemens, L. G., Wallen, K., & Gorski, R. Mating behavior: Facilitation in the female rat after cortical application of potassium chloride. *Science,* 1967, *157,* 1208–1209.

Clore, G. L., & Byrne, D. A reinforcement-affect model of attraction. In T. L. Huston (Ed.), *Foundations of interpersonal attraction*. New York: Academic Press, 1974.

Cloudsley-Thompson, J. L. *Animal conflict and adaptation*. Chester Springs, Pa.: Dufour, 1965.

Cofer, C. N., & Appley, M. H. *Motivation: Theory and research*. New York: Wiley, 1964.

Cohen, M. L., Garofalo, R., Boucher, R., & Seghorn, T. The psychology of rapists. *Seminars in Psychiatry*, 1971, *3*(3), 307–327.

Cole, T. Sexuality and physical disabilities. *Archives of Sexual Behavior*, 1975, *4*, 389–403.

Collias, N. E., & Collias, E. C. Size of breeding colony related to attraction of mates in a tropical passerine bird. *Ecology*, 1969, *50*, 481–488.

Conan, P. Males with an XYY chromosome complement. *Journal of Medical Genetics*, 1968, *5*, 341–359.

Conner, R. L. Hormones, biogenic amines, and aggression. In S. Levine (Ed.), *Hormones and behavior*. New York: Academic Press, 1972.

Conti, G. L'erection du penis human et ses bases morphologicovasculaires. *Acta Anatomica*, 1952, *14*, 217–262.

Cooper, A. J., Ismail, A. A. A., Phanjoo, A. L., & Love, D. L. Antiandrogen (Cyproterone Acetate) therapy in deviant hypersexuality. *British Journal of Psychiatry*, 1972, *120*, 59–63.

Costa, P. J., & Bonnycastle, D. D. Effect of DCA, compound E, testosterone, progesterone and ACTH in modifying "agene-induced" convulsions in dogs. *Archives Internationales de Pharmacodynamie et de Thérapy*, 1952, *91*, 330–338.

Court-Brown, W. M. *Human population cytogenetics*. New York: Wiley, 1967.

Cowden, J. Adventures with South Africa's black eagles. *National Geographic*, 1969, *136*, 533–551.

Craig, K. D., & Wood, K. Autonomic components of observers' responses to pictures of homicide victims and nude females. *Journal of Experimental Research in Personality*, 1971, *5*, 304–309.

Crépault, C., Abraham, G., Porto, R., & Couture, M. Erotic imagery in women. In R. Gemme & C. C. Wheeler (Eds.), *Progress in sexology*. New York: Plenum Press, 1977.

Crook, J. H., & Butterfield, P. A. Effects of testosterone propionate and luteinizing hormone on agonistic and nest building behavior of *Quela quela*. *Animal Behaviour*, 1968, *16*, 370–384.

Crosby, E. C., Humphrey, T., & Lauer, E. W. *Correlative anatomy of the nervous system*. New York: Macmillan, 1962.

Crouch, J. E. *Functional human anatomy* (3rd ed.). Philadelphia: Lea & Febiger, 1978.

Crow, J. F., & Kimura, M. *An introduction to population genetics theory*. New York: Harper & Row, 1970.

Crowley, W. R., Popolow, H. B., & Ward, O. B., Jr. From dud to stud: Copulatory behavior elicited through conditioned arousal in sexually inactive male rats. *Physiology and Behavior*, 1973, *10*, 391–394.

Dalton, K. Menstruation and acute psychiatric illnesses. *British Medical Journal*, 1959, *1*(5115), 148–149.

Dalton, K. Effect of menstruation on schoolgirls' weekly work. *British Medical Journal*, 1960, *1*(5169), 326–327. (a)

Dalton, K. Menstruation and accidents. *British Medical Journal*, 1960, *2*(5210), 1425–1426. (b)

Dalton, K. *The premenstrual syndrome*. Springfield, Ill.: Thomas, 1964.

Daly, R. F. Mental illness and patterns of behavior in 10 XYY males. *Journal of Nervous and Mental Disease*, 1969, *149*, 318–327.

Dannecker, M., & Reiche, R. *Der gewöhnliche Homosexuelle*. Frankfurt: Fischer, 1974.

Darling, F. F. *A herd of red deer*. Garden City, N.Y.: Anchor Books, 1964.

Dart, R. A. The Kisoro pattern of mountain gorilla preservation. *Current Anthropology*, 1961, *2*, 510–511.

Darwin, C. *On the origin of species by means of natural selection*. New York: Appleton, 1887. (Originally published, 1859.)

Davenport, W. Sexual patterns and their regulation in a society of the Southwest Pacific. In F. A. Beach (Ed.), *Sex and behavior*. New York: Wiley, 1965.

Davenport, W. H. Sex in cross-cultural perspective. In F. A. Beach (Ed.), *Human sexuality in four perspectives*. Baltimore: Johns Hopkins University Press, 1976.

Davidson, J. M. Activation of male rats' sexual behavior by intracerebral implantation of androgen. *Endocrinology*, 1966, *79*, 783–794.

Davidson, J. M., Camargo, C. A., & Smith, E. R. Effects of androgen on sexual behavior in hypogonadal men. *Journal of Clinical Endocrinology and Metabolism*, 1979, *48*, 955–958.

Davidson, T. *Conjugal crime: Understanding and changing the wifebeating pattern*. New York: Hawthorn Books, 1978.

Davison, G. C. Elimination of a sadistic fantasy by a client-controlled counterconditioning technique. *Journal of Abnormal Psychology*, 1968, *73*, 84–90.

Davison, G. C. Elimination of a sadistic fantasy by a client-controlled counterconditioning technique: A case study. In J. Fischer & H. L. Gochros (Eds.), *Handbook of behavior therapy with sexual problems* (Vol. 2). *Approaches to specific problems*. New York: Pergamon Press, 1977.

Day, K. D. *The effect of music differing in excitatory potential and hedonic valence on provoked aggression*. Unpublished doctoral dissertation, Indiana University, 1980.

Delgado, J. M. R. Aggression and defense under cerebral radio control. In C. D. Clemente & D. B. Lindsley (Eds.), *Aggression and defense: Neural mechanisms and social patterns* (Vol. 5). *Brain function*. Berkeley: University of California Press, 1967. (a)

Delgado, J. M. R. Social rank and radio-stimulated aggressiveness in monkeys. *Journal of Nervous and Mental Disease*, 1967, *144*, 383–390. (b)

Delgado, J. M. R. Offensive–defensive behaviour in free monkeys and chimpanzees induced by radio stimulation of the brain. In S. Garattini & E. B. Sigg (Eds.), *Aggressive behaviour*. New York: Wiley, 1969. (a)

Delgado, J. M. R. *Physical control of the mind: Toward a psychocivilized society*. New York: Harper & Row, 1969. (b)

Delgado, J. M. R., Roberts, W. W., & Miller, N. E. Learning motivated by electrical stimulation of the brain. *American Journal of Physiology*, 1954, *179*, 587–593.

de Molina, F., & Hunsperger, R. W. Affective reactions obtained by electrical stimulation of the amygdala. *Journal of Physiology* (Proceedings of the Physiological Society), 1957, *138*, 29–30.

de Molina, F. A., & Hunsperger, R. W. Central representation of affective reactions in forebrain and brain stem: Electrical stimulation of amygdala, stria terminalis and adjacent structures. *Journal of Physiology*, 1959, *145*, 251–265.

de Riencourt, A. *Sex and power in history*. New York: McKay, 1974.

DeRiver, J. *The sexual criminal: A psychoanalytic study*. Springfield, Ill.: Thomas, 1956.

de Sade, D. A. F. *Les crimes de l'amour*. Paris: Pauvert, 1955. (Originally published, 1799.)

Deutsch, H. *The psychology of women*. New York: Grune & Stratton, 1944.

Deutsch, J. A., & Deutsch, D. *Physiological psychology*. Homewood Ill.: Dorsey Press, 1966.

Dewsbury, D. A. Diversity and adaptation in rodent copulatory behavior. *Science*, 1975, *190*, 947–955.

DiCara, L. V. Plasticity in the autonomic nervous system: Instrumental learning of visceral and glandular responses. In F. O. Schmitt (Ed.), *The neurosciences: Second study program*. New York: Rockefeller University Press, 1970.

Dienstbier, R. A. Emotion-attribution theory: Establishing roots and exploring future perspectives. In H. E. Howe & R. A. Dienstbier (Eds.), *Nebraska Symposium on Motivation* (Vol. 26). Lincoln: University of Nebraska Press, 1979.

Dobzhansky, T. *Genetics of the evolutionary process*. New York: Columbia University Press, 1970.

Doering, C. H., Brodie, H. K. H., Kraemer, H., Becker, H., & Hamburg, D. A. Plasma testosterone levels and psychologic measures in men over a 2-month period. In R. C. Friedman, R. M. Richart, & R. L. vande Wiele (Eds.), *Sex differences in behavior*. New York: Wiley, 1974.

Dollard, J., Doob, L. W., Miller, N. E., Mowrer, O. H., & Sears, R. R. *Frustration and aggression*. New Haven, Conn.: Yale University Press, 1939.

Donnerstein, E. Aggressive erotica and violence against women. *Journal of Personality and Social Psychology*, 1980, *39*, 269–277.

Donnerstein, E., & Barrett, G. Effects of erotic stimuli on male aggression toward females. *Journal of Personality and Social Psychology*, 1978, *36*, 180–188.

Donnerstein, E., & Berkowitz, L. Victim reactions in aggressive erotic films as a factor in violence against women. *Journal of Personality and Social Psychology*, 1981, *41*, 710–724.

Donnerstein, E., Donnerstein, M., & Evans, R. Erotic stimuli and aggression: Facilitation or inhibition. *Journal of Personality and Social Psychology*, 1975, *32*, 237–244.

Donnerstein, E., & Hallam, J. Facilitating effects of erotica on aggression against women. *Journal of Personality and Social Psychology*, 1978, *36*, 1270–1277.

Driscoll, R., Davis, K. E., & Lipetz, M. E. Parental interference and romantic love: The Romeo and Juliet effect. *Journal of Personality and Social Psychology*, 1972, *24*, 1–10.

Dua, S., & MacLean, P. D. Localization for penile erection in medial frontal lobe. *American Journal of Physiology*, 1964, *207*, 1425–1434.

Duffy, E. The psychological significance of the concept of "arousal" or "activation." *Psychological Review*, 1957, *64*, 265–275.

Duffy, E. *Activation and behavior*. New York: Wiley, 1962.

Dutton, D. G., & Aron, A. P. Some evidence for heightened sexual attraction under conditions of high anxiety. *Journal of Personality and Social Psychology*, 1974, 30, 510–517.

Eaton, G. G., Goy, R. W., & Phoenix, C. H. Effects of testosterone treatment in adulthood on sexual behaviour of female pseudo-hermaphrodite rhesus monkeys. *Nature* [New Biology], 1973, *242*, 119–120.

Eaton, G. G., & Resko, J. A. Plasma testosterone and male dominance in a Japanese macaque (*Macaca fuscata*) troop compared with repeated measures of testosterone in laboratory males. *Hormones and Behavior*, 1974, *5*, 251–259.

Eckhardt, C. Untersuchungen über die Erektion des Penis beim Hunde. *Beiträge zur Anatomie, Physiologie, und Pathologie*, 1863, *3*, 123.

Edwards, D. A. Neonatal administration of androstenedione, testosterone or testosterone propionate: Effects on ovulation, sexual receptivity and aggressive behavior in female mice. *Physiology and Behavior*, 1971, *6*, 223–228.

Egger, M. D., & Flynn, J. P. Effect of electrical stimulation of the amygdala on hypothalamically eclicited attack behavior in cats. *Journal of Neurophysiology*, 1963, *26*, 705–720.

Ehrenkranz, J., Bliss, E., & Sheard, M. H. Plasma testosterone: Correlation with aggressive behavior and social dominance in men. *Psychosomatic Medicine*, 1974, *36*, 469–475.

Ehrhardt, A. A. Prenatal androgenization and human psychosexual behavior. In J. Money & H. Musaph (Ed.), *Handbook of sexology* (Vol. 1). Amsterdam: Excerpta Medica, 1977.

Ehrhardt, A. A., & Baker, S. W. Fetal androgens, human central nervous system differentiation, and behavior sex differences. In R. C. Friedman, R. M. Richart, & R. L. vande Wiele (Eds.), *Sex differences in behavior*. New York: Wiley, 1974.

Ehrhardt, A. A., Epstein, K., & Money, J. Fetal androgens and female gender identity in the early treated andrenogenital syndrome. *Johns Hopkins Medical Journal*, 1968, *122*, 160–167.

Eibl-Eibesfeldt, I. *Ethology: The biology of behavior*. New York: Holt, Rinehart & Winston, 1970.

Eibl-Eibesfeldt, I. *Der vorprogrammierte Mensch: Das Ererbte als bestimmender Faktor im menschlichen Verhalten*. Wien: Molden, 1973.

Eibl-Eibesfeldt, I. *Love and hate: The natural history of behavior patterns*. New York: Schocken Books, 1974.

Ekman, P. Universals and cultural differences in facial expressions of emotion. In J. K. Cole (Ed.), *Nebraska Symposium on Motivation* (Vol. 19). Lincoln: University of Nebraska Press, 1972.

Ellis, A., & Abarbanel, A. (Eds.). *The encyclopedia of sexual behavior* (Vols. 1 & 2). New York: Hawthorn Books, 1961.

Ellis, H. *Studies in the psychology of sex* (Vol. 7). Philadelphia: Davis, 1928.

Ellis, H. *My life*. Boston: Mifflin, 1939.

Elmadjian, F. Excretion and metabolism of epinephrine and norepinephrine in various emotional states. *Editorial Sesator*, Lima, Peru, 1963, pp. 341–370.

Englander-Golden, P., Whitmore, M. R., & Dienstbier, R. A. Menstrual cycle as focus of study and self-reports of moods and behaviors. *Motivation and Emotion*, 1978, *2*, 75–86.

Englander-Golden, P., Willis, K. A., & Dienstbier, R. A. Stability of perceived tension as a function of the menstrual cycle. *Journal of Human Stress*, 1977, *3*, 14–21.

Estes, R. D. Territorial behavior of the wildebeest (*Connochaetes taurinus Burchell*) 1923. *Zeitschrift für Tierpsychologie*, 1969, *26*, 284–370.

Etkin, W., & Freedman, D. G. *Social behavior from fish to man*. Chicago: University of Chicago Press, 1964.

Euler, U. S., von, Gemzell, C. A., Levi, L., & Ström, G. Cortical and medullary adrenal activity in emotional stress. *Acta Endocrinologica*, 1959, *30*, 567–573.

Everitt, B. J., Herbert, J., & Hamer, J. D. Sexual receptivity of bilateral adrenalectomized female rhesus monkeys. *Physiology and Behavior*, 1971, *8*, 409–415.

Eysenck, H. J. *Sex and personality*. Austin: University of Texas Press, 1976.

Eysenck, H. J., & Wilson, G. *The experimental study of Freudian theories*. London: Methuen, 1974.

Farkas, G. M. *Trait and state determinants of male sexual arousal to descriptions of coercive sexuality*. Unpublished doctoral dissertation, University of Hawaii, 1979.

Faulk, M. Sexual factors in marital violence. *Medical Aspects of Human Sexuality*, October 1977, pp. 30–38.

Feder, H. H. Specificity of steroid hormone activation of sexual behaviour in rodents. In J. B. Hutchison (Ed.), *Biological determinants of sexual behaviour*. Chichester: Wiley, 1978.

Feder, H. H., & Whalen, R. E. Feminine behavior in neonatally castrated and estrogen-treated male rats. *Science*, 1965, *147*, 306–307.

Feshbach, S., & Malamuth, N. Sex and aggression: Proving the link. *Psychology Today*, November 1978, pp. 111–114; 116–117; 122.

Feshbach, S., Malamuth, N., & Drapkin, R. *The effects of aggression inhibition and aggression facilitation on sexual responsiveness*. Paper presented at the meeting of the International Society for Research on Aggression, Toronto, September 1974.

Festinger, L. *A theory of cognitive dissonance*. Stanford, Calif.: Stanford University Press, 1957.

Festinger, L. *Conflict, decision, and dissonance*. Stanford, Calif.: Stanford University Press, 1964.

Finck, H. T. *Romantic love and personal beauty: Their development, causal relations, historic and national peculiarities*. London: Macmillan, 1891.

Finkelhor, D. *Sexually victimized children*. New York: Free Press, 1979.

Finkelhor, D., & Yllo, K. Forced sex in marriage: A preliminary research report. *Crime and Delinquency*, 1982, *28*, 459–478.

Fisher, A. E. Effects of stimulus variation on sexual satiation in the male rat. *Journal of Comparative and Physiological Psychology*, 1962, *55*, 614–620.

Fisher, J. L., & Harris, M. B. Modeling, arousal, and aggression. *Journal of Social Psychology*, 1976, *100*, 219–226.

Fisher, R. A. *The genetical theory of natural selection* (Rev. ed.). New York: Dover, 1958.

Fitting, M., Salisbury, S., Davis, N., & Mayclin, D. Self-concept and sexuality of spinal cord injured women. *Archives of Sexual Behavior*, 1978, *7*, 143–156.

Flaceliere, R. *Love in ancient Greece*. New York: Crown, 1962.

Flerkó, B., & Mess, B. Reduced estradiol-binding capacity of androgen sterilized rats. *Acta Physiologica Academiae Scientiarum Hungaricae*, 1968, *33*, 111–113.

Flerkó, B., Mess, B., & Illei-Donhoffer, A. On the mechanism of androgen sterilization. *Neuroendocrinology*, 1969, *4*, 164–169.

Fonberg, E., & Delgado, J. M. R. Avoidance and alimentary reactions during amygdaloid stimulation. *Journal of Neurophysiology*, 1961, *24*, 651–664.

Ford, C. S., & Beach, F. A. *Patterns of sexual behavior*. New York: Harper, 1951.

Fossey, D. The imperiled mountain gorilla. *National Geographic*, 1981, *159*, 501–523.

Fowler, H., & Whalen, R. E. Variation in incentive stimulus and sexual behavior in the male rat. *Journal of Comparative and Physiological Psychology*, 1961, *54*, 68–71.

Fox, C. A., & Fox, B. Blood pressure and respiratory patterns during human coitus. *Journal of Reproduction and Fertility*, 1969, *19*, 405–415.

Fox, C. A., Ismail, A. A., Love, D. N., Kirkham, K. E., & Loraine, J. A. Studies on the relationship between plasma testosterone levels and human sexual activity. *Journal of Endocrinology*, 1972, *52*, 51–58.

Frankenhaeuser, M. Psychoneuroendocrine approaches to the study of emotion as related to stress and coping. In H. E. Howe & R. A. Dienstbier (Eds.), *Nebraska Symposium on Motivation* (Vol. 26). Lincoln: University of Nebraska Press, 1979.

Freud, S. Drei Abhandlungen zur Sexualtheorie. In *Gesammelte Werke* (Vol. 5). London: Imago, 1942. (Originally published, 1905.)

Freud, S. Beiträge zur Psychologie des Liebeslebens. In *Gesammelte Werke* (Vol. 8). London: Imago, 1943. (Originally published, 1912.)

Freud, S. Triebe und Triebschicksale. In *Gesammelte Werke* (Vol. 10). London: Imago, 1946. (Originally published, 1915.)

Freud, S. Vorlesungen zur Einführung in die Psychoanalyse. In *Gesammelte Werke* (Vol. 11). London: Imago, 1940. (Originally published, 1917.)

Freud, S. Jeuseits des Lustprinzips. In *Gesammelte Werke* (Vol. 13). London: Imago, 1940. (Originally published, 1920.)

Freud, S. Warum Krieg? In *Gesammelte Werke* (Vol. 16). London: Imago, 1950. (Originally published, 1933.)

Freud, S. *Abriss der Psychoanalyse*. Frankfurt: Fischer Bücherei, 1958. (Originally published, 1938.)

Freud, S. Das ökonomische Problem des Masochismus. In *Gesammelte Werke* (Vol. 13). London: Imago, 1940.

Friedman, P. Sexual deviations. In S. Arieti (Ed.), *American handbook of psychiatry* (Vol. 2, Part 4). New York: Basic Books, 1959.

Fromm, E. *The art of loving*. New York: Harper, 1956.

Fromm, E. *The anatomy of human destructiveness*. New York: Holt, Rinehart & Winston, 1973.

Funkenstein, D. H. Nor-epinephrine-like and epinephrine-like substances in relation to human behavior. *Journal of Nervous and Mental Disease*, 1956, *124*, 58–68.

Gager, N., & Schurr, C. *Sexual assault: Confronting rape in America*. New York: Grosset & Dunlap, 1976.

Gagnon, J. H. Scripts and the coordination of sexual conduct. In J. K. Cole & R. Dienstbier (Eds.), *Nebraska Symposium on Motivation* (Vol. 21). Lincoln: University of Nebraska Press, 1973.

Gajdusek, D. C. Physiological and psychological characteristics of Stone Age man. In *Engineering and Science*. Pasadena: Symposium on Biological Bases of Human Behavior, California Institute of Technology, March 1970, pp. 26–33; 56–62.

Garn, S. M., & Clark, L. L. The sex differences in the basic metabolic rate. *Child Development*, 1953, *24*, 215–224.

Gebhard, P. H. Fetishism and sadomasochism. *Science and Psychoanalysis*, 1969, *15*, 71–80.

Gebhard, P. H., & Johnson, A. B. *The Kinsey data: Marginal tabulations of the 1938–1963 interviews conducted by the Institute for Sex Research*. Philadelphia: Saunders, 1979.

Geen, R. G. *Aggression*. Morristown, N.J.: General Learning Press, 1972.

Geen, R. G., Rakosky, J. J., & Pigg, R. Awareness of arousal and its relation to aggression. *British Journal of Social and Clinical Psychology,* 1972, *11,* 115–121.

Gelles, R. J. On the association of sex and violence in the fantasy production of college students. *Suicide,* 1975, *5*(2), 78–85.

Gelles, R. J. *Family violence.* Beverly Hills, Calif.: Sage Publications, 1979.

Gellhorn, E. Motion and emotion: The role of proprioception in the physiology and pathology of the emotions. *Psychological Review,* 1964, *71,* 457–472.

Gil, D. G. *Violence against children: Physical child abuse in the United States.* Cambridge, Mass.: Harvard University Press, 1973.

Ginsburg, B. E. Coaction of genetical and nongenetical factors influencing sexual behavior. In F. A. Beach (Ed.), *Sex and behavior.* New York: Wiley, 1965.

Ginsburg, B. E. *Wolf social behavior.* Paper presented at the meeting of the New England Psychological Association, Boston, November 1970.

Goddard, G. V. Functions of the amygdala. *Psychological Bulletin,* 1964, *62,* 89–109.

Goldfoot, D. A., Feder, H. H., & Goy, R. W. Development of bisexuality in the male rat treated neonatally with androstenedione. *Journal of Comparative and Physiological Psychology,* 1969, *67,* 41–45.

Goodall, J. Chimpanzees of the Gombe Stream Reserve. In I. DeVore (Ed.), *Primate behavior: Field studies of monkeys and apes.* New York: Holt, Rinehart & Winston, 1965.

Gorski, R. A., Gordon, J. H., Shryne, J. E., & Southam, A. M. Evidence for a morphological sex difference within the medial preoptic area of the rat brain. *Brain Research,* 1978, *148,* 333–346.

Gottschalk, L. A., Kaplan, S. M., Gleser, G. C., & Winget, C. M. Variations in magnitude of emotion: A method applied to anxiety and hostility during phases of the menstrual cycle. *Psychosomatic Medicine,* 1962, *24,* 300–311.

Goy, R. Early hormonal influences on the development of sexual and sex-related behavior. In F. O. Schmitt, G. C. Quarton, T. Melnechuck, & G. Adelman (Eds.), *The neurosciences: Second study program.* New York: Rockefeller University Press, 1970.

Goy, R. W., Bridson, W. E., & Young, W. C. Period of maximum susceptibility of the prenatal female guinea pig to the masculinizing actions of testosterone propionate. *Journal of Comparative and Physiological Psychology,* 1964, *57,* 166–174.

Goy, R. W., & McEwen, B. S. (Eds.) *Sexual differentiation of the brain.* Cambridge, Mass.: MIT Press, 1980.

Goy, R. W., Wolf, J. E., & Eisele, S. G. Experimental female hermaphroditism in rhesus monkeys: Anatomical and psychological characteristics. In J. Money & H. Musaph (Eds.), *Handbook of sexology* (Vol. 1). Amsterdam: Excerpta Medica, 1977.

Grady, K. L., Phoenix, C. H., & Young, W. C. Role of the developing rat testis in differentiation of the neural tissues mediating mating behavior. *Journal of Comparative and Physiological Psychology,* 1965, *59,* 176–182.

Gray, J. A. Sex differences in emotional behavior in mammals including man: Endocrine bases. *Acta Psychologica,* 1971, *35,* 29–46.

Green, J. D., Clemente, C. D., & de Groot, J. Rhinecephalic lesions and behavior in cats. *Journal of Comparative Neurology,* 1957, *108,* 505–545.

Green, R., Luttge, W. G., & Whalen, R. E. Uptake and retention of tritiated estradiol in brain and peripheral tissues of male, female, and neonatally androgenized female rats. *Endocrinology,* 1969, *85,* 373–378.

Greenough, W. T., Carter, C. S., Steerman, C., & de Voogd, T. J. Sex difference in dendritic branching patterns in hamster preoptic area. *Brain Research,* 1977, *126,* 63–72.

Grings, W. W., & Dawson, M. E. *Emotions and bodily responses: A psychophysiological approach.* New York: Academic Press, 1978.

Groth, A. N. *Men who rape: The psychology of the offender.* New York: Plenum Press, 1979.

Groth, A. N., & Burgess, A. W. Rape: A sexual deviation. *American Journal of Orthopsychiatry,* 1977, *47,* 400–406.

Grumbach, M. M., & Conte, F. A. Disorders of sex differentiation. In R. H. Williams (Ed.), *Textbook of endocrinology* (6th ed.). Philadelphia: Saunders, 1981.

Grunt, J. A., & Young, W. C. Psychological modification of fatigue following orgasm (ejaculation) in the male guinea pig. *Journal of Comparative and Physiological Psychology*, 1952, *45*, 508–510.

Gustafson, J. E., Winokur, G., & Reichlin, S. The effect of psychic-sexual stimulation on urinary and serum acid phosphatase and plasma nonesterified fatty acids. *Psychosomatic Medicine*, 1963, *25*, 101–105.

Guyton, A. C. *Structure and function of the nervous system*. Philadelphia: Saunders, 1972.

Hale, E. B., & Almquist, J. O. Relation of sexual behavior to germ cell output in farm animals. In The effect of germ cell damage on animal reproduction. *Journal of Dairy Science*, 1960, *43*(Suppl.), 145–169.

Hall, K. R. L. Social vigilance behaviour of the chacma baboon (*Papio ursinus*). *Behaviour*, 1960, *16*, 261–294.

Hall, K. R. L. Social organization of the old-world monkeys and apes. In P. C. Jay (Ed.), *Primates: Studies in adaptation and variability*. New York: Holt, Rinehart & Winston, 1968. (a)

Hall, K. R. L. Tool-using performances as indicators of behavioral adaptability. In P. C. Jay (Ed.), *Primates: Studies in adaption and variability*. New York: Holt, Rinehart & Winston, 1968. (b)

Hall, K. R. L., & DeVore, I. Baboon social behavior. In I. DeVore (Ed.), *Primate behavior: Field studies of monkeys and apes*. New York: Holt, Rinehart & Winston, 1965.

Hamburg, D. A. Effects of progesterone on behavior. In Association for Research in Nervous and Mental Disease, *Research Publications* (Vol. 43). *Endocrines and the central nervous system*. Baltimore: Williams & Wilkins, 1966.

Hamburg, D. A., Moos, R. H., & Yalom, I. D. Studies of distress in the menstrual cycle and the postpartum period. In R. P. Michael (Ed.), *Endocrinology and human behaviour*. London: Oxford University Press, 1968.

Hamilton, G. V. A study of sexual tendencies in monkeys and baboons. *Journal of Animal Behavior*, 1914, *4*, 295–318.

Harding, C. F., & Leshner, A. I. The effects of adrenalectomy on the aggressiveness of differently housed mice. *Physiology and Behavior*, 1972, *8*, 437–440.

Hare, R., Wood, K., Britain, S., & Frazelle, J. Autonomic responses to affective visual stimulation: Sex differences. *Journal of Experimental Research in Personality*, 1971, *5*, 14–22.

Hariton, B. E., & Singer, F. L. Women's fantasies during sexual intercourse: Normative and theoretical implications. *Journal of Consulting and Clinical Psychology*, 1974, *42*, 313–322.

Harlow, H. F. Sexual behavior in the rhesus monkey. In F. A. Beach (Ed.), *Sex and behavior*. New York: Wiley, 1965.

Harlow, H. F. Lust, latency and love: Simian secrets of successful sex. *Journal of Sex Research*, 1975, *11*, 79–90.

Harris, G. W., & Levine, S. Sexual differentiation of the brain and its experimental control. *Journal of Physiology* (Proceedings of the Physiological Society), 1962, *163*, 42–43.

Harris, G. W., & Levine, S. Sexual differentiation of the brain and its experimental control. *Journal of Physiology*, 1965, *181*, 379–400.

Hart, B. Sexual reflexes and mating behavior in the male dog. *Journal of Comparative and Physiological Psychology*, 1967, *64*, 388–399.

Hart, B. Alteration of quantitative aspects of sexual reflexes in spinal male dogs by testosterone. *Journal of Comparative and Physiological Psychology*, 1968, *66*, 726–730.

Hart, B. Gonadal hormones and sexual reflexes in the female rat. *Hormones and Behavior*, 1969, *1*, 65–71.

Hart, B. L. Hormones, spinal reflexes, and sexual behaviour. In J. B. Hutchison (Ed.), *Biological determinants of sexual behaviour*. Chichester: Wiley, 1978.

Hauser, A. *Philosophie der Kunstgeschichte*. München: Beck'sche Verlagsbuchhandlung, 1958.

Hautojärvi, S., & Lagerspetz, K. The effects of socially-induced aggressiveness or nonaggressiveness on the sexual behaviour of inexperienced male mice. *Scandinavian Journal of Psychology*, 1968, *9*, 45–49.

Healey, M. C. Aggression and self-regulation of population size in deermice. *Ecology*, 1967, *48*, 377–392.

Heath, R. G. Electrical self-stimulation of the brain in man. *American Journal of Psychiatry*, 1963, *120*, 571–577.

Heath, R. G., & Mickle, W. A. Evaluation of seven years' experience with depth electrode studies in human patients. In E. R. Ramey & D. S. O'Doherty (Eds.), *Electrical studies on the unanesthetized brain*. New York: Hoeber, 1960.

Hediger, H. Die Bedeutung von Miktion und Defäkation bei Wirbeltieren. *Schweizerische Zeitschrift für Psychologie*, 1944, *3*, 170–182.

Hediger, H. Environmental factors influencing the reproduction of zoo animals. In F. A. Beach (Ed.), *Sex and behavior*. New York: Wiley, 1965.

Heider, K. G. Dani sexuality: A low energy system. *Man*, 1976, *11*, 188–201.

Heider, K. G. *Grand Valley Dani: Peaceful warriors*. New York: Holt, Rinehart & Winston, 1979.

Heiman, J. R. A psychophysiological exploration of sexual arousal patterns in females and males. *Psychophysiology*, 1977, *14*, 266–274.

Heimberger, R. R. Stereotaxic amygdalotomy. *Journal of the American Medical Association*, 1966, *198*, 741–745.

Heimer, L., & Larsson, K. Impairment of mating behavior in male rats following lesions in the preoptic-anterior hypothalamic continuum. *Brain Research*, 1967, *3*, 248–263.

Henderson, V. E., & Roepke, M. H. On the mechanism of erection. *American Journal of Physiology*, 1933, *106*, 441–448.

Hennessy, J. W., & Levine, S. Stress, arousal, and the pituitary-adrenal system: A psychoendocrine hypothesis. In J. M. Sprague & A. N. Epstein (Eds.), *Progress in psychobiology and physiological psychology*. New York: Academic Press, 1979.

Henriques, F. *Modern sexuality*. London: McGibbon & Kee, 1968.

Herbert, J. Some functions of hormones and the hypothalamus in the sexual activity of primates. *Progress in Brain Research*, 1974, *41*, 331–348.

Herbert, J. The neuroendocrine basis of sexual behavior in primates. In J. Money & H. Musaph (Eds.), *Handbook of sexology* (Vol. 1). Amsterdam: Excerpta Medica, 1977.

Herbert, J. Neuro-hormonal integration of sexual behaviour in female primates. In J. B. Hutchison (Ed.), *Biological determinants of sexual behaviour*. Chichester: Wiley, 1978.

Hess, E. H. Imprinting. *Science*, 1959, *130*, 133–141.

Hess, W. R. Stammganglien-Reizversuche. *Berichte über die gesamte Physiologie und experimentelle Pharmakologie*, 1928, *42*, 554–555.

Hess, W. R. *Diencephalon: Autonomic and extrapyramidal functions*. New York: Grune & Stratton, 1954.

Hess, W. R., & Brügger, M. Das subkortikale Zentrum der affektiven Abwehrreaktion. *Helvetica Physiologica et Pharmacologia Acta*, 1943, *1*, 33–52.

Hess, W. R., Brügger, M., & Bucher, V. Zur Physiologie von Hypothalamus Area präoptica und Septum, sowie angrenzender Balken- und Stirnhirnbereiche. *Monatsschrift für Psychiatrie und Neurologie*, 1945, *111*, 17–59.

Hill, W. C. O. A note on integumental colours with special references to the genus Mandrillus. *Säugetierkundliche Mitteilungen*, 1955, *3*, 145–151.

Hinde, R. A. *Animal behaviour: A synthesis of ethology and comparative psychology* (2nd ed.). New York: McGraw-Hill, 1970.

Hohmann, G. W. Some effects of spinal cord lesions on experienced emotional feelings. *Psychophysiology*, 1966, *3*, 143–156.

Holmberg, A. R. *The Siriono*. Unpublished doctoral dissertation, Yale University, 1946.

Homans, G. C. *The human group*. New York: Harcourt, 1950.

Hook, E. B., & Kim, D. Height and antisocial behavior in XY and XYY boys. *Science*, 1971, *172*, 21–29.

Hoon, P. W., Wincze, J. P., & Hoon, E. F. A test of reciprocal inhibition: Are anxiety and sexual arousal in women mutually inhibitory? *Journal of Abnormal Psychology*, 1977, *86*, 65–74.

Howard, J. L., Reifler, C. B., & Liptzin, M. B. Effects of exposure to pornography. In *Technical Report of The Commission on Obscenity and Pornography* (Vol. 8). Washington, D.C.: U.S. Government Printing Office, 1971.

Hull, C. L. *Principles of behavior: An introduction to behavior theory*. New York: Appleton-Century-Crofts, 1943.

Hull, C. L. *A behavior system: An introduction to behavior theory concerning the individual organism*. New York: Wiley, 1952.

Hunsperger, R. W. Affektreaktionen auf elektrische Reizung im Hirnstamm der Katze. *Helvetica Physiologica et Pharmacologia Acta*, 1956, *14*, 70–92.

Hunsperger, R. W. Les représentations centrales des réactions affectives dans le cerveau antérieur et dans le tronc cérébral. *Neurochirurgie*, 1959, *5*, 207–233.

Hunt, M. *Sexual behavior in the 1970s*. New York: Dell Books, 1974.

Hurst, F. *Five and ten*. New York: Harper, 1929.

Hutchinson, R. R. The environmental causes of aggression. In J. K. Cole & D. D. Jensen (Eds.), *Nebraska Symposium on Motivation* (Vol. 20). Lincoln: University of Nebraska Press, 1972.

Hutchison, J. B. (Ed.). *Biological determinants of sexual behaviour*. Chichester: Wiley, 1978.

Hyorth, I. Reproductive behavior in Tetraonidae, with special reference to males. *Viltrevy*, 1970, *7*, 271–328.

Ingram, W. R. Brain stem mechanisms and behavior. *Electroencephalography and Clinical Neurophysiology*, 1952, *4*, 395–406.

Istvan, J., Griffitt, W., & Weidner, G. *Sexual arousal and the polarization of perceived sexual attractiveness*. Unpublished manuscript, Kansas State University, 1982.

Ivey, M. E., & Bardwick, J. M. Patterns of affective fluctuation in the menstrual cycle. *Psychosomatic Medicine*, 1968, *30*, 336–345.

Izard, C. E. *Human emotions*. New York: Plenum Press, 1977.

Izard, C. E., & Caplan, S. Sex differences in emotional responses to erotic literature. *Journal of Consulting and Clinical Psychology*, 1974, *42*, 468.

Jackson, B. T. A case of voyeurism treated by counterconditioning. In J. Fischer & H. L. Gochros (Eds.), *Handbook of behavior therapy with sexual problems* (Vol. 2). *Approaches to specific problems*. New York: Pergamon Press, 1977.

Jacobs, P., Brenton, M., Melville, M., Brittain, R., & McClemont, W. Aggressive behavior, mental subnormality and the XYY male. *Nature*, 1965, *208*, 1351–1353.

Jaffe, Y. *Sex and aggression: An intimate relationship*. Unpublished doctoral dissertation, University of California at Los Angeles, 1974.

Jaffe, Y. Sexual stimulation: Effects on prosocial behavior. *Psychological Reports*, 1981, *48*, 75–81.

Jaffe, Y., Malamuth, N., Feingold, J., & Feshbach, S. Sexual arousal and behavioral aggression. *Journal of Personality and Social Psychology*, 1974, *30*, 759–764.

James, W. H. The distribution of coitus within the human intermenstrum. *Journal of Biosocial Science*, 1971, *3*, 159–171.

Janda, L. H., & Klenke-Hamel, K. E. *Human sexuality*. New York: Van Nostrand, 1980.

Jaspers, K. *General psychopathology*. Manchester: Manchester University Press, 1963.

Jay, P. The common langur of North India. In I. DeVore (Ed.), *Primate behavior: Field studies of monkeys and apes*. New York: Holt, Rinehart & Winston, 1965.

Jensen, G. D. Human sexual behavior in primate perspective. In J. Zubin & J. Money (Eds.), *Contemporary sexual behavior: Critical issues in the 1970s*. Baltimore: Johns Hopkins University Press, 1973.

Johnson, R. N. *Aggression in man and animals.* Philadelphia: Saunders, 1972.

Kaada, B. R., Anderson, P., & Jansen, J., Jr. Stimulation of the amygdaloid nuclear complex in unanaesthetized cats. *Neurology,* 1954, *4,* 48–64.

Kahn, M. W. The effect of socially learned aggression or submission on the mating behavior of C57 mice. *Journal of Genetic Psychology,* 1961, *98,* 211–217.

Kahneman, D., Tursky, B., Shapiro, D., & Crider, A. Pupillary, heart rate, and skin resistance changes during a mental task. *Journal of Experimental Psychology,* 1969, *79,* 164–167.

Kanin, E. J. Male aggression in dating-courtship relations. *American Journal of Sociology,* 1957, *63,* 197–204.

Kanin, E. J. Reference groups and sex conduct norm violations. *The Sociological Quarterly,* 1967, *8,* 495–504.

Karpman, B. *The sexual offender and his offenses.* New York: Julian Press, 1954.

Kaufmann, H. *Aggression and altruism: A psychological analysis.* New York: Holt, Rinehart & Winston, 1970.

Kaunitz, P. E. Sadomasochistic marriages. *Medical Aspects of Human Sexuality,* February 1977, pp. 66–69; 74; 79–80.

Kelley, K. *Variety is the spice of erotica: Repeated exposure, novelty, and sexual attitudes.* Paper presented at the meeting of the Eastern Psychological Association, Baltimore, April 1982.

Kelley, K., Miller, C. T., Byrne, D., & Bell, P. A. Facilitating sexual arousal via anger, aggression, or dominance. *Motivation and Emotion,* 1983, in press.

Kenrick, D. T., & Cialdini, R. B. Romantic attraction: Misattribution versus reinforcement explanations. *Journal of Personality and Social Psychology,* 1977, *35,* 381–391.

Kenrick, D. T., Cialdini, R. B., & Linder, D. E. Misattribution under fear-producing circumstances: Four failures to replicate. *Personality and Social Psychology Bulletin,* 1979, *5,* 329–334.

Kercher, G. A., & Walker, C. E. Reactions of convicted rapists to sexually explicit stimuli. *Journal of Abnormal Psychology,* 1973, *81,* 46–50.

Kessel, N., & Coppen, A. The prevalence of common menstrual symptoms. *Lancet,* July 13, 1963, 61–64.

Kim, Y. K., & Umbach, W. Combined stereotaxic lesions for treatment of behavior disorders and severe pain. In L. V. Laitenen & K. E. Livingston (Eds.), *Surgical approaches to psychiatry.* Baltimore: University Park Press, 1973.

Kimmel, H. D. Instrumental conditioning of autonomically mediated responses in human beings. *American Psychologist,* 1974, *29,* 325–335.

King, F. A. Effects of septal and amygdaloid lesions on emotional behavior and conditioned avoidance responses in the rat. *Journal of Nervous and Mental Disease,* 1958, *126,* 57–63.

King, H. E. Psychological effects of excitation in the limbic system. In D. E. Sheer (Ed.), *Electrical stimulation of the brain.* Austin: University of Texas Press, 1961.

King, J. Sexual behavior of C57BL/10 mice and its relation to early social experience. *Journal of Genetic Psychology,* 1956, *88,* 223–229.

Kinsey, A. C., Pomeroy, W. B., & Martin, C. E. *Sexual behavior in the human male.* Philadelphia: Saunders, 1948.

Kinsey, A. C., Pomeroy, W. B., Martin, C. E., & Gebhard, P. H. *Sexual behavior in the human female.* Philadelphia: Saunders, 1953.

Kirchshofer, R. Einige bemerkenswerte Verhaltensweisen bei Saimiris im Vergleich zu verwandten Arten. *Zeitschrift für Morphologie und Anthropologie,* 1963, *53,* 77–91.

Klein, H. Masochism. *Medical Aspects of Human Sexuality,* November 1972, pp. 33–35; 39; 41; 44; 48; 53.

Kling, A., Orbach, J., Schwartz, N. B., & Towne, J. C. Injury to the limbic system and associated structures in cats (chronic behavioral and physiological effects). *Archives of General Psychiatry,* 1960, *3,* 391–420.

Klumbies, G., & Kleinsorge, H. Das Herz im Orgasmus. *Medizinische Klinik,* 1950, *45,* 952–958.

Klüver, H., & Bucy, P. C. "Psychic blindness" and other symptoms following bilateral temporal lobectomy in rhesus monkeys. *American Journal of Physiology*, 1937, *119*, 352–353.

Komisaruk, B. R., Larsson, K., & Cooper, R. *Intense lordosis in the absence of ovarian hormones after septal ablations in rats.* Paper presented at the Second Annual Meeting of the Society for Neuroscience, Houston, November 1972.

Kopell, B. S., Lunde, D. T., Clayton, R. B., & Moos, R. H. The variations in some measures of arousal during the menstrual cycle. *Journal of Nervous and Mental Disease*, 1969, *148*, 180–187.

Kostowski, W., Rewerski, W., & Piechocki, T. Effects of some steroids on aggressive behavior in mice and rats. *Neuroendocrinology*, 1970, *6*, 311–318.

Kraemer, H. C., Becker, H. B., Brodie, H. K. H., Doering, C. H., Moos, R. H., & Hamburg, D. A. Orgasmic frequency and plasma testosterone levels in normal human males. *Archives of Sexual Behavior*, 1976, *5*, 125–132.

Kreuz, L. E., & Rose, R. M. Assessment of aggressive behavior and plasma testosterone in a young criminal population. *Psychosomatic Medicine*, 1972, *34*, 321–332.

Kreuz, L. E., Rose, R. M., & Jennings, J. R. Suppression of plasma testosterone levels and psychological stress. *Archives of General Psychiatry*, 1972, *26*, 479–482.

Kummer, H. *Primate societies: Group techniques of ecological adaptation.* Chicago: Aldine, 1971.

Kunkel, P., & Kunkel, L. Beiträge zur Ethologie des Hausmeerschweinchens *Cavia aperea f. porcellus* (L.). *Zeitschrift für Tierpsychologie*, 1964, *21*, 602–641.

Kuntz, A. *The autonomic nervous system* (4th ed.). Philadelphia: Lea & Febiger, 1953.

Kutner, S. J., & Brown, W. L. Types of oral contraceptives, depression and premenstrual symptoms. *Journal of Nervous and Mental Disease*, 1972, *155*, 153–162.

Lagerspetz, K., & Hautojärvi, S. The effect of prior aggressive or sexual arousal on subsequent aggressive or sexual reactions in male mice. *Scandanavian Journal of Psychology*, 1967, *8*, 1–6.

Lagerspetz, K. M. J., & Lagerspetz, K. Y. H. The expression of the genes of aggressiveness in mice: The effect of androgen on aggression and sexual behavior in females. *Aggressive Behavior*, 1975, *1*, 291–296.

Lagerspetz, K. Y. H., Tirri, R., & Lagerspetz, K. M. J. Neurochemical and endocrinological studies of mice selectively bred for aggressiveness. *Scandinavian Journal of Psychology*, 1968, *9*, 157–160.

Laidlaw, J. Catamenial epilepsy. *Lancet*, July 21, 1956, 1235–1237.

Langer, W. L. Checks on population growth: 1750–1850. *Scientific American*, 1972, *226*, 92–99.

Langer, W. L. Infanticide: A historical survey. *History of Childhood Quarterly*, 1974, *1*(3), 363–365.

Langley, L. L. *Physiology of man* (4th ed.). New York: Van Nostrand Reinhold, 1971.

Larsson, K. Mating behavior in male rats after cerebral cortex ablation. II. Effects of lesions in the frontal lobes compared to lesions in the posterior half of the hemispheres. *Journal of Experimental Zoology*, 1964, *155*, 203–214.

Laschet, U. Antiandrogen in the treatment of sex offenders: Mode of action and therapeutic outcome. In J. Zubin & J. Money (Eds.), *Contemporary sexual behavior: Critical issues in the 1970s.* Baltimore: Johns Hopkins University Press, 1973.

Laschet, U., & Laschet, L. Die Behandlung der pathologisch gesteigerten und abartigen Sexualität des Mannes mit dem Antiandrogen Cyproteronacetat. In *13th Symposium der Deutschen Gesellschaft für Endokrinologie, Würzburg, March 1967.* Berlin: Springer, 1968.

Lawick-Goodall, J. van. The behavior of free-living chimpanzees in the Gombe Stream Reserve. *Animal Behaviour Monographs*, 1968, *1*(3), 161–311.

Laws, D. *Non-aversive treatment alternatives of hospitalized pedophiles: An automated fading procedure to alter sexual responsiveness.* Paper presented at the meeting of the American Psychological Association, New Orleans, September 1974.

Le Beau, J. The cingular and precingular areas in psychosurgery (agitated behaviour, obsessive compulsive states, epilepsy). *Acta Psychiatrica et Neurologica*, 1952, *27*, 305–316.

Le Boeuf, B. J., & Peterson, R. S. Social status and mating activity in elephant seals. *Science,* 1969, *163,* 91–93.

Lederer, L. (Ed.). *Take back the night: Women on pornography.* New York: Morrow, 1980.

Leonard, K. E., & Taylor, S. P. Exposure to pornography, permissive and nonpermissive cues, and male aggression toward females. *Motivation and Emotion,* 1983, *7,* 291–299.

Leshner, A. I. *An introduction to behavioral endocrinology.* New York: Oxford University Press, 1978.

Leshner, A. I., & Candland, D. K. Endocrine effects of grouping and dominance rank in squirrel monkeys. *Physiology and Behavior,* 1972, *8,* 441–445.

Lester, D. *Unusual sexual behavior: The standard deviations.* Springfield, Ill.: Thomas, 1975.

Leventhal, H. Emotions: A basic problem for social psychology. In C. Nemeth (Ed.), *Social Psychology: Classic and contemporary integrations.* Chicago: Rand McNally, 1974.

Leventhal, H. A perceptual-motor processing model of emotion. In P. Pliner, K. R. Blankstein, & I. M. Spigel (Eds.), *Advances in the study of communication and affect* (Vol. 5). *Perception of emotion in self and others.* New York: Plenum Press, 1979.

Levi, L. The urinary output of adrenalin and noradrenalin during experimentally induced emotional stress in clinically different groups. *Acta Psychotherapeutica et Psychosomatica,* 1963, *11,* 218–227.

Levi, L. The urinary output of adrenalin and noradrenalin during pleasant and unpleasant emotional states: A preliminary report. *Psychosomatic Medicine,* 1965, *27,* 80–85.

Levi, L. Sympatho-adrenomedullary responses to emotional stimuli: Methodologic, physiologic and pathologic considerations. In E. Bajusz (Ed.), *An introduction to clinical neuroendocrinology.* Basel: Karger, 1967.

Levi, L. Sympatho-adrenomedullary activity, diuresis, and emotional reactions during visual sexual stimulation in human females and males. *Psychosomatic Medicine,* 1969, *31,* 251–268.

Levi, L. Stress and distress in response to psychosocial stimuli: Laboratory and real life studies on sympathoadrenomedullary and related reactions. *Acta Medica Scandinavica,* 1972, Supplement 528.

Levine, M. D., Gordon, T. P., Peterson, R. H., & Rose, R. M. Urinary 17-OHCS response of high- and low-aggressive rhesus monkeys to shock avoidance. *Physiology and Behavior,* 1970, *5,* 919–924.

Levine, S. (Ed.). *Hormones and behavior.* New York: Academic Press, 1972.

Levy, J., & King, J. A. The effects of testosterone propionate on fighting behaviour in young male C57BL/10 mice. *Anatomical Record,* 1953, *117,* 562–563. (Abstract)

Lincoln, G. A. The role of antlers in the behaviour of red deer. *Journal of Experimental Zoology,* 1972, *182,* 233–250.

Lindsey, B., & Evans, W. *The companionate marriage.* New York: Boni & Liveright, 1927.

Lindsley, D. B. Emotion. In S. S. Stevens (Ed.), *Handbook of experimental psychology.* New York: Wiley, 1951.

Lindsley, D. B. Psychophysiology and motivation. In M. R. Jones (Ed.), *Nebraska Symposium on Motivation* (Vol. 5). Lincoln: University of Nebraska Press, 1957.

Lisk, R. D. Diencephalic placement of estradiol and sexual receptivity in the female rat. *American Journal of Physiology,* 1962, *203,* 493–496.

Litman, R. E., & Swearingen, C. Bondage and suicide. *Archives of General Psychiatry,* 1972, *27,* 80–85.

Logothetis, J., Harner, R., Morrell, F., & Torres, F. The role of estrogens in catamenial exacerbation of epilepsy. *Neurology,* 1959, *9,* 352–360.

LoPiccolo, J., Stewart, R., & Watkins, B. Case study: Treatment of erectile failure and ejaculatory incompetence of homosexual etiology. *Journal of Behavior Therapy and Experimental Psychiatry,* 1972, *3,* 233–236.

Lorenz, K. Z. The comparative method in studying innate behaviour patterns. *Symposia of the Society for Experimental Biology,* 1950, *4,* 221–268.

Lorenz, K. Z. Phylogenetische Anpassung und adaptive Modifikation des Verhaltens. *Zeitschrift für Tierpsychologie*, 1961, *18*, 139–187.

Lorenz, K. *Das sogenannte Böse: Zur Naturgeschichte der Aggression*. Wien: Borotha-Schoeler, 1963.

Lorenz, K. Ritualized fighting. In J. D. Carthy & F. J. Ebling (Eds.), *The natural history of aggression*. New York: Academic Press, 1964.

Lorenz, K. Z. *Evolution and modification of behavior*. Chicago: University of Chicago Press, 1965.

Lubs, H. A., & Ruddle, F. H. Chromosomal abnormalities in the human population: Estimation of rates based on New Haven newborn study. *Science*, 1970, *169*, 495–497.

Lundberg, P. O. Sexual dysfunction in patients with neurological disorders. In R. Gemme & C. C. Wheeler (Eds.), *Progress in sexology: Selected papers from the proceedings of the 1976 International Congress of Sexology*. New York: Plenum Press, 1977.

Luria, Z., & Rose, M. D. *Psychology of human sexuality*. New York: Wiley, 1979.

Luttge, W. G. The role of gonadal hormones in the sexual behavior of the rhesus monkey and human: A literature survey. *Archives of Sexual Behavior*, 1971, *1*, 61–68.

Maccoby, E. (Ed.). *The development of sex differences*. Stanford, Calif.: Stanford University Press, 1966.

Maccoby, E. E., & Jacklin, C. N. *The psychology of sex differences*. Stanford, Calif.: Stanford University Press, 1974.

MacKinnon, P. C., & MacKinnon, I. L. Hazards of the menstrual cycle. *British Medical Journal*, 1956, *1*(4966), 555.

MacLean, P. D. Some psychiatric implications of physiological studies on frontotemporal portion of limbic system (visceral brain). *Electroencephalography and Clinical Neurophysiology*, 1952, *4*, 407–418.

MacLean, P. D. New findings relevant to the evolution of psychosexual functions of the brain. *Journal of Nervous and Mental Disease*, 1962, *135*, 289–301.

MacLean, P. D. Phylogenesis. In P. H. Knapp (Ed.), *Expression of the emotions in man*. New York: International Universities Press, 1963.

MacLean, P. D. Man and his animal brains. *Modern Medicine*, 1964, *32*, 95–106. (a)

MacLean, P. D. Mirror display in the squirrel monkey (*Saimiri sciureus*). *Science*, 1964, *146*, 950–952. (b)

MacLean, P. D. The brain in relation to empathy and medical education. *Journal of Nervous and Mental Disease*, 1967, *144*, 374–382.

MacLean, P. D. Alternative neural pathways to violence. In L. Ng (Ed.), *Alternatives to violence: A stimulus to dialogue*. New York: Time-Life Books, 1968. (a)

MacLean, P. D. Contrasting functions of limbic and neocortical systems of the brain and their relevance to psychophysiological aspects of medicine. In E. Gellhorn (Ed.), *Biological foundations of emotion*. Glenview, Ill.: Scott, Foresman, 1968. (b)

MacLean, P. D. The triune brain, emotion, and scientific bias. In F. O. Schmitt (Ed.), *The neurosciences: Second study program*. New York: Rockefeller University Press, 1970.

MacLean, P. D. Special Award Lecture: New findings on brain function and sociosexual behavior. In J. Zubin & J. Money (Eds.), *Contemporary sexual behavior: Critical issues in the 1970s*. Baltimore: Johns Hopkins University Press, 1973.

MacLean, P. D., & Delgado, J. M. R. Electrical and chemical stimulation of frontal-temporal portion of limbic system in the waking animal. *Electroencephalography and Clinical Neurophysiology*, 1953, *5*, 91–100.

MacLean, P. D., Denniston, R. H., & Dua, S. Further studies on cerebral representation of penile erection: Caudal thalamus, midbrain, and pons. *Journal of Neurophysiology*, 1963, *26*, 273–293.

MacLean, P. D., Denniston, R. H., Dua, S., & Ploog, D. W. Hippocampal changes with brain stimulation eliciting penile erection. In *Physiologie de l'hippocampe*. Paris: Colloques Internationaux du Centre National de la Recherche Scientifique, 1962, *107*, 491–510.

MacLean, P. D., Dua, S., & Denniston, R. H. Cerebral localization for scratching and seminal discharge. *Archives of Neurology,* 1963, *9,* 485–497.

MacLean, P. D., & Ploog, D. W. Cerebral representation of penile erection. *Journal of Neurophysiology,* 1962, *25,* 29–55.

MacLusky, N. J., & Naftolin, F. Sexual differentiation of the central nervous system. *Science,* 1981, *211,* 1294–1303.

Magnus, O., & Lammers, H. J. The amygdaloid complex. Part I. Electrical stimulation of the amygdala and periamygdaloid cortex in the waking cat. *Folia Psychiatrica, Neurologica et Neurochirurgica Neerlandica,* 1956, *55,* 555–581.

Malamuth, N. M. Rape fantasies as a function of exposure to violent sexual stimuli. *Archives of Sexual Behavior,* 1981, *10,* 33–47. (a)

Malamuth, N. M. Rape proclivity among males. *Journal of Social Issues,* 1981, *37,* 138–157. (b)

Malamuth, N. M., & Check, J. V. P. Penile tumescence and perceptual responses to rape as a function of victim's perceived reactions. *Journal of Applied Social Psychology,* 1980, *10,* 528–547. (a)

Malamuth, N. M., & Check, J. V. P. Sexual arousal to rape and consenting depictions: The importance of the woman's arousal. *Journal of Abnormal Psychology,* 1980, *89,* 763–766. (b)

Malamuth, N. M., Feshbach, S., & Jaffe, Y. Sexual arousal and aggression: Recent experiments and theoretical issues. *Journal of Social Issues,* 1977, *33,* 110–133.

Malamuth, N. M., Haber, S., & Feshbach, S. Testing hypotheses regarding rape: Exposure to sexual violence, sex differences, and the "normality" of rapists. *Journal of Research in Personality,* 1980, *14,* 121–137.

Malamuth, N. M., Heim, M., & Feshbach, S. Sexual responsiveness of college students to rape depictions: Inhibitory and disinhibitory effects. *Journal of Personality and Social Psychology,* 1980, *38,* 399–408.

Malinowski, B. *The sexual life of savages in North-Western Melanesia.* New York: Readers League of America, 1929.

Malmo, R. B. Activation: A neuropsychological dimension. *Psychological Review,* 1959, *66,* 367–386.

Mandler, G. *Mind and emotions.* New York: Wiley, 1975.

Mandler, G., & Kahn, M. Discrimination of changes in heart rate: Two unsuccessful attempts. *Journal for the Experimental Analysis of Behavior,* 1960, *3,* 21–25.

Mandler, G., & Kremen, I. Autonomic feedback: A correlational study. *Journal of Personality,* 1958, *26,* 388–399.

Mandler, G., Mandler, J. M., Kremen, I., & Sholiton, R. D. The response to threat: Relations among verbal and physiological indices. *Psychological Monographs,* 1961, *75*(9, Whole No. 513).

Mann, J., Berkowitz, L., Sidman, J., Starr, S., & West, S. Satiation of the transient stimulating effect of erotic films. *Journal of Personality and Social Psychology,* 1974, *30,* 729–735.

Mann, J., Sidman, J., & Starr, S. Effects of erotic films on sexual behavior of married couples. In *Technical Report of The Commission on Obscenity and Pornography* (Vol. 8). Washington, D.C.: U.S. Government Printing Office, 1971.

Marcuse, H. *Eros und Kultur: Ein philosophischer Beitrag zu Sigmund Freud.* Stuttgart: Klett, 1957.

Marinari, K. T., Leshner, A. I., & Doyle, M. P. Menstrual cycle status and adrenocortical reactivity to psychological stress. *Psychoneuroendocrinology,* 1976, *1,* 213–218.

Mark, V. H., & Ervin, F. R. *Violence and the brain.* New York: Harper & Row, 1970.

Mark, V. H., Sweet, W., & Ervin, F. Deep temporal lobe stimulation and destructive lesions in episodically violent temporal lobe epileptics. In W. S. Fields & W. H. Sweet (Eds.), *Neural bases of violence and aggression.* St. Louis: Green, 1975.

Marler, P., & Hamilton, W. J. *Mechanisms of animal behavior.* New York: Wiley, 1968.

Marshall, D. S. *Ra'ivavae: An expedition to the most fascinating and mysterious island in Polynesia.* New York: Doubleday, 1961.

Marshall, D. S. Sexual behavior on Mangaia. In D. S. Marshall & R. C. Suggs (Eds.), *Human sexual behavior: Variations in the ethnographic spectrum.* New York: Basic Books, 1971.

Marshall, D. S., & Suggs, R. C. (Eds.). *Human sexual behavior: Variations in the ethnographic spectrum.* New York: Basic Books, 1971.

Marshall, W. The modification of sexual fantasies: A combined treatment approach to the reduction of deviant sexual behaviour. *Behaviour Research and Therapy,* 1973, *11,* 557–564.

Marshall, W., & McKnight, R. An integrated treatment program for sexual offenders. *Canadian Psychiatric Association Journal,* 1975, *20,* 133–138.

Marshall, W., & Williams, S. *A behavioral treatment program for incarcerated sex offenders: Some tentative results.* Paper presented at the meeting of the Association for Advancement of Behavior Therapy, San Francisco, December 1975.

Martin, R. D. Reproduction and ontogeny in tree-shrews (*Tupaia belangeri*) with reference to their general behaviour and taxonomic relationships. *Zeitschrift für Tierpsychologie,* 1968, *25,* 1409–1495.

Mason, J. W., Mangan, G., Brady, J. V., Conrad, D., & Rioch, D. McK. Concurrent plasma epinephrine, norepinephrine and 17-hydroxycorticosteroid levels during conditioned emotional disturbances in monkeys. *Psychosomatic Medicine,* 1961, *23,* 344–353.

Mason, W. A. Field and laboratory studies of social organization in *Saimiri* and *Callicebus.* In L. A. Rosenblum (Ed.), *Primate behavior: Developments in field and laboratory research* (Vol. 2). New York: Academic Press, 1971.

Masserman, J. H. Is the hypothalamus a center of emotion? *Psychosomatic Medicine,* 1941, *3,* 3–25.

Masters, W. H., & Johnson, V. *Human sexual response.* Boston: Little, Brown, 1966.

McCary, J. L. *McCary's human sexuality* (3rd ed.). New York: Van Nostrand, 1978.

McGuire, J. L., & Lisk, R. D. Oestrogen receptors in androgen or oestrogen sterilized female rats. *Nature,* 1969, *221,* 1068–1069.

McGuire, R. J., Carlisle, J. M., & Young, B. G. Sexual deviations as conditioned behaviour: A hypothesis. *Behaviour Research and Therapy,* 1965, *2,* 185–190.

McKinney, T. D., & Desjardins, C. Postnatal development of the testis, fighting behavior and fertility in house mice. *Biology of Reproduction,* 1973, *9,* 279–294.

Melges, F. T., & Hamburg, D. A. Psychological effects of hormonal changes in women. In F. A. Beach (Ed.), *Human sexuality in four perspectives.* Baltimore: Johns Hopkins University Press, 1976.

Mertens, T. R. *Human genetics.* New York: Wiley, 1975.

Messenger, J. C. *Inis Beag: Isle of Ireland.* New York: Holt, Rinehart & Winston, 1969.

Messenger, J. C. Sex and repression in an Irish folk community. In D. S. Marshall & R. C. Suggs (Eds.), *Human sexual behavior: Variations in the ethnographic spectrum.* New York: Basic Books, 1971.

Meyer, T. P. The effects of sexually arousing and violent films on aggressive behavior. *Journal of Sex Research,* 1972, *8,* 324–333.

Meyer-Bahlburg, H. F. L., Boon, D. A., Sharma, M., & Edwards, J. A. Aggressiveness and testosterone measures in man. *Psychosomatic Medicine,* 1974, *36,* 269–274.

Meyers, R. Three cases of myoclonus alleviated by bilateral ansotomy, with a note on postoperative alibido and impotence. *Journal of Neurosurgery,* 1962, *19,* 71–81.

Michael, R. P., & Herbert, J. Menstrual cycle influences grooming behavior and sexual activity in the rhesus monkey. *Science,* 1963, *140,* 500–501.

Michael, R. P., & Zumpe, D. Potency in male rhesus monkeys: Effects of continuously receptive females. *Science,* 1978, *200,* 451–453.

Miller, C. T., Byrne, D., & Bell, P. A. *Facilitating sexual arousal: Anger or dominance?* Paper presented at the meeting of the Midwestern Psychological Association, Chicago, May 1977.

Miller, N. E. The frustration-aggression hypothesis. *Psychological Review*, 1941, *48*, 337–342.

Mills, J., & Mintz, P. M. Effect of unexplained arousal on affiliation. *Journal of Personality and Social Psychology*, 1972, *24*, 11–13.

Mishkin, M. Visual discrimination performance following partial ablations of the temporal lobe: II. Ventral surface vs. hippocampus. *Journal of Comparative and Physiological Psychology*, 1954, *47*, 187–193.

Mishkin, M., & Pribram, K. H. Visual discrimination performance following partial ablations of the temporal lobe: I. Ventral vs. lateral. *Journal of Comparative and Physiological Psychology*, 1954, *47*, 14–20.

Mittwoch, U. *Sex chromosomes*. New York: Academic Press, 1967.

Money, J. Prenatal hormones and postnatal socialization in gender identity differentiation. In J. K. Cole & R. Dienstbier (Eds.), *Nebraska Symposium on Motivation* (Vol. 21). Lincoln: University of Nebraska Press, 1973.

Money, J. Role of fantasy in pair-bonding and erotic performance. In R. Gemme & C. C. Wheeler (Eds.), *Progress in sexology*. New York: Plenum Press, 1977.

Money, J., & Ehrhardt, A. A. *Man and woman, boy and girl: The differentiation and dimorphism of gender identity from conception to maturity*. Baltimore: Johns Hopkins University Press, 1972.

Money, J., Gaskin, R. J., & Hull, H. Impulse, aggression and sexuality in the XYY syndrome. *St. John's Law Review*, 1970, *44*, 220–235.

Money, J., & Pollitt, E. Cytogenetic and psychosexual ambiguity: Klinefelter's syndrome and transvestism compared. *Archives of General Psychiatry*, 1964, *11*, 589–595.

Money, J., & Schwartz, M. F. Fetal androgens in the early treated adrenogenital syndrome of 46 XX hermaphroditism: Influence on assertive and aggressive types of behavior. *Aggressive Behavior*, 1976, *2*, 19–30.

Money, J., & Schwartz, M. F. Dating, romantic and nonromantic friendships and sexuality in 17 early-treated adrenogenital females, ages 16 to 25. In P. A. Lee, L. P. Plotnick, A. A. Kowarski, & C. J. Migeon (Eds.), *Congenital adrenal hyperplasia*. Baltimore: University Park Press, 1977.

Money, J., & Schwartz, M. Biosocial determinants of gender identity differentiation and development. In J. B. Hutchison (Ed.), *Biological determinants of sexual behaviour*. Chichester: Wiley, 1978.

Money, J., Wiedeking, C., Walker, P., Migeon, C., Meyer, W., & Borgaonkar, D. 47,XYY and 46,XY males with antisocial and/or sex-offending behavior: Antiandrogen therapy plus counseling. *Psychoneuroendocrinology*, 1975, *1*, 165–178.

Montagu, A. Chromosomes and crime. *Psychology Today*, October 1968, pp. 42–49.

Moore-Čavar, E. C. *International inventory of information on induced abortion*. New York: International Institute for the Study of Human Reproduction, Columbia University, 1974.

Moos, R. H., Kopell, B. S., Melges, F. T., Yalom, I. D., Lunde, D. T., Clayton, R. B., & Hamburg, D. A. Fluctuations in symptoms and moods during the menstrual cycle. *Journal of Psychosomatic Research*, 1969, *13*, 37–44.

Morris, D. *The naked ape*. New York: McGraw-Hill, 1968.

Morton, J. H., Addison, R., Hunt, L., & Sullivan, J. Clinical study of premenstrual tension. *American Journal of Obstetrics and Gynecology*, 1953, *65*, 1182–1191.

Mosher, D. L. Sex callousness toward women. In *Technical Report of the Commission on Obscenity and Pornography* (Vol. 8). Washington, D.C.: U.S. Government Printing Office, 1971.

Mosher, D. L., & Cross, H. J. Sex guilt and premarital sexual experiences of college students. *Journal of Consulting and Clinical Psychology*, 1971, *36*, 27–32.

Munro, D., Horne, H. W., Jr., & Paull, D. P. The effect of injury to the spinal cord and cauda equina on the sexual potency of men. *New England Journal of Medicine*, 1948, *239*, 903–911.

Nakao, H. Emotional behavior produced by hypothalamic stimulation. *American Journal of Physiology*, 1958, *194*, 411–418.

Narabayashi, H. Stereotaxic amygdalotomy for behavioral and emotional disorders. *Brain Nerve*, 1964, *16*, 800–804.

Narabayashi, H., & Uno, M. Long range results of stereotaxic amygdalotomy for behavioral disorders. *Confinia Neurologica*, 1966, *27*, 168–171.

Neel, J. V. Lessons from a "primitive" people. *Science*, 1970, *170*, 815–822.

Newcomb, T. M. *The acquaintance process*. New York: Holt, 1961.

Newman, H. F., Northrup, J. D., & Devlin, J. Mechanism of human penile erection. *Investigative Urology*, 1964, *1*, 350–353.

Oaks, W. W., Melchiode, G. A., & Ficher, I. (Eds.). *Sex and the life cycle*. New York: Grune & Stratton, 1976.

Olds, J. Hypothalamic substrates of reward. *Physiological Reviews*, 1962, *42*, 554–604.

Olds, J., & Milner, P. Positive reinforcement produced by electrical stimulation of septal area and other regions of rat brain. *Journal of Comparative and Physiological Psychology*, 1954, *47*, 419–427.

Ottow, B. *Biologische Anatomie der Genitalorgane und der Fortpflanzung der Säugetiere*. Jena: Fischer, 1955.

Ovid. *[The art of love, and other poems]* (J. H. Mozley, trans.). Cambridge, Mass.: Harvard University Press, 1947.

Paige, K. E. Effects of oral contraceptives on affective fluctuations associated with the menstrual cycle. *Psychosomatic Medicine*, 1971, *33*, 515–537.

Papez, J. W. *Comparative neurology*. New York: Crowell, 1929.

Papez, J. W. A proposed mechanism of emotion. *Archives of Neurology and Psychiatry*, 1937, *38*, 725–743.

Parlee, M. B. The premenstrual syndrome. *Psychological Bulletin*, 1973, *80*, 454–465.

Pátkai, P. Catecholamine excretion in pleasant and unpleasant situations. *Acta Psychologica*, 1971, *35*, 352–363. (a)

Pátkai, P. The diurnal rhythm of adrenaline secretion in subjects with different working habits. *Acta Physiologica Scandinavica*, 1971, *81*, 30–34. (b)

Perachio, A. A., Alexander, M., & Marr, L. D. Hormonal and social factors affecting evoked sexual behavior in rhesus monkeys. *American Journal of Physical Anthropology*, 1973, *38*, 227–232.

Perachio, A., Alexander, M., & Robinson, B. Sexual behavior evoked by telestimulation. In H. O. Hofer (Ed.), *Proceedings of the Second International Congress of Primatology* (Vol. 3). Basel: Karger, 1969.

Persky, H., Smith, K. D., & Basu, G. K. Relation of psychologic measures of aggression and hostility to testosterone production in men. *Psychosomatic Medicine*, 1971, *33*, 265–277.

Phoenix, C. H., Goy, R. W., Gerall, A. A., & Young, W. C. Organizing action of prenatally administered testosterone propionate on the tissues mediating mating behavior in the female guinea pig. *Endocrinology*, 1959, *65*, 369–382.

Pick, J. *The autonomic nervous system*. Philadelphia: Lippincott, 1970.

Pirke, K. M., Kockott, G., & Dittmar, F. Psychosexual stimulation and plasma testosterone in man. *Archives of Sexual Behavior*, 1974, *3*, 577–584.

Ploog, D. Biologische Grundlagen aggressiven Verhaltens. In H. E. Ehrhardt (Ed.), *Aggressivität, Dissozialität, Psychohygiene*. Bern: Huber, 1975.

Ploog, D., Hopf, S., & Winter, P. Ontogenese des Verhaltens von Totenkopf-Affen (*Saimiri sciureus*). *Psychologische Forschung*, 1967, *31*, 1–41.

Ploog, D. W., & MacLean, P. D. Display of penile erection in squirrel monkey (*Saimiri sciureus*). *Animal Behaviour,* 1963, *11,* 32–39.

Polani, P. A. Abnormal sex chromosomes and mental disorder. *Nature,* 1969, *223,* 680–686.

Pool, J. L. The visceral brain of man. *Journal of Neurosurgery,* 1954, *11,* 45–63.

Prescott, J. W. Phylogenetic and ontogenetic aspects of human affectional development. In R. Gemme & C. C. Wheeler (Eds.), *Progress in sexology: Selected papers from the Proceedings of the 1976 International Congress of Sexology.* New York: Plenum Press, 1977.

Pribram, K. H. Interrelations of Psychology and the neurological disciplines. In S. Koch (Ed.), *Psychology: A study of a science* (Vol. 4). New York: McGraw-Hill, 1962.

Pribram, K. H., & Bagshaw, M. Further analysis of the temporal lobe syndrome utilizing fronto-temporal ablations. *Journal of Comparative Neurology,* 1953, *99,* 347–375.

Price, W. H., & Whatmore, P. B. Behaviour disorders and pattern of crime among XYY males identified at a maximum security hospital. *British Medical Journal,* 1967, *1,* 533–536.

Rachman, S. Sexual disorders and behavior therapy. *American Journal of Psychiatry,* 1961, *118,* 235–240.

Rachman, S. Sexual fetishism: An experimental analogue. *Psychological Record,* 1966, *16,* 293–296.

Rada, R. T., Laws, D. R., & Kellner, R. Plasma testosterone levels in the rapist. *Psychosomatic Medicine,* 1976, *38,* 257–268.

Rado, S. An adaptational view of sexual behavior. In P. H. Hoch & J. Zubin (Eds.), *Psychosexual development in health and disease.* New York: Grune & Stratton, 1949.

Raisman, G. Evidence for a sex difference in the neuropil of the rat preoptic area and its importance for the study of sexually dimorphic functions. In Association for Research in Nervous and Mental Disease, *Research Publications* (Vol. 52). Baltimore: William & Wilkins, 1974.

Ramirez, J., Bryant, J., & Zillmann, D. Effects of erotica on retaliatory behavior as a function of level of prior provocation. *Journal of Personality and Social Psychology,* 1982, *43,* 971–978.

Reichlin, S. Neuroendocrinology. In R. H. Williams (Ed.), *Textbook of endocrinology* (4th ed.). Philadelphia: Saunders, 1968.

Reifler, C. B., Howard, J., Lipton, M. A., Liptzin, M. B., & Widmann, D. E. Pornography: An experimental study of effects. *American Journal of Psychiatry,* 1971, *128,* 575–582.

Reinisch, J. M. Prenatal exposure to synthetic progestins increases potential for aggression in humans. *Science,* 1981, *211,* 1171–1173.

Reisenzein, R., & Gattinger, E. Salience of arousal as a mediator of misattribution of transferred excitation. *Motivation and Emotion,* 1982, *6,* 315–328.

Resnick, H. Erotized repetitive hangings. *American Journal of Psychotherapy,* 1972, *26,* 4–21.

Reynolds, V., & Reynolds, F. Chimpanzees of the Budongo Forest. In I. DeVore (Ed.), *Primate behavior: Field studies of monkeys and apes.* New York: Holt, Rinehart & Winston, 1965.

Robinson, B. W., & Mishkin, M. Penile erection evoked from forebrain structures in *Macaca mulatta. Archives of Neurology,* 1968, *19,* 184–198.

Roeder, K. D. The control of tonus and locomotor activity in the praying mantis (*Mantis religiosa* L.). *Journal of Experimental Zoology,* 1937, *76,* 353–374.

Roeder, K. D. *Nerve cells and insect behavior.* Cambridge, Mass.: Harvard University Press, 1963.

Roeder, K. D., Tozian, L., & Weiant, E. A. Endogenous nerve activity and behaviour in the mantis and cockroach. *Journal of Insect Physiology,* 1960, *4,* 45–62.

Rogers, J. *Endocrine and metabolic aspects of gynecology.* Philadelphia: Saunders, 1963.

Root, W. S., & Bard, P. The mediation of feline erection through sympathetic pathways with some remarks on sexual behavior after deafferentation of the genitalia. *American Journal of Physiology,* 1947, *151,* 80–90.

Rose, J. W., Claybough, C., Clemens, L. G., & Gorski, R. A. Short latency induction of oestrous behaviour with intracerebral gonadal hormones in ovariectomized rats. *Endocrinology,* 1971, *89,* 32–38.

Rose, R. M. The psychological effects of androgens and estrogens: A review. In R. I. Shader (Ed.), *Psychiatric complications of medical drugs*. New York: Raven Press, 1972.

Rose, R. M., Holaday, J. W., & Bernstein, I. S. Plasma testosterone, dominance rank and aggressive behavior. *Nature*, 1971, *231*, 366–368.

Rose, S. S. An investigation in sterility after lumbar ganglionectomy. *British Medical Journal*, 1953, *1*, 247–250.

Rosene, J. M. *The effects of violent and sexually arousing film content: An experimental study*. Unpublished doctoral dissertation, Ohio University, 1971.

Rosenthal, R. *Experimenter effects in behavioral research*. New York: Appleton, 1966.

Rosvold, H. E., Mirsky, A. F., & Pribram, K. H. Influence of amygdalectomy on social behavior in monkeys. *Journal of Comparative and Physiological Psychology*, 1954, *47*, 173–178.

Rothschild, B. Psychiatrisch-klinische Erfahrungen mit einem Antiandrogenpräparat. *Schweizerische Medizinische Wochenschrift*, 1970, *100*, 1918–1924.

Rowell, T. E. Female reproductive cycle and social behaviour in primates. In D. S. Lehrman, R. A. Hinde, & E. Shaw (Eds.), *Advances in the study of behaviour* (Vol. 4). New York: Academic Press, 1972.

Rubin, Z. From liking to loving: Patterns of attraction in dating relationships. In T. L. Huston (Ed.), *Foundations of interpersonal attraction*. New York: Academic Press, 1974.

Ruitenbeek, H. M. *The new sexuality*. New York: New Viewpoints, 1974.

Russell, B. *Marriage and morals*. New York: Liveright, 1929.

Russell, B. *The autobiography of Bertrand Russell: The middle years 1914–1944*. New York: Bantam, 1969.

Russell, D. *The politics of rape: The victim's perspective*. New York: Stein & Day, 1975.

Russell, D. E. H. Pornography and violence: What does the new research say? In L. Lederer (Ed.), *Take back the night: Women on pornography*. New York: Morrow, 1980. (a)

Russell, D. *The prevalence and impact of marital rape in San Francisco*. Paper presented at the meeting of the American Sociological Association, New York, August 1980. (b)

Sade, D. S. Seasonal cycle in size of testes of free-ranging *Macaca mulatta*. *Folia Primatologica*, 1964, *2*, 171–180.

Sade, D. S. Inhibition of son-mother mating among free-ranging rhesus monkeys. *Science and Psychoanalysis*, 1968, *12*, 18–38.

Sadleir, R. M. F. S. The relationship between agonistic behavior and population changes in the deermouse, *Peromyscus maniculatus* (Wagner). *Journal of Animal Ecology*, 1965, *34*, 331–351.

Salmon, U. J., & Geist, S. H. Effect of androgens upon libido in women. *Journal of Clinical Endocrinology*, 1943, *3*, 235–238.

Saltman, J. *Abortion today*. Springfield, Ill.: Thomas, 1973.

Salzman, L. The psychodynamic approach to sex deviation. In H. Resnik & M. Wolfgang (Eds.), *Sexual behavior*. Boston: Little, Brown, 1972.

Sano, K. Sedative neurosurgery: With special reference to postero-medial hypothalamotomy. *Neurologia Medico Chirurgica*, 1962, *4*, 112–142.

Sano, K. Posterior hypothalamic lesions in the treatment of violent behavior. In W. S. Fields & W. H. Sweet (Eds.), *Neural bases of violence and aggression*. St. Louis: Green, 1975.

Sano, K., Yoshioka, M., Ogashiwa, M., Ishijima, B., & Ohye, C. Postero-medial hypothalamotomy in the treatment of aggressive behaviors. *Second International Symposium on Stereoencephalotomy, Confinia Neurologica*, 1966, *27*, 164–167.

Sapolsky, B. S., & Zillmann, D. The effect of soft-core and hard-core erotica on provoked and unprovoked hostile behavior. *Journal of Sex Research*, 1981, *17*, 319–343.

Sawa, M., Ueki, Y., Arita, M., & Harada, T. Preliminary report on the amygdaloidectomy on the psychotic patients, with interpretation of oral-emotional manifestation in schizophrenics. *Folia Psychiatrica et Neurologica Japonica*, 1954, *7*, 309–329.

Schachter, S. *The psychology of affiliation: Experimental studies of the sources of gregariousness*. Stanford, Calif.: Stanford University Press, 1959.

Schachter, S. The interaction of cognitive and physiological determinants of emotional state. In L. Berkowitz (Ed.), *Advances in experimental social psychology* (Vol. 1). New York: Academic Press, 1964.

Schaller, G. B. Life with the king of beasts. *National Geographic,* 1969, *135,* 494–519.

Schein, M. W., & Hale, E. B. Stimuli eliciting sexual behavior. In F. A. Beach (Ed.), *Sex and behavior.* New York: Wiley, 1965.

Schmidt, G. Male–female differences in sexual arousal and behavior during and after exposure to sexually explicit stimuli. *Archives of Sexual Behavior,* 1975, *4,* 353–365.

Schmidt, G., & Sigusch, V. Sex differences in responses to psychosexual stimulation by films and slides. *Journal of Sex Research,* 1970, *6,* 268–283.

Schram, D. D. Rape. In J. R. Chapman & M. Gates (Eds.), *The victimization of women.* Beverly Hills, Calif.: Sage Publications, 1978.

Schreiner, L., & Kling, A. Behavioral changes following rhinencephalic injury in cat. *Journal of Neurophysiology,* 1953, *16,* 643–658.

Schreiner, L., & Kling, A. Rhinencephalon and behavior. *American Journal of Physiology,* 1956, *184,* 486–490.

Schultz, A. H. Vergleichende Untersuchungen an einigen menschlichen Spezialisationen. *Bulletin der Schweizerischen Gesellschaft für Anthropologie und Ethnologie,* 1951, *28,* 25–37.

Schwartz, G. E. Self-regulation of response patterning: Implications for psychophysiological research and therapy. *Biofeedback and Self-Regulation,* 1976, *1,* 7–30.

Schwartz, G. E. Biofeedback and patterning of autonomic and central processes: CNS-cardiovascular interactions. In G. E. Schwartz & J. Beatty (Eds.), *Biofeedback: Theory and Research.* New York: Academic Press, 1977.

Scott, J. P. *Aggression.* Chicago: University of Chicago Press, 1958. (a)

Scott, J. P. *Animal Behavior.* Chicago: University of Chicago Press, 1958. (b)

Sears, R. R. Development of gender role. In F. A. Beach (Ed.), *Sex and behavior.* New York: Wiley, 1965.

Selander, R. K. On mating systems and sexual selection. *American Naturalist,* 1965, *99,* 129–140.

Seligman, M. E. P. On the generality of the laws of learning. *Psychological Review,* 1970, *77,* 406–418.

Selye, H. Studies concerning the anesthetic action of steroid hormones. *Journal of Pharmacology and Experimental Therapeutics,* 1941, *73,* 127–141.

Selye, H. *The stress of life* (2nd ed.). New York: McGraw-Hill, 1976.

Sem-Jacobsen, C. W., & Torkildsen, A. Depth recording and electrical stimulation in the human brain. In E. R. Ramey & D. S. O'Doherty (Eds.), *Electrical studies on the unanesthetized brain.* New York: Hoeber, 1960.

Semans, J. H., & Langworthy, O. R. Observations on the neurophysiology of sexual function in the male cat. *Journal of Urology,* 1938, *40,* 836–846.

Shainess, N. Vulnerability to violence: Masochism as process. *American Journal of Psychotherapy,* 1979, *33*(2), 174–189.

Shealy, C. N., & Peele, T. L. Studies on amygdaloid nucleus of cat. *Journal of Neurophysiology,* 1957, *20,* 125–139.

Sigg, E. B. Relationship of aggressive behaviour to adrenal and gonadal function in male mice. In S. Garattini & E. B. Sigg (Eds.), *Aggressive behaviour.* New York: Wiley, 1969.

Sigusch, V., Schmidt, G., Reinfeld, A., & Wiedemann-Sutor, I. Psychosexual stimulation: Sex differences. *Journal of Sex Research,* 1970, *6,* 10–24.

Sillitoe, P. Big men and war in New Guinea. *Man,* 1978, *13,* 252–271.

Simon, W. The social, the erotic, and the sensual: The complexities of sexual scripts. In J. K. Cole & R. Dienstbier (Eds.), *Nebraska Symposium on Motivation* (Vol. 21). Lincoln: University of Nebraska Press, 1973.

Simon, W., & Gagnon, J. H. On psychosexual development. In D. A. Goslin (Ed.), *Handbook of socialization theory and research.* Chicago: Rand McNally, 1969.

Simonds, P. E. The bonnet macaque in South India. In I. DeVore (Ed.), *Primate behavior: Field studies of monkeys and apes.* New York: Holt, Rinehart & Winston, 1965.

Singer, J. Hypothalamic control of male and female sexual behavior in female rats. *Journal of Comparative and Physiological Psychology,* 1968, *66,* 738–742.

Skinner, B. F. *Contingencies of reinforcement: A theoretical analysis.* New York: Appleton-Century-Crofts, 1969.

Smith, G. P. Adrenal hormones and emotional behavior. In E. Stellar & J. M. Sprague (Eds.), *Progress in physiological psychology.* New York: Academic Press, 1973.

Smith, S. L. Mood and the menstrual cycle. In E. J. Sachar (Ed.), *Topics in psychoendocrinology.* New York: Grune & Stratton, 1975.

Snow, D. W. Courtship ritual: The dance of the manakins. *Animal Kingdom,* 1956, *59,* 86–91.

Sopchak, A. L., & Sutherland, A. M. Psychological impact of cancer and its treatment. VII. Exogenous hormones and their relation to lifelong adaptation in women with metastatic cancer of the breast. *Cancer,* 1960, *13,* 528–531.

Sorenson, R. *Adolescent sexuality in contemporary America.* New York: World Publishing Co., 1973.

Southwick, C. H. Experimental studies of intragroup aggression in rhesus monkeys. *American Zoologist,* 1966, *6,* 301.

Southwick, C. H. Aggressive behaviour of rhesus monkeys in natural and captive groups. In S. Garattini & E. B. Sigg (Eds.), *Aggressive behaviour.* New York: Wiley, 1969.

Spengler, A. Manifest sadomasochism of males: Results of an empirical study. *Archives of Sexual Behavior,* 1977, *6*(6), 441–456.

Spiegel, E. A., Kletzkin, M., & Szekely, E. G. Pain reactions upon stimulation of the tectum mesencephali. *Journal of Neuropathology and Experimental Neurology,* 1954, *13,* 212–220.

Spiegel, E. A., Miller, H. R., & Oppenheimer, M. J. Forebrain and rage reactions. *Journal of Neurophysiology,* 1940, *3,* 538–548.

Spiegel, E. A., & Wycis, H. T. *Stereoencephalotomy: Thalamotomy and related procedures* (Part 1). *Methods and stereotaxic atlas of the human brain.* New York: Grune & Stratton, 1952.

Spiegel, E. A., & Wycis, H. T. *Stereoencephalotomy: Thalamotomy and related procedures* (Part 2). *Clinical and physiological applications.* New York: Grune & Stratton, 1962.

Steel, B. F., & Pollack, D. B. A psychiatric study of parents who abuse infants and small children. In R. E. Helfer & C. H. Kempe (Eds.), *The battered child.* Chicago: University of Chicago Press, 1968.

Steinmetz, S. K., & Straus, M. A. *Violence in the family.* New York: Dodd, Mead, 1974.

Stekel, W. *Sadism and masochism: The psychology of hatred and cruelty* (Vols. 1 & 2). New York: Liveright, 1929.

Stephan, W., Berscheid, E., & Walster, E. Sexual arousal and heterosexual perception. *Journal of Personality and Social Psychology,* 1971, *20,* 93–101.

Stern, R. M., Farr, J. H., & Ray, W. J. Pleasure. In P. H. Venables & M. J. Christie (Eds.), *Research in psychophysiology.* London: Wiley, 1975.

Sternbach, R. *Principles of psychophysiology.* New York: Academic Press, 1966.

Sternbach, R. A. *Pain: A psychophysiological analysis.* New York: Academic Press, 1968.

Stoller, R. J. *Perversion: The erotic form of hatred.* New York: Pantheon Books, 1975.

Storr, A. *Human aggression.* New York: Atheneum, 1968.

Straus, M. A., Gelles, R. J., & Steinmetz, S. K. *Behind closed doors: Violence in the American family.* Garden City, N.Y.: Anchor Books, 1980.

Sugiyama, Y. Social organization of Hanuman langurs. In S. A. Altmann (Ed.), *Social communication among primates.* Chicago: University of Chicago Press, 1967.

Sugiyama, Y. Social behavior of chimpanzees in the Budongo Forest, Uganda. *Primates,* 1969, *10,* 197–225.

Suinn, R. M. *Fundamentals of behavior pathology.* New York: Wiley, 1970.

Svare, B. B., Davis, P. G., & Gandelman, R. Fighting behavior in female mice following chronic androgen treatment during adulthood. *Physiology and Behavior,* 1974, *12,* 399–403.

Svare, B. B., & Gandelman, R. Aggressive behavior of juvenile mice: Influence of androgen and olfactory stimuli. *Developmental Psychobiology,* 1975, *8,* 405–415.

Swanson, E. M., & Foulkes, D. Dream content and the menstrual cycle. *Journal of Nervous and Mental Disease,* 1968, *145,* 358–363.

Sweet, W. H., Ervin, F., & Mark, V. H. The relationship of violent behavior to focal cerebral disease. In S. Garattini & E. B. Sigg (Eds.), *Aggressive behaviour.* New York: Wiley, 1969.

Szasz, T. S. *Pain and pleasure: A study of bodily feelings.* New York: Basic Books, 1957.

Szechtman, H., Caggiula, A. R., & Wulkan, D. Preoptic knife cuts and sexual behavior in male rats. *Brain Research,* 1978, *150,* 569–591.

Talbot, H. S. The sexual function in paraplegia. *Journal of Urology,* 1955, *73,* 91–100.

Tannenbaum, P. H., & Zillmann, D. Emotional arousal in the facilitation of aggression through communication. In L. Berkowitz (Ed.), *Advances in experimental social psychology* (Vol. 8). New York: Academic Press, 1975.

Tanner, J. M. Physical growth. In P. H. Mussen (Ed.), *Carmichael's manual of child psychology* (3rd ed.). New York: Wiley, 1970.

Tarpy, R. M. The nervous system and emotion. In D. K. Candland, J. P. Fell, E. Keen, A. I. Leshner, R. M. Tarpy, & R. Plutchik (Eds.), *Emotion.* Monterey, Calif.: Brooks/Cole, 1977.

Taylor, G. T. Male aggression in the presence of an estrous female. *Journal of Comparative and Physiological Psychology,* 1975, *89,* 246–252.

Tedeschi, J. T., Smith, R. B., III, & Brown, R. C., Jr. A reinterpretation of research on aggression. *Psychological Bulletin,* 1974, *81,* 540–562.

Terzian, H., & Ore, G. D. Syndrome of Klüver and Bucy reproduced in man by bilateral removal of the temporal lobes. *Neurology,* 1955, *5,* 373–380.

Thayer, R. E. Measurement of activation through self-report. *Psychological Reports,* 1967, *20,* 663–678.

Thayer, R. E. Activation states as assessed by verbal report and four psychophysiological variables. *Psychophysiology,* 1970, *7,* 86–94.

Thompson, R. F. *Foundations of physiological psychology.* New York: Harper & Row, 1967.

Thorpe, J. G., Schmidt, E., & Castell, D. A comparison of positive and negative (aversive) conditioning in the treatment of homosexuality. *Behaviour Research and Therapy,* 1963, *1,* 357–362.

Tieger, T. Self-rated likelihood of raping and the social perception of rape. *Journal of Research in Personality,* 1981, *15,* 147–158.

Tiger, L. *Men in groups.* New York: Random House, 1969.

Tiger, L., & Fox, R. *The imperial animal.* New York: Holt, Rinehart & Winston, 1971.

Tighe, T. J., & Leaton, R. N. (Eds.). *Habituation: Perspectives from child development, animal behavior, and neurophysiology.* Hillsdale, N.J.: Lawrence Erlbaum Associates, 1976.

Tinbergen, N. *Social behaviour in animals.* London: Methuen, 1953.

Tollman, J., & King, J. A. The effects of testosterone propionate on aggression in male and female C57BL/10 mice. *British Journal of Animal Behaviour,* 1956, *4,* 147–149.

Torghele, J. R. Premenstrual tension in psychotic women. *Journal-Lancet,* 1957, *77*(5), 163–170.

Tow, P. M., & Whitty, C. W. Personality changes after operations on the cingulate gyrus in man. *Journal of Neurology, Neurosurgery and Psychiatry,* 1953, *16,* 186–193.

Trimble, M. R., & Herbert, J. The effect of testosterone or oestradiol upon the sexual and associated behavior of the adult female rhesus monkey. *Journal of Endocrinology,* 1968, *42,* 171–185.

Trivers, R. L. Parental investment and sexual selection. In B. Campbell (Ed.), *Sexual selection and the descent of man.* Chicago: Aldine, 1972.

Turner, C. D., & Bagnara, J. T. *General endocrinology* (5th ed.). Philadelphia: Saunders, 1971.

Udry, J. R., & Morris, N. M. Distribution of coitus in the menstrual cycle. *Nature,* 1968, *220,* 593–596.

Udry, J. R., & Morris, N. M. Effect of contraceptive pills on the distribution of sexual activity in the menstrual cycle. *Nature*, 1970, *227*, 502–503.

Ullock, B., & Wagner, N. N. The evolution of human sexual behavior. In J. S. Lockard (Ed.), *The evolution of human social behavior*. New York: Elsevier, 1980.

Ursin, H. The effect of amygdaloid lesions on flight and defense behavior in cats. *Experimental Neurology*, 1965, *11*, 64–79.

Ursin, H., & Kaada, B. R. Functional localization within the amygdaloid complex in the cat. *Electroencephalography and Clinical Neurophysiology*, 1960, *12*, 1–20.

Valenstein, E. S. Brain stimulation and the origin of violent behavior. In W. L. Smith & A. Kling (Eds.), *Issues in brain/behavior control*. New York: Spectrum, 1976.

Valentine, G. H. *The chromosome disorders*. Philadelphia: Lippincott, 1969.

Vallois, H. V. The social life of early man: The evidence of skeletons. In S. L. Washburn (Ed.), *Social life of early man*. New York: Wenner-Gren Foundation for Anthropological Research, 1961.

van Dis, H., & Larsson, K. Induction of sexual arousal in the castrated male rat by intracranial stimulation. *Physiology and Behavior*, 1971, *6*, 85–86.

van Wagenen, G., & Hamilton, J. B. The experimental production of pseudohermaphroditism in the monkey. In *Essays in biology: In honor of Herbert M. Evans*. Berkeley: University of California Press, 1943.

Vatsyayana. *Kāma Sūtra*. New York: Dutton, 1962.

Vital Statistics of the United States, 1977 (Vol. 2). *Mortality* (Part B) (U.S. Department of Health and Human Services Publication No. (PHS) 80-1102). Washington, D.C.: U.S. Government Printing Office, 1980.

Vogel, W., Broverman, D. M., & Klaiber, E. L. EEG responses in regularly menstruating women and in amenorrheic women treated with ovarian hormones. *Science*, 1971, *173*, 388–391.

vom Saal, F. S., Gandelman, R., & Svare, B. Aggression in male and female mice: Evidence for changed neural sensitivity to neonatal but not adult androgen. *Physiology and Behavior*, 1976, *17*, 53–57.

vom Saal, F. S., Svare, B., & Gandelman, R. Time of neonatal androgen exposure influences length of testosterone treatment required to induce aggression in adult male and female mice. *Behavioral Biology*, 1976, *17*, 391–397.

von Krafft-Ebing, R. *Psychopathia sexualis: Eine klinisch-forensische Studie*. Stuttgart: Enke, 1886.

von Schrenck-Notzing, A. P. *Die Suggestionstherapie bei krankhaften Erscheinungen des Geschlechtssinnes mit besonderer Berücksichtigung der conträren Sexualempfindung*. Stuttgart: Enke, 1892.

Wagner, G. C., Beuving, L. J., & Hutchinson, R. R. The effects of gonadal hormone manipulations on aggressive target-biting in mice. *Aggressive Behavior*, 1980, *6*, 1–7.

Wagner, N. N. (Ed.). *Perspectives on human sexuality: Psychological, social, and cultural research findings*. New York: Behavioral Publications, 1974.

Walker, A. E., & Blumer, D. Long term effects of temporal lobe lesions on sexual behavior and aggressivity. In W. S. Fields & W. H. Sweet (Eds.), *Neural bases of violence and aggression*. St. Louis: Green, 1975.

Walker, A. E., Thomson, A. F., & McQueen, J. D. Behavior and the temporal rhinencephalon in the monkey. *Bulletin of the Johns Hopkins Hospital*, 1953, *93*, 65–93.

Walker, P. A. The role of antiandrogens in the treatment of sex offenders. In C. B. Qualls, J. P. Wincze, & D. H. Barlow (Eds.), *The prevention of sexual disorders: Issues and approaches*. New York: Plenum Press, 1978.

Walster, E. Passionate love. In B. I. Murstein (Ed.), *Theories of attraction and love*. New York: Springer, 1971.

Walster, E., & Berscheid, E. Adrenaline makes the heart grow fonder. *Psychology Today*, June 1971, pp. 47–62.

Walster, E., & Walster, G. W. *A new look at love*. Reading, Mass.: Addison-Wesley, 1978.

Walther, F. Zum Kampf- und Paarungsverhalten einiger Antilopen. *Zeitschrift für Tierpsychologie*, 1958, *15*, 340–380.

Ward, I. L. Differential effect of pre- and post-natal androgen on the sexual behavior of intact and spayed female rats. *Hormones and Behavior*, 1969, *1*, 25–36.

Washburn, S. L., & Lancaster, C. S. The evolution of hunting. In R. B. Lee & I. DeVore (Eds.), *Symposium on man the hunter*. Chicago: Aldine, 1968.

Waxenberg, S. E., Drellich, M. G., & Sutherland, A. M. The role of hormones in human behavior: I. Changes in female sexuality after adrenalectomy. *Journal of Clinical Endocrinology*, 1959, *19*, 193–202.

Waxenberg, S. E., Finkbeiner, J. A., Drellich, M. G., & Sutherland, A. M. The role of hormones in human behavior: II. Changes in sexual behavior in relation to vaginal smears of breast-cancer patients after oophorectomy and adrenalectomy. *Psychosomatic Medicine*, 1960, *22*, 435–442.

Weiskrantz, L. Behavioral changes associated with ablation of the amygdaloid complex in monkeys. *Journal of Comparative and Physiological Psychology*, 1956, *49*, 381–391.

Weisman, A. D. Self-destruction and sexual perversion. In E. S. Shneidman (Ed.), *Essays in self-destruction*. New York: Science House, 1967.

Weiss, H. D. The physiology of human penile erection. *Annals of Internal Medicine*, 1972, *76*, 793–799.

Welch, J., Borgaonkar, D., & Herr, H. Psychopathy, mental deficiency, aggressiveness and the XYY syndrome. *Nature*, 1967, *214*, 500–501.

Wendt, H. *The sex life of the animals*. New York: Simon & Schuster, 1965.

Wenger, M. A., Jones, F. N., & Jones, M. H. *Physiological psychology*. New York: Holt, 1956.

Whalen, R. E. Sexual motivation. *Psychological Review*, 1966, *73*, 151–163.

Whalen, R. E. Differentiation of the neural mechanisms which control gonadotropin secretion and sexual behavior. In M. Diamond (Ed.), *Perspectives in reproduction and sexual behavior*. Bloomington: Indiana University Press, 1968.

Whalen, R. E. The ontogeny of sexuality. In H. Moltz (Ed.), *The ontogeny of vertebrate behavior*. New York: Academic Press, 1971.

Whalen, R. E. Brain mechanisms controlling sexual behavior. In F. A. Beach (Ed.), *Human sexuality in four perspectives*. Baltimore: Johns Hopkins University Press, 1976.

Whalen, R. E., & Edwards, D. A. Sexual reversibility in neonatally castrated male rats. *Journal of Comparative and Physiological Psychology*, 1966, *62*, 307–310.

Whalen, R. E., & Edwards, D. A. Hormonal determinants of the development of masculine and feminine behavior in male and female rats. *Anatomical Record*, 1967, *157*, 173–180.

Whalen, R. E., Edwards, D. A., Luttge, W. G., & Robertson, R. T. Early androgen treatment and male sexual behavior in female rats. *Physiology and Behavior*, 1969, *4*, 33–40.

Whalen, R. E., & Robertson, R. T. Sexual exhaustion and recovery of masculine copulatory behavior in virilized female rats. *Psychonomic Science*, 1968, *11*, 319–320.

White, G. L., Fishbein, S., & Rutstein, J. Passionate love and the misattribution of arousal. *Journal of Personality and Social Psychology*, 1981, *41*, 56–62.

White, L. A. Erotica and aggression: The influence of sexual arousal, positive affect, and negative affect on aggressive behavior. *Journal of Personality and Social Psychology*, 1979, *37*, 591–601.

Whitelaw, G. P., & Smithwick, R. H. Some secondary effects of sympathectomy: With particular reference to disturbance of sexual function. *New England Journal of Medicine*, 1951, *245*, 121–130.

Wickler, W. Socio-sexual signals and their intra-specific imitation among primates. In D. Morris (Ed.), *Primate ethology*. Chicago: Aldine, 1967.

Wickler, W. *The sexual code: The social behavior of animals and men*. Garden City, N.Y.: Doubleday, 1972.

Wilder, J. The law of initial values in neurology and psychiatry: Facts and problems. *Journal of Nervous and Mental Disease*, 1957, *125*, 73–86.

Wilson, A. P., & Boelkins, C. Evidence for seasonal variation in aggressive behaviour by *Macaca mulatta*. *Animal Behaviour*, 1970, *18*, 719–724.

Wilson, J. A., Kuehn, R. E., & Beach, F. A. Modification of the sexual behavior of male rats produced by changing the stimulus female. *Journal of Comparative and Physiological Psychology*, 1963, *56*, 636–644.

Wolchik, S. A., Beggs, V. E., Wincze, J. P., Sakheim, D. K., Barlow, D. H., & Mavissakalian, M. The effect of emotional arousal on subsequent sexual arousal in men. *Journal of Abnormal Psychology*, 1980, *89*, 595–598.

Wolfgang, M. E. *Patterns in criminal homicide*. Philadelphia: University of Pennsylvania, 1958.

Wolfgang, M. E., & Ferracuti, F. *The subculture of violence: Towards an integrated theory in criminology*. London: Tavistock, 1967.

Wood, C. D. Behavioral changes following discrete lesions of temporal lobe structures. *Neurology*, 1958, *8*, 215–220.

Woods, J. W. "Taming" of the wild Norway rat by rhinencephalic lesions. *Nature*, 1956, *178*, 869.

Woolley, D. E., & Timiras, P. S. The gonad-brain relationship: Effects of female sex hormones on electroshock convulsions in the rat. *Endocrinology*, 1962, *70*, 196–209.

Wyer, R. S., & Srull, T. K. Category accessibility: Some theoretical and empirical issues concerning the processing of social stimulus information. In E. T. Higgins, C. P. Herman, & M. P. Zanna (Eds.), *Social cognition: The Ontario Symposium on Personality and Social Psychology*. Hillsdale, N.J.: Lawrence Erlbaum Associates, 1980. (a)

Wyer, R. S., & Srull, T. K. The processing of social stimulus information: A conceptual integration. In R. Hastie, T. Ostrom, E. Ebbesen, R. Wyer, D. Hamilton, & D. Carlston (Eds.), *Cognitive bases of impression formation and person memory*. Hillsdale, N.J.: Lawrence Erlbaum Associates, 1980. (b)

Wynne-Edwards, V. C. *Animal dispersion in relation to social behavior*. New York: Hafner, 1962.

Yablonsky, L. *The violent gang*. New York: Macmillan, 1962.

Yoshiba, K. Local and intertroop variability in ecology and social behavior of common Indian langurs. In P. C. Jay (Ed.), *Primates: Studies in adaptation and variability*. New York: Holt, Rinehart & Winston, 1968.

Young, W., Goy, R., & Phoenix, C. Hormones and sexual behavior. *Science*, 1964, *143*, 212–218.

Young, W. C., & Orbison, W. D. Changes in selected features of behavior in oppositely sexed chimpanzees during the sexual cycle after ovariectomy. *Journal of Comparative Psychology*, 1944, *37*, 107–143.

Zajonc, R. B. Attitudinal effects of mere exposure. *Journal of Personality and Social Psychology Monograph Supplement*, 1968, *9*, 1–27.

Zeitlin, A. B., Cottrell, T. L., & Lloyd, F. A. Sexology of the paraplegic male. *Fertility and Sterility*, 1957, *8*, 337–344.

Zillmann, D. Excitation transfer in communication-mediated aggressive behavior. *Journal of Experimental Social Psychology*, 1971, *7*, 419–434.

Zillmann, D. Attribution and misattribution of excitatory reactions. In J. H. Harvey, W. J. Ickes, & R. F. Kidd (Eds.), *New directions in attribution research* (Vol. 2). Hillsdale, N.J.: Lawrence Erlbaum Associates, 1978.

Zillmann, D. *Hostility and aggression*. Hillsdale, N.J.: Lawrence Erlbaum Associates, 1979.

Zillmann, D. Anatomy of suspense. In P. H. Tannenbaum (Ed.), *The entertainment functions of television*. Hillsdale, N.J.: Lawrence Erlbaum Associates, 1980.

Zillmann, D. Arousal and aggression. In R. G. Geen & E. Donnerstein (Eds.), *Aggression: Theoretical and empirical reviews*. New York: Academic Press, 1983. (a)

Zillmann, D. Transfer of excitation in emotional behavior. In J. T. Cacioppo & R. E. Petty (Eds.), *Social psychophysiology*. New York: Guilford Press, 1983. (b)

Zillmann, D., & Bryant, J. Pornography, sexual callousness, and the trivialization of rape. *Journal of Communication,* 1982, *32*(4), 10–21.

Zillmann, D., & Bryant, J. Effects of massive exposure to pornography. In N. M. Malamuth & E. Donnerstein (Eds.), *Pornography and sexual aggression.* New York: Academic Press, 1983.

Zillmann, D., Bryant, J., Cantor, J. R., & Day, K. D. Irrelevance of mitigating circumstances in retaliatory behavior at high levels of excitation. *Journal of Research in Personality,* 1975, *9,* 282–293.

Zillmann, D., Bryant, J., & Carveth, R. A. The effect of erotica featuring sadomasochism and bestiality on motivated intermale aggression. *Personality and Social Psychology Bulletin,* 1981, *7,* 153–159.

Zillmann, D., Bryant, J., Comisky, P. W., & Medoff, N. J. Excitation and hedonic valence in the effect of erotica on motivated intermale aggression. *European Journal of Social Psychology,* 1981, *11,* 233–252.

Zillmann, D., Hoyt, J. L., & Day, K. D. Strength and duration of the effect of aggressive, violent, and erotic communications on subsequent aggressive behavior. *Communication Research,* 1974, *1,* 286–306.

Zillmann, D., Katcher, A. H., & Milavsky, B. Excitation transfer from physical exercise to subsequent aggressive behavior. *Journal of Experimental Social Psychology,* 1972, *8,* 247–259.

Zillmann, D., & Sapolsky, B. S. What mediates the effect of mild erotica on annoyance and hostile behavior in males. *Journal of Personality and Social Psychology,* 1977, *35,* 587–596.

Zuckerman, M. Physiological measures of sexual arousal in the human. *Psychological Bulletin,* 1971, *75,* 297–329.

Zuckerman, S. *The social life of monkeys and apes.* London: Kegan Paul, Trench, Trubner, 1932.

Author Index

Subject Index